A Maverick Eye

THE STREET PHOTOGRAPHY OF JOHN DEAKIN

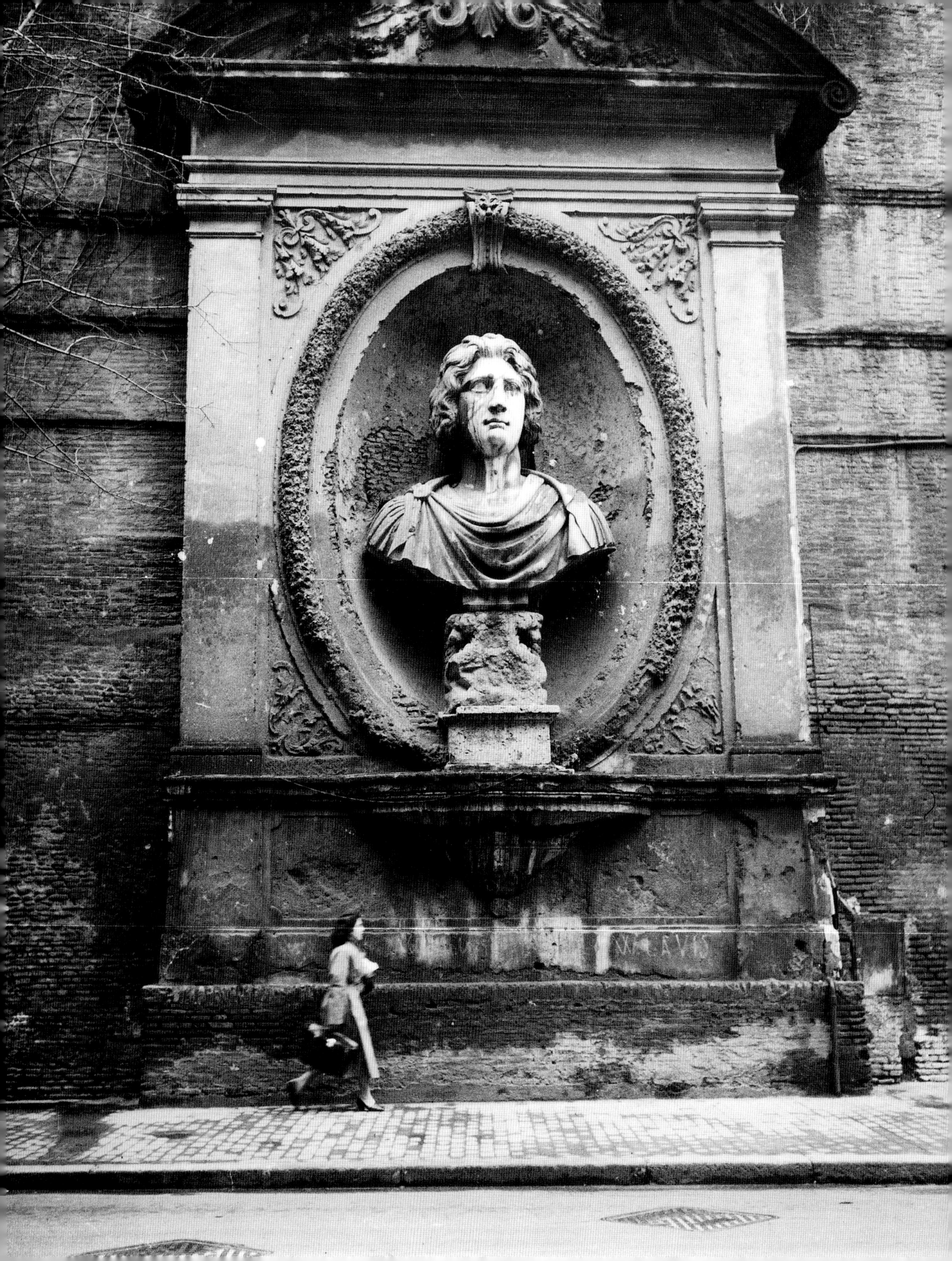

Robin Muir

A Maverick Eye
The Street Photography of John Deakin

With 192 photographs in duotone and color

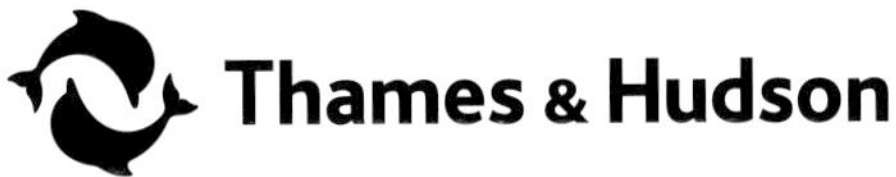
Thames & Hudson

The vintage prints used in the production of this book were made under the supervision of John Deakin himself. In many instances they were his own working prints, which accounts for their occasional distressed appearance. They are now in the collection of James Moores. The publishers would like to express their gratitude to James Moores for lending these irreplaceable prints, and for allowing these images to be published in this book.

Designed by Martin Harrison

Any copy of this book issued by the publisher as a paperback is sold subject to the condition that it shall not by way of trade or otherwise be lent, resold, hired out or otherwise circulated without the publisher's prior consent in any form of binding or cover other than that in which it is published and without a similar condition including these words being imposed on a subsequent purchaser.

© 2002 Thames & Hudson Ltd, London

The photographs on the following pages are reproduced courtesy of *Vogue* © The Condé Nast Publications Ltd: 8, 9 (left), 47, 60, 61, 79. All other photographs, except those on pages 7, 15, 28, 29 and 206, copyright © The Estate of John Deakin

First published in hardback in the United States of America in 2002 by Thames & Hudson Inc.,
500 Fifth Avenue, New York, New York 10110
thamesandhudsonusa.com

Library of Congress Catalog Card Number 2001093085
ISBN 0-500-54244-9

All Rights Reserved. No part of this publication may be reproduced or transmitted in any form or by any means, electronic or mechanical, including photocopy, recording or any other information storage and retrieval system, without prior permission in writing from the publisher.

Printed and bound in Germany by Steidl, Göttingen

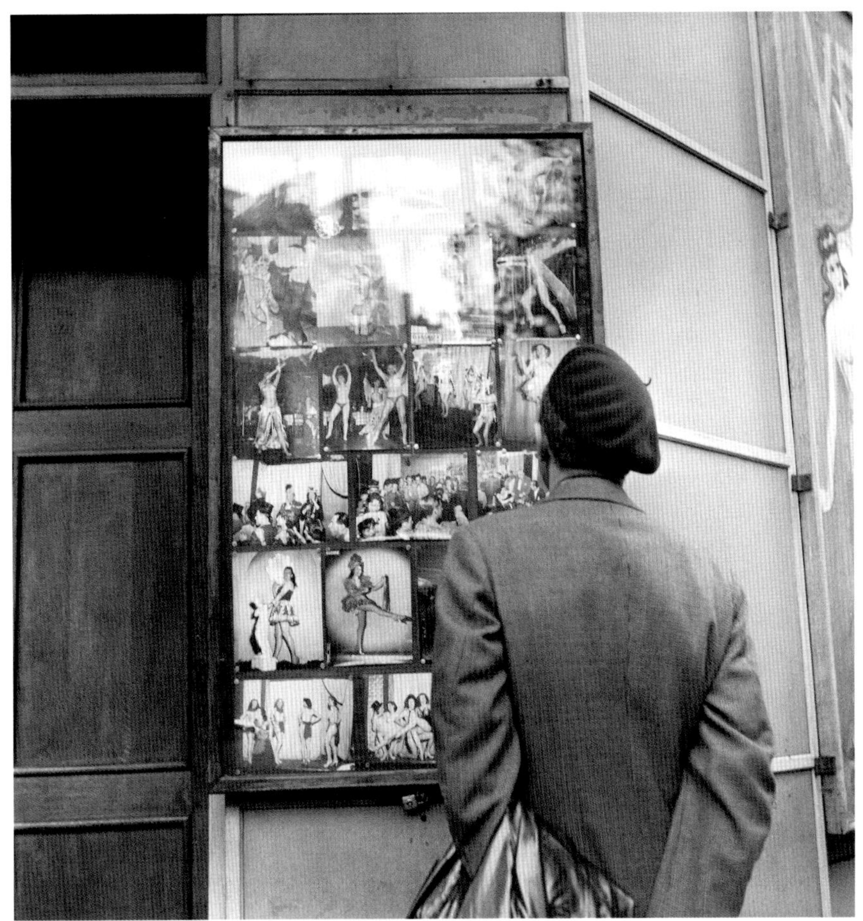

Outside a club, Paris, 1950s

Contents

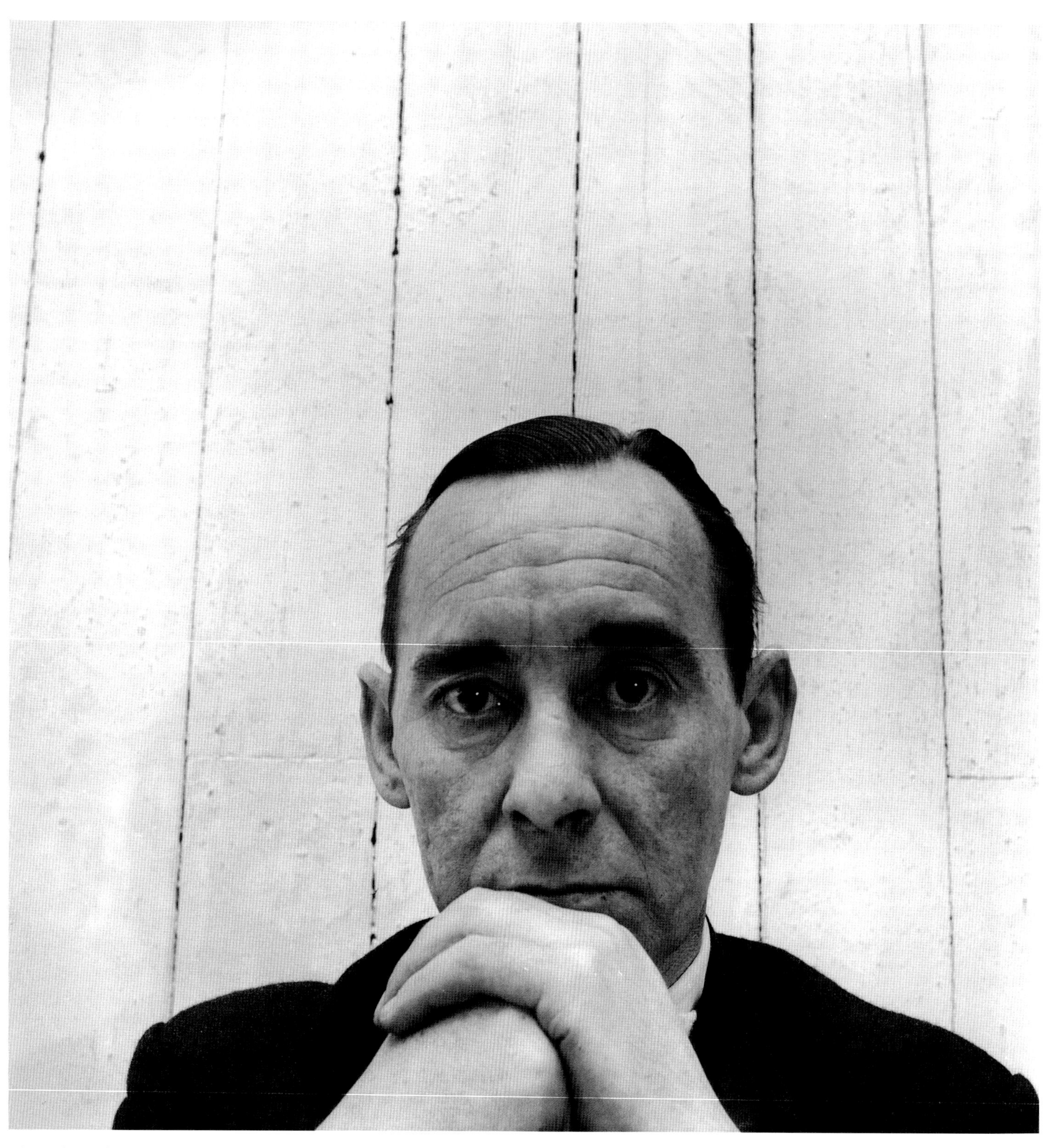

John Deakin, self-portrait, 1952

Frontispiece, page 2: Via Campania, Rome, 1950s

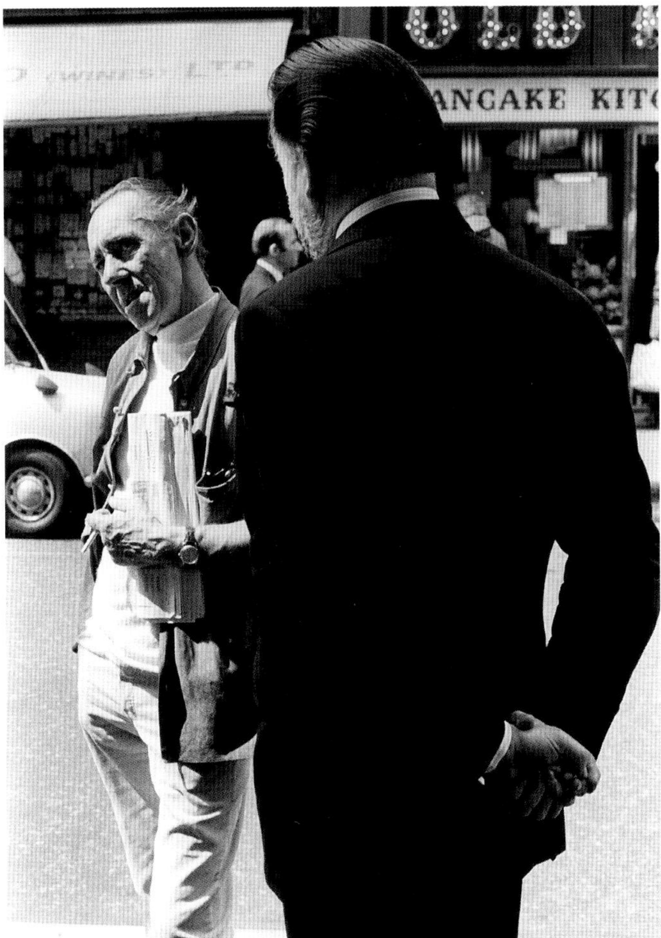

John Deakin in Soho, early 1960s. Photo Harry Diamond

A Maverick Eye

Lying in a bed at the Westminster Hospital in early April 1972 recovering from an operation to stop the spread of cancer, the photographer John Deakin was unconcerned that large parts of his lungs had been removed. Instead, he was planning an ambitious trip to the Greek Islands: 'Operation over and successful,' he wrote on 11 April to the writer and broadcaster Dan Farson, 'an *early* cancer, all removed. Should be out and Poros-bound in a fortnight.' On 7 May, in a further letter to Farson, he admitted he would have to learn, as he put it, 'to breathe all over again'. By the end of the month he was dead. He had discharged himself from hospital to convalesce at his friend Francis Bacon's expense at the Old Ship Hotel, Brighton. There he suffered heart failure the day after a marathon drinking binge with a friend whose capacity for alcohol was, according to Farson, even greater than his. During Deakin's final stay in hospital he had named Bacon as his next-of-kin. Though it was known that the artist was his occasional benefactor – Bacon had once given him the proceeds from the sale of a painting, had sometimes paid his rent and had commissioned photographs from him – Farson suspected Deakin had given Bacon's name chiefly to impress the doctor who asked. Bacon was required to identify the body: 'It was the last dirty trick he played on me,' he remarked.[1] Another friend, the writer Bruce Bernard, was probably the last person to speak to him: 'I phoned Deakin and he told me he had rung for tea and would I call him back. It was the maid who brought the tea that found him dead.'[2]

From under Deakin's bed in his flat in Berwick Street, Soho, Bernard retrieved several cardboard boxes of his documentary photographs and, in far from pristine condition, many of the monumental close-cropped headshots which Bernard first showed to the public in an exhibition of Deakin's portraits at the Victoria and Albert Museum, London, in 1984.[3] These survivors from the wreckage of a brief career, plus the archive of commissioned portraits still held by *Vogue* (he had first worked for the magazine in 1947), show Deakin's range at its best: portraits, fashion pictures, poignant moments of urban life, reportage, graffiti, tattooed servicemen, transvestites and drag queens, photo-essays on heavy industry and, most haunting of all, the documentary work he took for himself and never found the time or inclination

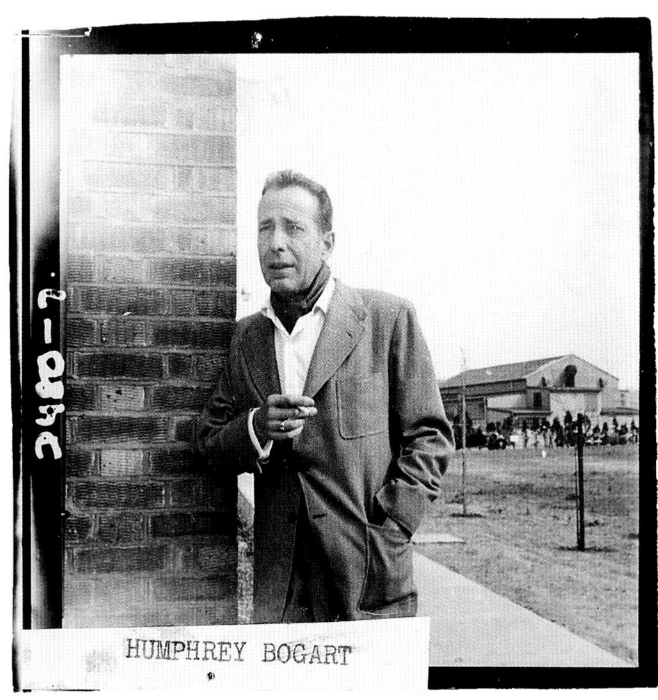

Humphrey Bogart, actor, 1953

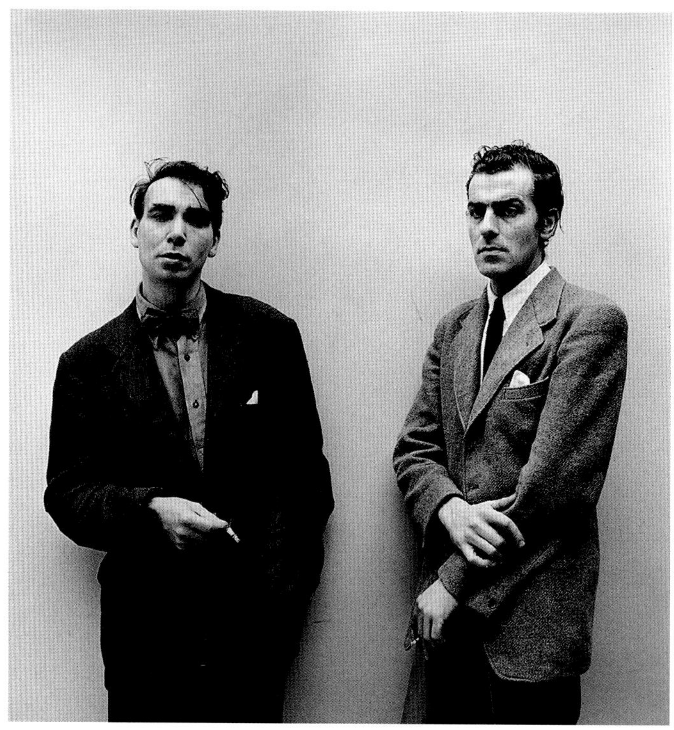

Robert MacBryde and Robert Colquhoun, artists, 1951

to do much with. These evocations of life on the streets of Paris, Rome and London, found in hundreds of negatives, torn prints and stained contact sheets wrapped in brittle and desiccated brown paper, reveal that Deakin's eye was not as pitiless as many of the more famous portraits suggest. Occasionally it could be sympathetic. Like Vittorio de Sica, whose stark neo-realist films he much admired, he found compassion and an unexpected beauty in the chaos and poverty of postwar Roman life. His pictures of lamplighters, fairground workers, dog walkers, balloon sellers, priests, nuns and shopkeepers reveal a magnanimity unanticipated in one so memorably described as 'a vicious little drunk of such inventive malice and implacable bitchiness that it's surprising he didn't choke on his own venom'.[4]

The editor of *Vogue*, Audrey Withers, whose patience Deakin drove to breaking point with a catalogue of misdemeanours (broken tripods, weeping models, exposure meters mislaid in taxicabs, provoked fashion editors and unduly high entertaining expenses), allowed the following to be written in her magazine: '[Deakin] has travelled widely, and only recently returned from living abroad in Rome and Paris, where he took many extraordinary photographs seen through his own highly individual eye-view of heightened realism. Deakin's eye selects the Gothic, the darkly romantic, often the grotesque sidewalks and alleyways of city life, and emphasizes their individuality, their emotional strength and their forlorn dignity.'[5] Withers always remained an admirer of Deakin's documentary work. She was impressed above all by the Paris pictures, which she first saw in 1947. She even tried to find them a book publisher, enlisting the help (fruitlessly) of American *Vogue*'s art director, Alexander Liberman.[6] These photographs were what persuaded her to sign Deakin for *Vogue*, and it was with great reluctance that she ended up firing him, twice: first in 1948 and for the second and final time in 1954.

Deakin did not make a happy transition to fashion pictures (which all staff photographers were required to carry out) and recognized that his strength lay on the features pages. His fashion work, recalled one editor, 'was a bit hit-and-miss. A lot of the time miss-and-miss, really.'[7] Occasionally, however, as sessions with his discovery the model Cassie Chaney show, his fashion photographs, high on contrast, could burn through the pages of the magazine, eclipsing those of his rivals. But these were rare occasions and, in Miss Chaney's case, successful because he was allowed to treat the fashion photograph as if it were a portrait.

Deakin's portraits for *Vogue* were conspicuously brilliant, laid out with sympathy by John Parsons, the magazine's art director, and his assistant Tommy Hawkyard, both of whom were supportive of, though often uneasy with, Deakin's confrontational style. More than one subject recalled that a sitting was more like an interrogation, while the actor

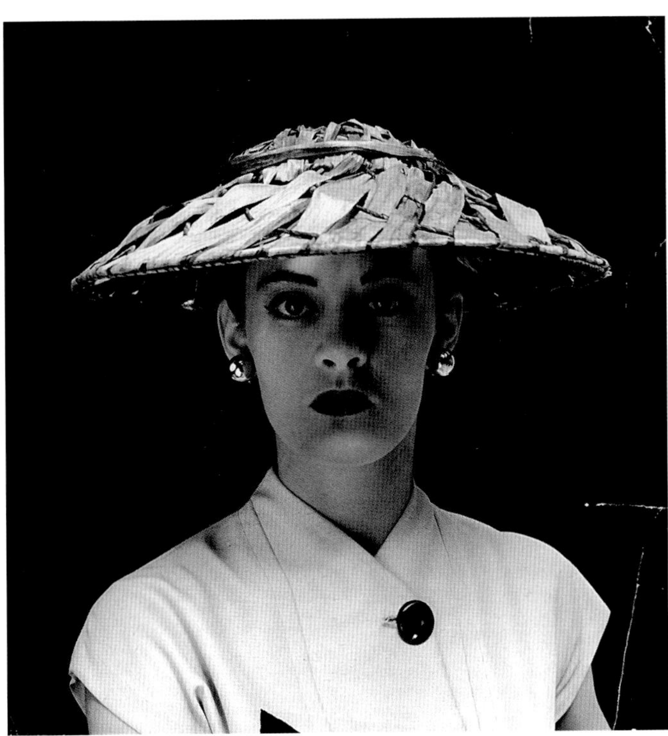

Cassie Chaney, fashion model, 1952

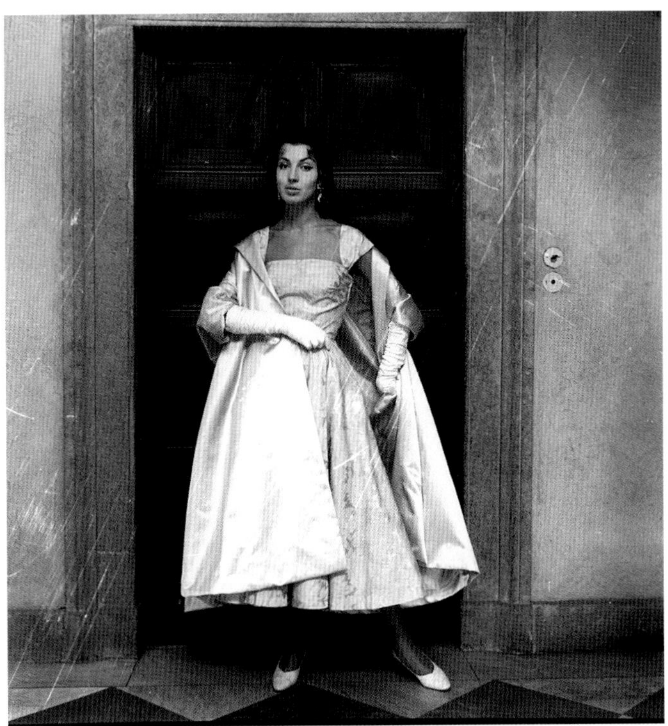

Fashion shot, Paris, 1950s

Paul Scofield remembered Deakin as 'giving the impression of dampness...I remember thinking uncomfortably that he didn't like me.'[8] Certainly no one was producing for *Vogue* at that time such tightly cropped headshots with no pretence to flattery, no concessions to the sitters' vanity and scant regard for what the magazine really wanted. They resemble nothing so much as the police mugshots that Daniel Farson first recognized them for,[9] and it was bold of the editor to publish so many so frequently. Granted she invariably allowed them to be cropped and reduced on the page, sensing that readers, in an age when the theatrical whimsy of Cecil Beaton was still *de rigueur*, would be repelled by such frank, unvarnished pictures of their favourite stars. In the years that followed Deakin at *Vogue*, only the photographers David Bailey and Richard Avedon would ever come near to matching his raw quality and the deep black tones of his enlargements. Perhaps only Irving Penn, one of the few photographers he is known to have admired, shared contemporaneously the same vision – stripped-down and free of artifice.

Needless to say, Deakin kept to one side of the *Vogue* pantheon of imagemakers and was never part of the wider photographic establishment, best exemplified at the time by the realism of Bill Brandt and the dominance of *Picture Post*'s romantic, occasionally gritty, notion of English life. He admired Brandt's vision of London, as outlined in the book *Camera in London* (1949), but Cecil Beaton, a contemporary at *Vogue*, he loathed. He took gleeful pleasure in taunting another colleague, Norman Parkinson, for wearing an embroidered hat as a good-luck charm. Deakin belonged more to the artistic demi-monde of London's bohemian quarter, Soho, the lure of whose pubs, clubs and parties led him away from permanent employment. He was naturally at ease not with the grandes dames of the fashion world but with the creative souls and maverick talents that defined the metropolitan cultural life of his times.

Many of the *Vogue* portraits included studies of these Soho figures, most famously the painters whom he knew well and whose number he had hoped to join – Francis Bacon, Lucian Freud, John Minton, Eduardo Paolozzi, Michael Andrews, Roberts Colquhoun and MacBryde, Frank Auerbach, Timothy Behrens, Keith Vaughan, William Scott and many others. An *artist manqué*, his eye would always be quick to recognize genius in painting, while affecting to care little, if anything at all, for the achievements of photographers. In addition, under his bed, there were portraits of the lesser known, the 'dubious' characters of Soho, such as Gerald Hamilton, the alleged model for 'Mr Norris' in Christopher Isherwood's first Berlin novel. Other portraits, also taken for *Vogue*, remain incisive documents of their time because their subjects were leading figures of literature, the theatre and film: poets like Dylan Thomas and W. H. Auden, directors like

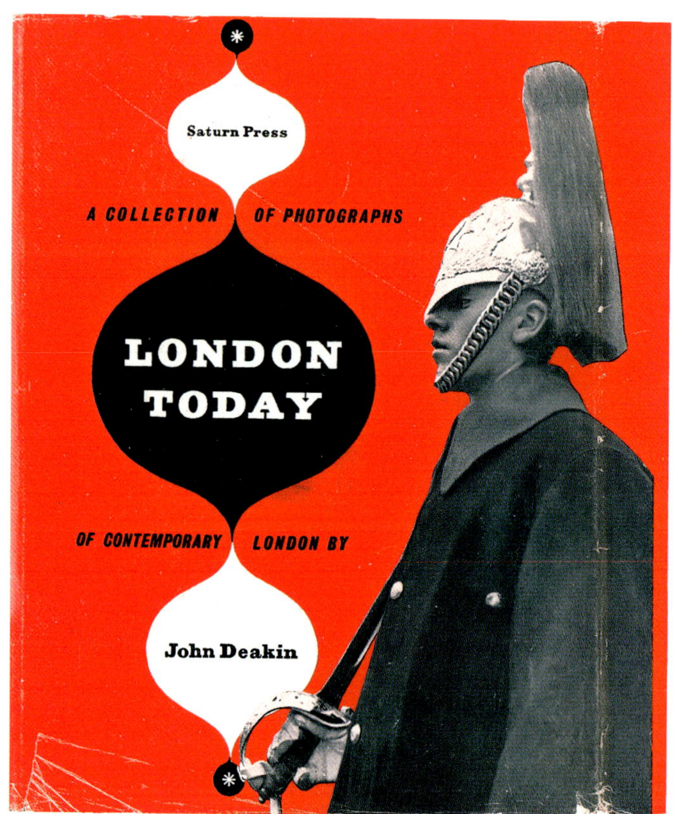

Left to right: Cover of *London Today*, with text and photographs by Deakin, 1949; announcement of the exhibition 'John Deakin's Paris' which opened at the Parton Gallery in Soho on 9 July 1956; cover of *Rome Alive*, by Christopher Kininmonth, with photographs by Deakin, 1951.

David Lean and John Huston, actors such as Humphrey Bogart and Yves Montand.

These portraits have remained largely intact, though haphazardly looked after by the magazine that commissioned them, but Deakin's street photographs appear mostly to have slipped from view, not least because in the end he cared more about painting than about photography. Dan Farson lamented particularly the loss of his series on the 'clochards', the down-and-outs of Paris, while Bruce Bernard wrote that 'Deakin unfortunately didn't care much for what he did best and I'm sure he resented the fact that it was just that. Perhaps never believing in photography's ultimate refinements gave him his cutting edge.'[10]

Recuperating during April and May in the 'Marie Celeste Ward' of the Westminster Hospital (the irony did not escape him), Deakin was only a little exhausted by 'the spilt champagnes, the vintage port, the fine champagne cognac, the endless visitors, flowers everywhere. The whole thing was quite out of hand...'[11] One visitor helped himself to a glass of water: 'I nearly choked. The decanter was full of neat gin. God knows how he does it, but he does seem to be having a ball.'[12] He was also preoccupied with his travel plans and ideas for the future. In the Berwick Street flat he still kept the maquettes of several unfinished book projects abandoned when he decided to give up photography in the 1960s. There was one on a steelworks and a tyre factory in Genoa and one on Paris, which had developed out of an exhibition he had held in 1956 at the Parton Gallery, below David Archer's Bookshop in Soho. There were the layouts for 'Eight Portraits', a projected book of character sketches in words and photographs of those few people he had found especially interesting. (He didn't need to like or admire them – or they him. Of Stephen Spender, one of the eight, he wrote: 'I had and have no feelings whatsoever about him except one of slight wonder that anyone should make me disapprove of myself so much.'[13]) There were also the first few pages of a larger

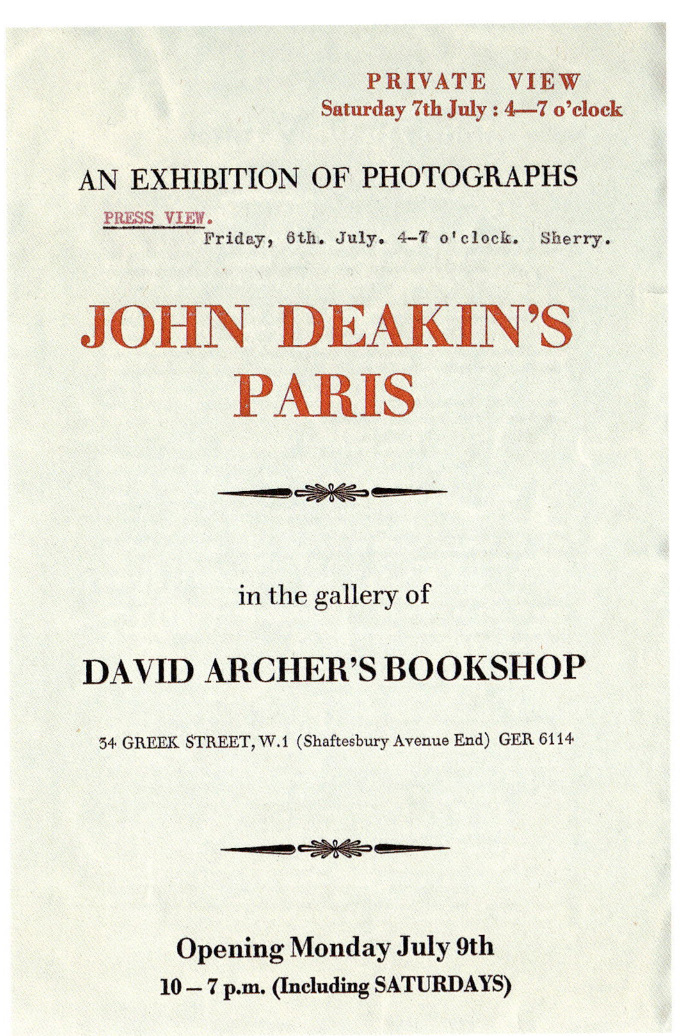

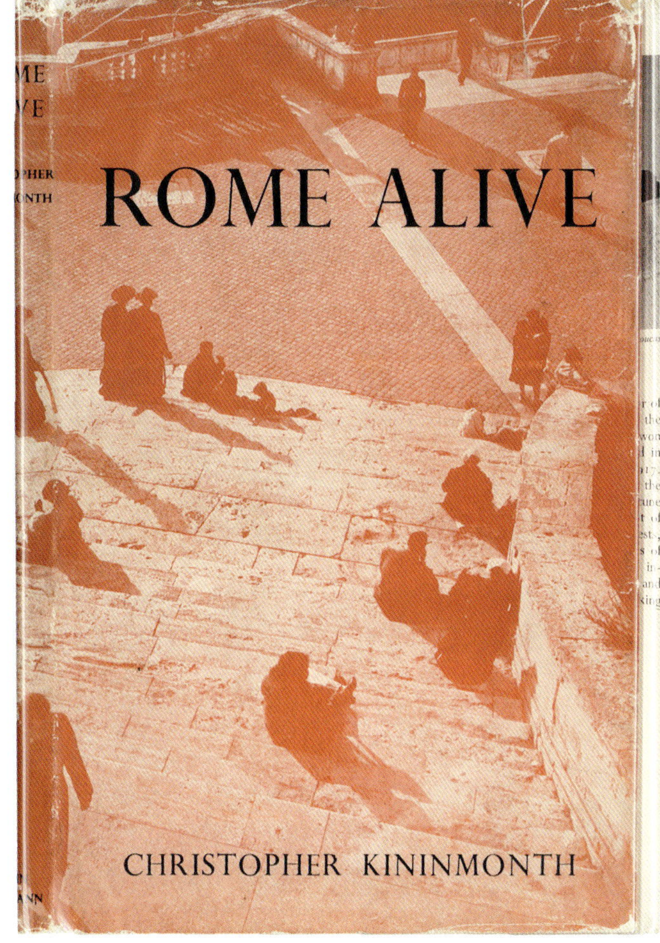

book of portraits which it is believed he wanted Elizabeth Smart, a friend and the author of *By Grand Central Station I Sat Down and Wept* (1945), to introduce. There is evidence too of a second book of Rome photographs (the first was published as *Rome Alive* in 1951) and some mounted prints that suggest he had been working on a book of tattoos and skin decoration.[14] Lastly there are maquettes of two uncompleted books: 'London Walls' and 'Paris Walls'. These two were to be Deakin's document of a vanishing vernacular, fleeting signals from another age: chalked-up children's games, graffitied messages of love or anger to the world and the richly textured shapes and surfaces of street signs, peeling walls, window shutters and shop-front banners.

The manuscript for 'Eight Portraits' is intriguing because its eight handwritten pages are as near to a photographic manifesto as Deakin ever came to articulating: 'In taking one photograph a good photographer is really taking two, one with the camera in his hands, and one with the visual imagination. The photograph in his head is a photograph of his idea of the sitter and he needs perception and study to have the idea. The other is easy. But the two photographs have to be superimposed one on the other in some peculiar and inexplicable way at the moment when the camera clicks, and that is very hard indeed.

'Being fatally drawn to the human race, what I want to do when I photograph it is to make a revelation about it. So my sitters turn into my victims. But I would like to add that it is only those with a daemon, however small and of whatever kind, whose faces lend themselves to be victimised at all. And the only complaints I have ever had from my victims have been from the bad ones, the vainies, the meanies.'[15]

Though he was frequently scornful of photography and its practitioners (especially his former colleagues at *Vogue*), he carried out his work with an insouciance that hid a rigorous discipline and, as 'Eight Portraits' shows, a pride in the results. On rare occasions that pride was publicly displayed.

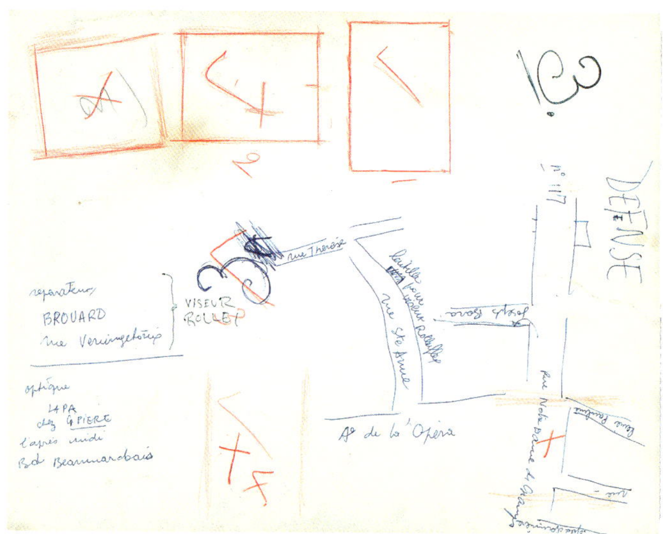

Sketch on the reverse of a photograph taken for the proposed book 'Paris Walls', 1950s

In the Gallery of David Archer's Bookshop
34 Greek Street W 1 (Shaftesbury Avenue end)

AN EXHIBITION OF PHOTOGRAPHS

JOHN DEAKIN'S ROME

PRIVATE VIEW: 3—7 PM Tuesday September 18th 1956

Daily 10—7 (Thursdays 10—1) GER 6114

Invitation to the opening of the exhibition 'John Deakin's Rome', September 1956

When Farson first met Deakin in the early 1950s, he remarked that he too was a part-time photographer, working for *Picture Post*. Deakin hastily arranged a viewing of his life's work. For the younger man the event was something of a personal epiphany, as recounted in at least four of his books. From his second volume of memoirs, Farson recalls: 'By now I had no illusions about the "art" of photography, knowing how much a photographer depends on other people...but as he laid his prints out on the floor with the wistful anxiety of a carpet-seller in a Turkish bazaar, I was stunned by their impact....The cruelty was deliberate.'[16]

All these projects remained unpublished and, despite Audrey Withers's efforts, there is little reason to believe that any publisher ever saw them or that, in the end, Deakin wanted them in book form at all. What reputation he had previously had as a photographer had now all but disappeared. This was partly due to his concentrating his efforts on trying to emulate the painters he knew with a cheerful style of 'Sunday painting' (though he took it very seriously) and partly because the louche glamour that had clung to him as an 'ex-*Vogue* photographer' had dissipated in the fifteen years since his sacking from the magazine. Despite this lack of recognition, which he had done much to encourage, he was aware of the international reputations of friends and acquaintances, such as Bacon and Lucian Freud, and of his own unique position as an intimate of both and, as court jester, a vital part of the circles surrounding them. 'He somehow managed to manipulate the court with malevolent glee,' observed Jeffrey Bernard, Bruce's younger brother, 'He could be very funny and a cap with bells would have gone down well with his obligatory pink gin.'[17] The oldest Bernard brother, Oliver, remembers his 'wide-open, voracious gaze'.[18]

Deakin was the best chronicler of their milieu, Soho, the recording angel of a time and place that shaped their futures and that had, by the early 1970s, drawn to a close. At times his eye was merciless, as his nude portraits of Henrietta Moraes (*c.* 1963) and contact sheets of a dissolute John Davenport (1952), the writer and critic, show. Equally, he could reveal moments of compassion and pathos in portraits of friends such as the doomed painters John Minton (1951) and Robert Colquhoun and Robert MacBryde (1951). His photograph of Dylan Thomas in the graveyard at Laugharne (1949) is perhaps his best-known. In a letter, Thomas describes how he was photographed 'inside the railings of a tomb, my hair, uncut for months, either completely covering my face (I think he liked that) or blown up like a great, dancing, mousey busby'.[19] Francis Bacon, who owned a print of the Thomas photograph, considered Deakin's portraits to be 'the best since Nadar and Julia Margaret Cameron'.[20]

Freud and Bacon appear as two of the 'Eight Portraits'. Deakin photographed the former on dozens of occasions

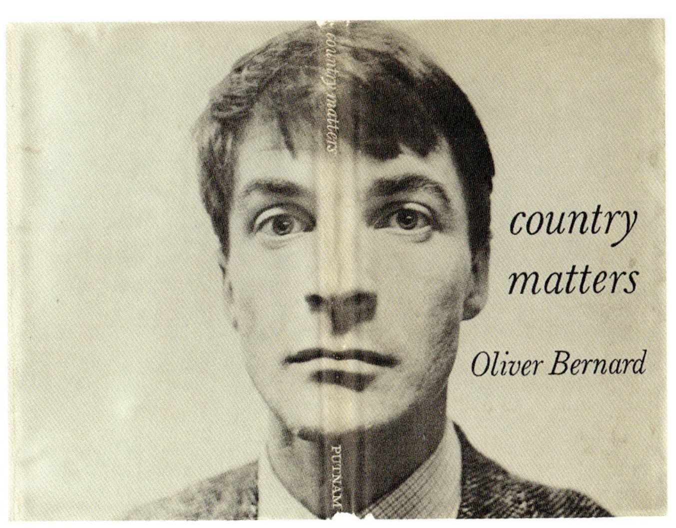

Oliver Bernard photographed by John Deakin, on the cover of the poet's 1960 collection, *Country Matters*

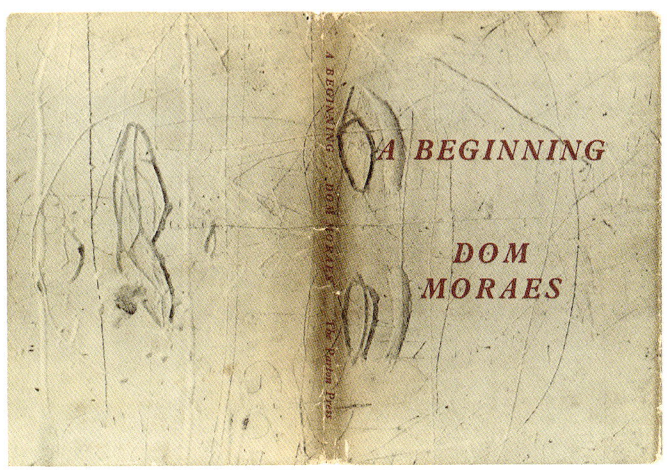

Cover of *A Beginning*, poems by Dom Moraes (1957), with Deakin's photograph of Paris graffiti

and in 1963 Freud painted a small likeness of the self-styled man with the 'huge Mickey Mouse smile'.[21] It was written up in the *Daily Telegraph* in 1968 under the headline 'Studies of Compelling Nastiness'.[22] To Deakin this more than made up for the interminable sittings. Freud, noting Deakin's mixture of vulnerability and rancour, described him as 'like Cinderella and the Ugly Sisters at the same time'.[23] For his part, Deakin made the following observation of Freud: 'He is such a strange, fox-like person, but he does like creating small fusses.'[24] Deakin undertook portrait commissions of Bacon's friends for the artist to use as aide-mémoires when painting their likenesses. Many of these finished prints lay on Bacon's studio floor, creased, abraded, spattered with paint and abandoned when their usefulness was over. He took many portraits of the painter himself in the *Vogue* studio, in his own studio, on street corners in Soho, attending exhibitions, travelling on the Orient Express and drinking in Soho, Limehouse and beyond. And of Bacon he wrote in 'Eight Portraits': 'He's an odd one, wonderfully tender and generous by nature, yet with curious streaks of cruelty, especially to his friends. I think that in this portrait I managed to catch something of the fear which must underlie these contradictions in his character.'[25]

In October 1971, six months before the onset of his final illness, Deakin had travelled to Paris as part of Bacon's entourage to attend the painter's retrospective at the Grand Palais. The two had previously had a row and Bacon had withdrawn Deakin's tickets to the opening. Though unwell, Deakin insisted on making the trip and Bacon relented enough partly to pay his way. 'At the top of the grandest of grand staircases', Deakin wrote to Farson, 'he [Bacon] hugged me and begged forgiveness. Surprising as his motto is never to apologise...'[26] Deakin's surviving letters from this time are exuberant, displaying a zest for life despite financial worries and a serious skin disease: '...mouth and throat full of ulcers, unable to eat, poisoned big toe oozing pus, itching blisters round my arse and my prick skinned and raw'. He continued: 'The [Bacon] show was of such magnificence it was worth the unspeakable agony.'[27] Such generosity towards the successes of friends was uncharacteristic. 'Deakin', Farson wrote in his memoirs, 'was almost physically ill when I had good luck.' He added: 'Many people found Deakin pathetic. Spellbound as I was by the force of his personality, I found him as pathetic as Goebbels. He was treacherous to his friends and possessed a skill in playing one against the other...'[28]

It would be Deakin's last visit to Paris, the city which he regarded as his second home and where some forty years before he had first picked up a camera. In return for the fare, Deakin's role this time – though it was only casually expressed – was to ensure that Bacon's lover George Dyer stayed out of trouble, which meant, though it did not need to be spelt out, that he was to be kept away from bars or

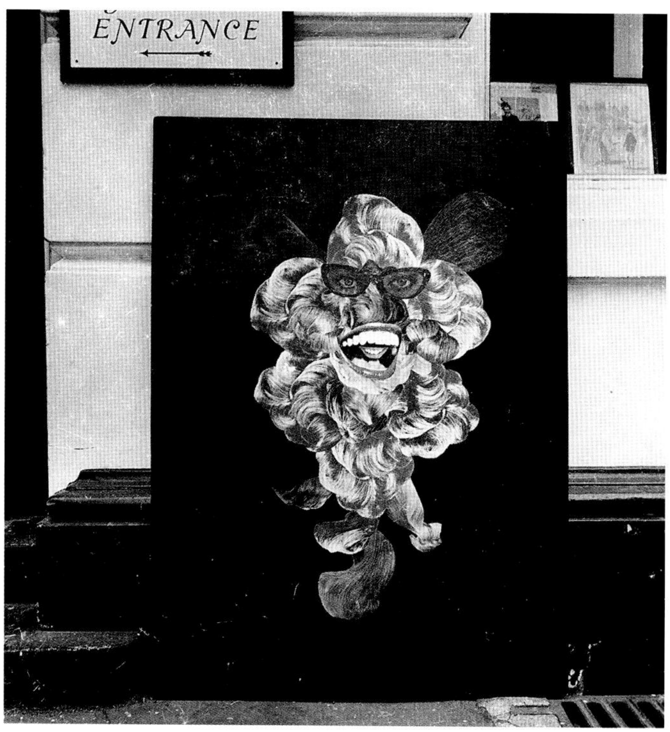

Collage by John Deakin, 1960s

anywhere else he might buy alcohol. Bacon's relationship with Dyer was waning. Deakin later reported that in London, before the party set off, 'Georgey [was] morose and not drinking...just out of a home for his sixth cure.'[29] In the event, Deakin failed Bacon greatly, for Dyer died drunk, unattended and having taken an overdose in the bathroom of his hotel suite on the morning of 24 October, the day before the official opening of Bacon's show and the lavish reception for the artist. Neglecting his charge, Deakin broke away from the Bacon party and used this time in Paris to walk the streets he had known since before the war. In a long letter written to Farson on 9 November, Deakin recounted the build-up to the exhibition, his own degenerating health – 'couldn't eat but lived on brandy to kill the pain' – gossip about mutual friends and exhortations to Farson to write to him in hospital. He hoped that Farson might find 'in your tea-chests...the negs. of my early Paris pix which I should dearly love to have'.[30] This was a surprising request. Deakin had never made any attempt previously to reacquire material. *Vogue* was still storing for him a large number of negatives, uncommissioned by the magazine, which it wanted to return (it never succeeded). Perhaps this is an indication of an interest in his œuvre rekindled by the Paris trip.

The death of George Dyer elicited only a line in the same letter to Farson, a postscript scrawled at the bottom of a page (and a post-postscript at that): 'PPS How about George's demise!'[31] A second letter, dated 17 November – a much fuller account of the Paris trip – did not mention the dead man at all. Paris had clearly enthralled Deakin again and he was thrilled to recount to Farson the last evening of the four-day celebrations, spent at La Coupole. A Frenchman at their table 'said in amazement "but the accent, it is pure Parisian, it is unbelievable!" Himself [Bacon] who was holding court immediately swung round and asked "WHOSE accent is pure Parisian?" I adjusted an invisible shoulder-strap and pointed a finger at my bosom, lowering my lashes in fake modesty. A very hard look I got.'[32]

Though Deakin's greatest pleasure was in painting, and in the company of painters, his own art has been judged harshly by history, art critics and even his most loyal friends. In his later life, his work was exhibited only occasionally and rarely well-received. In 1956 he showed in London at the St George's Gallery, St James's.[33] The exhibition was not the success he had hoped for, despite several pre-opening notices, including one in *Vogue*, which reproduced in its March issue his painting *The Coster*. 'He wanted to be an artist', remarked George Melly, 'like Man Ray wanted to be a painter. But his paintings? Oh no. I don't think so...'[34] Whatever its shortcomings, however, Deakin's is a distinctive style, if highly decorative, primitive and untutored. His approach resembles that of Camille Bombois, the circus-wrestler-turned-painter, whom he much admired and whom he photographed for *Vogue* in

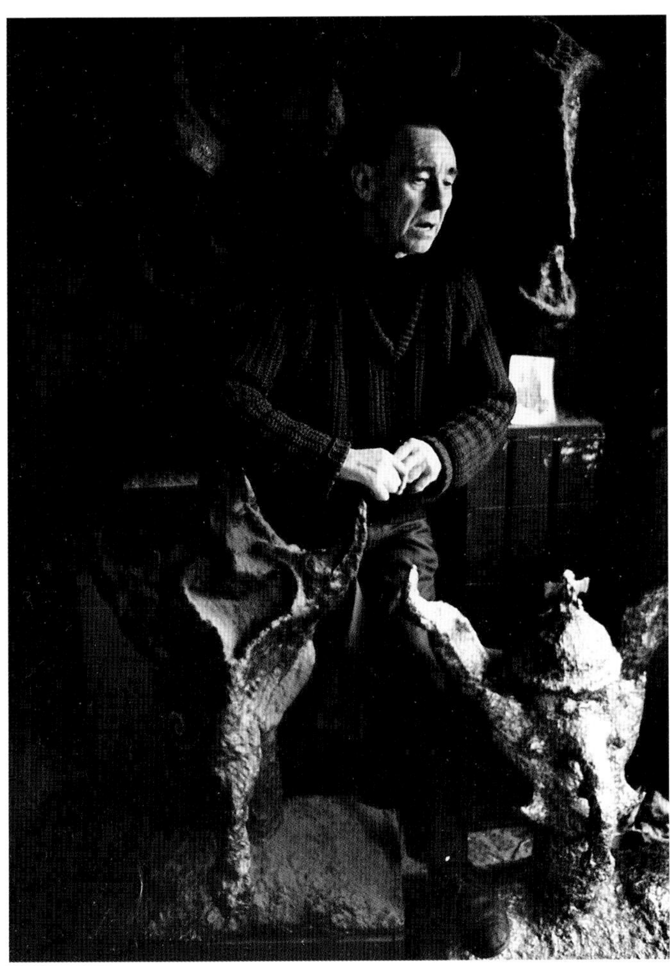

John Deakin with his papier-mâché sculptures, 1960s. Photographer unknown

1952. Deakin's medium was frequently gloss paint on board and his subject matter idiosyncratic: cameos of friends such as Bacon (tattooed) and Farson (with bright yellow hair), pearly kings and queens, monsters of the deep, idealized sailors, vases of flowers and imaginary landscapes. Farson considered 'sophisticates' to be a more accurate description of work so calculatedly artless, observing that Deakin feared success more than failure, and embraced the latter with a customary nonchalance.[35]

In the light of the judgments of his contemporaries, it is surprising to learn that his homespun naivety did have its admirers, including the American humorist S. J. Perelman, who bought a portrait of Queen Mary, and the ever-supportive Audrey Withers: '[his painting] is excellent', she wrote to a mutual acquaintance, qualifying it with 'of its "Sunday painter" type'.[36] *Portal Painters*, a survey of idiosyncratic British artists published in 1982, boldly compares his domestic interiors to the tradition of Vermeer and Van Eyck, but admits, 'his luck as a painter had been abysmal'.[37] Apart from painting, Deakin also made collages, superimposing pictures of eyes, ears and mouths torn from glossy magazines on to pictures of domestic utensils, fruits and vegetables. He gave them titles such as 'Mr Lionel Bart' and 'Miss Joan Littlewood', explaining to Farson, 'They won't be able to resist it when they see their own names!'[38] – but resist they invariably did. Farson recalled that the show's only notice ran in the *Daily Mail*: 'I hope', wrote the anonymous reviewer, 'that the artist's optimism in charging such prices is not matched by the public's enthusiasm.'[39] After that Deakin created sculpture of a kind, mounting broken doll's heads on plinths and threading their crania with transfers of ferns, and constructed 'grotesques' from papier-mâché and chicken wire. Neither met with popular success or critical approbation.

Apparently unknown to most of Deakin's friends – it is unmentioned in any of Farson's books and all subsequent articles or exhibition catalogues – some years previously he had enjoyed some small notoriety as a painter.[40] An exhibition held at the Mayor Gallery in London's West End in 1938 drew a considerable amount of press coverage, not least perhaps because the Museum of Modern Art, New York, had earlier the same year held a controversial show of similarly 'instinctive' artworks, 'Masters of Popular Painting'.

At least four critics recognized in Deakin's work the influence of Rouault – an 'unblushing influence', thought the *The Studio*'s critic.[41] His paintings were considered by another writer to be 'slightly Byzanto-Grotesque'.[42]

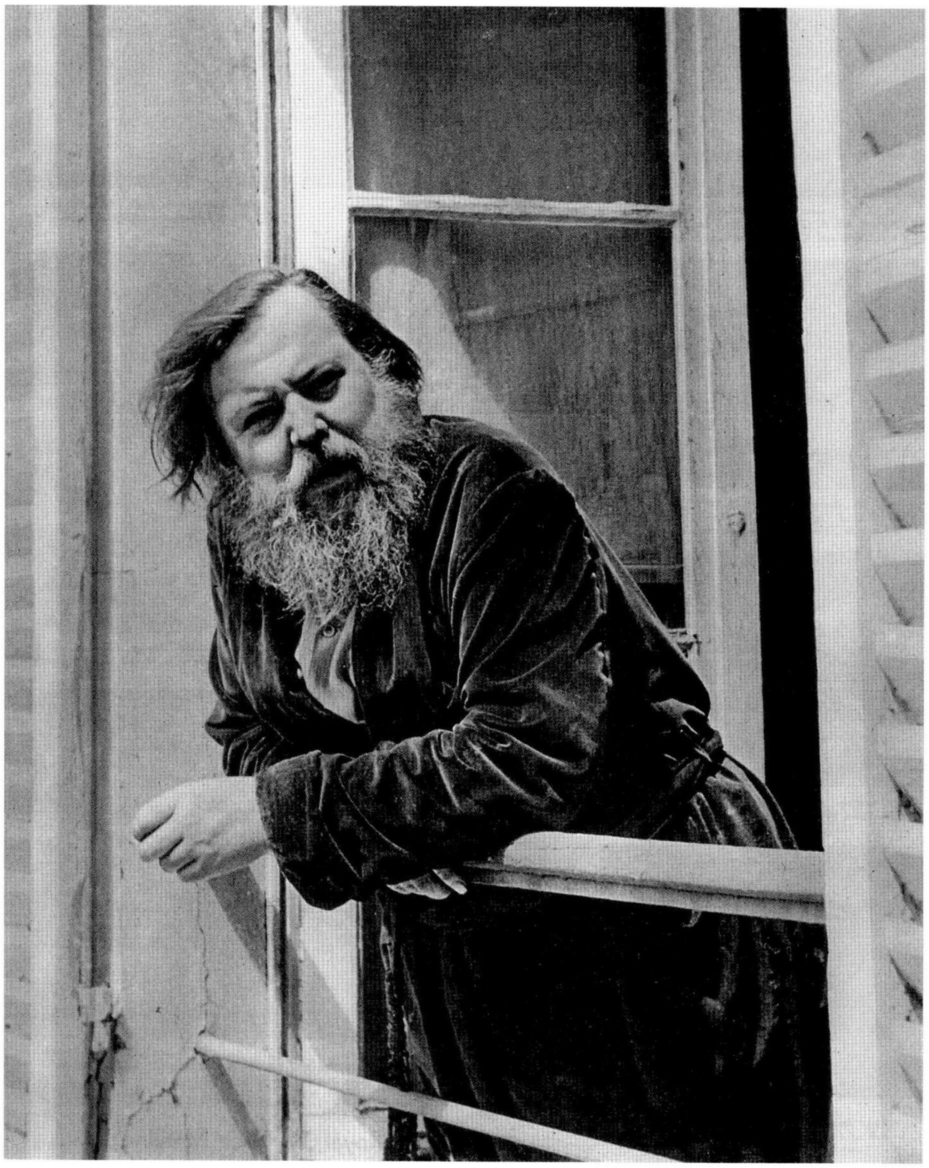

Christian Bérard, fashion illustrator and set designer, Paris, 1947

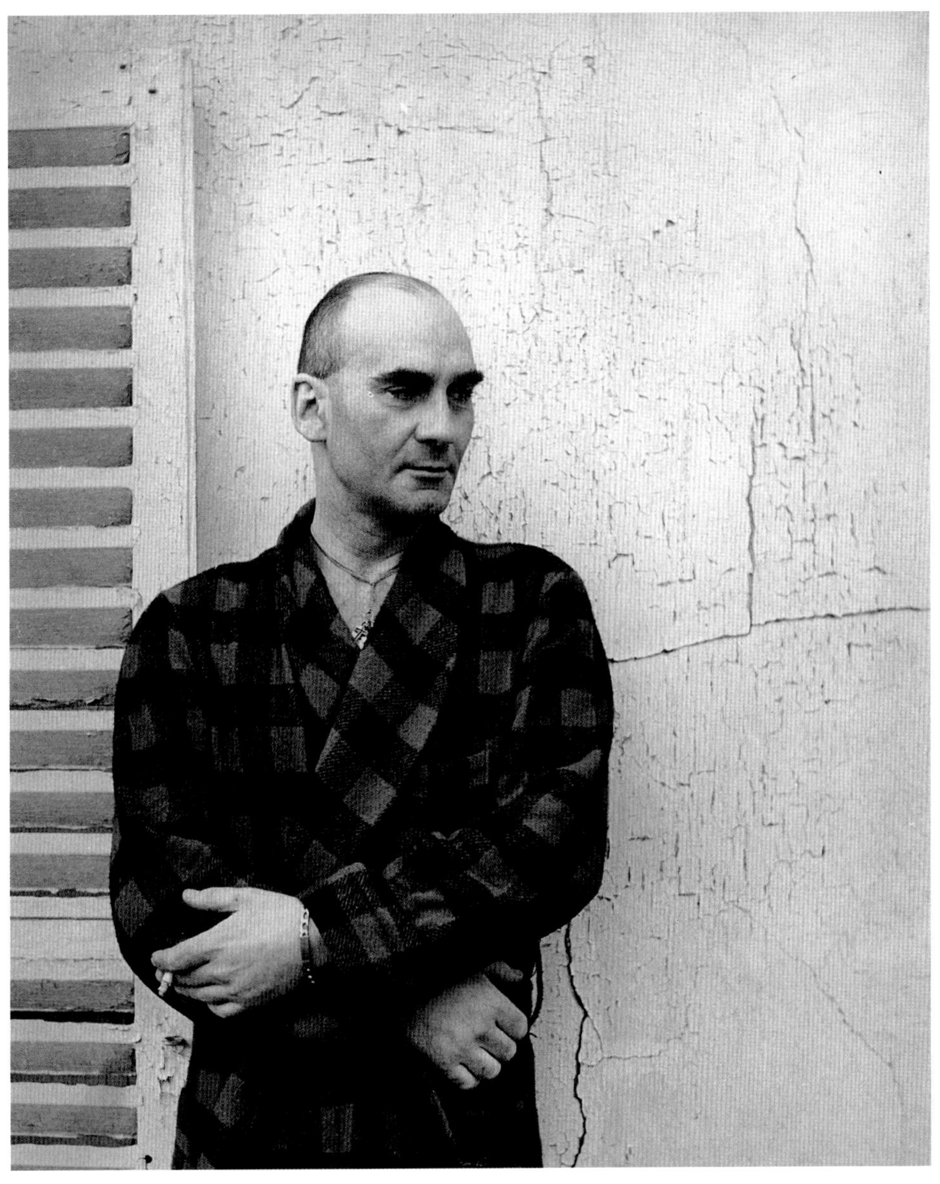

Boris Kochno, ballet dancer, Paris, 1947

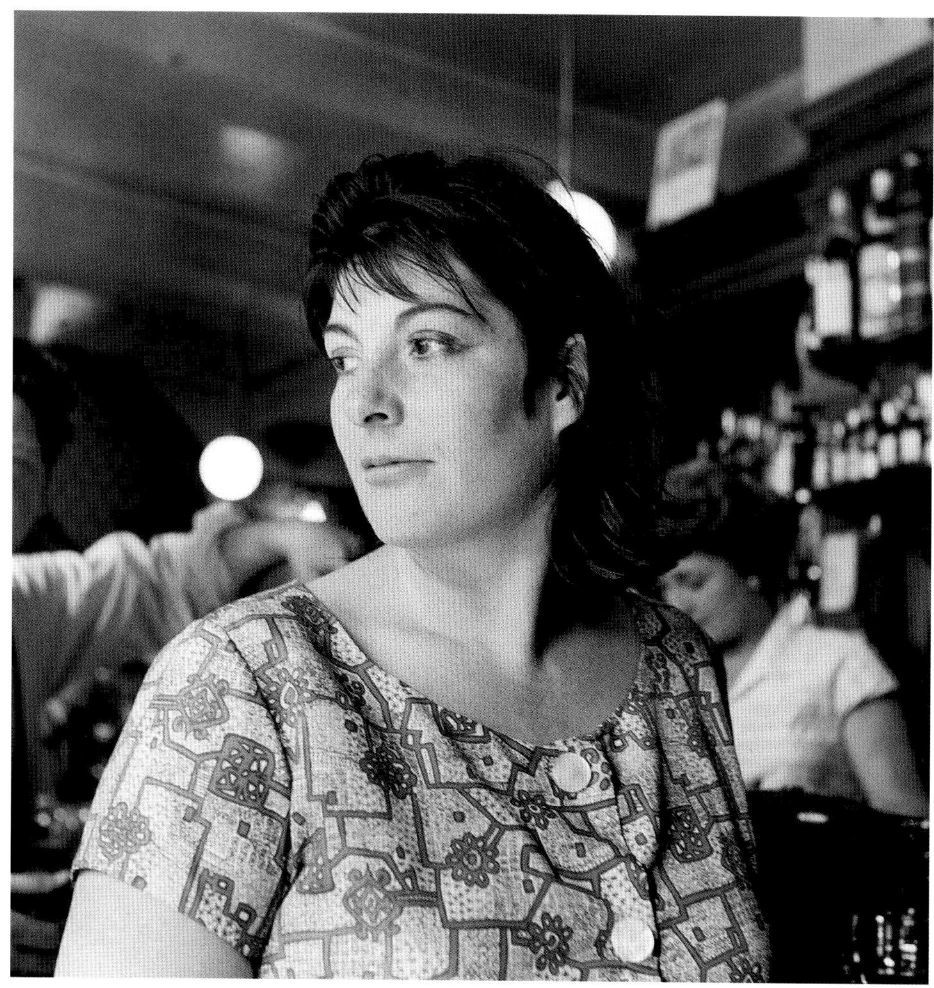

Henrietta Moraes, model for Francis Bacon and Lucian Freud, London, 1950s

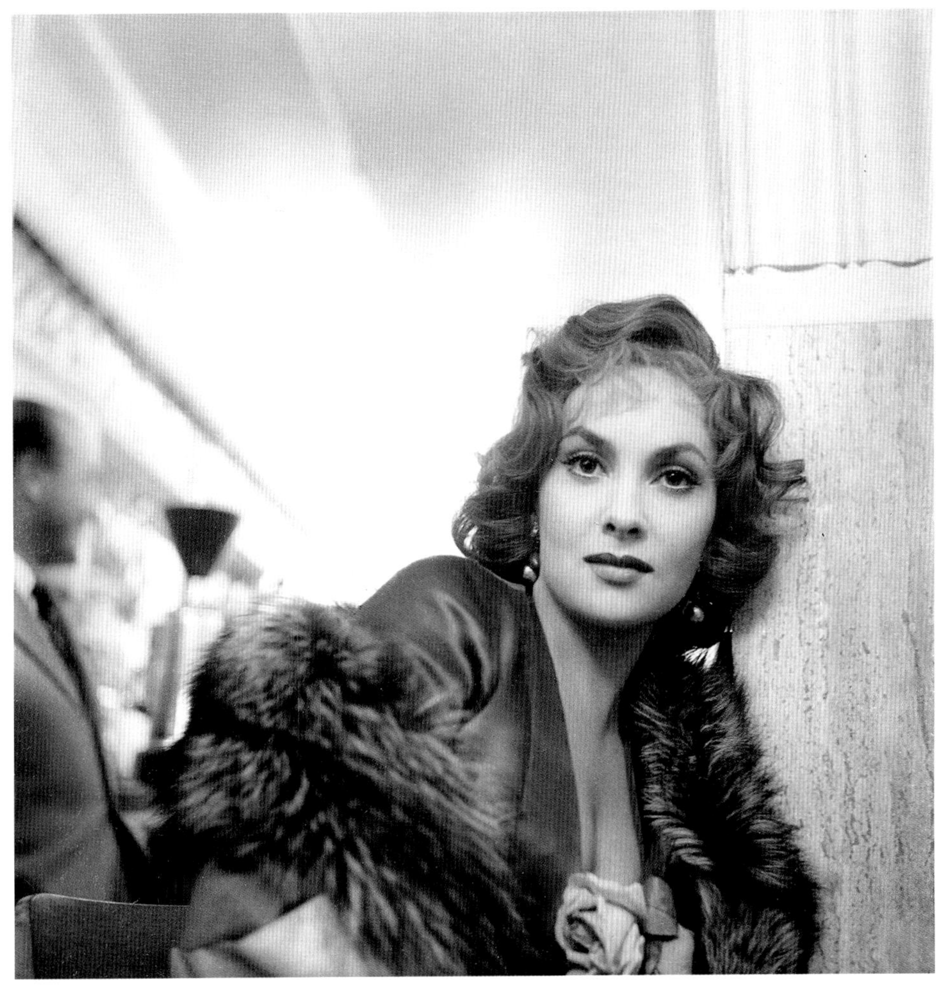

Gina Lollobrigida, actor, London, 1954

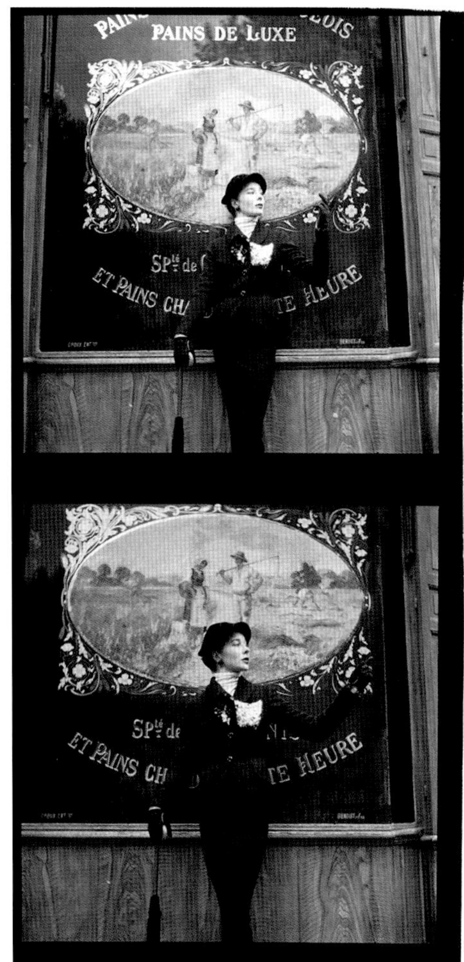

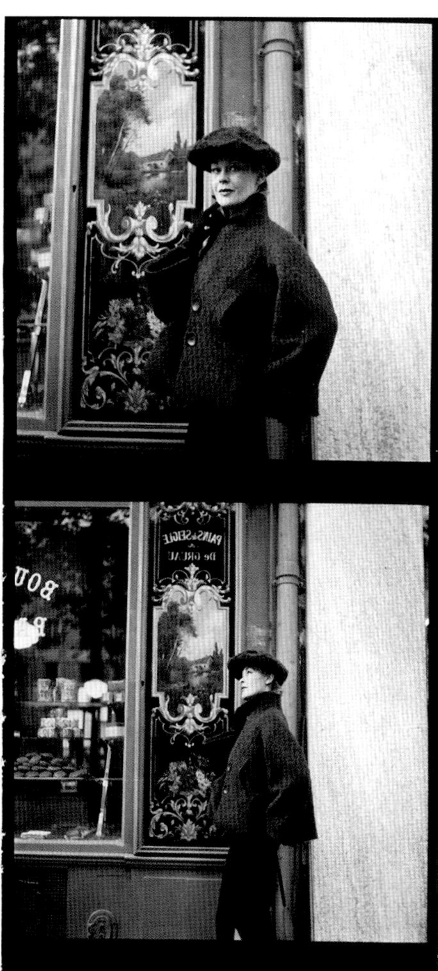

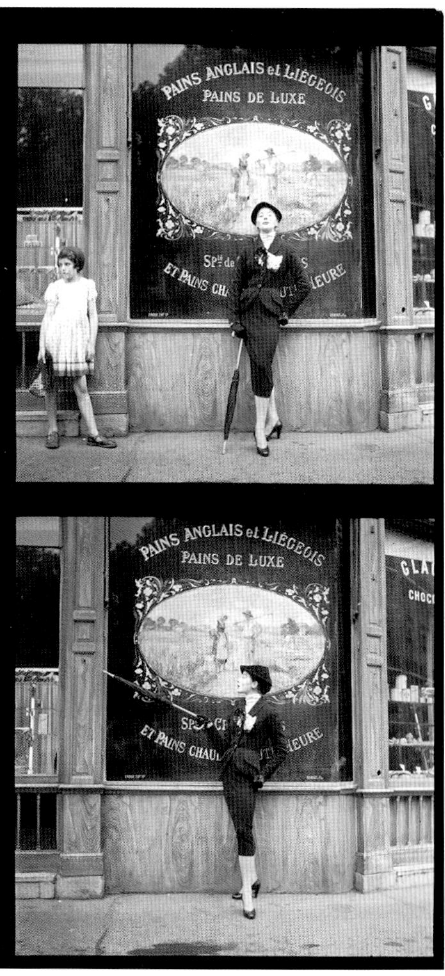

Above and opposite: Fashion photographs for 'L'Album de la mode de *Figaro*', Paris, 1950s

The reviewer for the *Sunday Times* stated admiringly that if one were to 'turn them upside down, they still make chromatic sense'.[43] Jan Gordon of *The Observer* believed the painter was 'certainly ear-marked for some sort of reputation'.[44] Most revealing of all is a short article, 'In Search of Paints', in the London *Evening Standard*. It relates details of Deakin's early life, which he invariably took pains to suppress, and sheds light on how the self-confessed (though inaccurately so) 'poor boy from the Liverpool slums' came to travel the world and eventually land up in Paris where his photographic career began: 'Mr Deakin has been painting on the island of Tahiti. One day he ran short of paints and discovered that, despite Tahiti's Gauguin tradition, the island was paintless. Leaving a half-finished canvas, he took ship for Fiji, six hundred miles away. But here too he drew a blank. A further week's journey brought him to the New Hebrides. In New Caledonia, some two thousand miles away from his starting point, he was lucky. He struck paint in a Chinese chemist's shop, returned to Tahiti after a month's absence and went on with his picture...'[45]

Deakin was notorious for his evasiveness, which led Jeffrey Bernard to lament that 'he never wrote down any of his fund of self-deprecatory anecdotes'.[46] Airy remarks about being born 'in Liverpool, near the Leper Colony...', for example, fed the sense of shadiness that already followed him everywhere, along with the habitual trail of dandruff, cigarette ash and spilt red wine.

That he was able to hold the exhibition at the Mayor Gallery and travel throughout Polynesia was entirely due to a wealthy patron, the American art collector Arthur Jeffress. Deakin became Jeffress's companion and travelled the world with him from the South Sea Islands to Mexico and the United States. His fine collection of paintings apart, Jeffress is chiefly remembered by art historians as an early benefactor of Francis Bacon and by social historians as a hugely extravagant and fervent party giver.[47] His notorious 'Red and White Party', held in 1931, predating his association with Deakin, led to his temporary exile abroad. Some guests arrived in red and white nuns' habits and the party eventually got out of hand when men gyrated

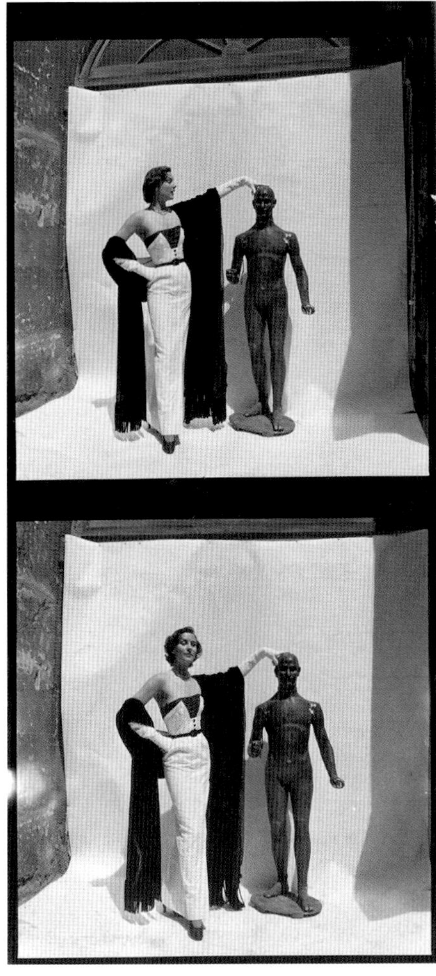
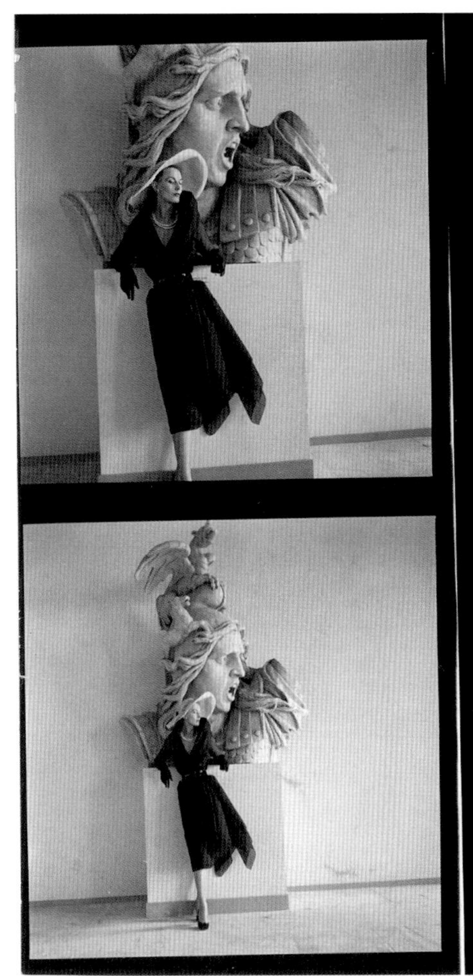
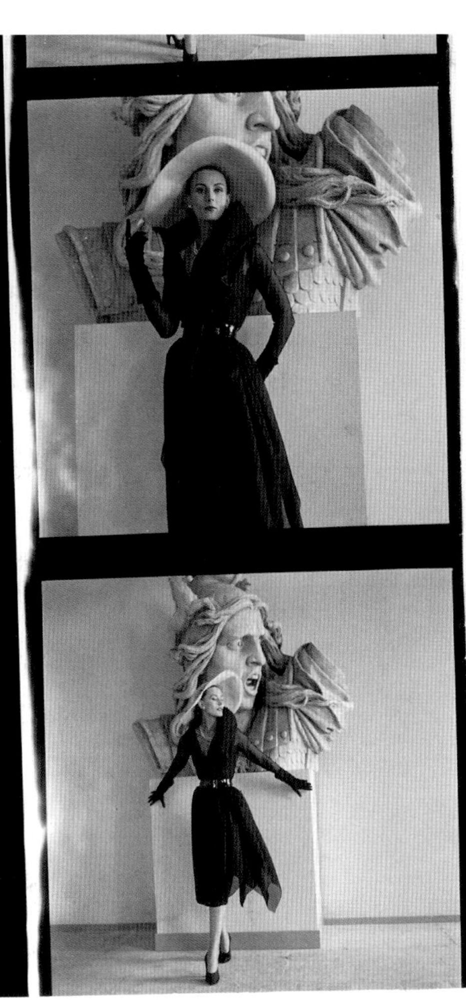

stripped to the waist, while one partygoer, dressed as Queen Elizabeth I in a doublet, pearls and scarlet wig, entertained his fellow guests with *Abide With Me* on the organ. Jeffress was photographed in what appeared to be an evening gown and the picture ran in several daily papers to great disapproval.[48] Much later, having settled in Venice, Jeffress was implicated in a blackmail case involving a gondolier, the local Chief of Police and the policeman's wife. The ramifications led to his booking himself in 1963 into a Paris hotel and there committing suicide. By that time he and Deakin had long parted company, but for one optimistic moment, according to Farson, Deakin imagined himself the heir to a fortune. After all, he had, he claimed, introduced Jeffress to Soutine and Bombois....[49]

It seems likely that Jeffress parted from Deakin in Paris sometime in the spring of 1939, the year in which Deakin accidentally discovered photography. Deakin's story of how this occurred is a highly colourful tale, one he continued to embroider over the years. Elizabeth Smart wrote her own account of it in 1956.[50] Asking herself the question: 'Who is John Deakin?', she replied, 'He is a photographer with extraordinary eyes.' She continued: 'John Deakin became a photographer because someone left a camera in his flat after a party in Paris. He woke up with a terrible hangover and went out and took six pictures. It was a cheap camera and he'd never taken a picture before, but his tyrannical eyes took over. From then on they lugged him and his camera all over Paris and half the world as well.'

In the light of Jeffress's generosity, the account becomes more romantic and somewhat implausible: 'He tramped holes in his shoes. He starved. He slept under the arches. Dizzy and lightheaded he followed his fanatical eyes, steeling himself to invade the privacy of suffering. "But at least they could beg. I couldn't." Anyhow, his eyes had no mercy.'

In those days, Deakin's guide around the streets of Paris was invariably one Paul Dieu, 'a threadbare aristocrat with sharp eyes and Parisian wit, who slept in the gutter with the grace of a renaissance angel'.[51] It seems probable that it

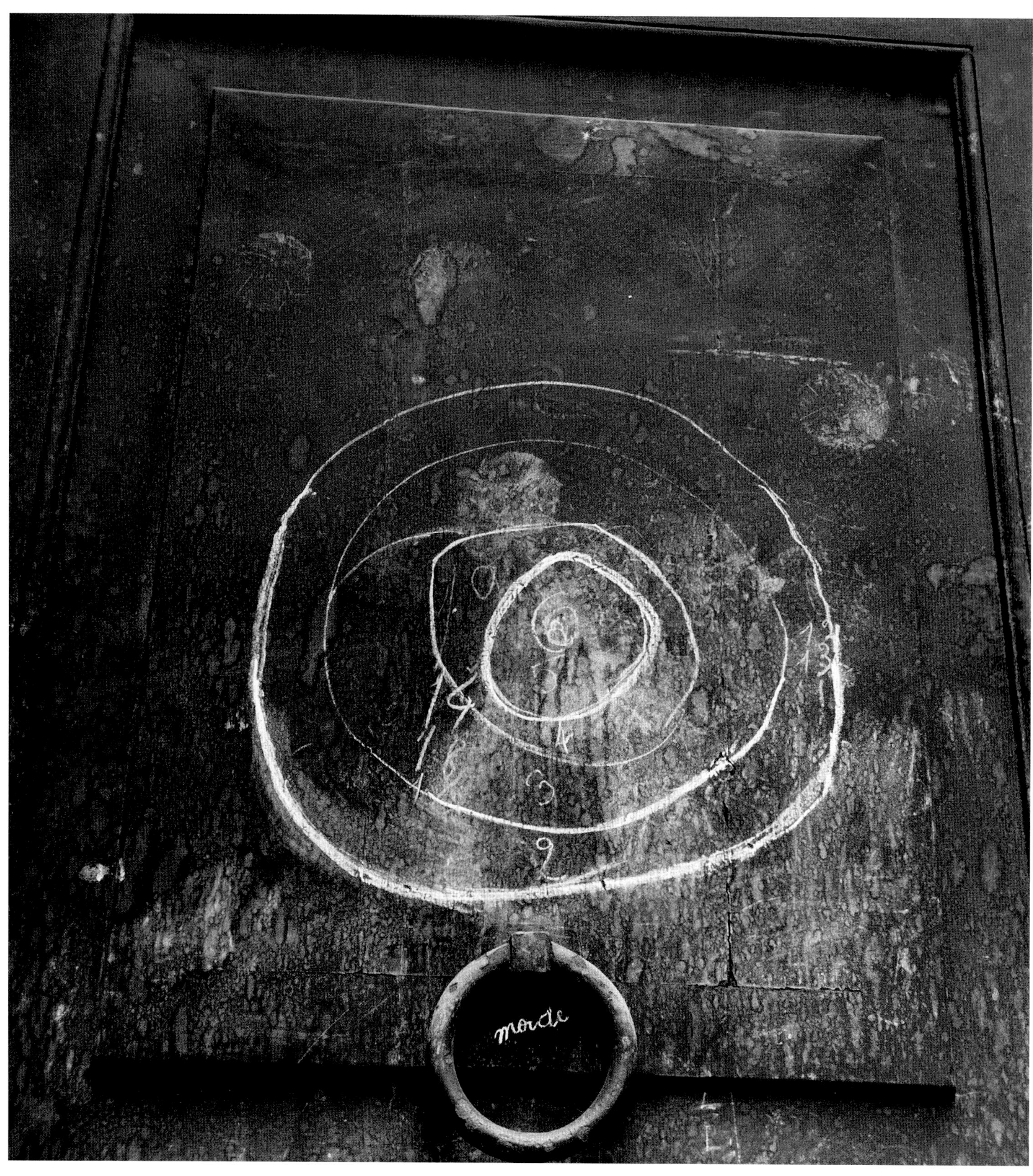

Target graffiti, Paris, 1950s

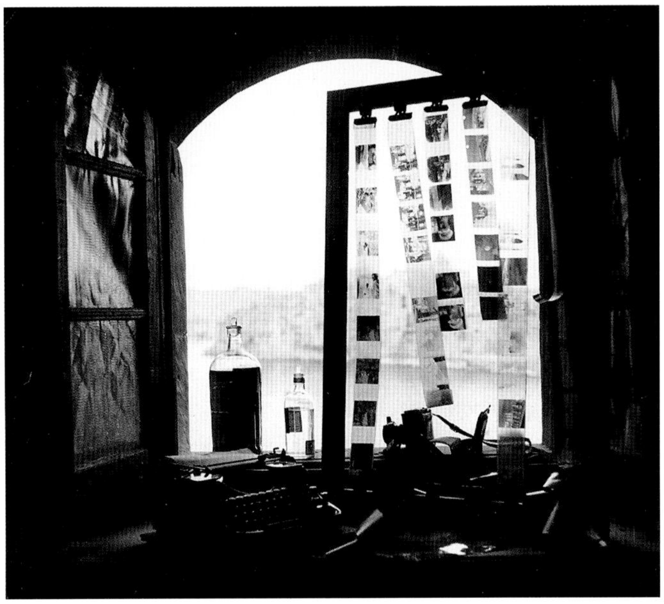

Sergeant John Deakin's quarters, Malta, 1942

was in Dieu's unconventional circle that Deakin met Christian Bérard, who in turn introduced him to Michel de Brunhoff, the editor of French *Vogue*. Though *Vogue* shut down during the Occupation, in 1939 the magazine was at its graphic and photographic peak and no one depicted the *folie de grandeur* of the times so convincingly and colourfully as its prized contributor Christian 'Bébé' Bérard. Skilled in many branches of the fine and applied arts, from set and interior design to portrait painting, he was most enduringly a fashion illustrator for *Vogue*. Towards the end of his life he became a chronic opium addict and Edna Woolman-Chase, Editor-in-Chief of American *Vogue*, lamented that 'his black beard was full of spaghetti and little active pets who lodged there.'[52] Bérard's dishevelled bohemianism is at its most pronounced in the photograph Deakin took of him squinting toward the lens from the balcony of his apartment (p. 16). He would have less than two years to live. If Deakin can be believed, by introducing him to de Brunhoff, Bérard was pivotal to his photographic career. Though de Brunhoff rarely used him, and not at all during 1939 or in the early months of *Vogue*'s revival in 1945, he was impressed enough by Deakin's work to recommend him in 1946 to Audrey Withers, his counterpart at the London office. This led in September 1947 to a full-time contract with *Vogue* as a staff photographer and perhaps the most creative and rewarding – certainly the most prolific – period of his brief career.

At the outbreak of the Second World War, however, Deakin had been practising photography for only a few months. But he returned to London from Paris and joined the Army Film and Photographic Unit, which suggests at least some technical competence with a camera. Apart from a few early Paris pictures, the photographs he took during the war years – now in the Imperial War Museum, the property still of the Ministry of War – are probably the earliest extant body of Deakin's work.

Sergeant Deakin was posted first to Egypt, then to Syria, before being recalled for a posting to Malta in August 1942. By December he was back in Egypt for Montgomery's North African campaign, joining the Eighth Army Film and Photographic Unit under the command of the legendary army photographer Geoffrey Keating who, according to the war correspondent Warwick Charlton, 'insisted they should share the dangers of battle with the soldier'.[53]

Deakin was typically flippant about his war experience. He claimed to have been drunk and left his lens cap on while carrying out aerial reconnaissance over Rommel's Afrika Corps.[54] At one of Montgomery's briefings before El Alamein, as the Field Marshall warned his men of the superior tank power massed against them, the anxious silence that followed was broken by Deakin's *sotto voce* comment: 'Do you think we're on the right side?'[55] In the

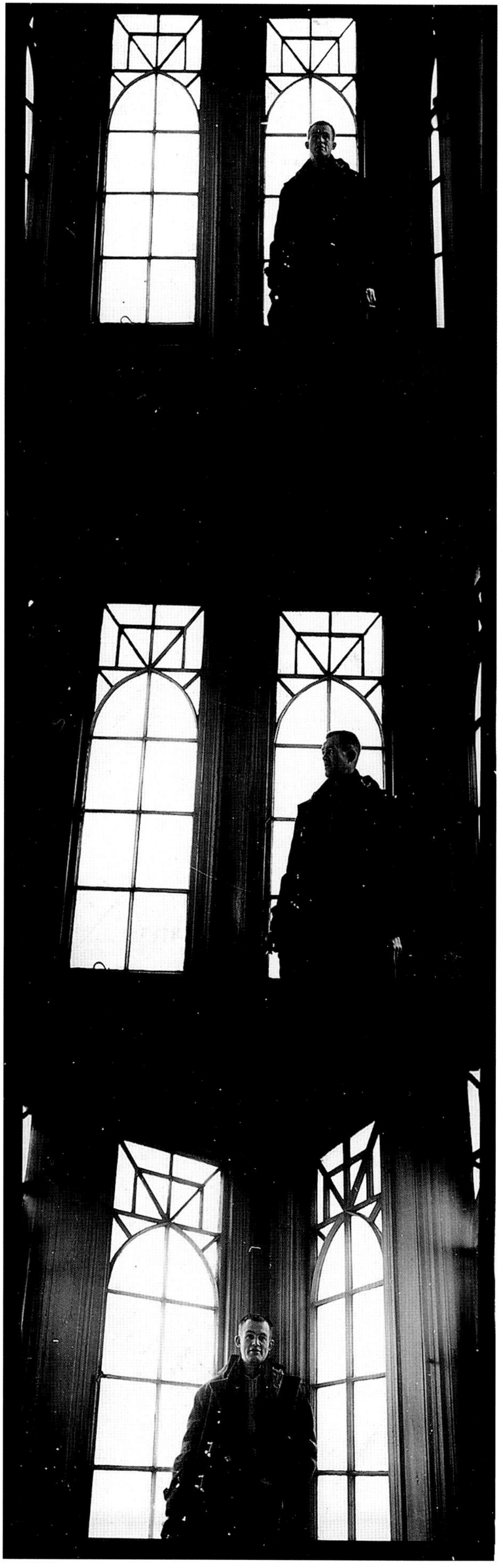

Colin MacInnes, novelist, London, 1950s

Opposite: Oliver Bernard, poet, London, 1960

event he showed considerable fearlessness. With Charlton as part of the advance party into Tripoli, 'his response to heavy fire', according to his colleague, 'was not to take cover but to remain busy with his camera'.[56] Deakin came under fire again when accompanying a gunboat patrol off the Libyan coast. Promoted to Lieutenant, he also saw service in Palestine.[57] His war photographs, the genesis of Deakin's documentary work, reveal themes and motifs he would return to later on the streets of Paris and Rome – nuns, tattoos, church statuary (albeit bomb-ravaged) and graffiti.[58]

The culmination of the Paris documentary work up to the mid-1950s was an exhibition in 1956 at the Parton Gallery in David Archer's Bookshop. Archer was a legendary Soho character, a genuine eccentric with no awareness of his own eccentricity. His modesty hid a remarkable prescience and his place in postwar literary life is assured by his having published the first slim volumes of the unknown poets Dylan Thomas, George Barker, David Gascoyne, W. S. Graham and Dom Moraes. He was also a patron of Deakin's and for a time they lived together in Archer's flat in Bayswater. Feeding off the fortunes of their drinking companions, Deakin greeted news of their disasters with relish, while Archer took pleasure in their triumphs – especially their literary successes – as if they had been his own. 'When a mutual friend received a bad

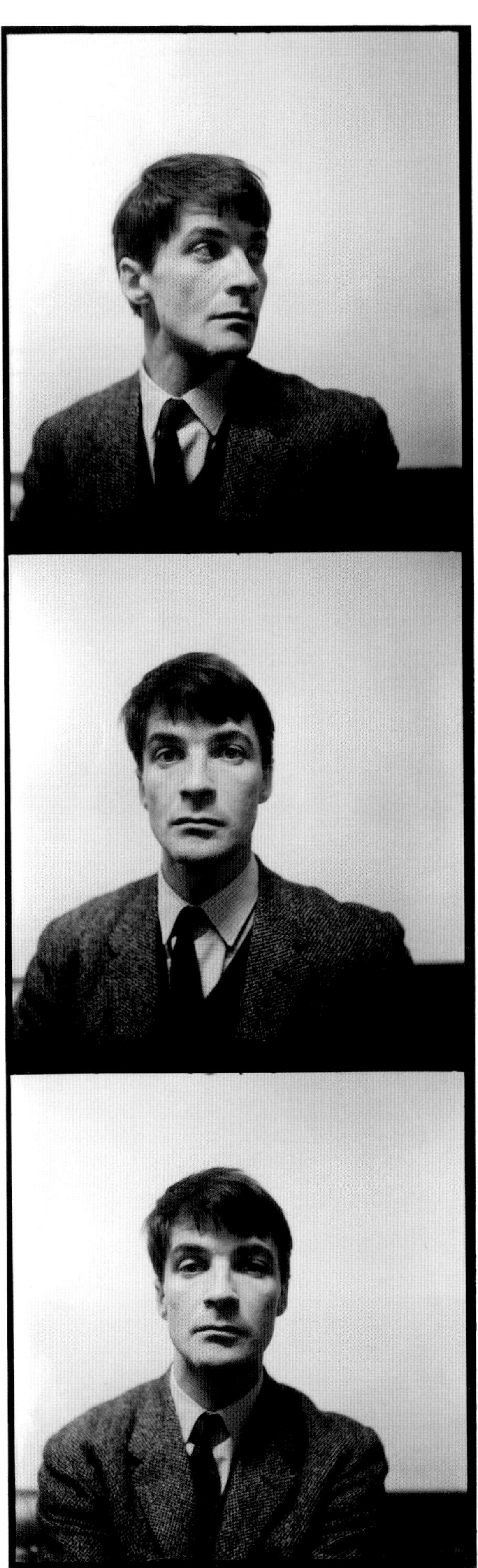

review', Dan Farson recalled, 'Archer actually kicked the critic.' It was, Archer confided to Farson, 'only a *tiny* kick...'[59] For the dustjacket of Moraes's book *A Beginning* (which would win the Hawthornden Prize), the author and publisher chose one of Deakin's pictures, the crude outline of a face etched into a Paris wall (p. 13). Moraes said in his memoirs: 'Deakin could not sell these photographs [of Paris] but they were very beautiful, and when he showed them to me I was fascinated by one of a wall...It was a pale, delicate grey, the loops and squiggles of the children contrasting with the cracked, worn texture of the wall itself.'[60]

In the gallery beneath his friend's bookshop, Deakin held two exhibitions two months apart: 'John Deakin's Paris' and 'John Deakin's Rome'. A third, 'John Deakin – Portraits', was advertised but never took place.[61] This account of the first comes from Bruce Bernard: 'One day in 1956 I found myself hanging some remarkable photographs on the walls of the basement gallery under David Archer's Bookshop in Greek Street. They were mostly of street scenes in Paris and there were also a few interesting portraits. Together they seemed to me the most interesting photographs I had ever seen. Their overwhelming feeling of directness gave them a mordant kind of power, and they seemed very different both to the good-natured photographs mostly taken with the 35mm camera that one had become so used

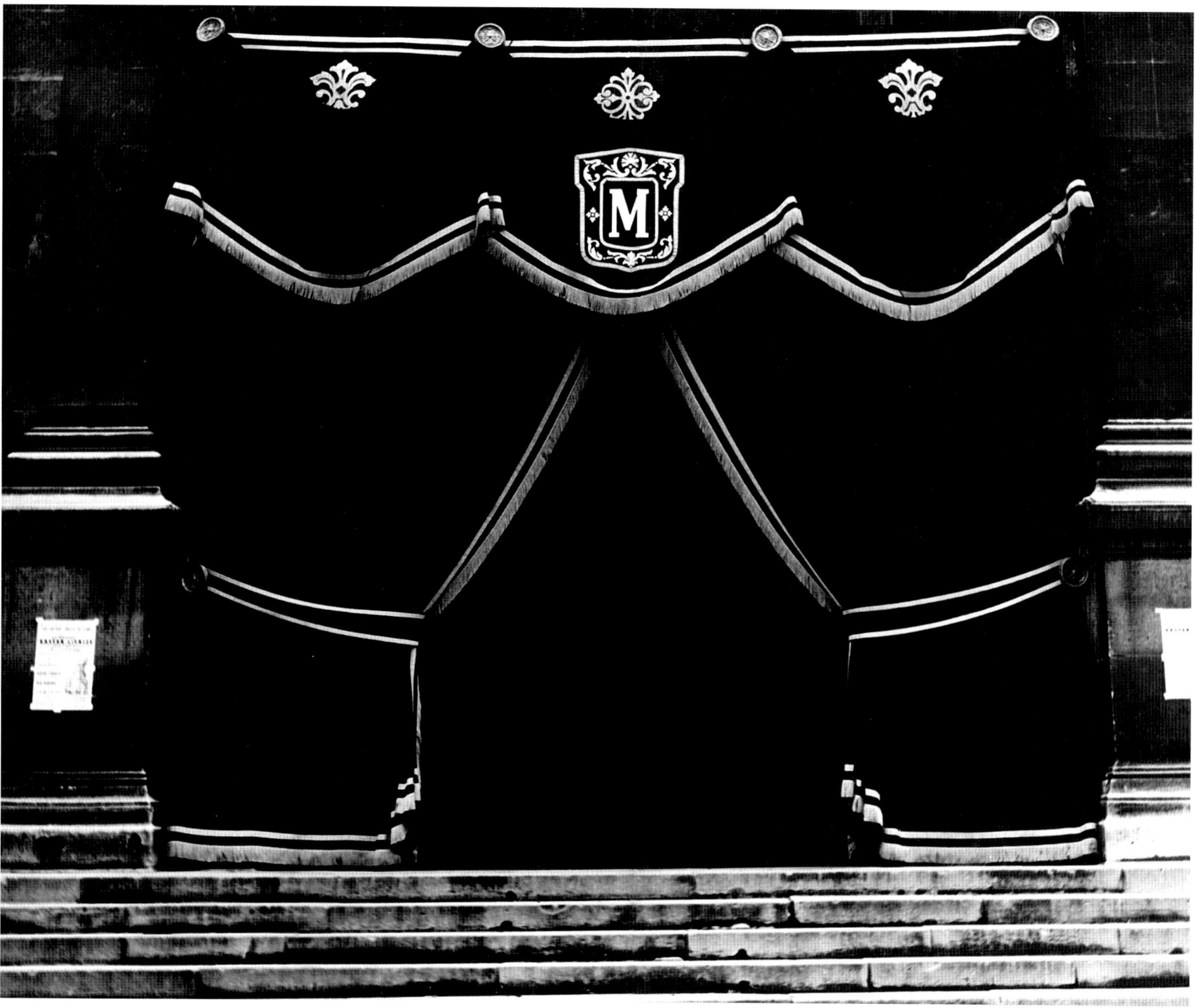

Funeral canopy, Paris, 1950s

to at the time in magazines like *Picture Post* and the little I had seen of the work of Cartier-Bresson and the other Magnum photographers. John Deakin had taken them with his Rolleiflex, a camera that seemed to suit him as well as the Leica suited the majority of other reportage photographers at the time.'[62]

The exhibition was modest in scale – there were fifty-five photographs – but its influence on a younger generation of London-based photographers was considerable.[63] *Vogue*, Deakin's former employers, praised it as 'a painful, monstrously beautiful view of the city that never appeared in any guidebook'.[64] David Sylvester reviewed it for *The Listener*: 'The pictures of Paris by John Deakin present a vision that is profoundly personal and profoundly strange, a vision which confounds and undermines all notions of where inanimate ends and animate takes over.'[65] The most satisfying for Deakin was surely Colin MacInnes's article in *The Times*. Having seen 'John Deakin's Paris' and Roger Mayne's 'Photographs from London', he believed that 'both Mr Deakin and Mr Mayne may lay unquestionable claim to being artists of the highest quality', continuing: 'Mr Deakin has an astonishing eye for the peculiar hidden in the ordinary: where the casual observer sees only a shop-front or the facade of a house, Mr Deakin sees one side of Alice's looking-glass, and the infinite mysteries that lie behind it....But there are deeper reasons for the compelling power of these images. One is that Mr Deakin has a high dramatic sense, that borders often on the bizarre, almost the macabre....The other explanation of the beauty of these photographs lies in the fund of affection, and at times of pity, that the artist clearly feels for his fellow

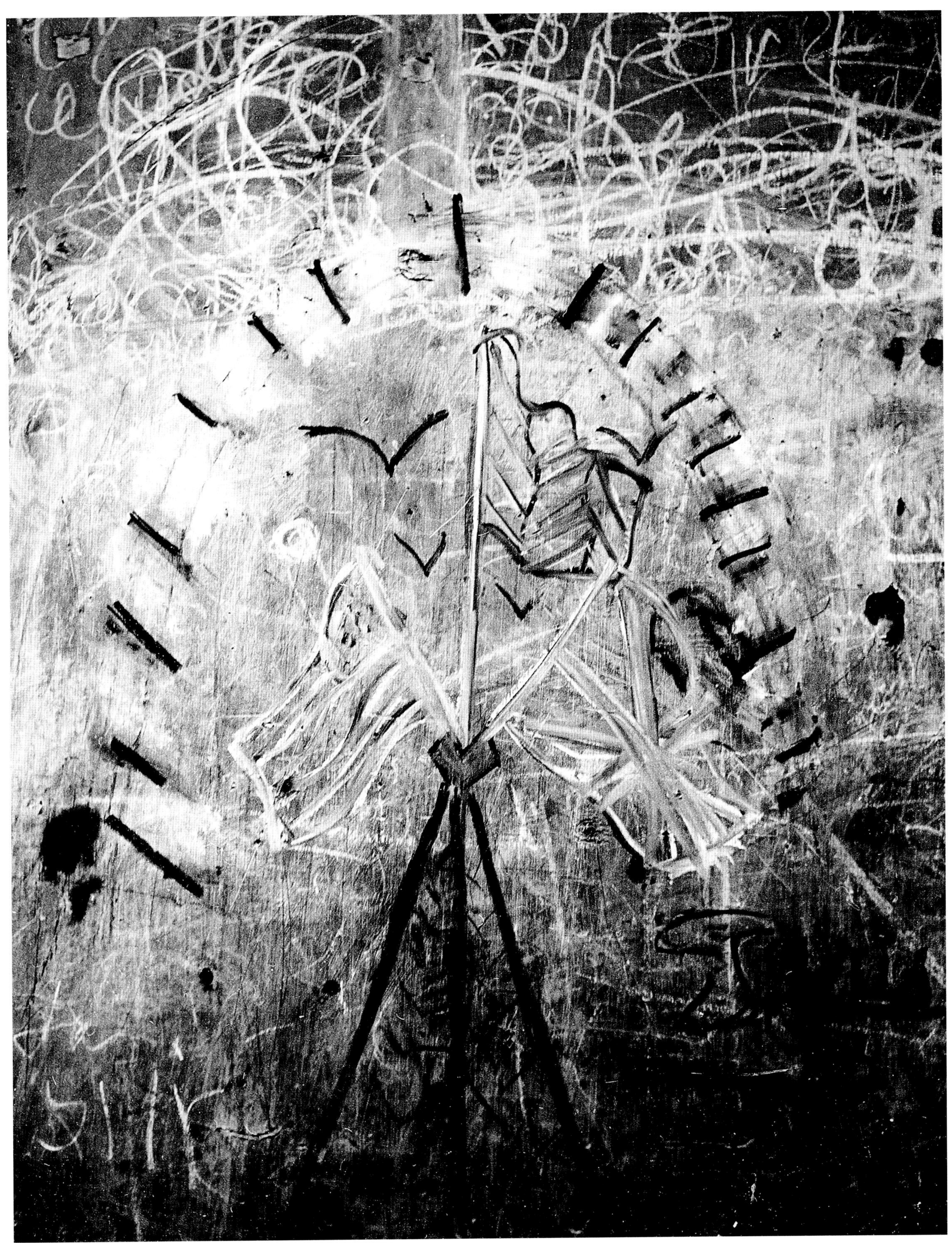

Flags of the Allies, graffiti, Paris, 1950s

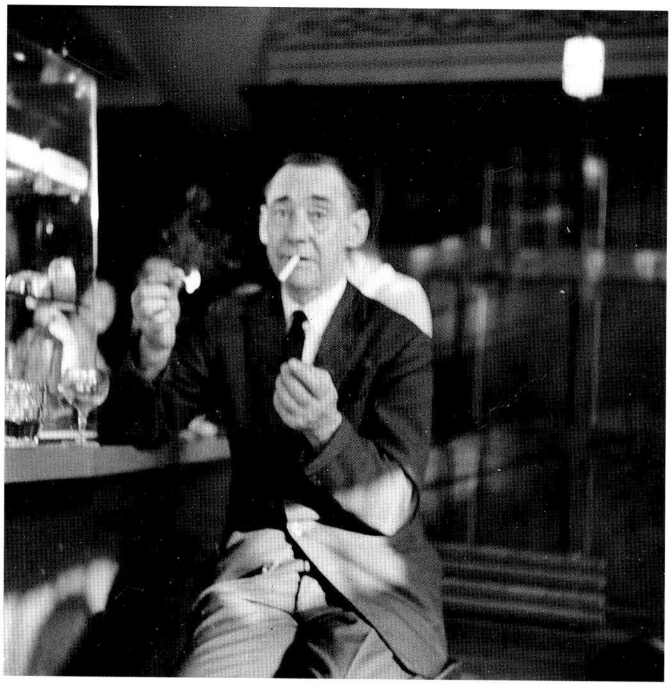

John Deakin in the Golden Lion pub, Soho, 1950s. Photograph attributed to Frank Auerbach

mortals. Many of those who, all unwittingly, were his sitters, are creatures crushed by life; and the artist, quite without condescension or sentimentality, sees the poignancy of their desperate will to live on in a world that has quite defeated them.'[66]

Deakin hoped to turn the Paris photographs into a book and had made several makeshift layouts as a dummy run of pictures to interest publishers. Alexander Liberman of American *Vogue*, whose help had been sought, felt with regret that 'there has been so much about Paris that it would be difficult indeed to find a new approach for another book...'[67]

One of the many books on the French capital that had appeared was *Days of Paris* (1945) by André Kertész. Laid out by Alexey Brodovitch (Liberman's counterpart at *Vogue*'s rival, *Harper's Bazaar*), it is just the book Deakin might have imagined for himself: poetical, poignant and with an entrancing sense of the surreal. The themes Deakin frequently returned to are similar to those of Kertész: shopkeepers and still lifes of their wares, the giant letters of street hoardings, children with animals and the staples of early morning and nocturnal urban life: street cleaners, lamplighters and tramps.

Deakin would surely have also been aware of another book, published four years after Kertész's: *Camera in Paris* by Brassaï. Many of the photographs in this classic of urban documentation were taken in the thirties, some contemporaneously with Deakin's – Deakin inevitably trod similar paths to Brassaï (occasionally exactly the same path).[68] Several decades later, Brassaï beat Deakin to print again, with a project close to the hearts of both men – he held a successful show of graffiti pictures in London in 1958, two years after 'John Deakin's Paris' (which included several of Deakin's own graffiti photographs), followed by the book *Graffiti*, published in 1960 but planned since 1932.[69] Graffiti had fascinated Deakin from the thirties too but after preparing some mounted prints he gave up trying to find a publisher for his own book, 'Paris Walls' (and its companion, 'London Walls'). Like Brassaï, Deakin was especially attracted to the impermanence of defacement, the naivety of children's chalk drawings – a strange juvenile world of symbols and messages made in the simplest ways. He was also drawn to images of happiness in smiling faces or of terror and anguish in death's-head motifs scraped into stone.

Deakin had already published two books of documentary work, which would be some consolation for the lack of interest in his Paris projects. The first, *London Today* (1949), also contained a text by him, the second, *Rome Alive* (1951), a guidebook, was written by Christopher Kininmonth. The former is by far the inferior. Containing sixty-two plates of the city's famous sights, it is in fact as much a vade-mecum as is the guide to Rome, indicating the likelihood that

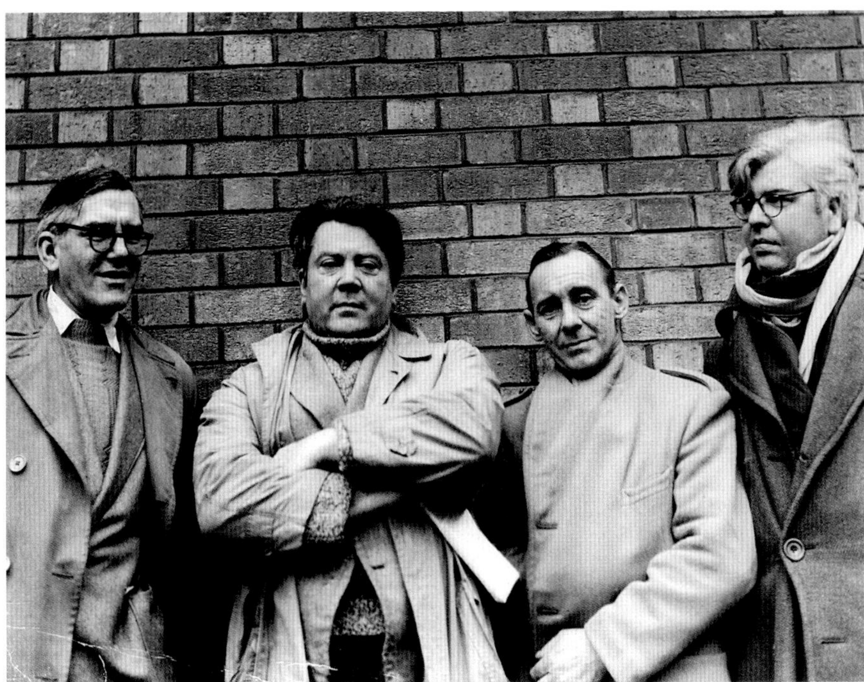

Anthony Carson, writer; John Davenport, literary critic; John Deakin; David Wright, poet; outside the York Minster pub, Soho, 1950s. Photograph by Daniel Farson

Deakin was photographing to order. Despite a few idiosyncratic vignettes, this is far from being Deakin's best street photography, not least because his London is deserted. He was at his most trenchant as documentarist of the chaos of the streets, unobserved among street entertainers and flea-market stall holders. He admits in his introduction to finding the city's lack of design and mixtures of styles 'bewildering', stating that 'the streets in general will not give away much of London life. They tend to be anonymous, and since there is no tradition of café society in London the real life goes on behind doors and lace-curtained windows.'[70]

The project certainly came at a fortuitous time, coinciding with Deakin's first sacking from *Vogue* and his attempt to open a studio. He had run one before, but closed it abruptly just before joining *Vogue*. The magazine's accountants, asked to unravel its financial state, were startled by Deakin's lack of acuity. Otherwise, he was at this time mostly subsisting on the generosity of friends (chiefly David Archer), while radiating a certain 'chic' as a former *Vogue* photographer. 'With Deakin', wrote Daniel Farson, 'my introduction to Soho was complete,' and it is in Soho itself that perhaps his best London photographs were taken.[71]

Much has been written about the allure of Soho – the route to the Colony Room by way of the Mandrake, the Golden Lion, the Caves de France and the York Minster – not least by Farson himself, who made this square mile of London's West End so entertainingly his own. A slight corrective to his version of recent social history can be found in the writings of many others, including contemporary accounts such as those of Colin MacInnes. In an essay for the literary magazine *Encounter* (1957), 'See You at Mabel's', the eponymous Mabel's, a drinking club, is a composite of many such establishments but draws most heavily on Muriel Belcher's Colony Room: 'As the gins slip down your throat and the dim electrics shine on the potted plants and on Muriel's lurid colour scheme of emerald, green and gold, you feel like the fish in the tank above the cash register – swimming aimlessly among water-weeds, mindless in warm water'.[72]

Despite Deakin's increasing dependency on alcohol, which helped hasten his departure from *Vogue*, and despite his frequent indifference to his work, it was plain to his peers that here was a photographer of extraordinary vision and range: Bruce Bernard considered a portrait of his brother Oliver, a low-angle head-and-shoulders snapshot taken against a wall, to be 'a masterpiece of portraiture'.[73] Indeed, its stark clarity and frontality of composition, which allow it little in common with the photographs of his contemporaries, led the art historian Alex Noble to observe that 'Deakin discarded over one hundred years of the photographic tradition of flattering his sitters and redefined the meaning of the word "photogenic".'[74] Deakin's pared-down

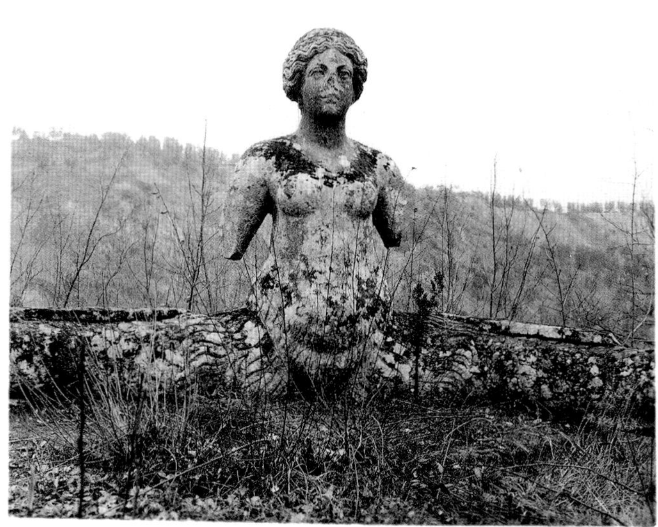

Sculpture carved from rock in the garden at Bomarzo, Italy, 1950s

technique can be seen in a photograph of Bruce and Jeffrey Bernard and their friend Terry Jones (p. 34): '[We] had just been counting our money at about a quarter past three outside the Mandrake Club hoping we had enough for a drink there but knowing we hadn't, when along waltzed Deakin, swinging his camera and seeming in his most insouciant mood. He glanced at the wall and with a mock imperious gesture commanded us to stand against it, upon which we laughingly insisted on drinks at the Mandrake as payment. Within two or three seconds of this badinage, which so often characterised encounters with him, he had transformed us into three serious and separate people being themselves but something else as well, forming a curiously true image of a time and place. My later experience with photographers has convinced me that only something like a great one could have done so in the circumstances.'[75]

At the time these portraits were first shown publicly, as part of Bruce Bernard's exhibition of Deakin's photographs at the Victoria and Albert Museum, Farson wrote this of their mutual friend's work: 'I am sure he will be seen as one of the most disturbing photographers of the century....The expressions of his victims look suitably appalled, for Deakin had no time for such niceties as "cheese" and the stark effect was magnified by the huge contrasty blow-ups with every pore, blemish and blood-shot eyeball exposed without mercy. In this way he combined the instant horror of the passport photo with a shock value all of his own.'[76]

Taken together, the 'Soho' portraits of figures such as George Dyer, Henrietta Moraes, Isabel Rawsthorne, Muriel Belcher, Bacon, the Bernard brothers, Robert Colquhoun, George Barker and many others comprise a collection of some of the most extraordinary street portraits in British photographic history, made more poignant by the lack of care the photographer took of them and the lack of value he placed on them.

Deakin had a life-long passion for travel, which was constantly thwarted by lack of funds. But he seemed to be able to conjure up benefactors, sponsors and patrons whenever he needed them most. There were those who could afford it, such as Jeffress, and those who could barely afford it but never refused, like David Archer. Deakin had long wanted to live in Rome. He had visited it with Jeffress in the early 1930s but the opportunity to spend time there – with pay – came by way of a project that also enabled him to continue the documentary concerns initiated by his time in Paris and by his work for *London Today*. Between 1949 and 1950 he took the photographs for *Rome Alive*. 'Of all the places he had been to', wrote Dan Farson, 'I believe Deakin was fondest of Rome, where the Italians relished his sense of mischief, apparently treating him like an attendant clown or a mascot.'[77] When the book was ready it was a perfect alliance of words and pictures. Christopher Kininmonth, who wrote the text, was, like Deakin, less interested in the familiar sights of the city, preferring to

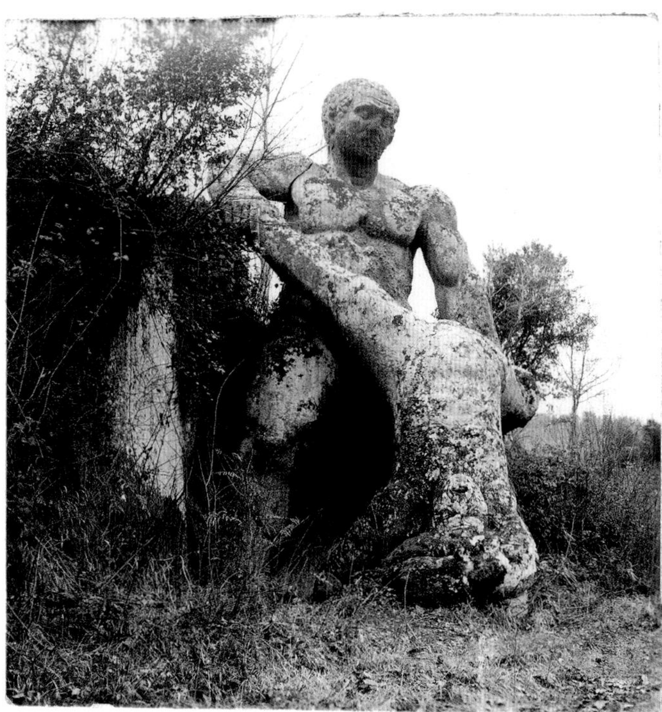

Sculpture carved from rock in the garden at Bomarzo, Italy, 1950s

linger below the facade: rent collection in the slum districts, the ruins of Mussolini's fascist stadia, the homeless and displaced surviving on the streets, squatters' rooms and all-night cafés. The book was published in 1951 and with uncharacteristic generosity Deakin presented Kininmonth with a giant composite of sixty-three contact prints, many of them the photographer's own favourites which had not been included in the finished work.[78] As much as the Paris pictures, these represent Deakin's greatest triumph as an observational photographer, and for some time afterwards he tried, though increasingly halfheartedly, to find a publisher for a separate book of Rome pictures.[79] Though unsuccessful in this attempt, he did hold a show of these photographs in 1956 at David Archer's Bookshop – and one of them appeared a few months later in *The Observer*.[80]

The spectre of death looms large over this part of Deakin's œuvre, for no other reason than that Italians appear always to have made much of death's rituals. In Rome these funerary monuments and relics appear to be more conspicuous, from the simple and elegant to the baroque and grotesque. As the number of extant contact sheets bears witness, Deakin clearly spent much time in the 'English Cemetery', the necropolis set aside by the Catholic Church for the burial of foreigners and non-Catholics. It famously contains the resting-places of the English Romantic poets Keats and Shelley. The white marble pyramid of Caius Cestius dominates several frames. In short, Rome was a city made for photography. Visiting Deakin there in 1961, Dan Farson wrote: 'Knowing and loving Rome, Deakin took pleasure in showing it off, taking me to the usual haunts like the Fontana di Trevi and his favourite catacombs, replete with skulls.'[81] Deakin was particularly fascinated with the then working-class district of Trastevere with its own traditions and patois. 'The Romans of Trastevere...and other such old quarters', wrote Kininmonth, 'are apt to retreat into their familiar habits and either ignore or despise the metropolitan ways of Romans by adoption, refusing at once to assimilate or imitate them.'[82]

Later, Deakin divided his time between Rome and Genoa, where he lived with a dress designer, Gianni Baldini, and his wife. He was technically married himself, having formed a liaison, purely for commercial gain, with a stateless Hungarian émigré. In Milan, in return for citizenship papers, his wife financed a new camera. Peter Ustinov suggested the happy event be announced in the births column of *The Times*: 'To John and Anna Deakin, a Rolleiflex was born.'[83]

In time, and to no one's surprise, Deakin quarrelled with the fashion designer, moved in with a princess and soon returned to Soho. From now until his death he mainly drifted from job to job. *The Observer* had kept him on a small retainer as a photographer since 1958 and he took for them mostly stills from films at press screenings.

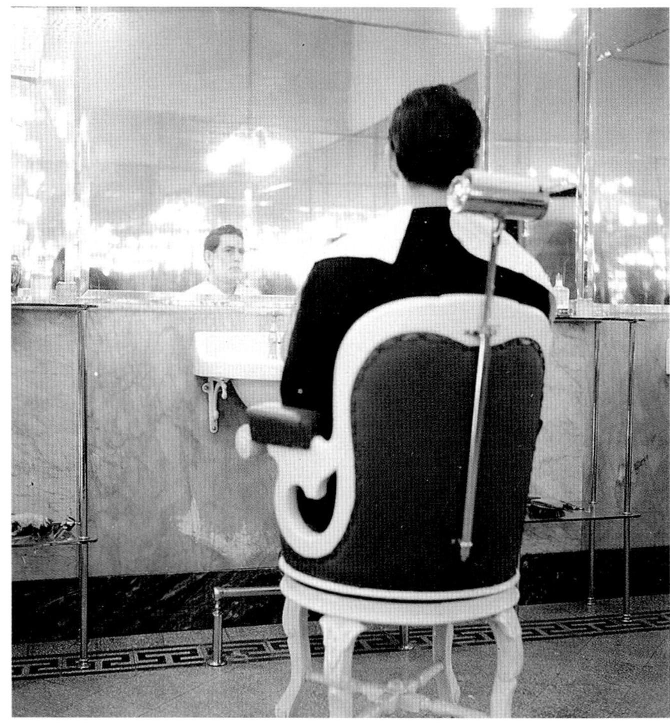

Above and opposite: Giancarlo Menotti, composer, at the barber's, Paris, 1953

Occasionally the paper printed one of his travel and documentary pictures, but Deakin now photographed with increasing rarity, preferring to paint. When his painting met with limited success, he held down a picture research post, helping Bruce Bernard and the graphic designer Germano Facetti on a partwork, a history of the first six decades of the twentieth century. And as the sixties turned into the seventies, his ill-health haunted and obsessed him: 'I am here for another two weeks I think,' he wrote to Daniel Farson on 17 November 1971 from St John's Hospital, Homerton, 'But you know me I use it like others use Aix-les-Bains or Elizabeth Arden Health Farms.'[84]

Deakin never expected his photographs to live on after his death, just as he never expected them to make him much of a living (nor did they). 'There is only one more thing I would like to say,' he wrote in 'Eight Portraits', 'That is, though I once worked on a fashion magazine, I have mainly photographed the great ones ['artists' is deleted] of my time, and never taken lucrative faces which did not interest me. But the great and the mighty rarely have tuppence to rub together, and it often vaguely annoys ['frightens' is deleted] me to think that were I willing to photograph lucrative faces, and falsify them, I might even now be living in dubious splendour.'[85]

He kept what remained of his photographs because in the end it was his life's work. He had no paintings left. A cache of them eventually reached an auction house when a dealer went bankrupt. Of the papier-mâché 'monsters', Farson recalled that 'they ended up in the gutter of Berwick Street, lying in strange attitudes, for the dustmen to consign to some rubbish dump.'[86]

Devious and charming by turns, Deakin was loved and loathed in equal measure and many, including eventually Bacon, found his wild, eccentric and drunken behaviour sometimes too much to bear. He had a caustic wit the match of Bacon's, so much so that the Woolworth heiress Barbara Hutton once referred to him as the 'second nastiest little man I have ever met' (prompting everyone to ask, much to Deakin's chagrin, who the first was).[87] There was no ignoring him and he became the subject of several character sketches both affectionate and acrimonious: in Elaine Dundy's *The Old Man and Me* (1964), he is Bollie the photographer, his 'eyes flirtatiously rolling upwards over the dry rot marks in the ceiling as if to entice them to come down and play with him'.[88] In *Ritual in the Dark* (1960) by Colin Wilson he makes an appearance as Carl Castering, 'one of the best photographers in London', with 'the liquid eyes of a drunk', who caresses the hand of Wilson's hero 'between two damp palms.'[89] Lately he has featured in Iain Sinclair's *Downriver* (1991), in Nigel Richardson's work of 'imaginative non-fiction', *Dog Days in Soho* (2000), and in John Maybury's film *Love Is the Devil* (1998), played by Karl Johnson.[90] He even appears in a

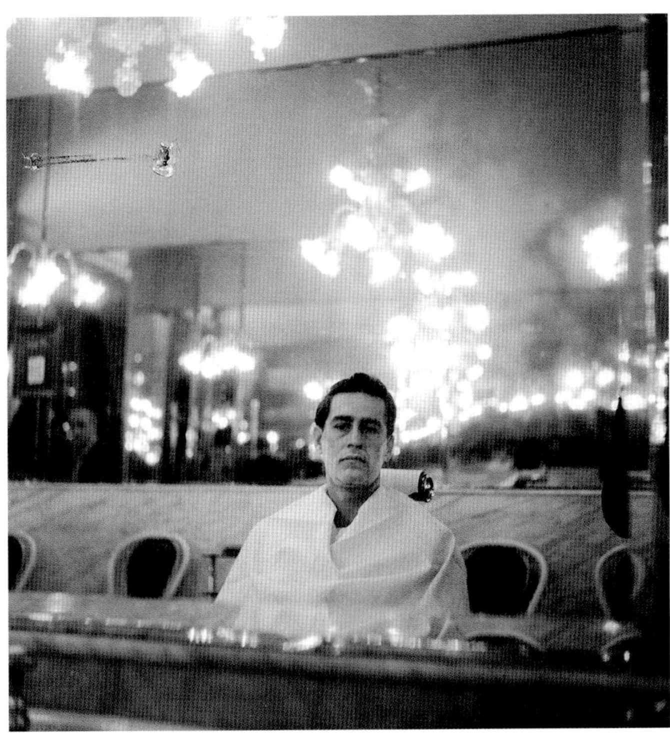

long poem by Martin Green, *The French Pub and the Snows of Yester-Year* (1996).[91]

That he slipped from view until recently, though reprehensible, is unsurprising. Deakin was an exception to the rule that good photographers are, on the whole, also good at self-promotion. The values embodied in the increasingly prevalent cult of the 'star photographer', which Deakin steadfastly rejected, usually demand a corrective. And Deakin's wilful, contrary example is just one such. His portraits still look starkly modern, half a century on. His street photographs are haunting documents too, a singular vision of three great cities. After two major retrospectives at London institutions, the Victoria and Albert Museum (1984/85) and the National Portrait Gallery (1996) and a future entry in *The New Dictionary of National Biography* (2004), his place in the pantheon of twentieth-century British photographers might finally be secured. 'It gives me satisfaction', wrote Bruce Bernard at the first retrospective, 'to have had a part in doing our dear, witty and wayward friend some of the justice he so strenuously denied himself, and I am confident that quite soon not to have heard of John Deakin will be seen as betraying a shameful ignorance of photographic history.'[92]

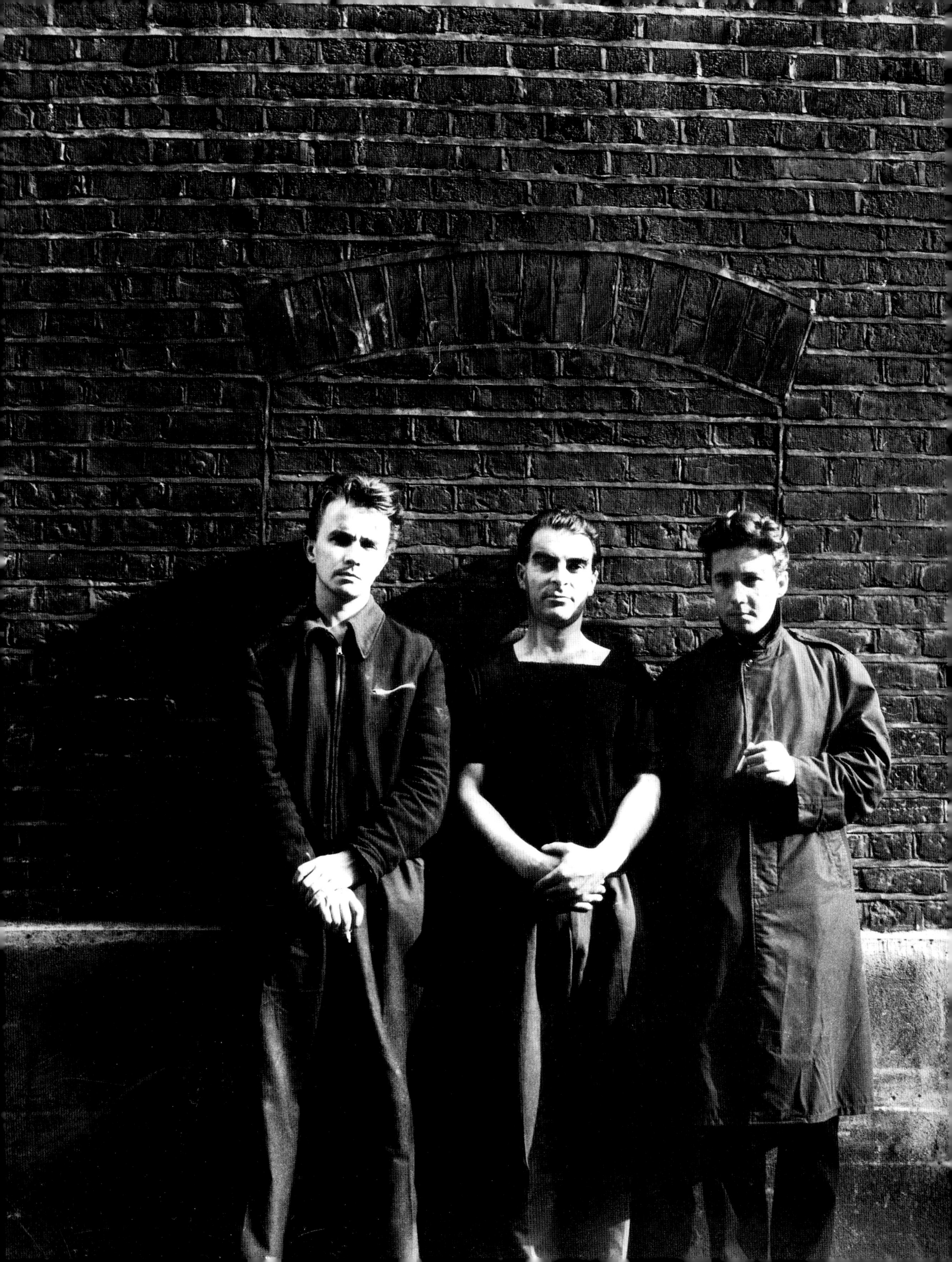

London

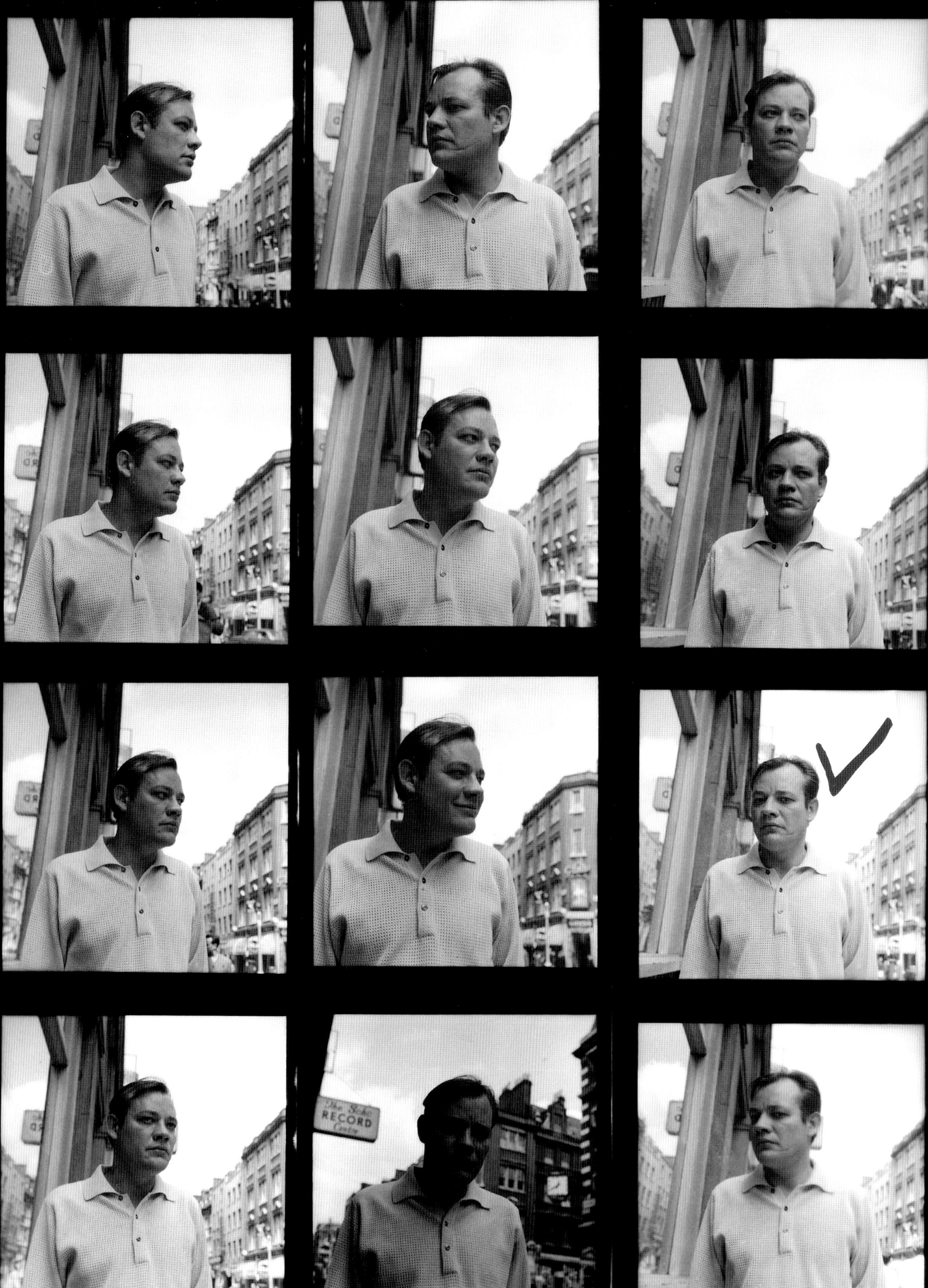
RECORD

Deakin's first published urban landscapes appear in the book *London Today* (1949), a meditation on the city at dusk and dawn, a time when, he wrote, 'London…holds most promise and mystery, timeless and inexhaustible, when the changing fashions and habits of its people seems insignificant'.[1] He hoped to follow this book swiftly with a similar exercise on the city of Paris, but this was never published.

Unusually for Deakin, *London Today* is uninhabited landscape. In the best of his documentary work – whether in London, Paris or Rome – the life of the city, peopled with a mix of fairground workers and street entertainers, passers-by and construction workers, is often the central theme. Of the London photographs, those of people in the streets of Soho, many taken in the 1950s and 1960s for Francis Bacon, are probably his most successful – certainly the best known. And his photographs of Bacon himself and his circle (Lucian Freud, George Dyer and others) prove to be the most intriguing.

The East End, which Deakin was encouraged to explore by Bacon and Daniel Farson, was a particularly fruitful location and he raked his lens over the old Chinese quarter of Limehouse and the decaying industrial wasteland of the bomb-ravaged postwar docklands. He recorded the dying arts of the dockers' tattooists, the ice-cream carrier and much of the vernacular of London life: street signs, graffiti, tattered municipal notices, peeling walls and the leftover signs and calligraphy of children's street games.

Opposite: Frank Norman, playwright, 1960s

Page 34: The writers and brothers, Bruce and Jeffrey Bernard, with their friend the stagehand Terry Jones (centre) in Meard Street, Soho, c. 1956–57

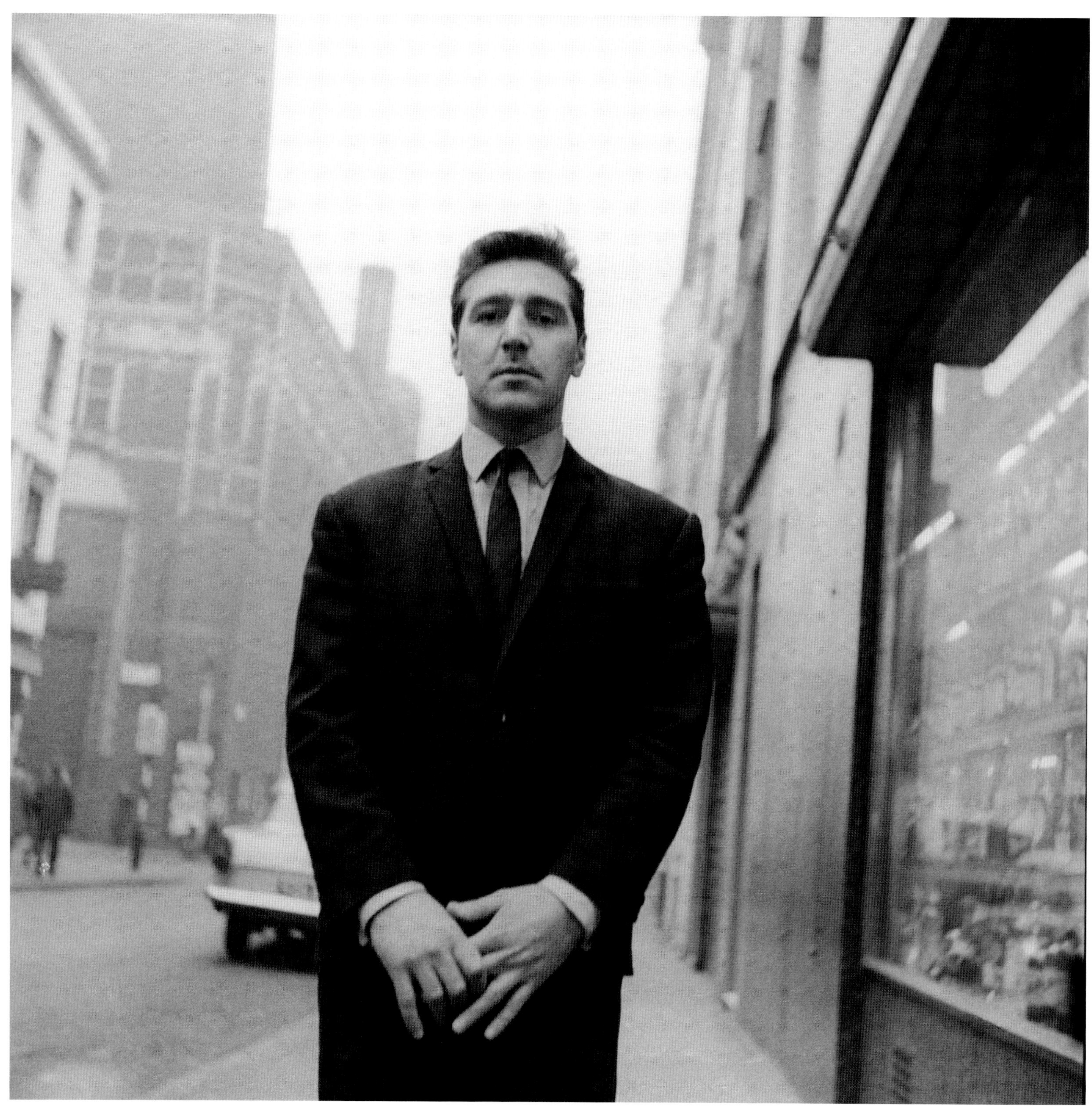

George Dyer, model for Francis Bacon, 1960s

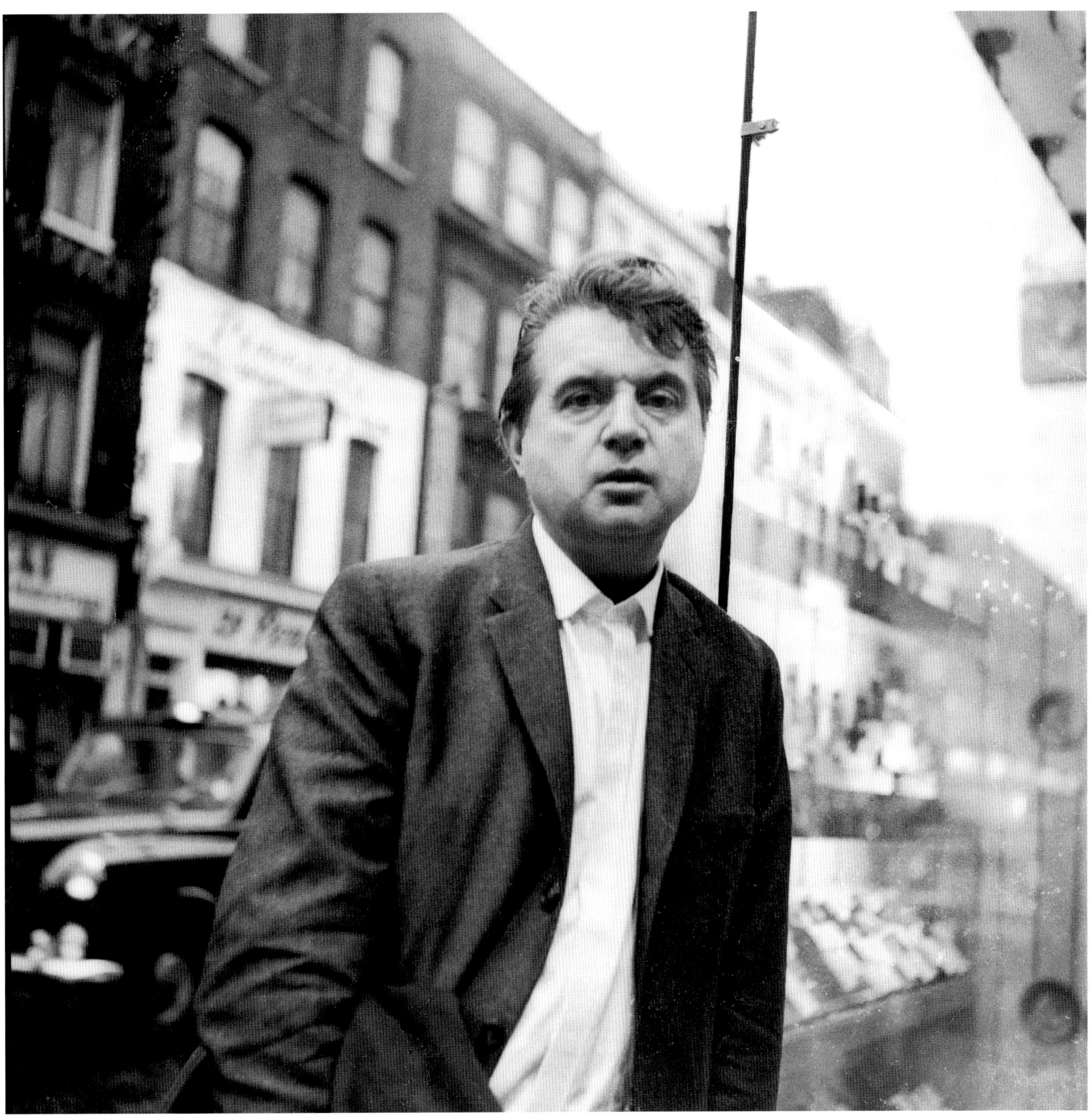

Francis Bacon, painter, 1960s

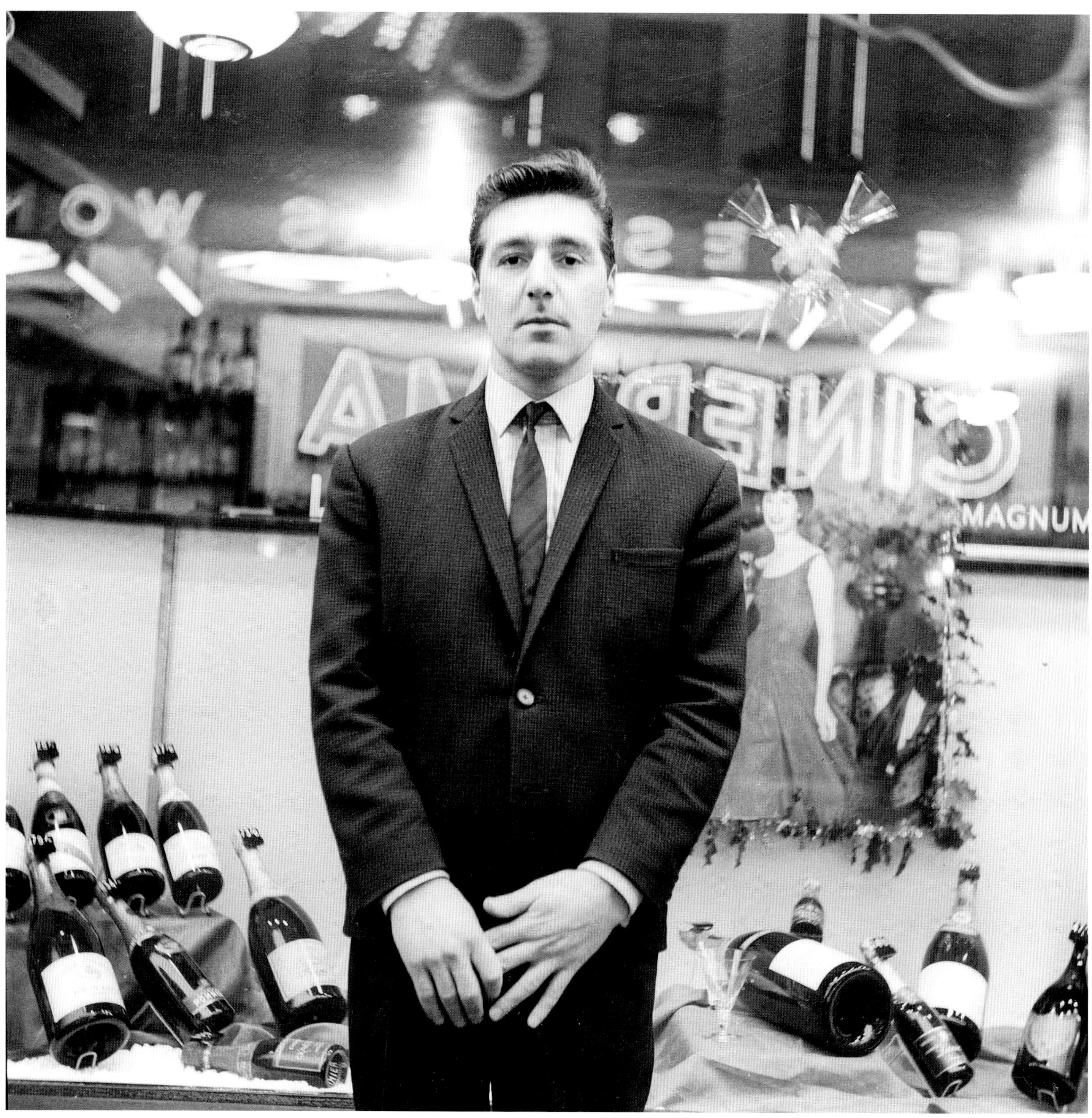

George Dyer, 1960s

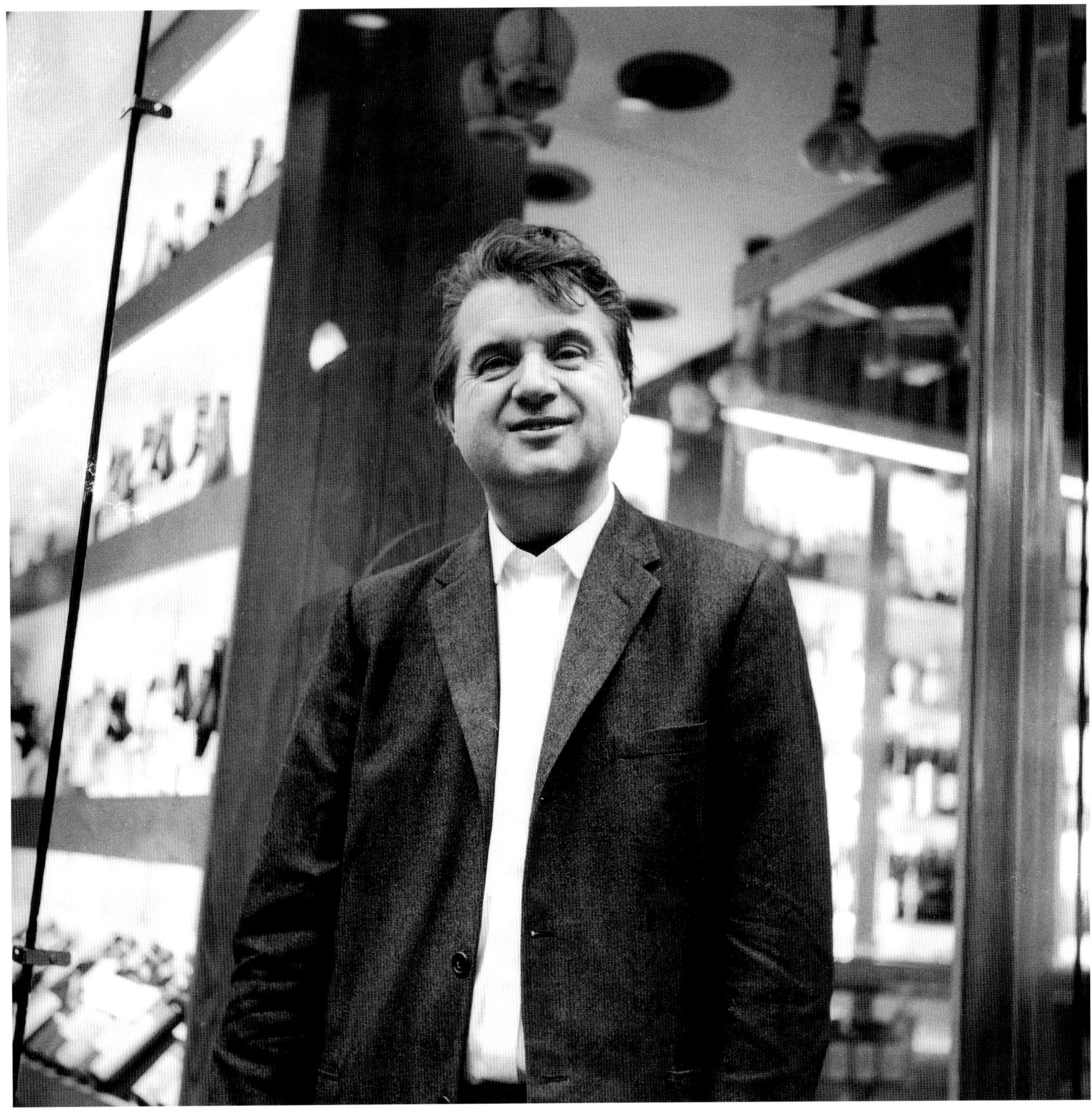

Francis Bacon, 1960s

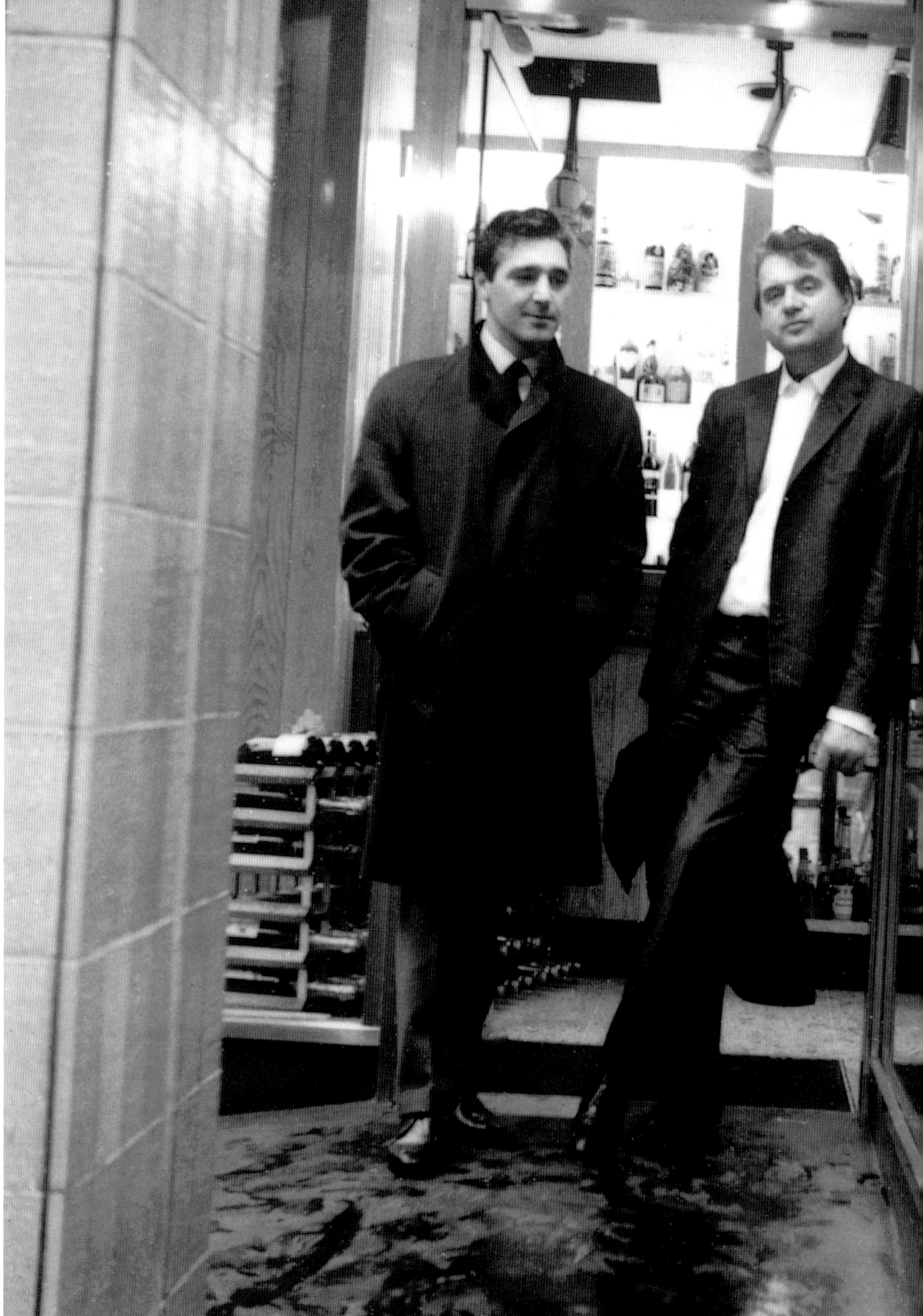

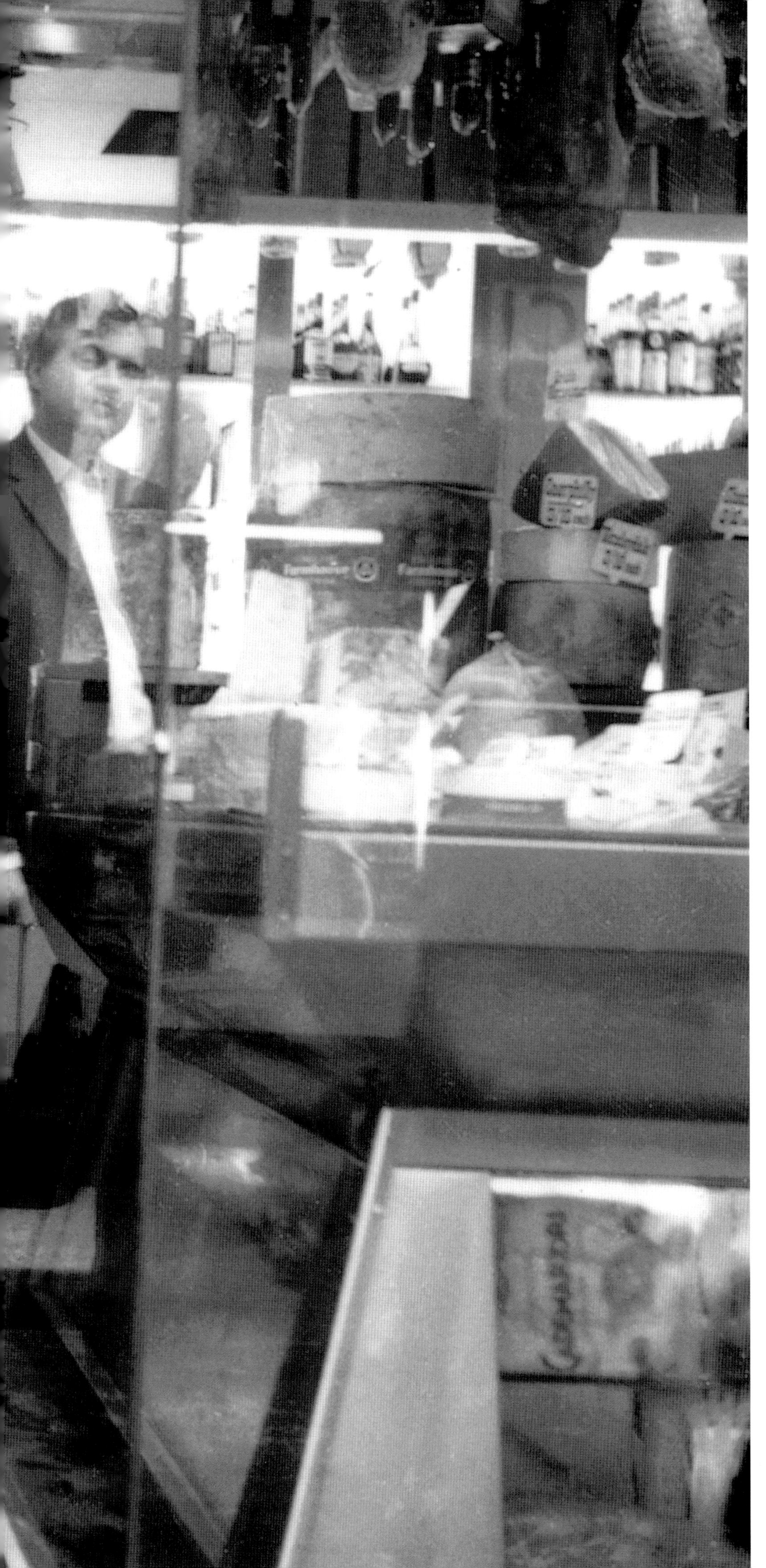

George Dyer and Francis Bacon, 1960s

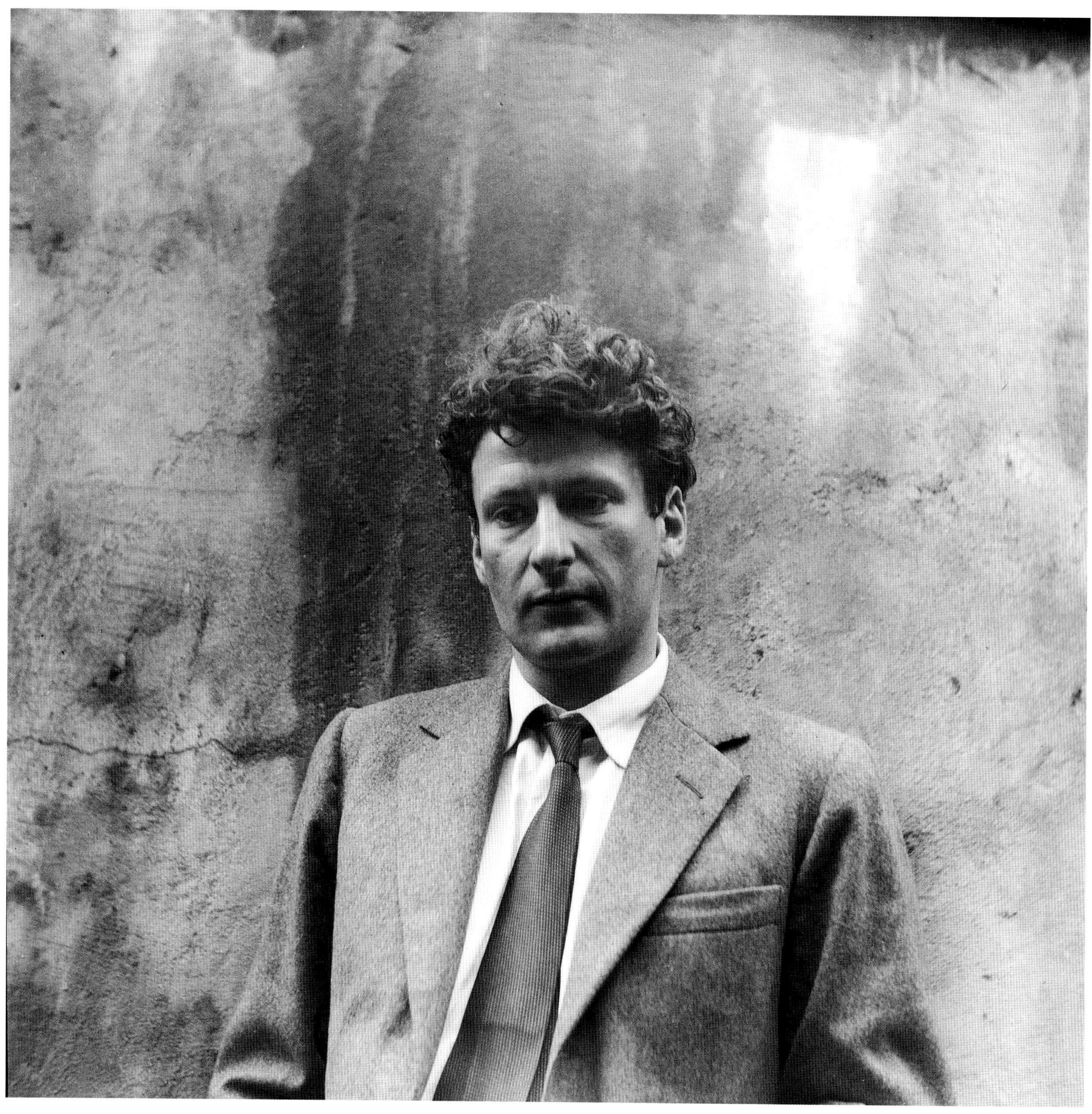

Lucian Freud, painter, c. 1961

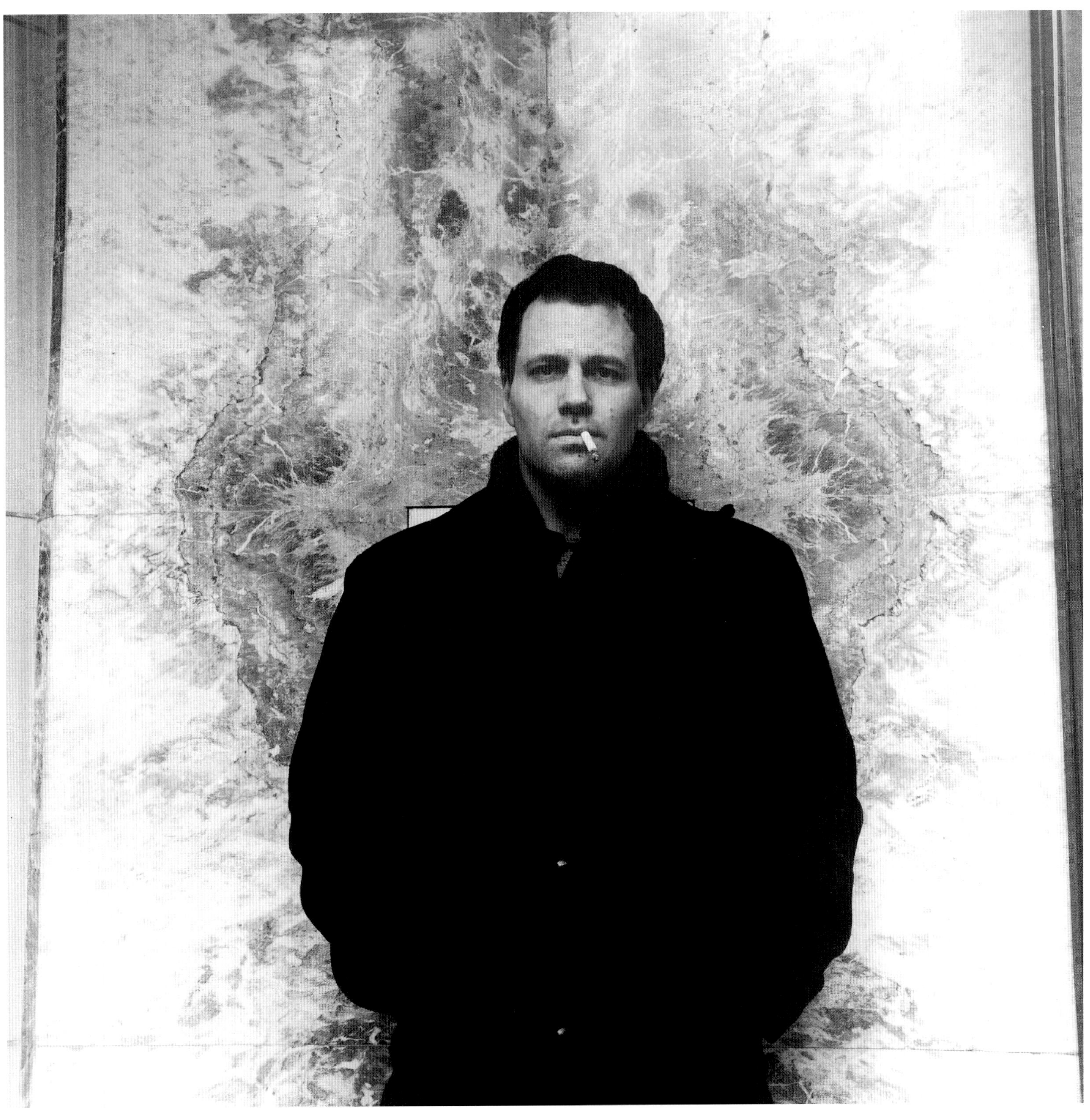

Frank Auerbach, painter, c. 1959

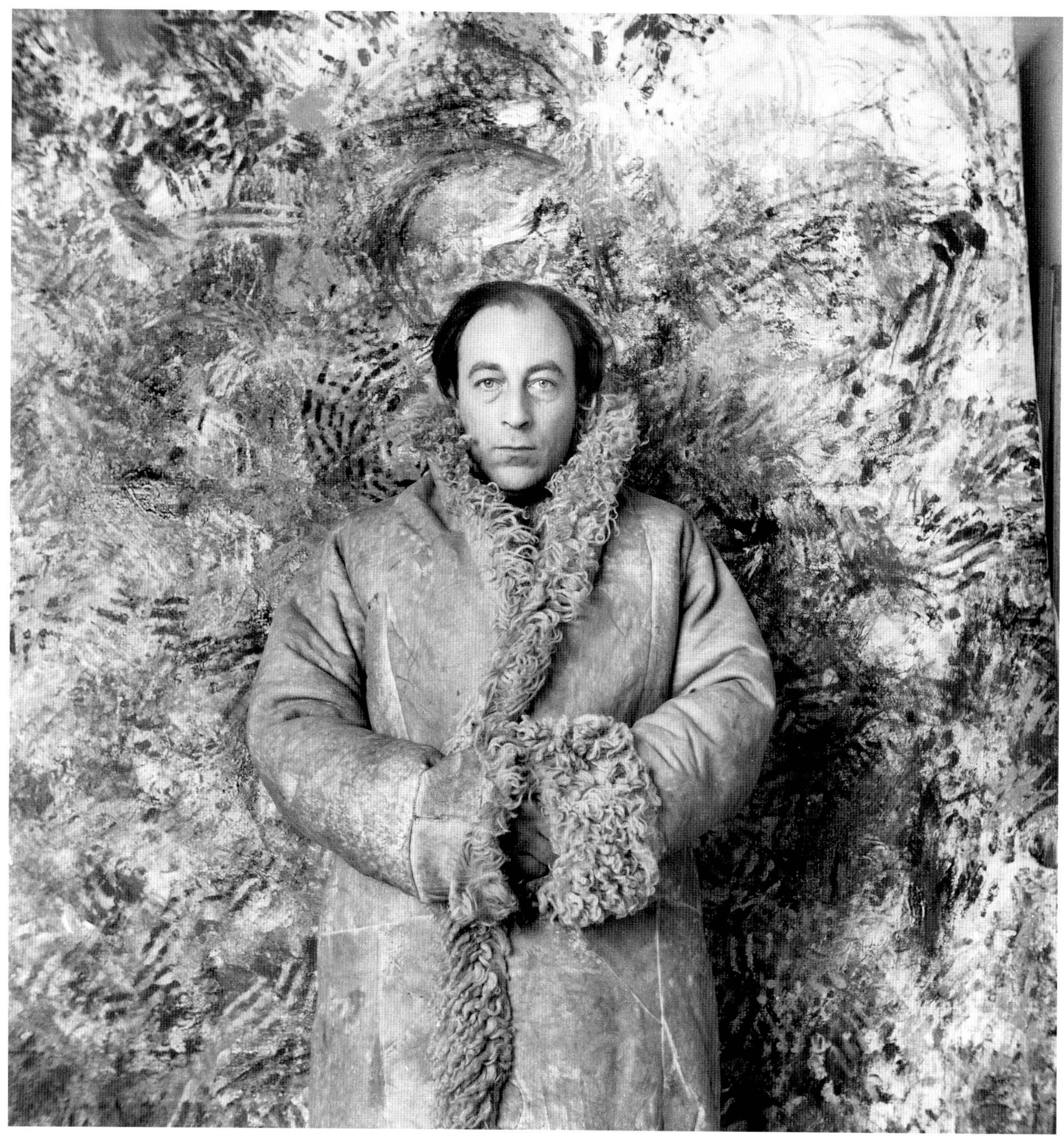

N. H. (Tony) Stubbing, painter, 1960s

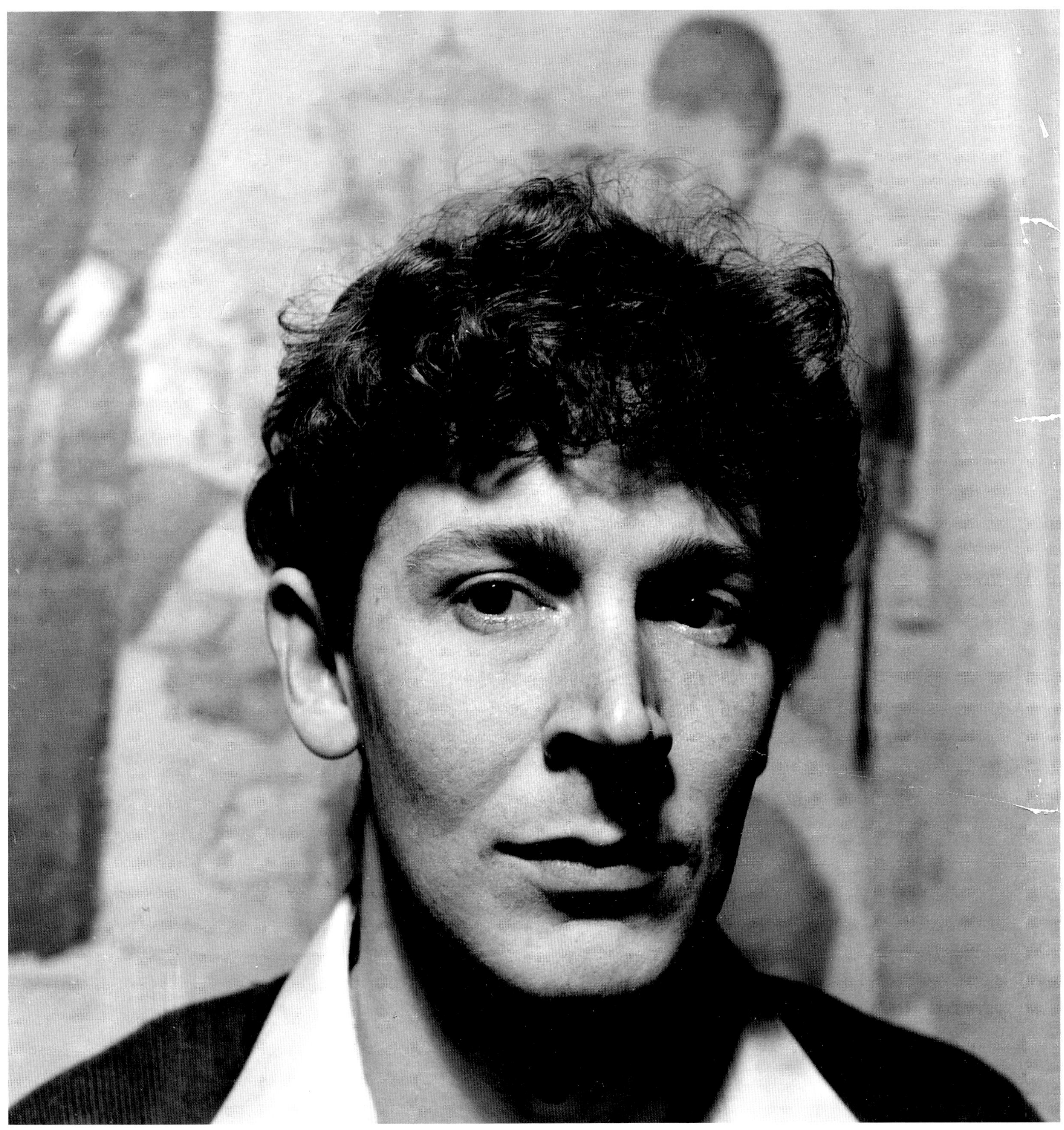

Michael Andrews, painter, 1952

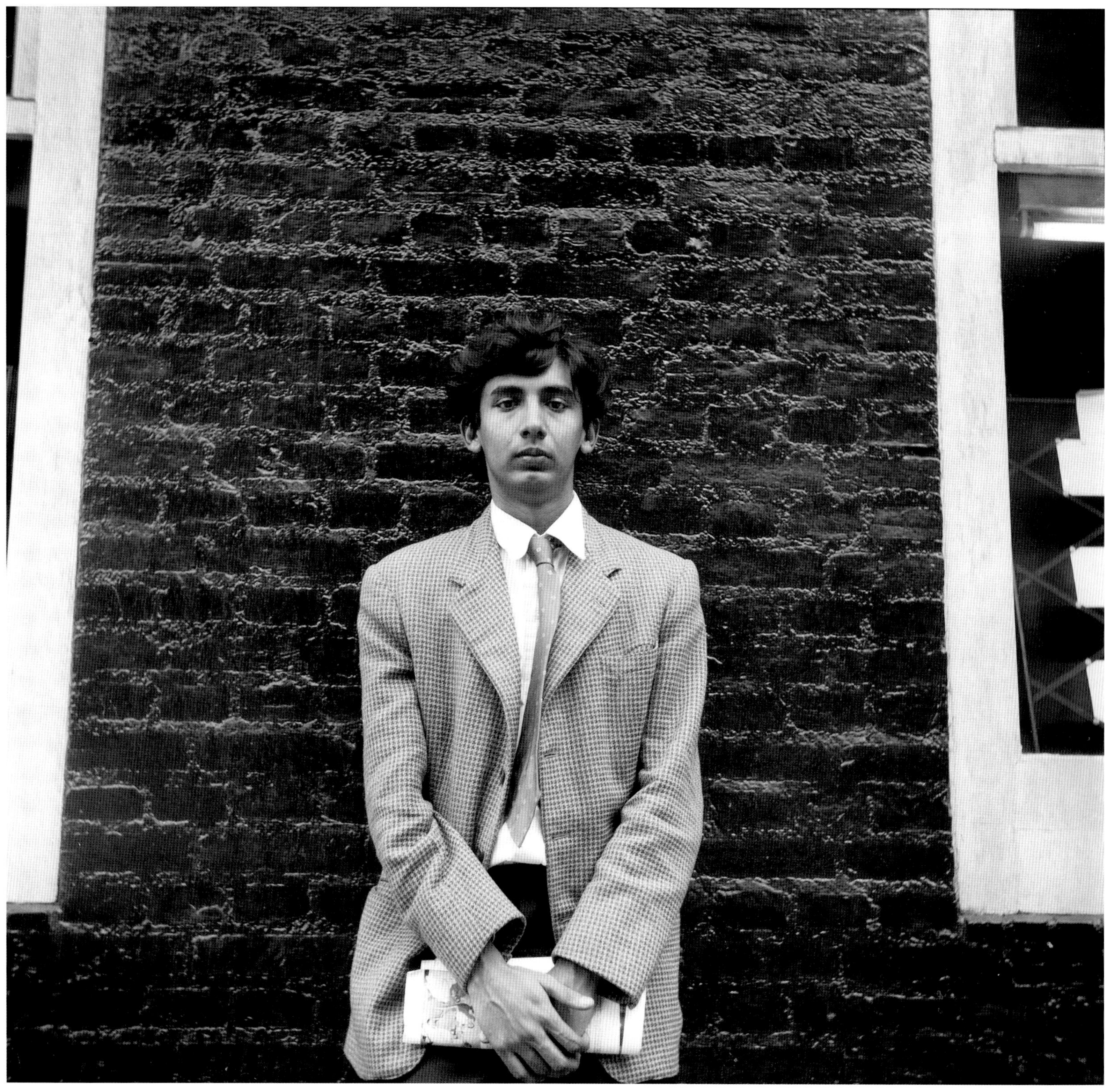

Dom Moraes, poet, 1960s

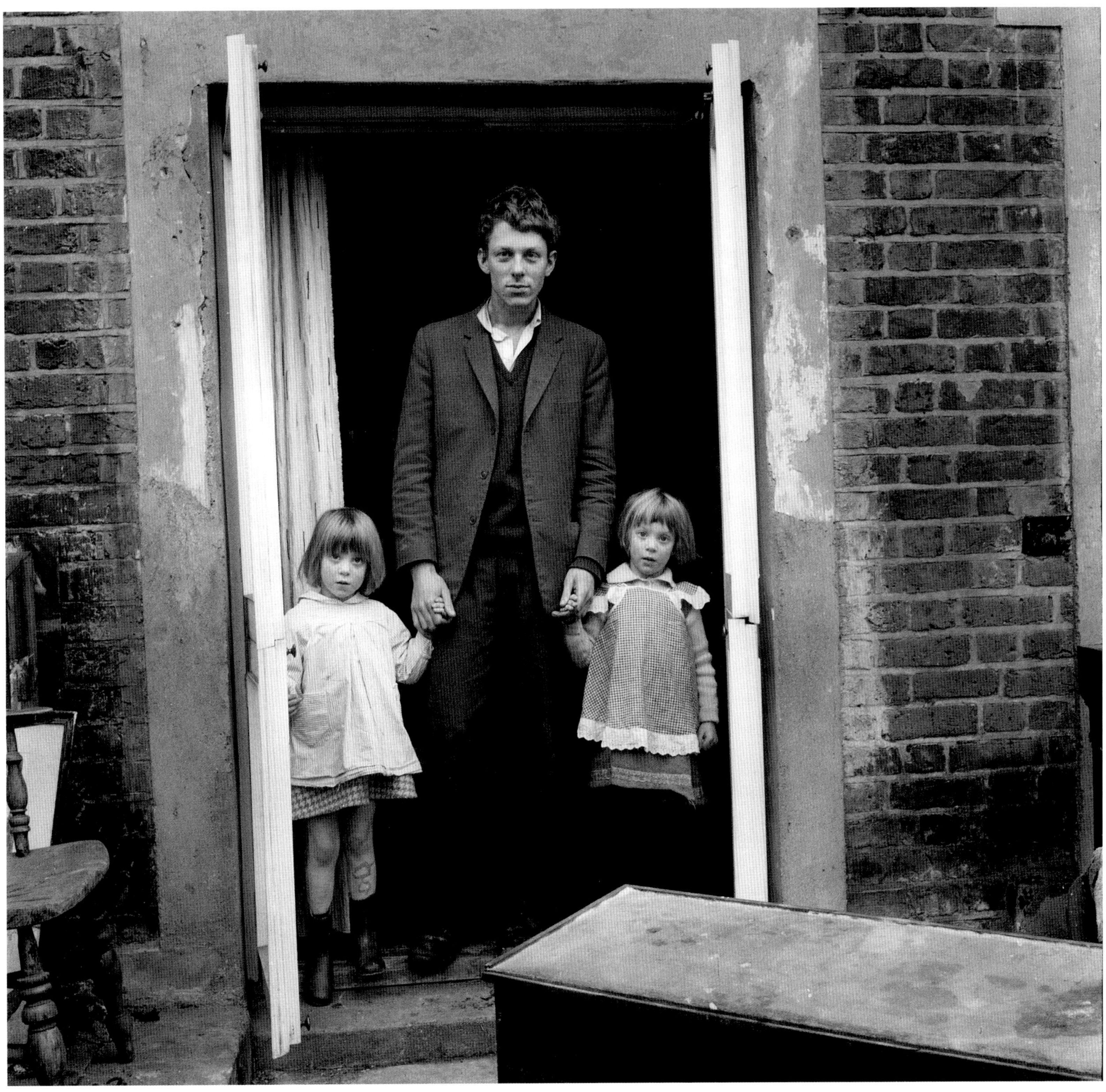

The painter Timothy Behrens and his daughters, 1960s

Page 50: Elizabeth Smart, writer, 1952

Page 51: David Archer, publisher and bookseller, 1952

Page 52: Lucian Freud, painter, 1960s

Page 53: Daniel Farson, photographer and journalist, 1952

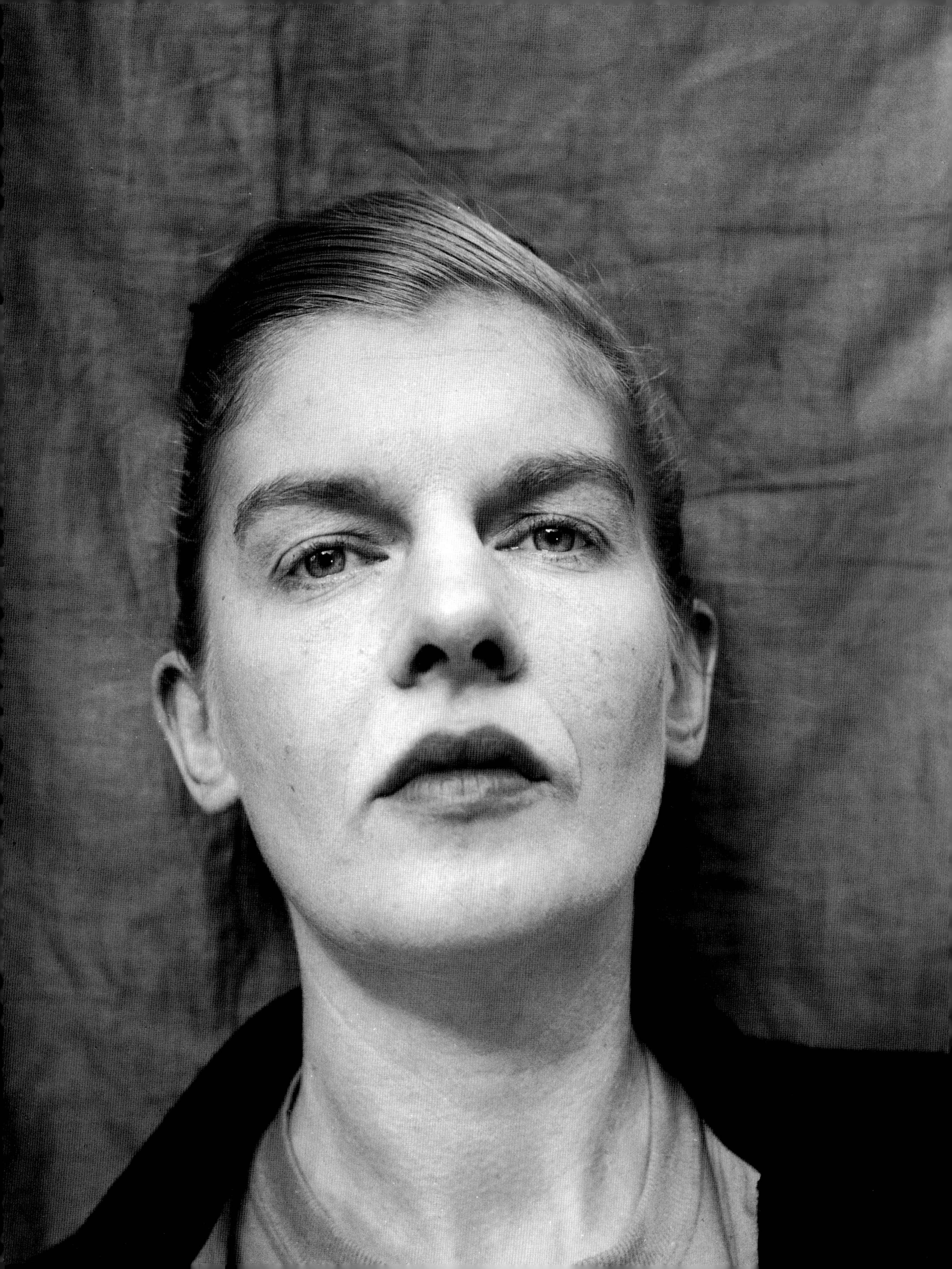

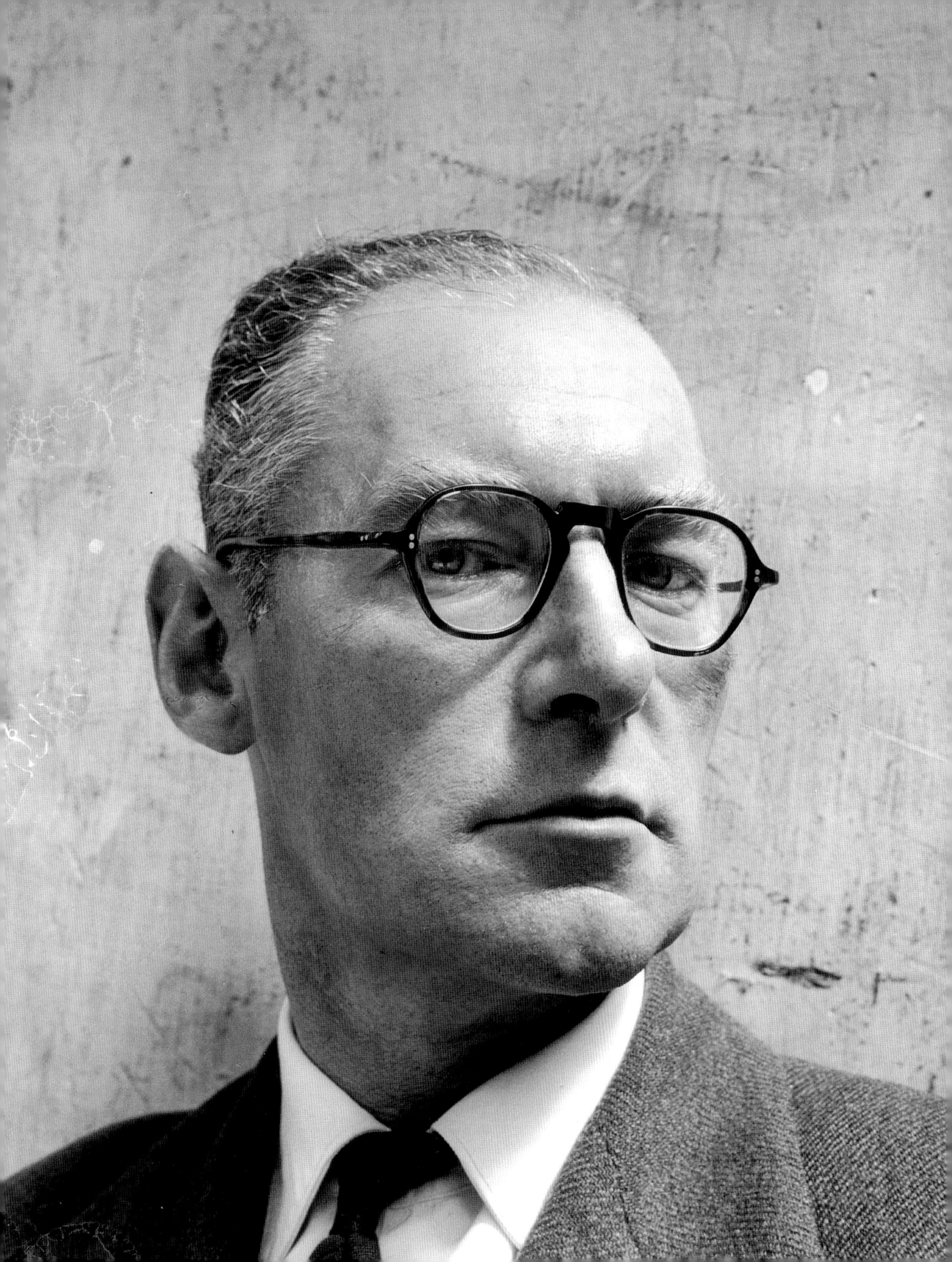

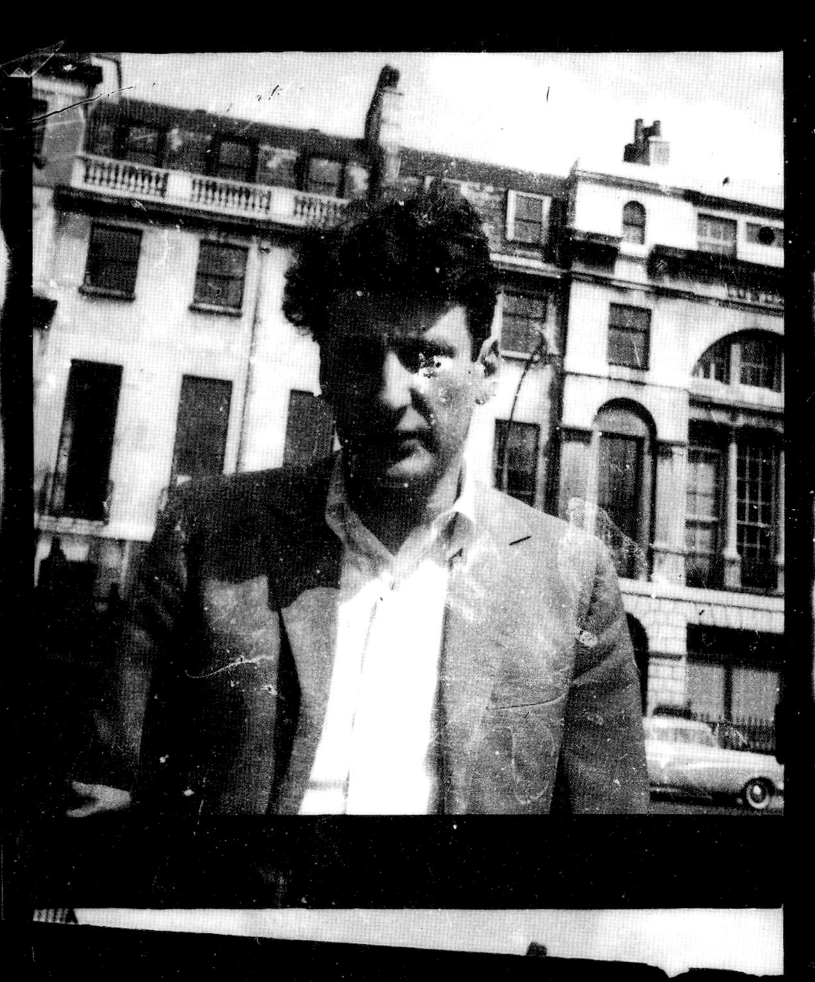
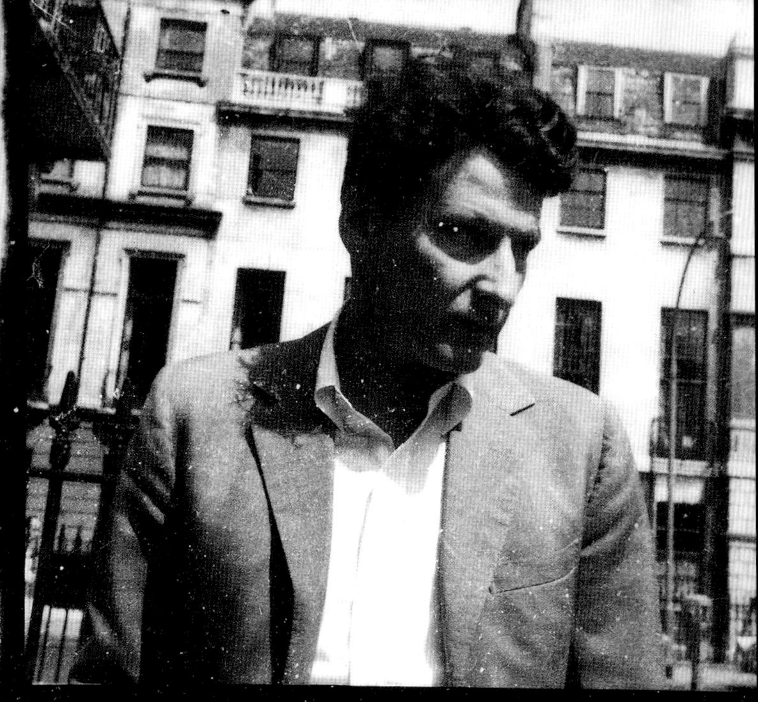
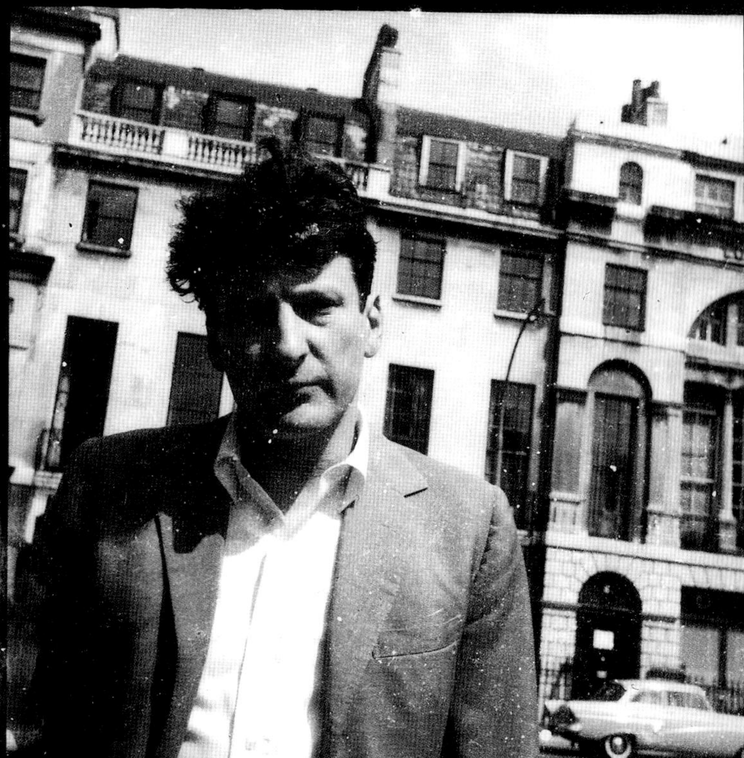
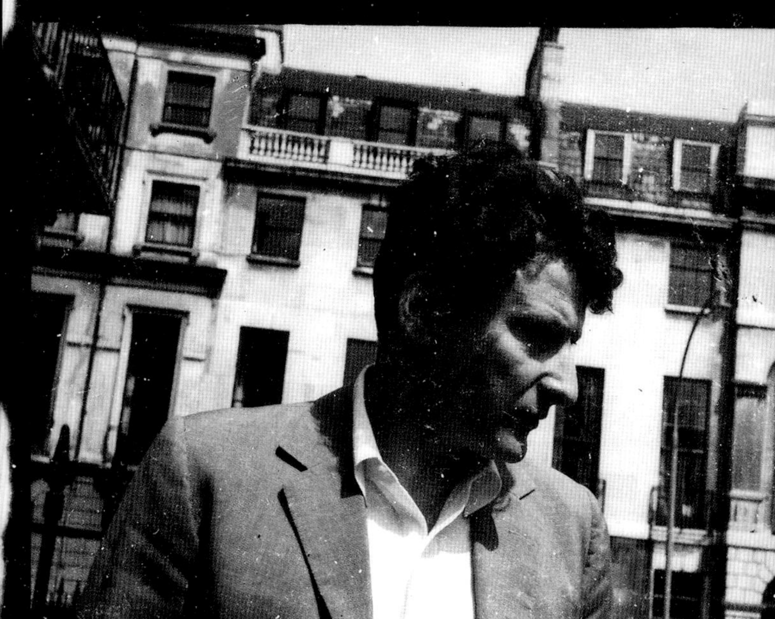

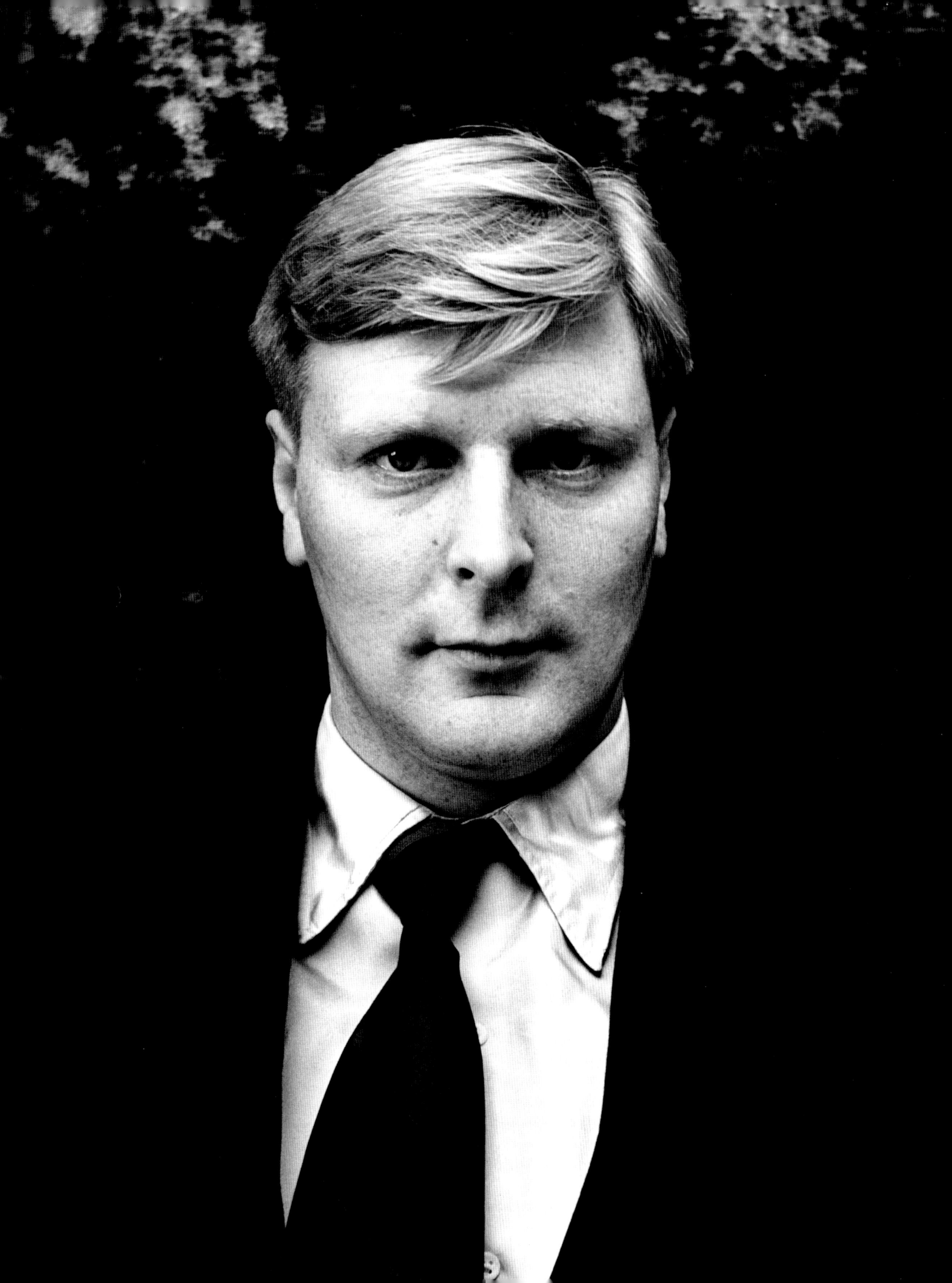

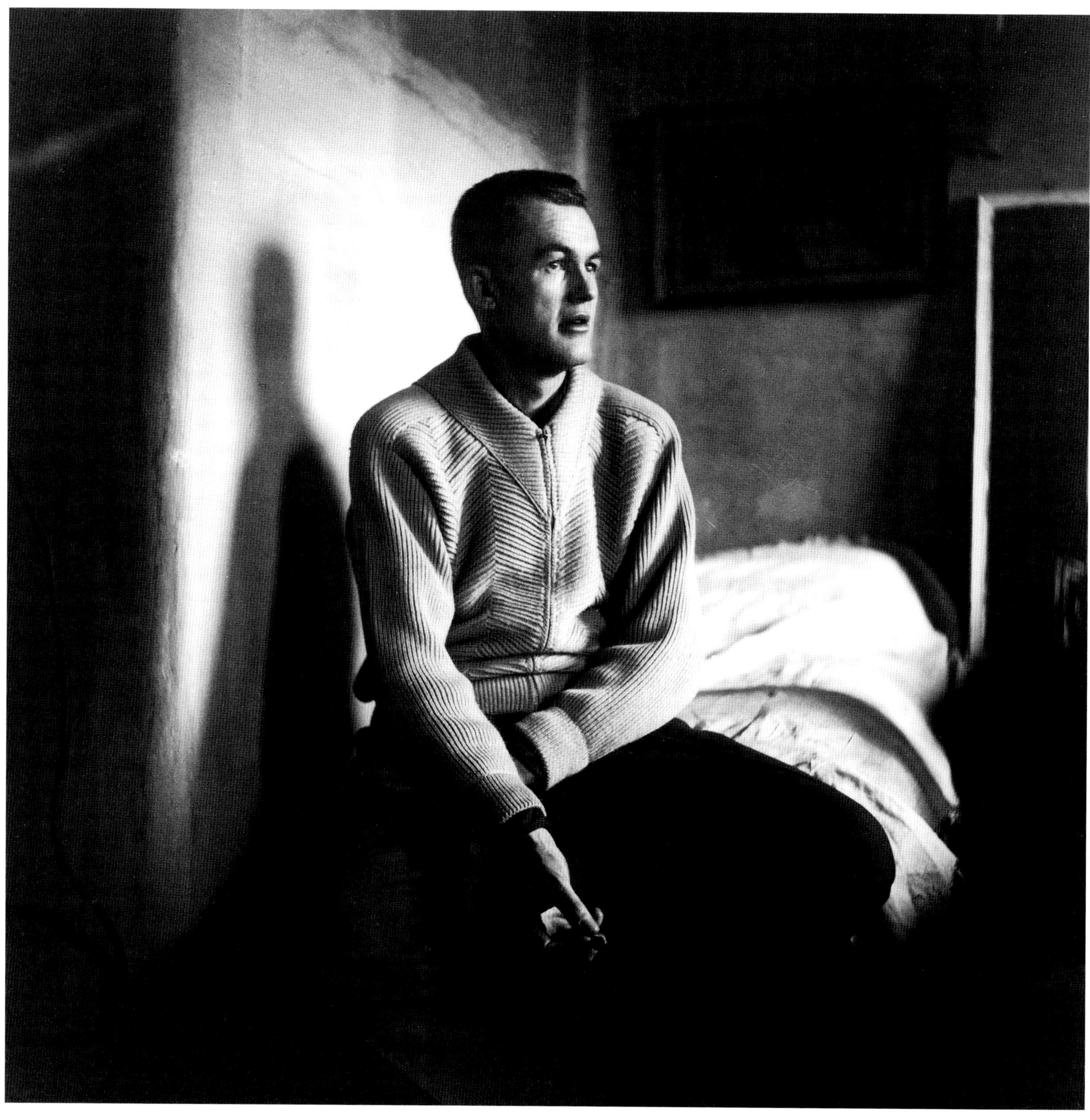

Colin MacInnes, novelist, 1950s

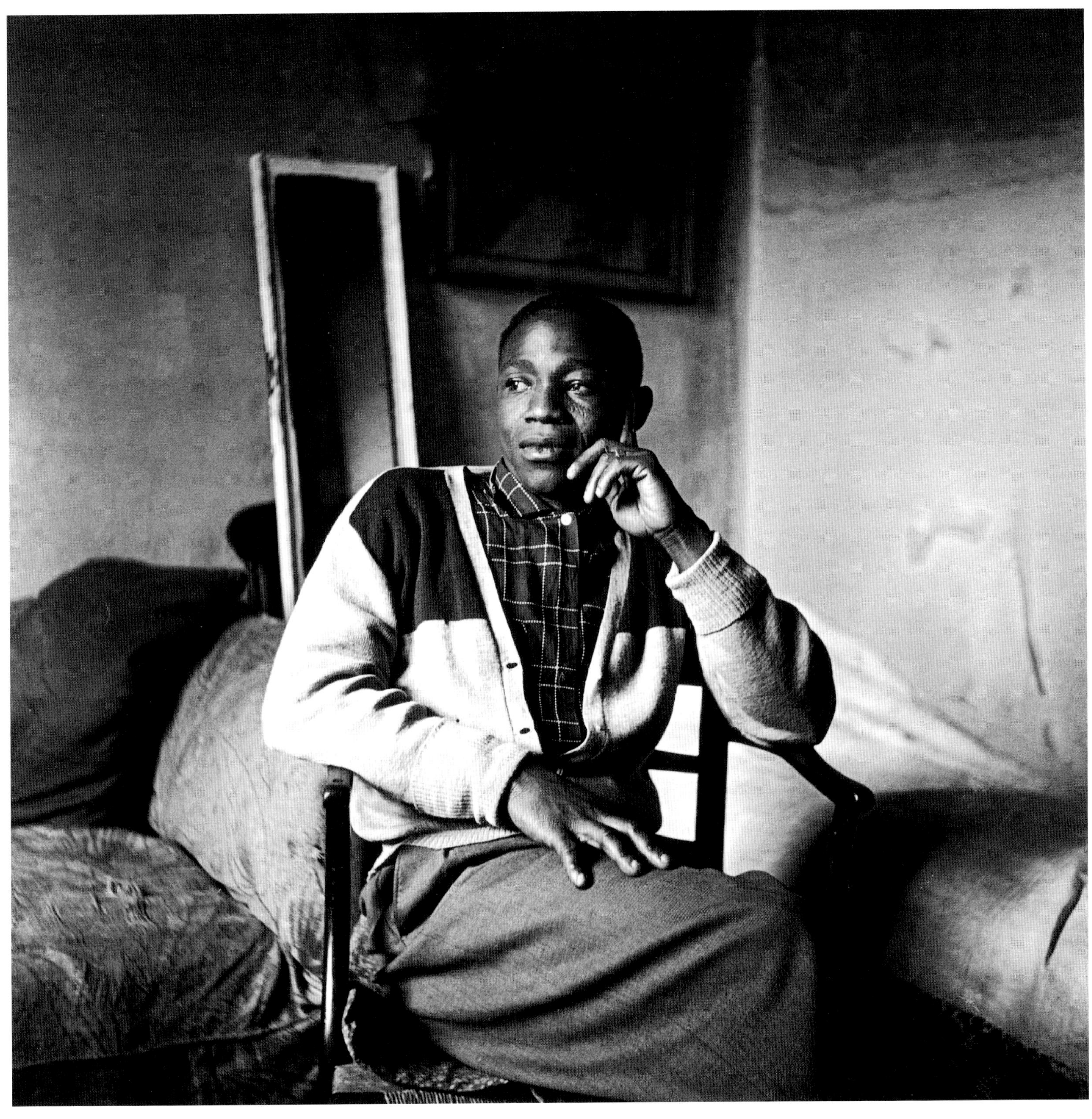

Unknown sitter, Colin MacInnes's flat, 1950s

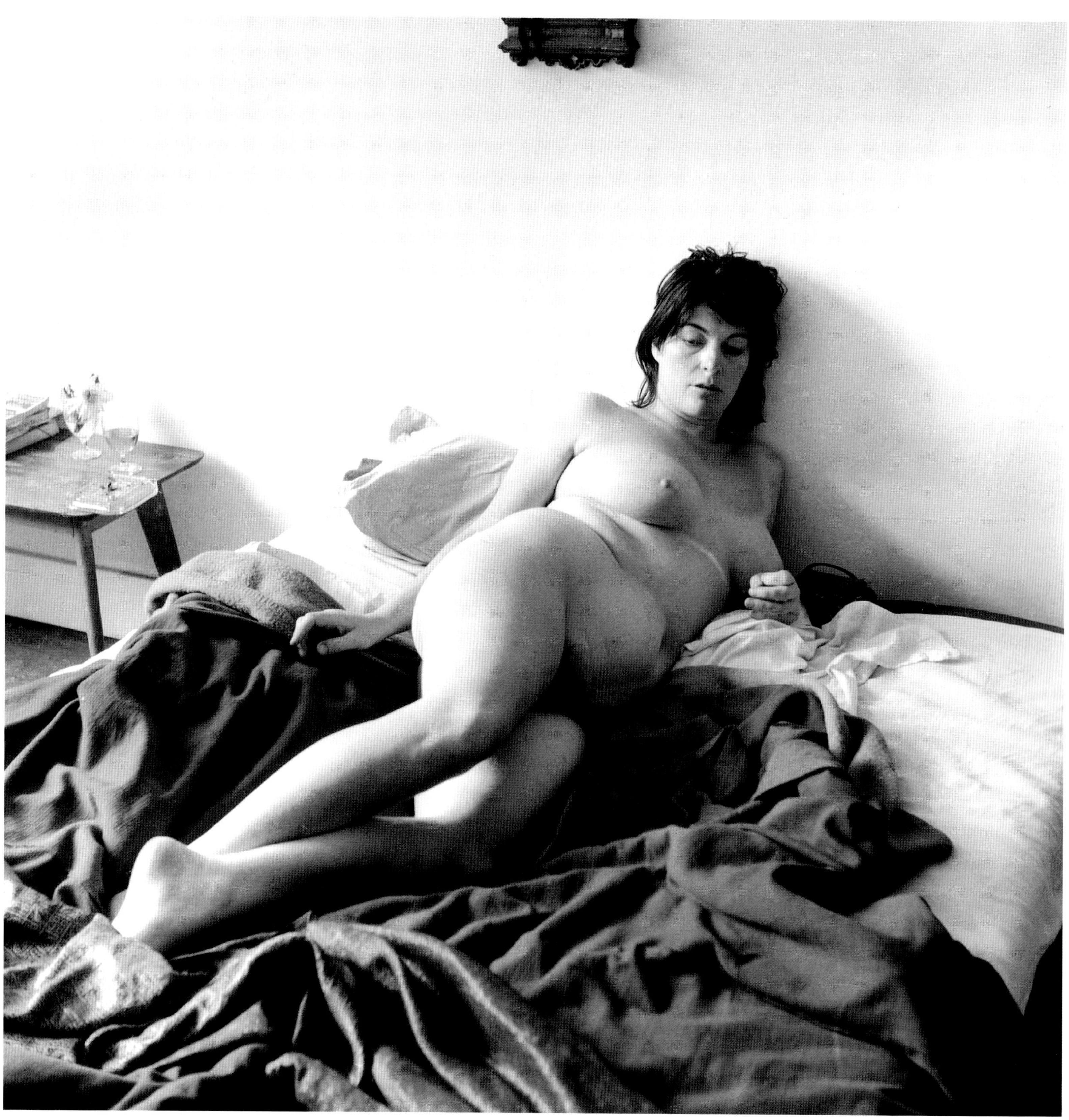

Henrietta Moraes, model for Francis Bacon, *c.* 1963

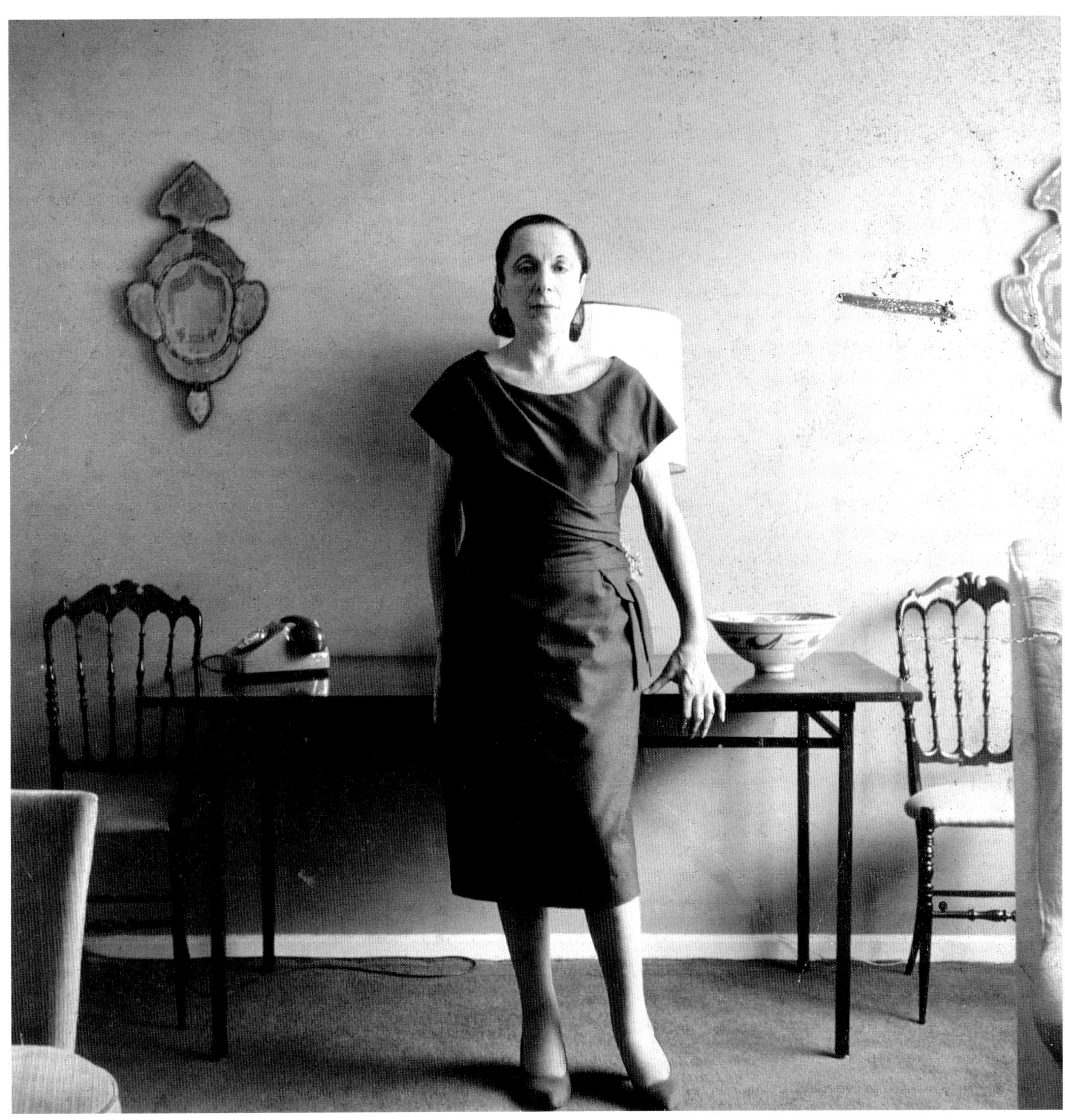

Muriel Belcher, proprietor of the Colony Room, 1960s

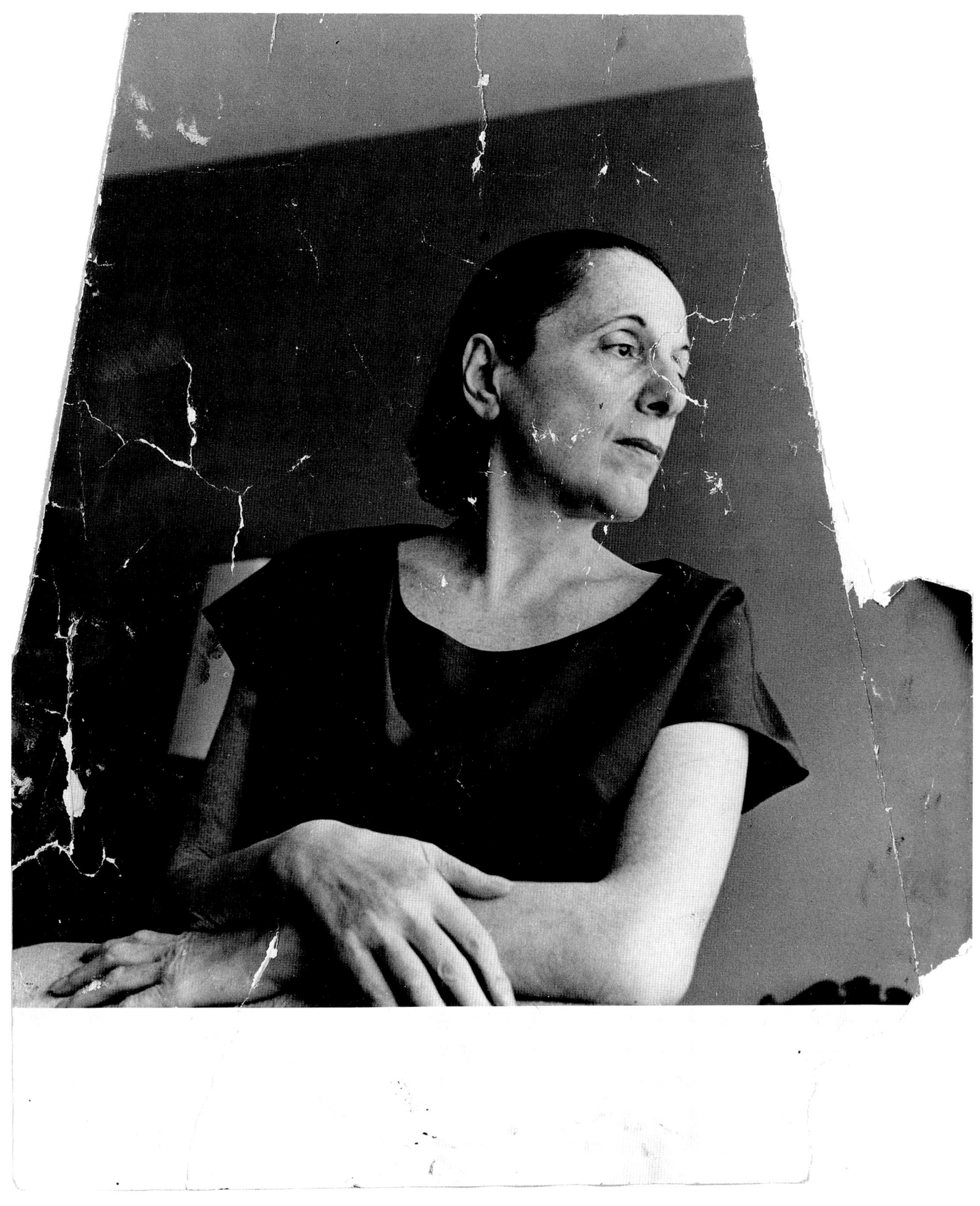

Muriel Belcher, 1960s

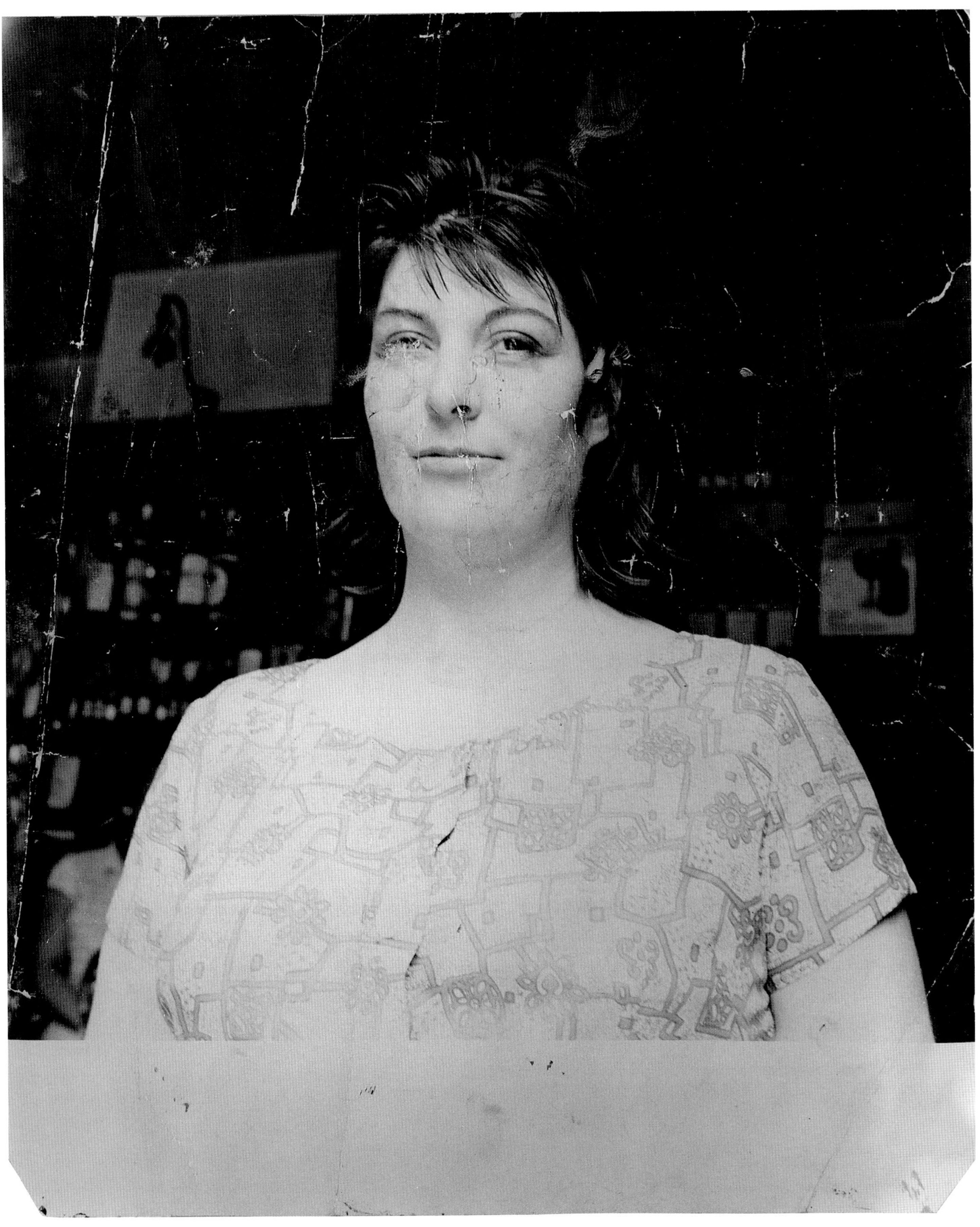

Henrietta Moraes, 1960s

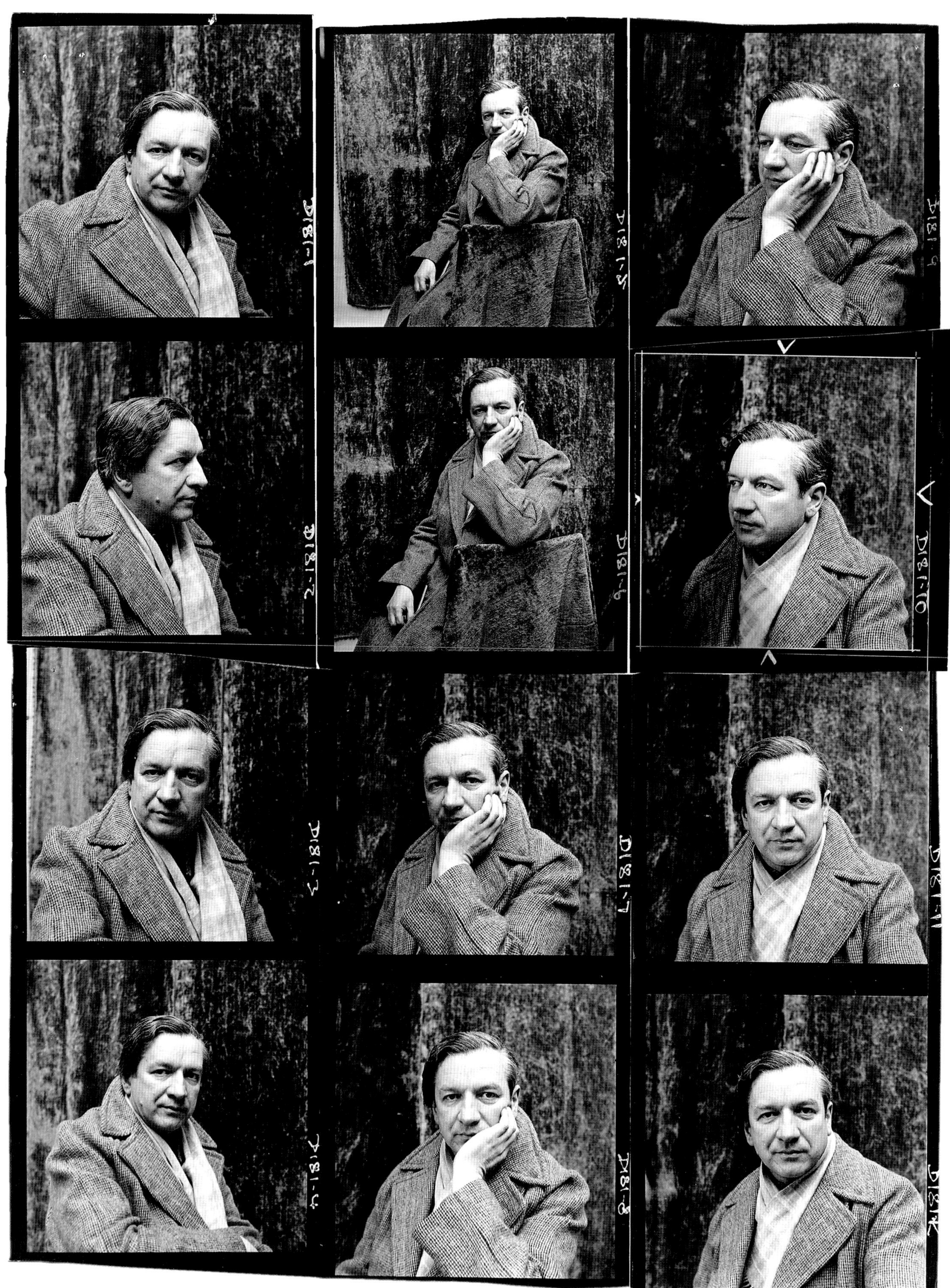

Ceri Richards, painter, 1952

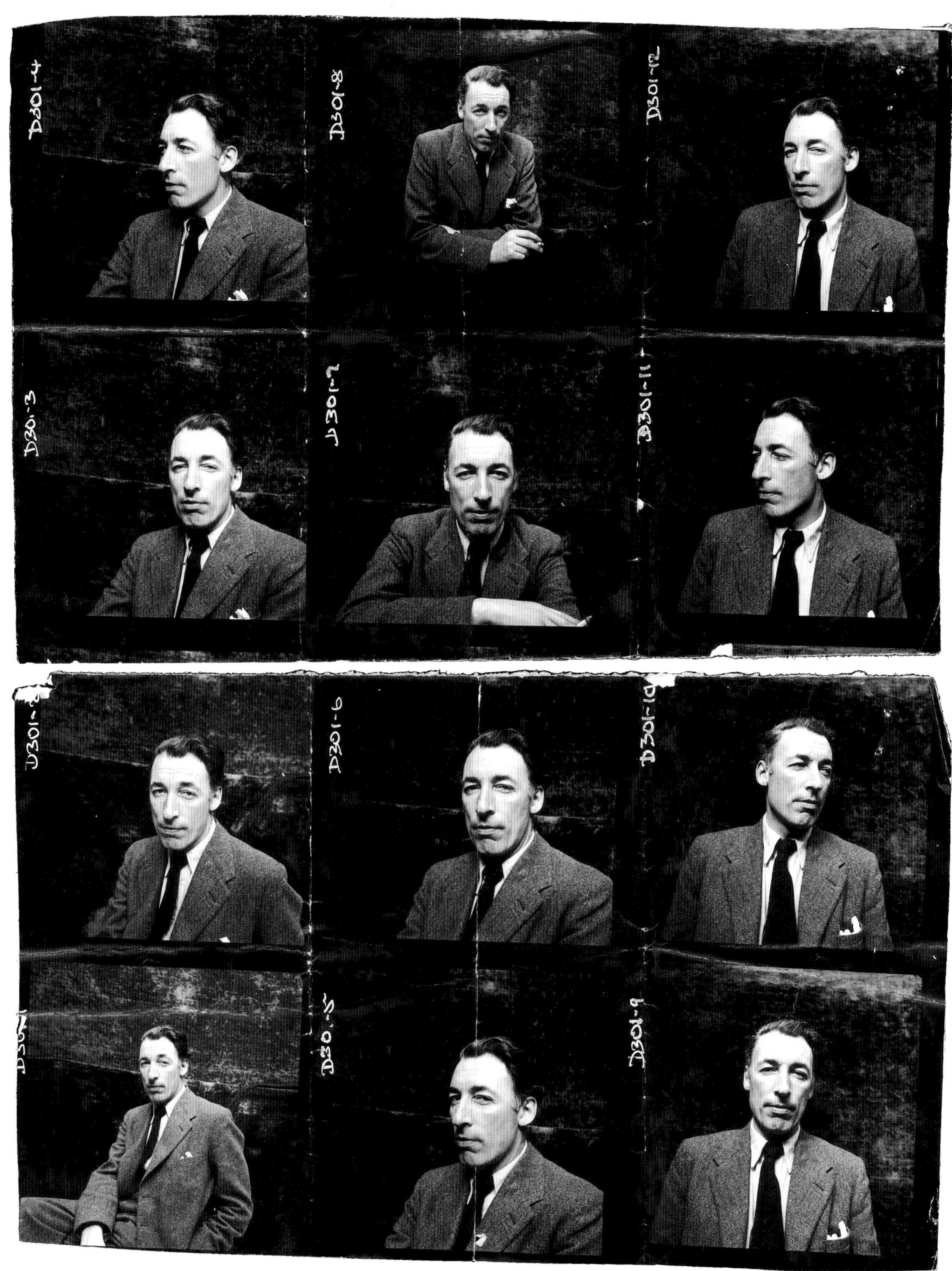

Louis MacNeice, poet, 1952

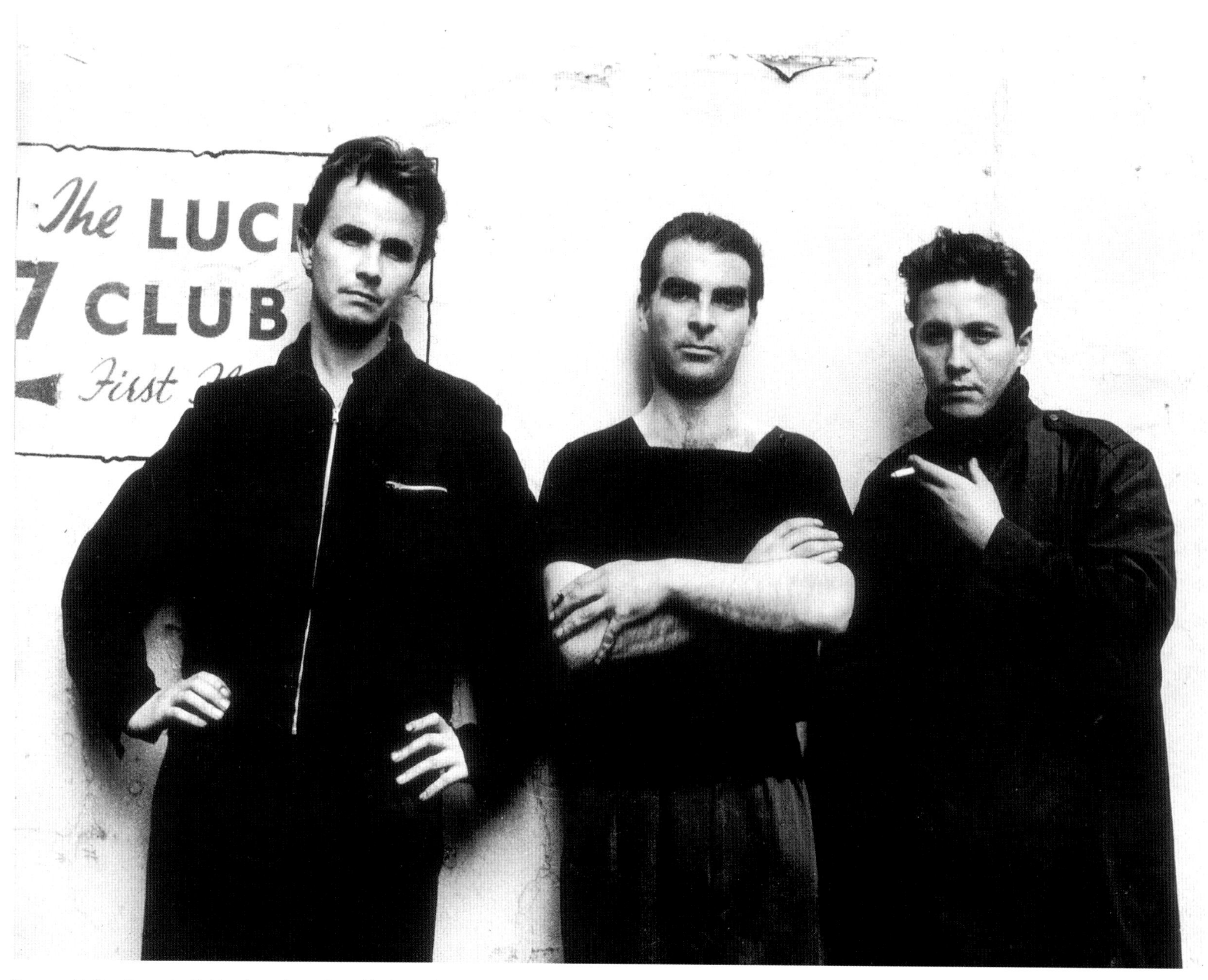

Bruce and Jeffrey Bernard with Terry Jones (centre) outside the Lucky 7 Club in Soho, c. 1956–57

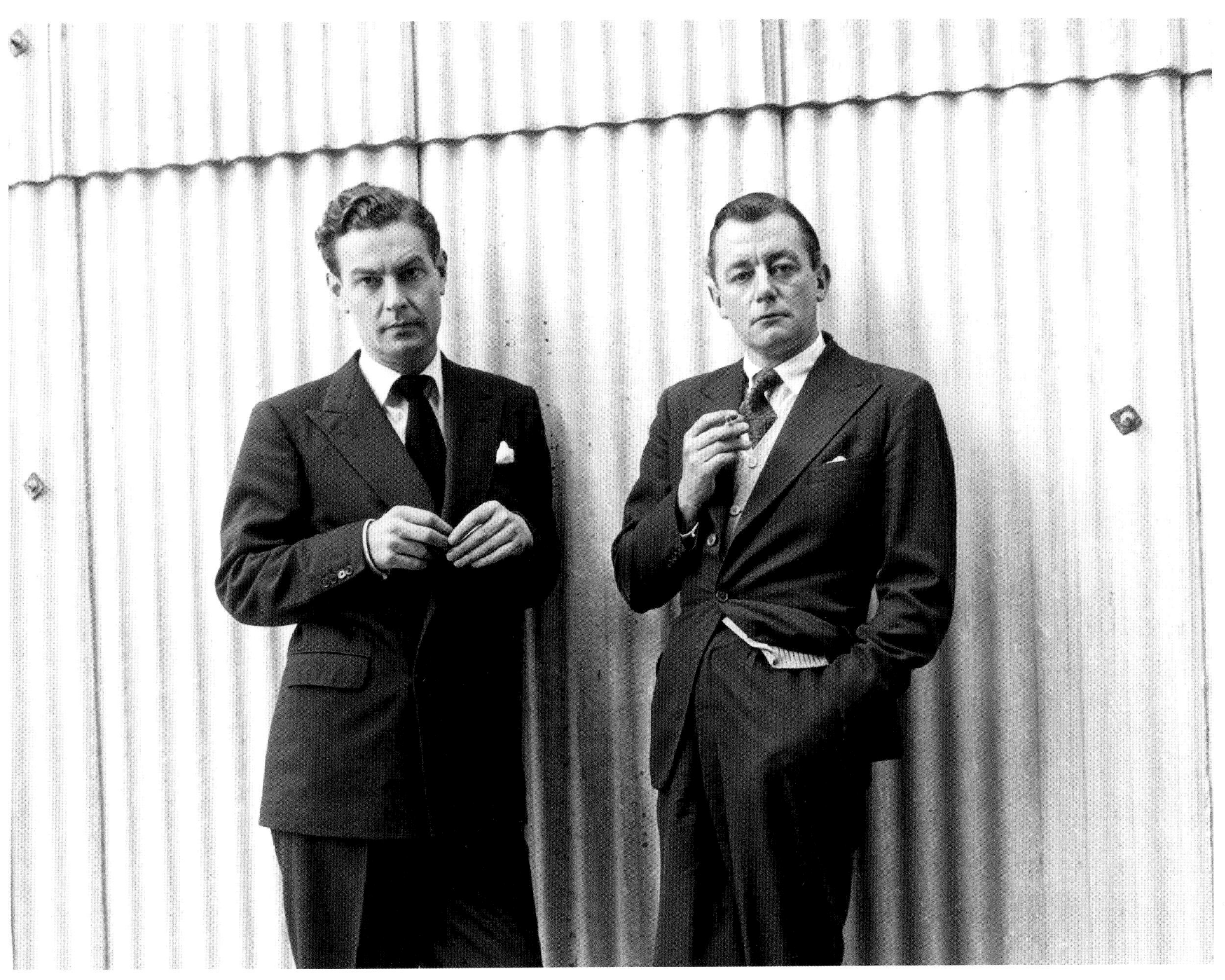

Michael Truman, film producer, and Robert Hamer, film director, 1952

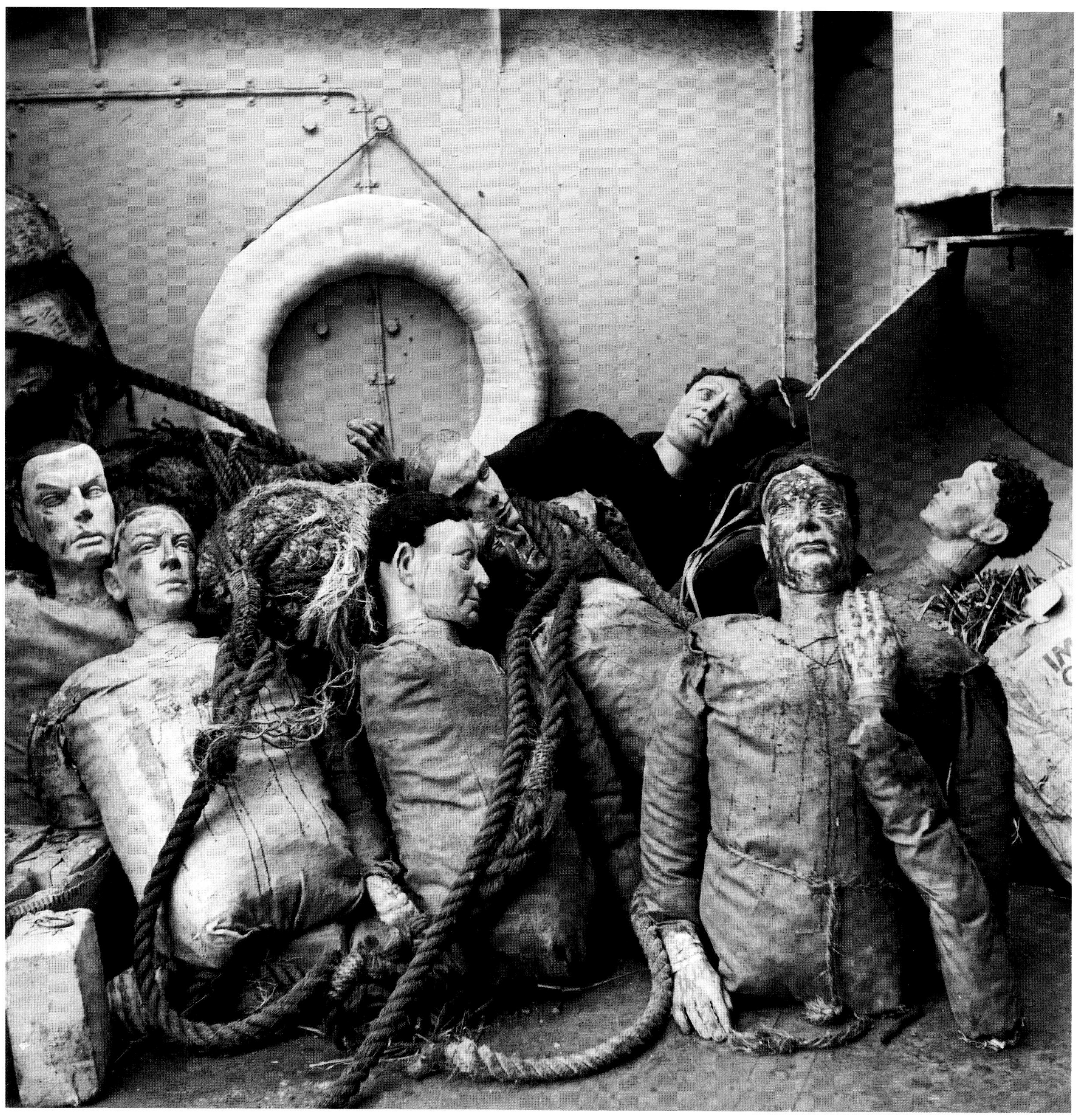

Dummies of drowned sailors for the 1952 film *The Cruel Sea*

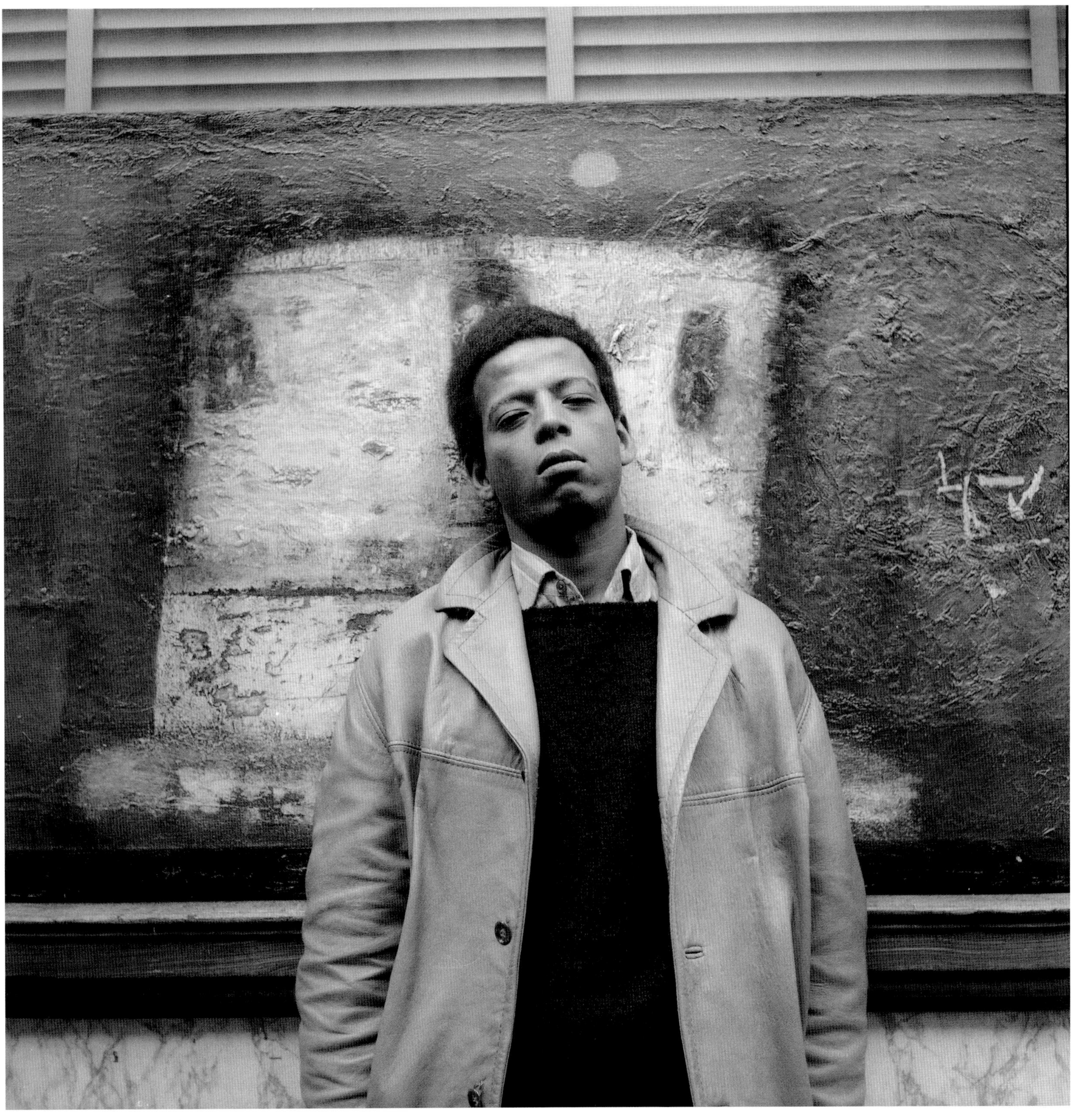

Hussain Sharif, painter, 1960s

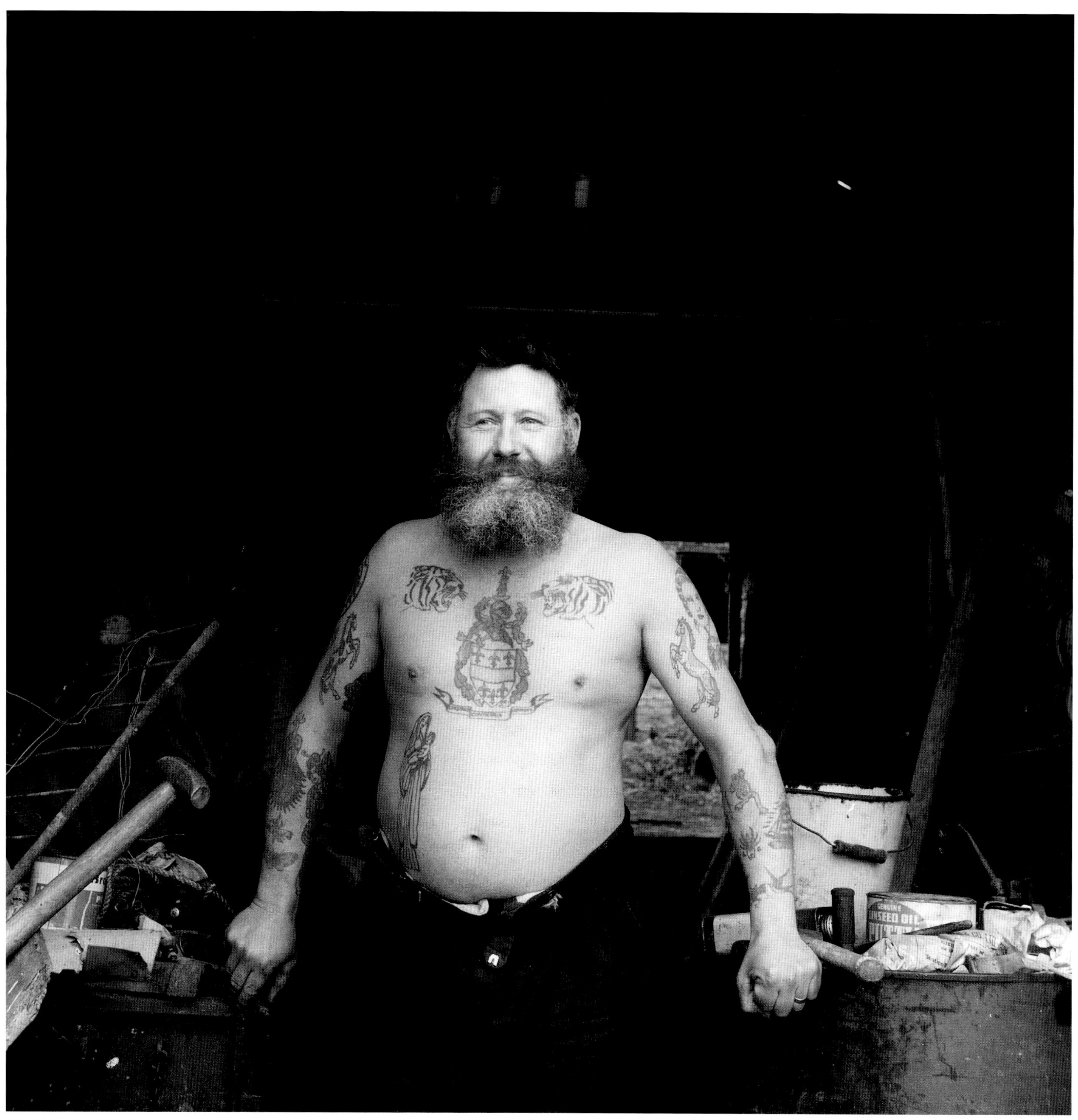

Tattooed man, 1950s

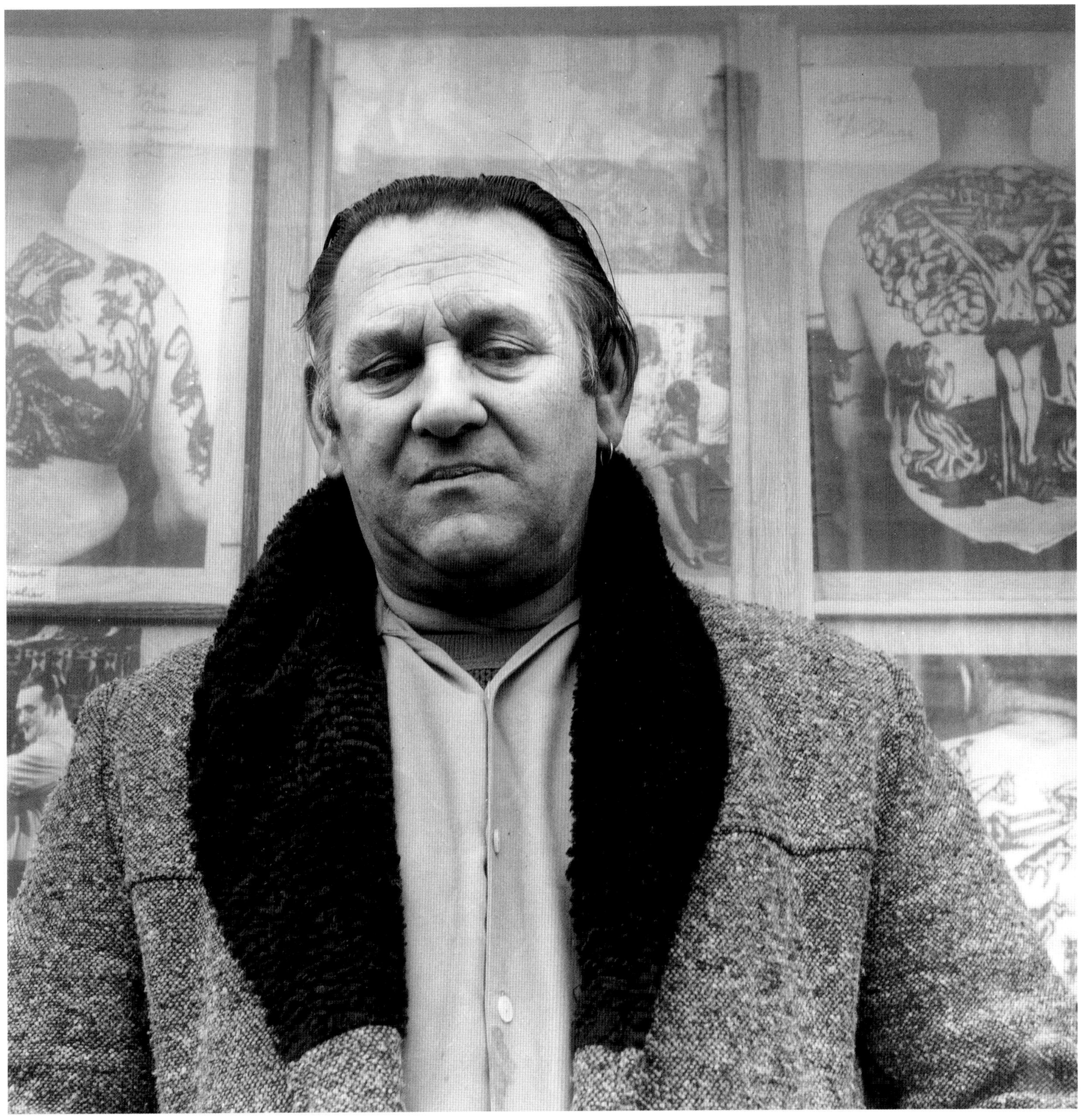

Frank Skuse, tattooist, 1950s

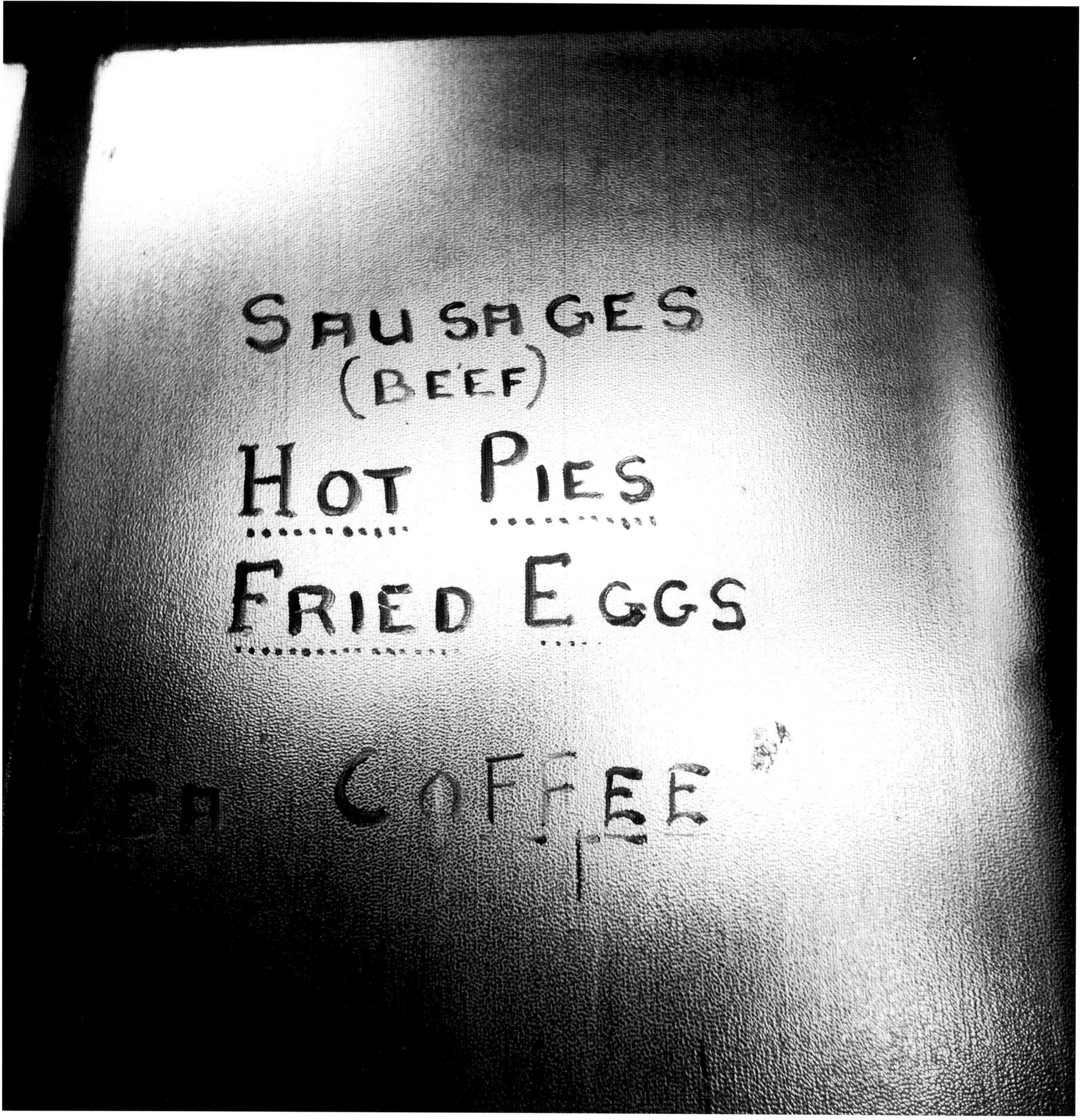

Café window, 1950s

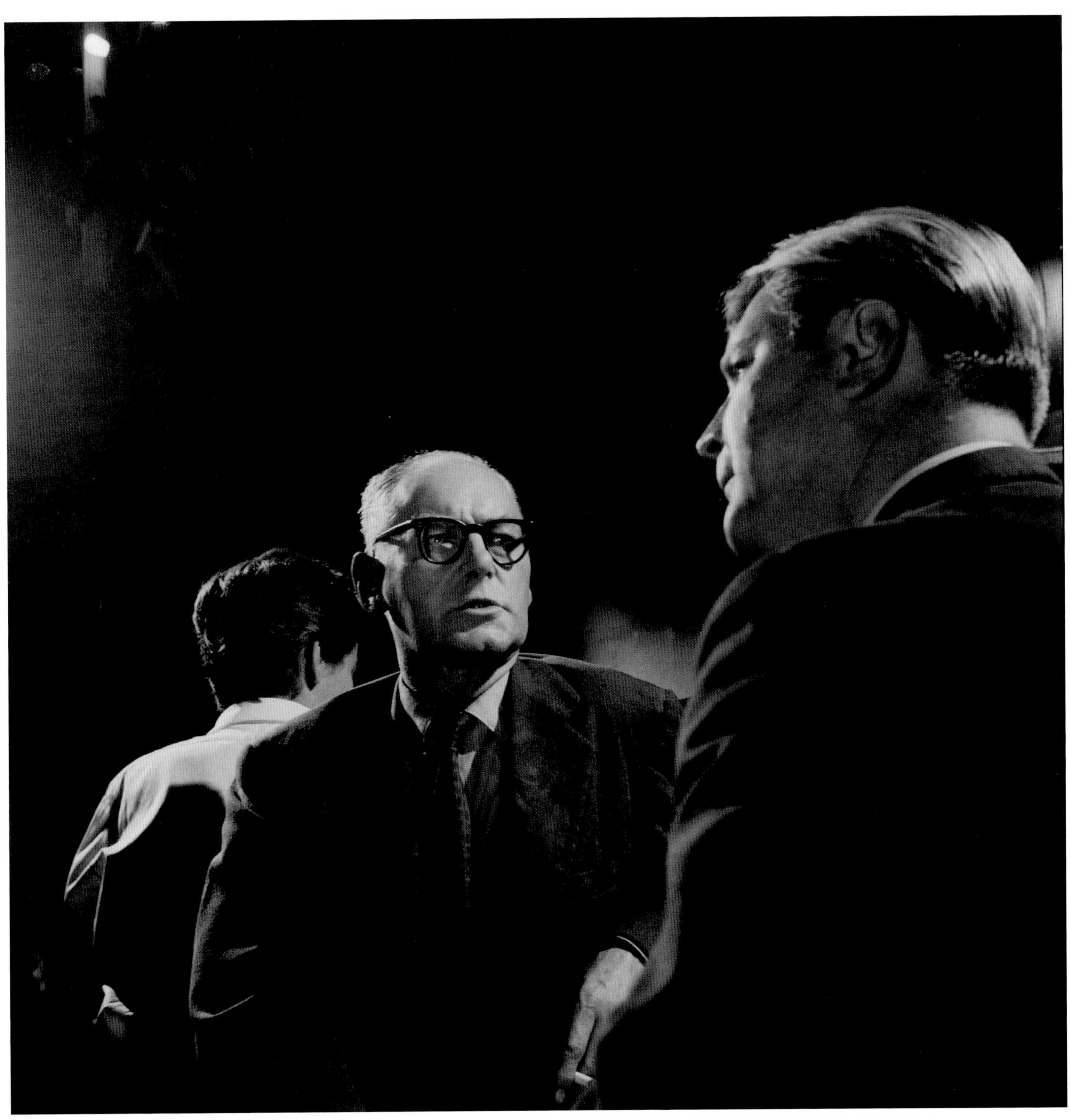

David Archer, publisher and bookseller, with the journalist Daniel Farson, c. 1958

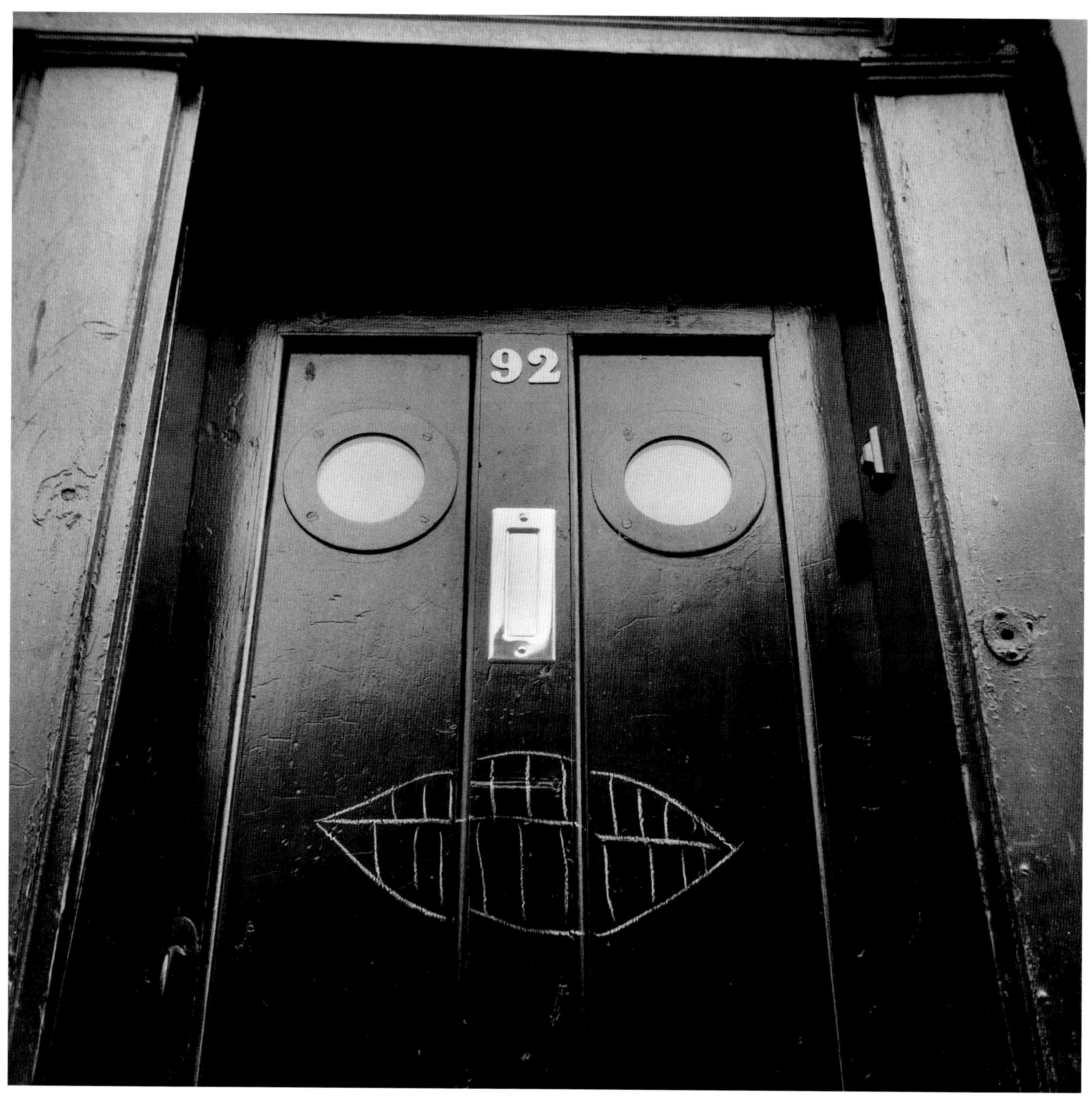

Graffitied doorway, 1960s

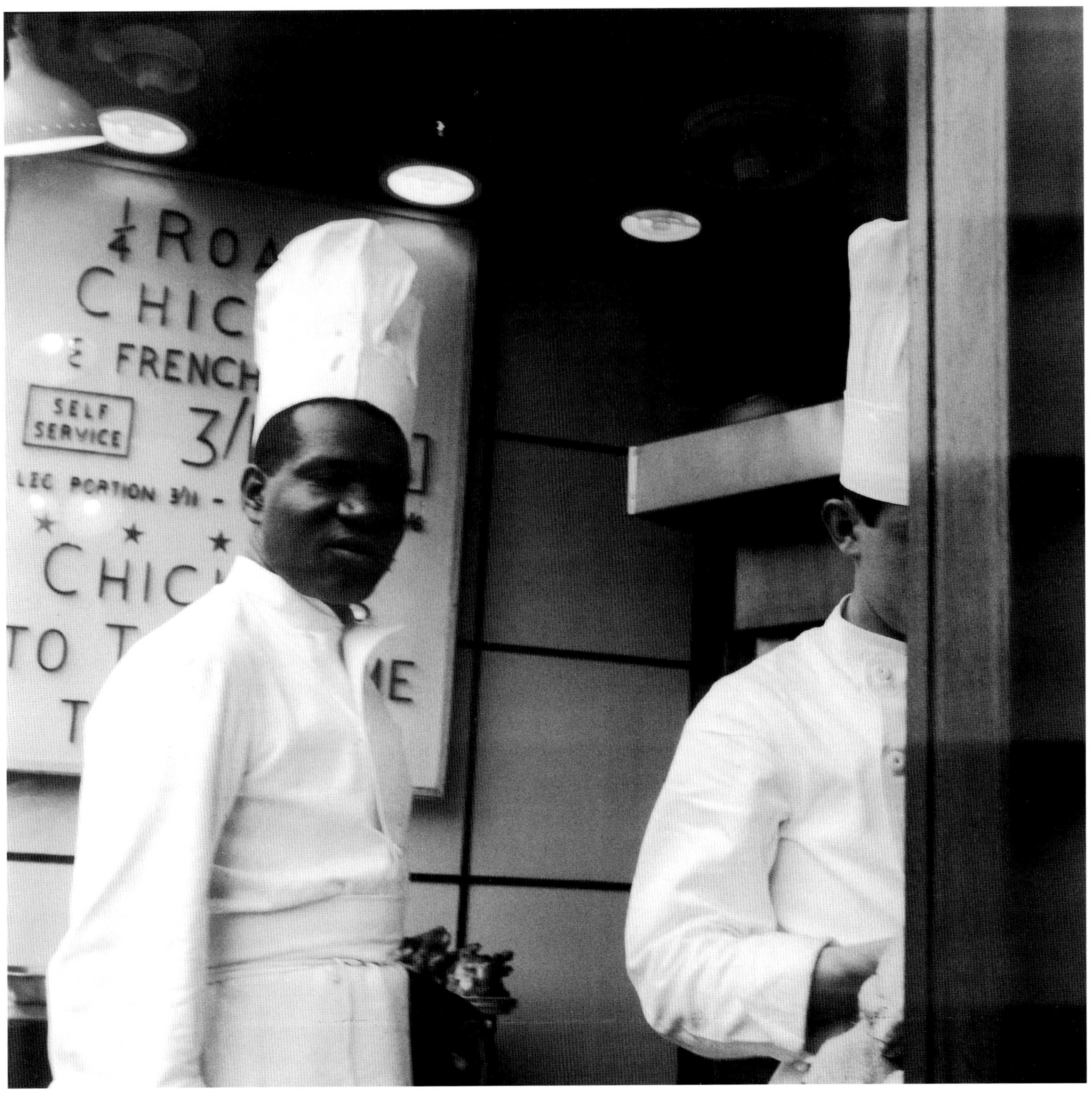

Chefs, Soho, 1957

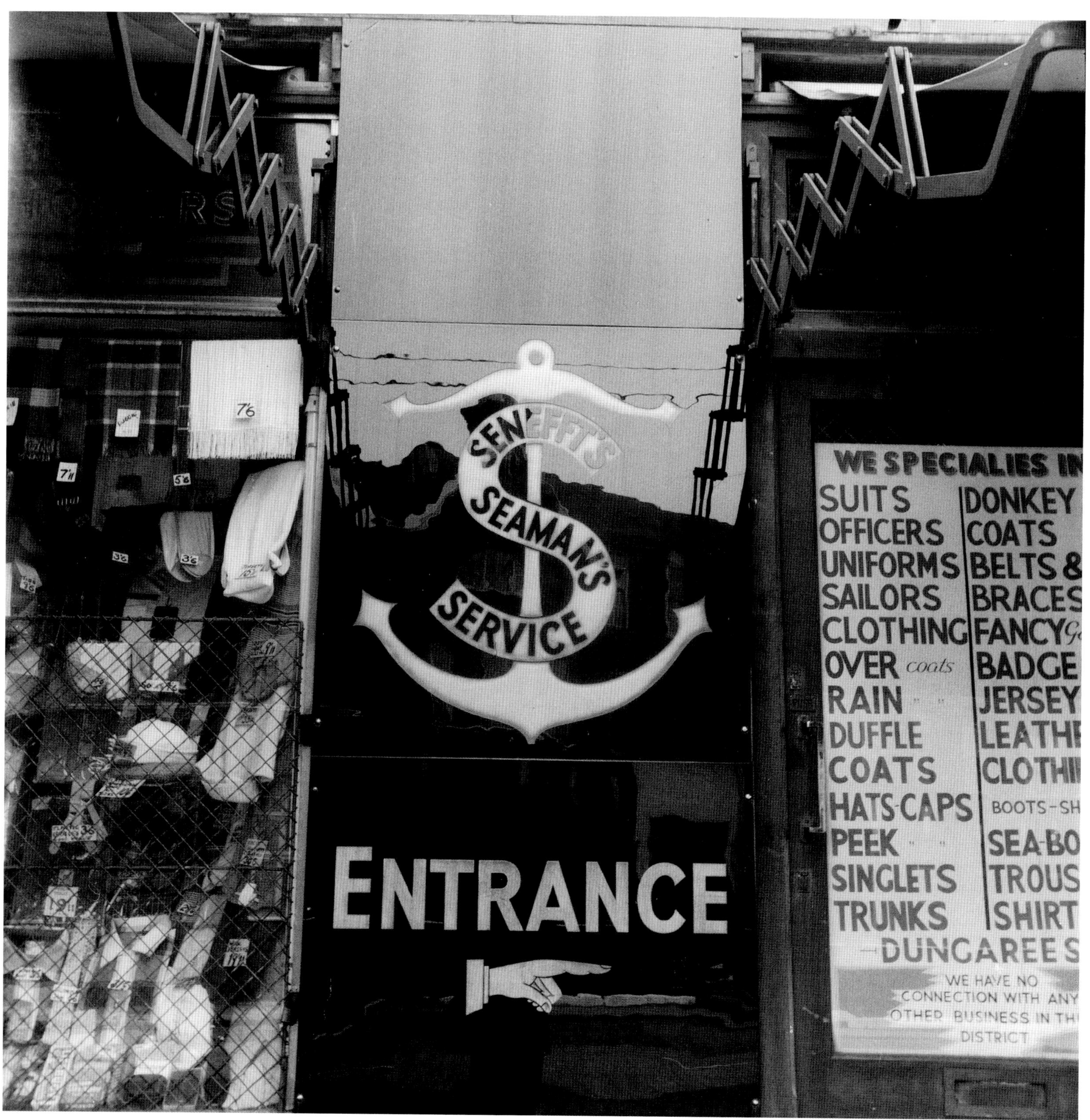

Marine outfitters, 1950s

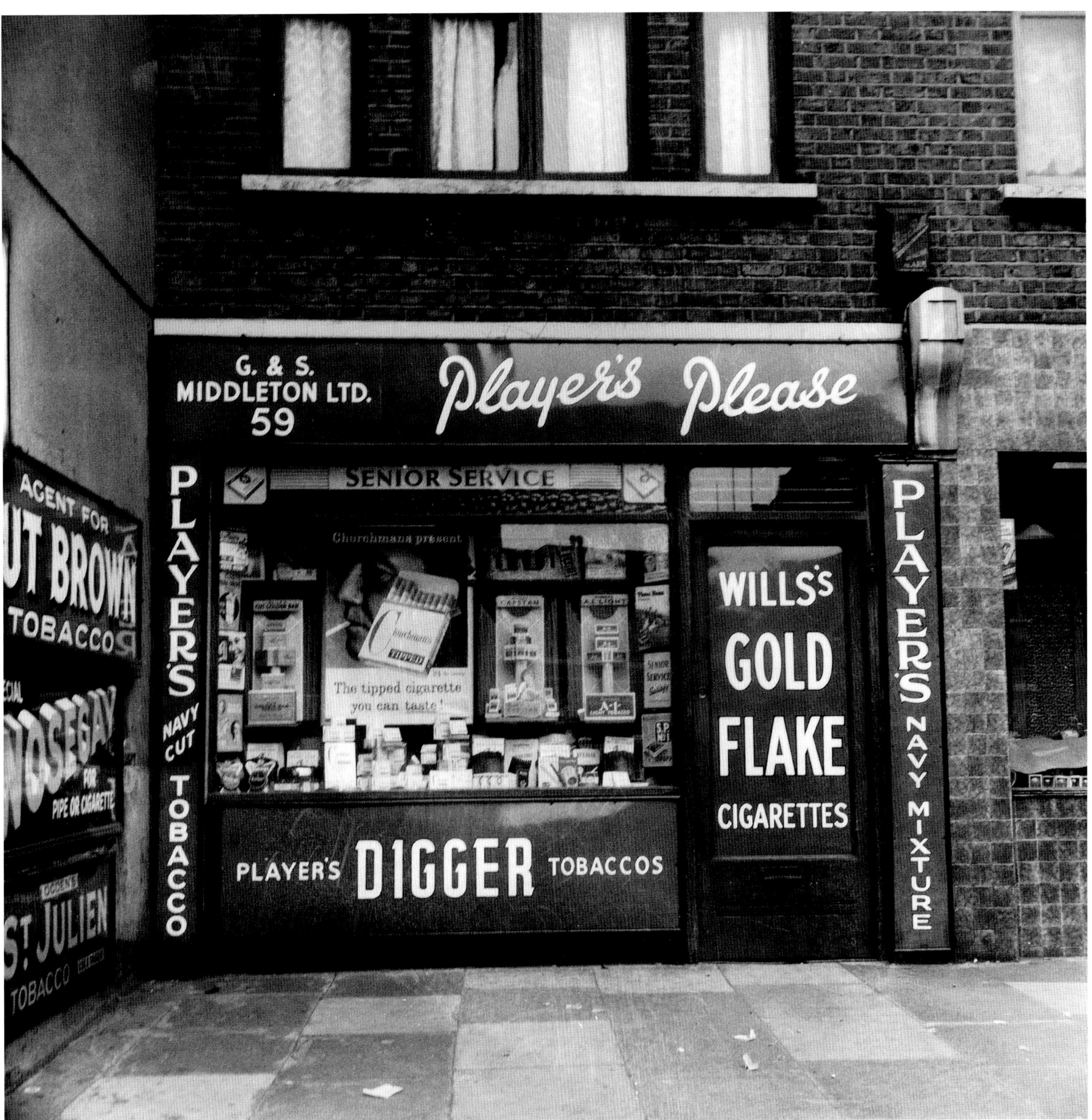

Tobacconist, East End, 1950s

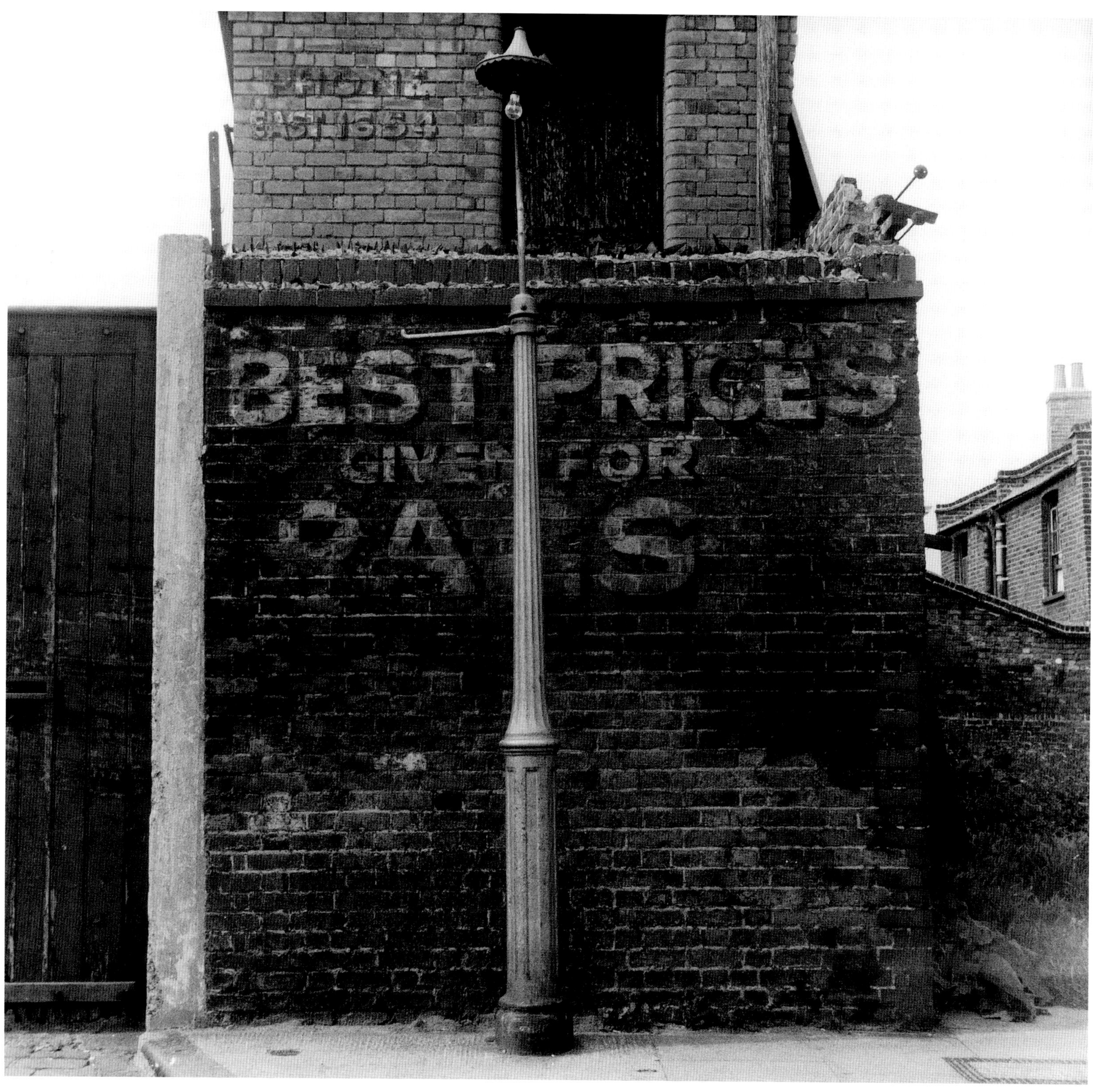

'Best Prices Given for Rags', for Deakin's proposed book 'London Walls', 1950s

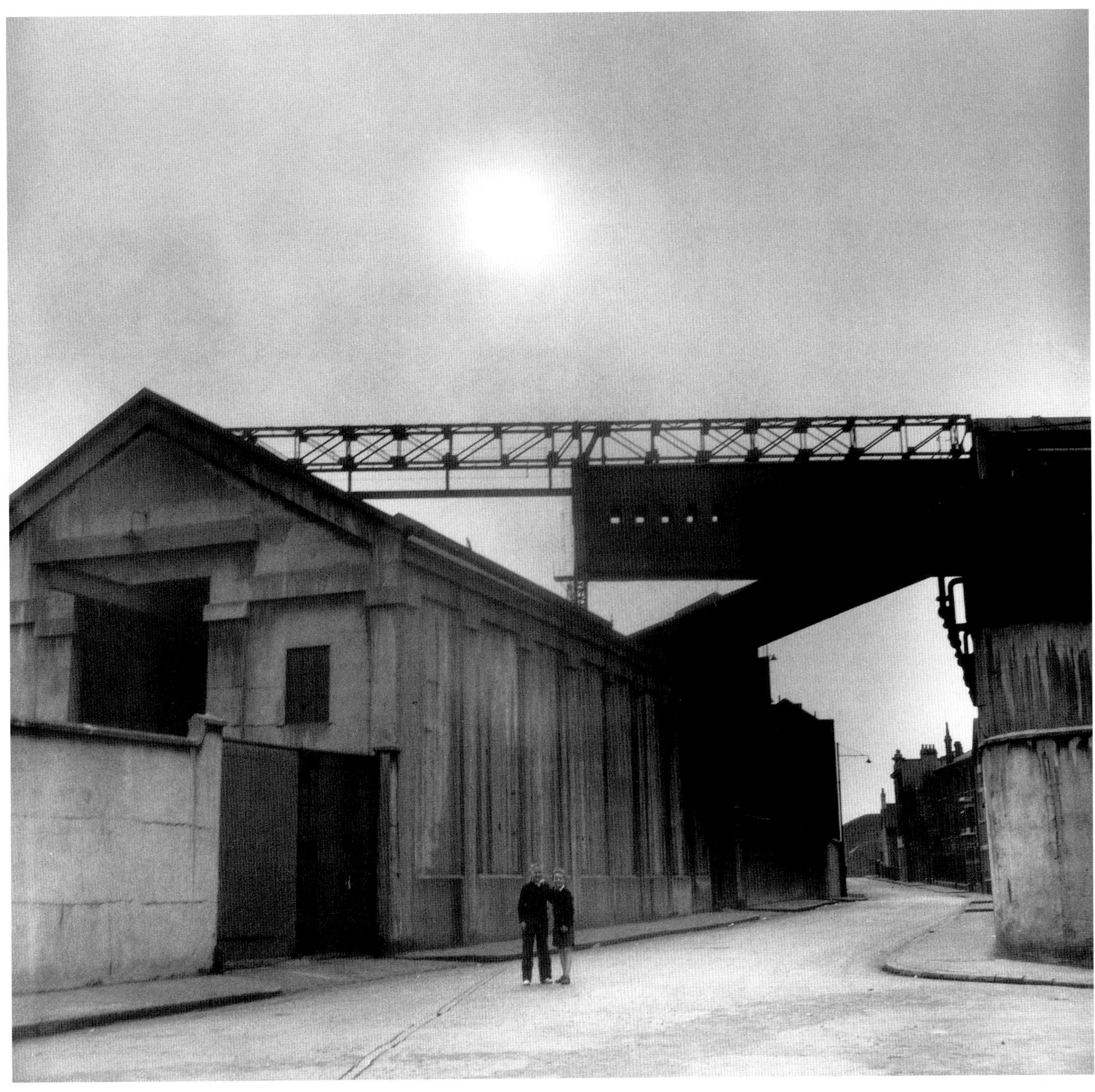

East London, 1950s

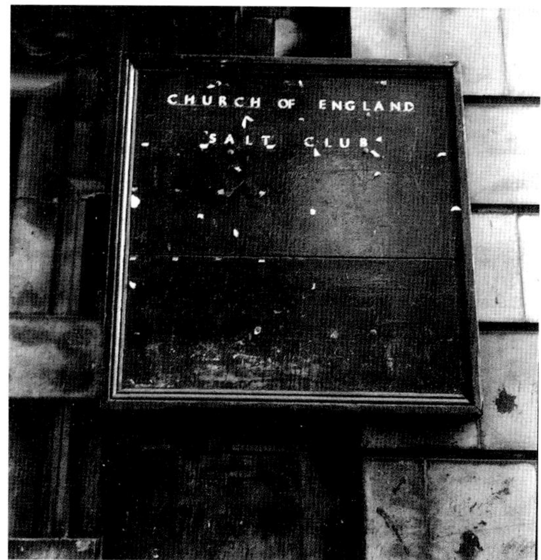

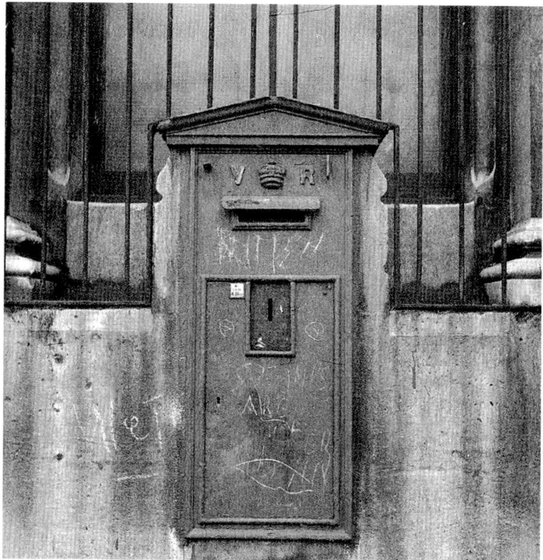

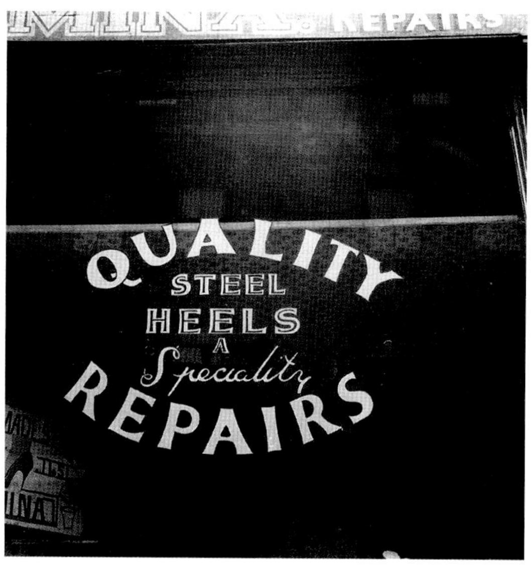

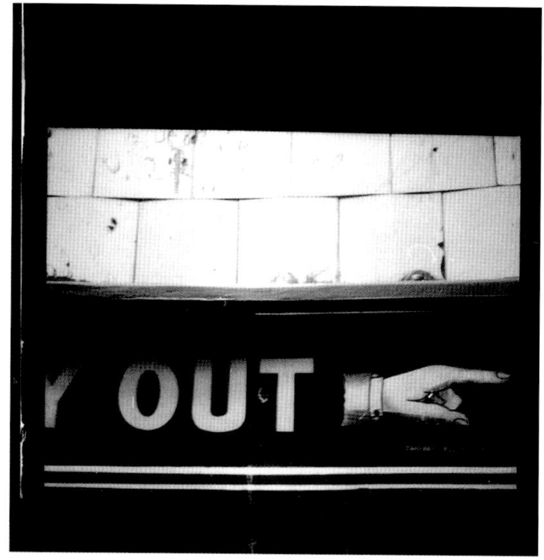

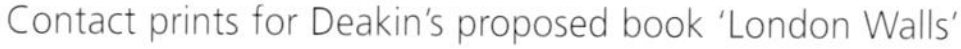
Contact prints for Deakin's proposed book 'London Walls'.

Deakin was an enthusiastic documentarist of the vernacular – shop fronts, advertising hoardings and road signs – as well as of the patterns created by the elements on plate glass windows and door panels. He delighted in the language of the streets as expressed in hand-rendered inscriptions and larger commercial messages. Unsurprisingly, in the light of his own artistic style, he found the 1951 exhibition 'Black Eyes and Lemonade'(*opposite*), a celebration of a century of popular art in London, particularly fascinating.

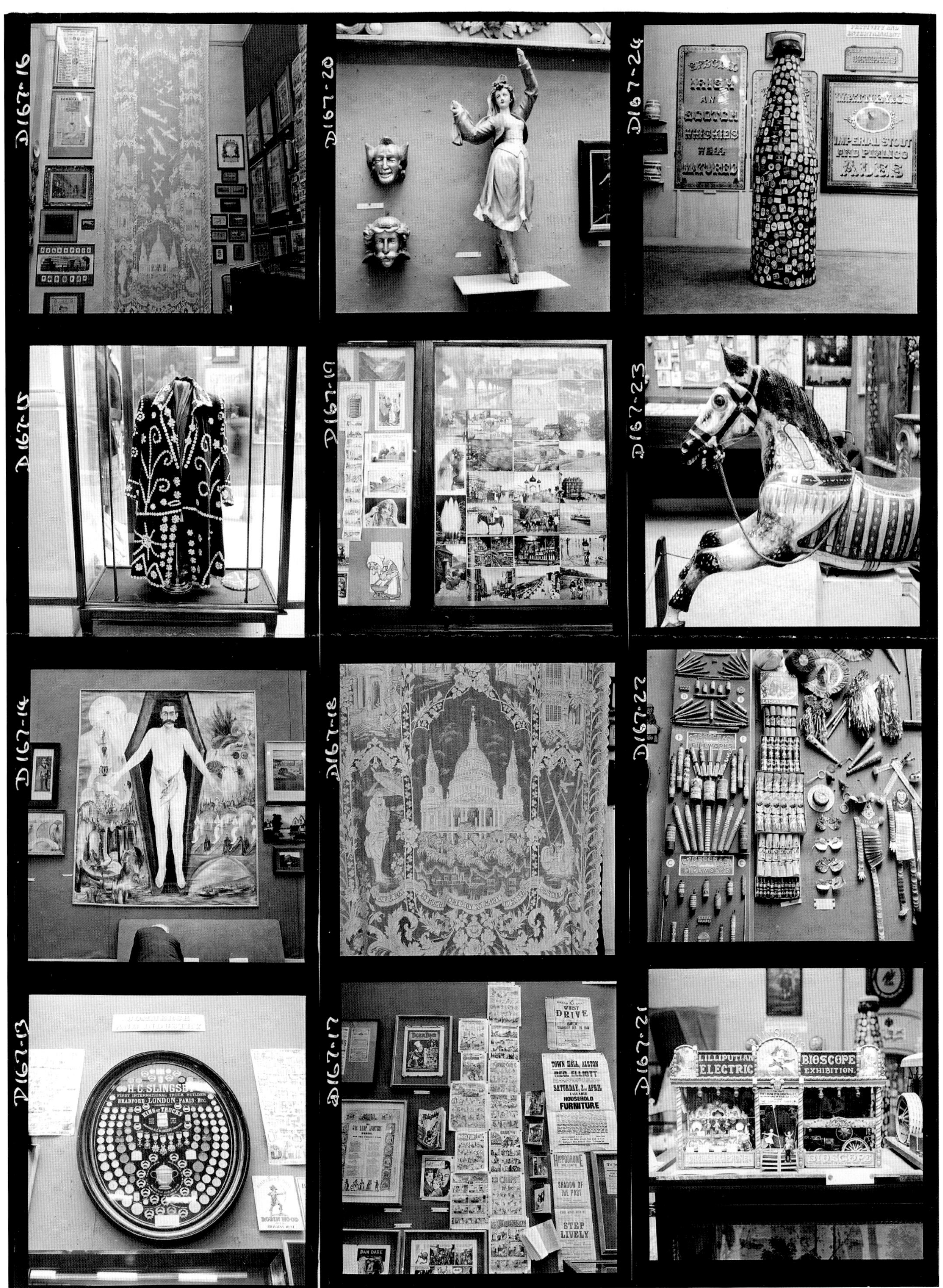

'Black Eyes and Lemonade', exhibition of folk art, Whitechapel Art Gallery, 1951

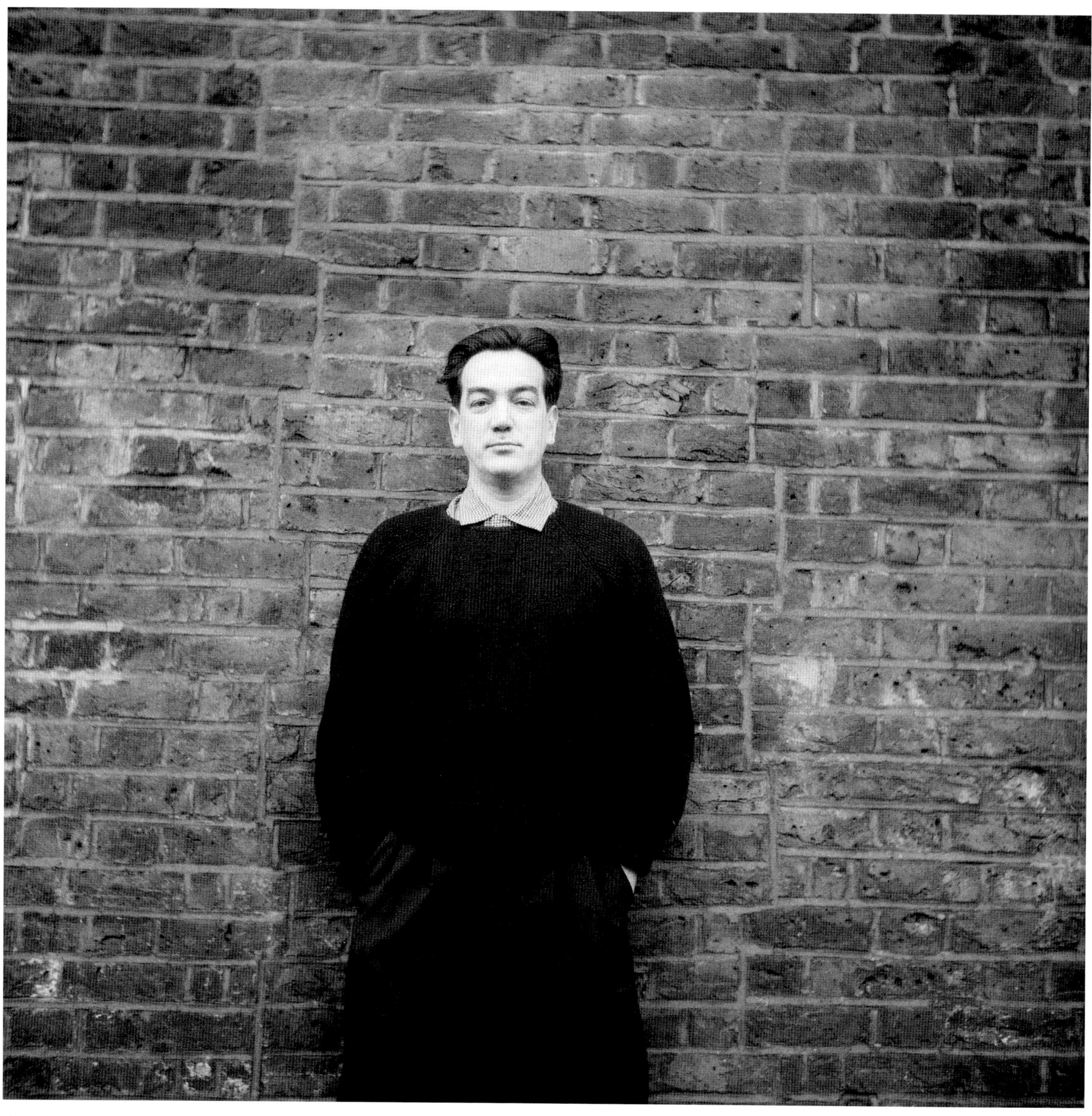

Alexander Mackendrick, film director, 1952

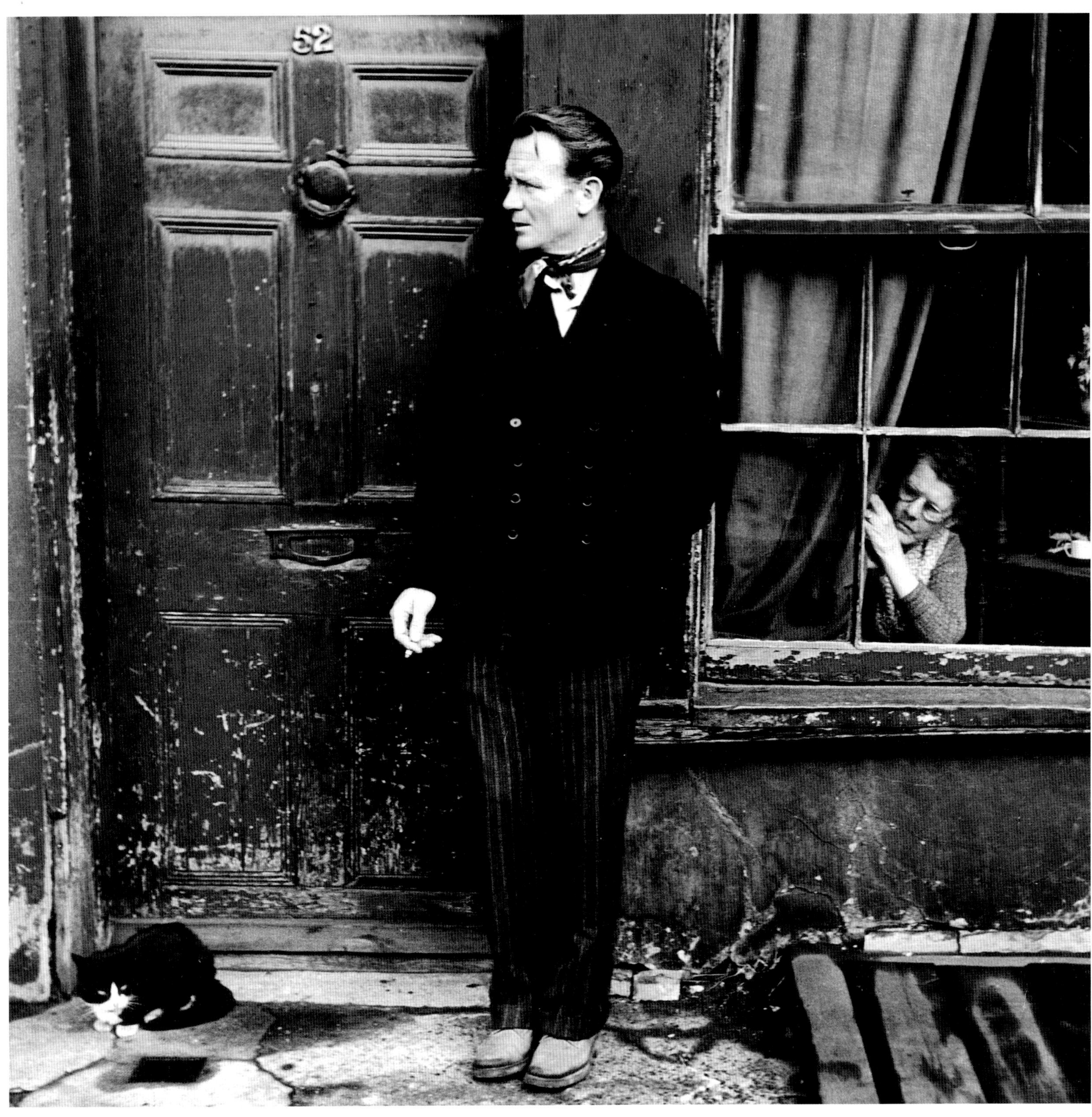

John Mills, actor, 1952

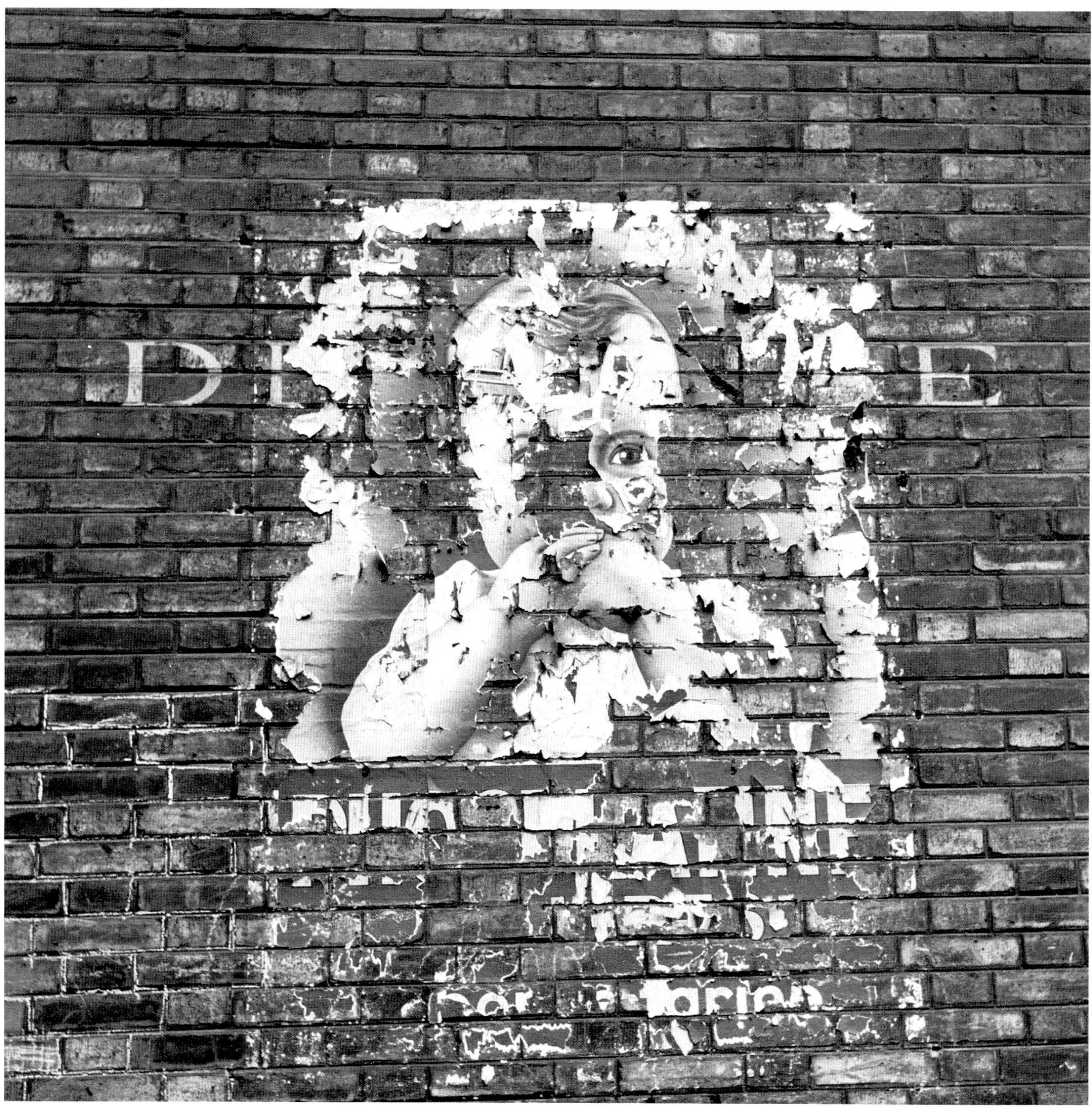

From 'London Walls', 1950s

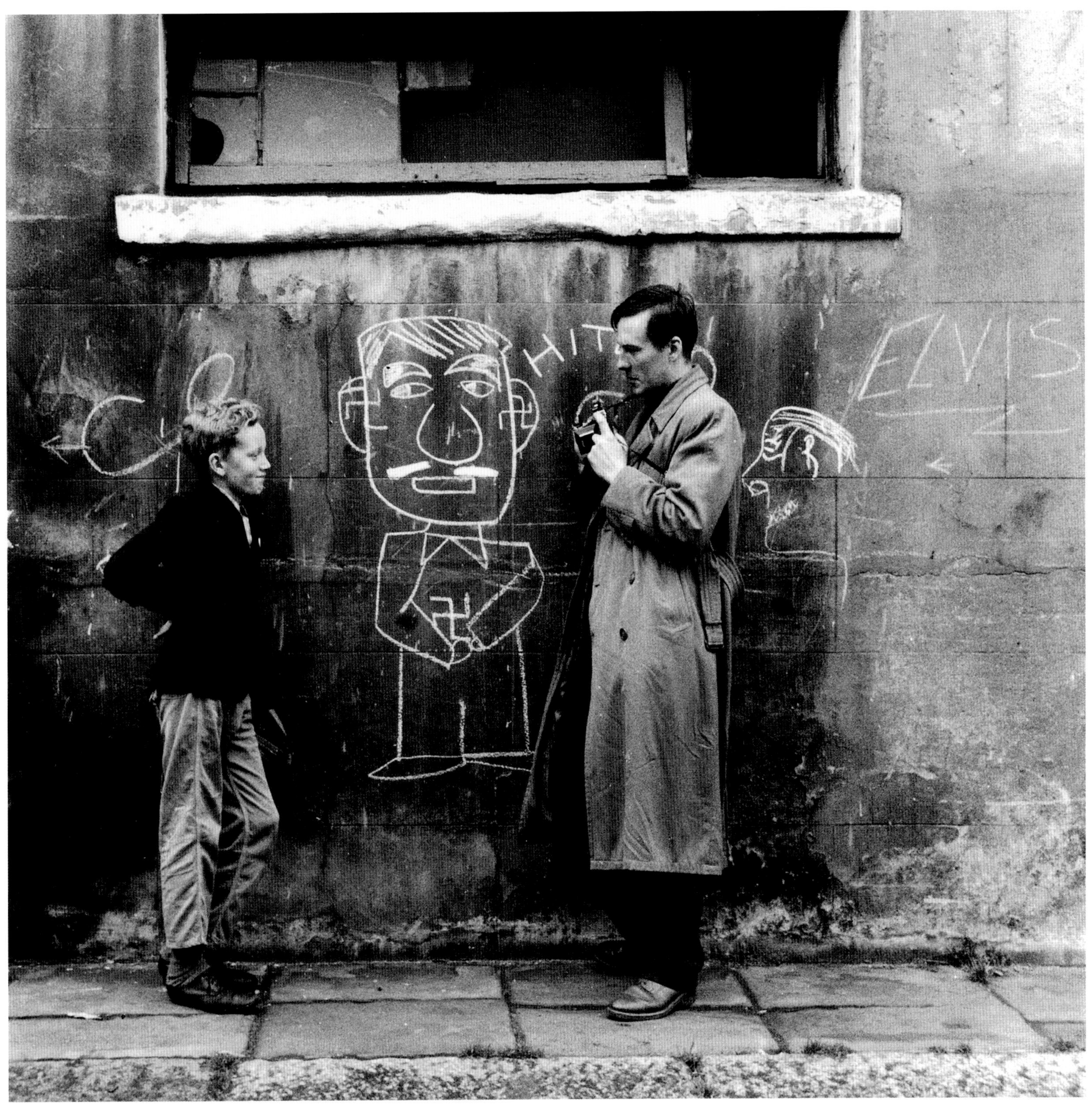

The photographer Roger Mayne and friend, Addison Place, North Kensington, 1957

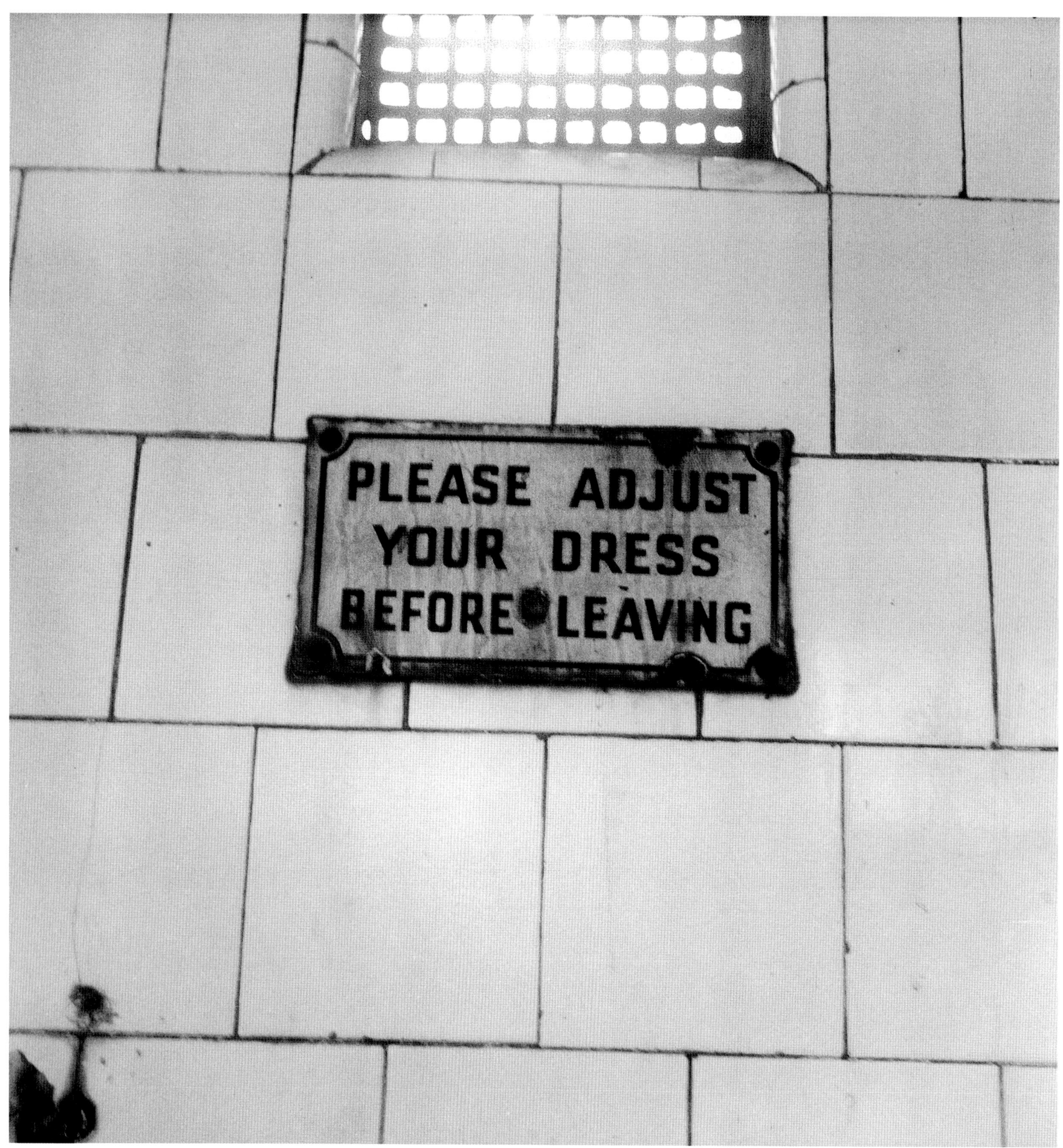

Public lavatory, 1950s

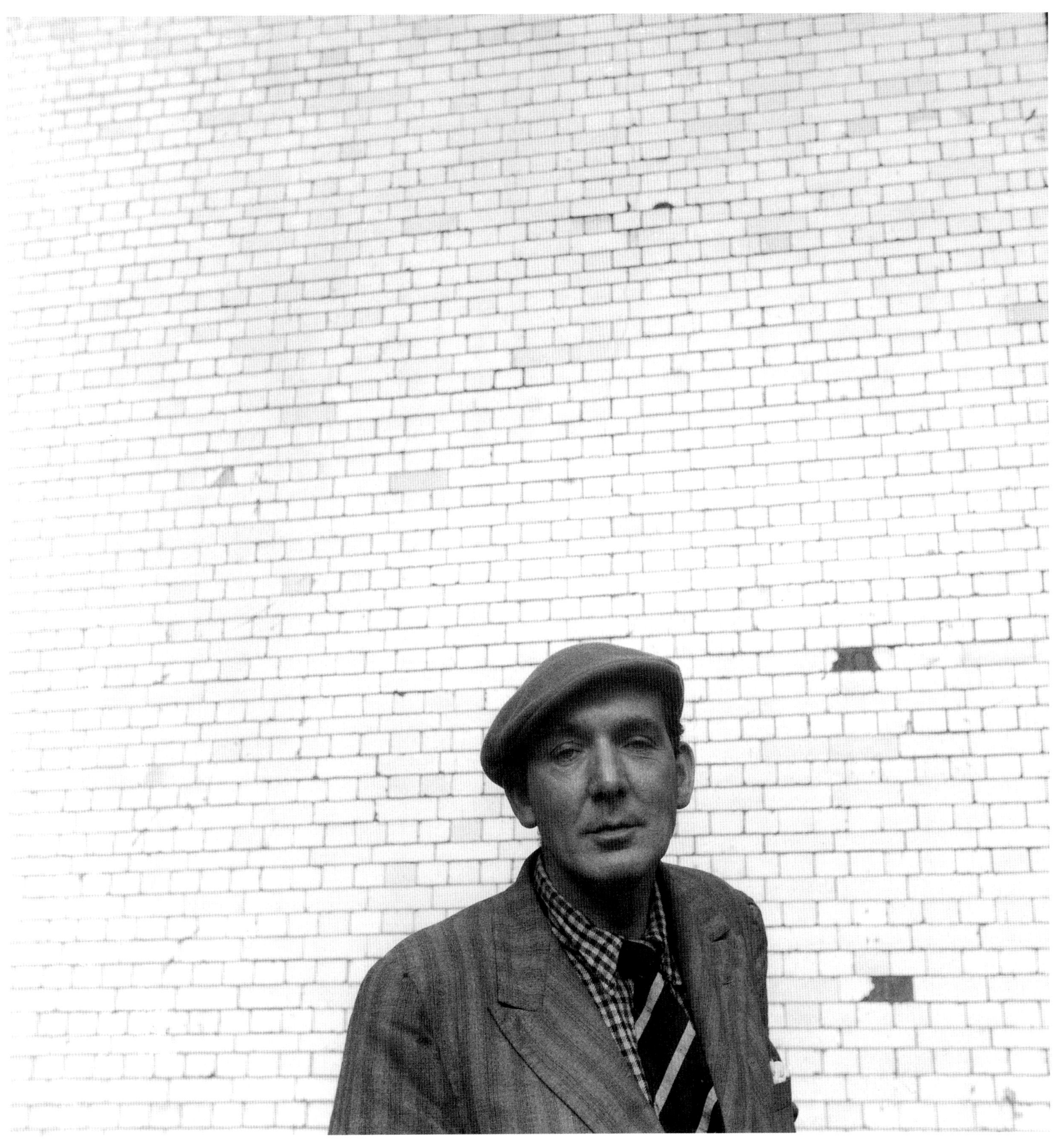

The poet George Barker, against a lavatory wall, 1952

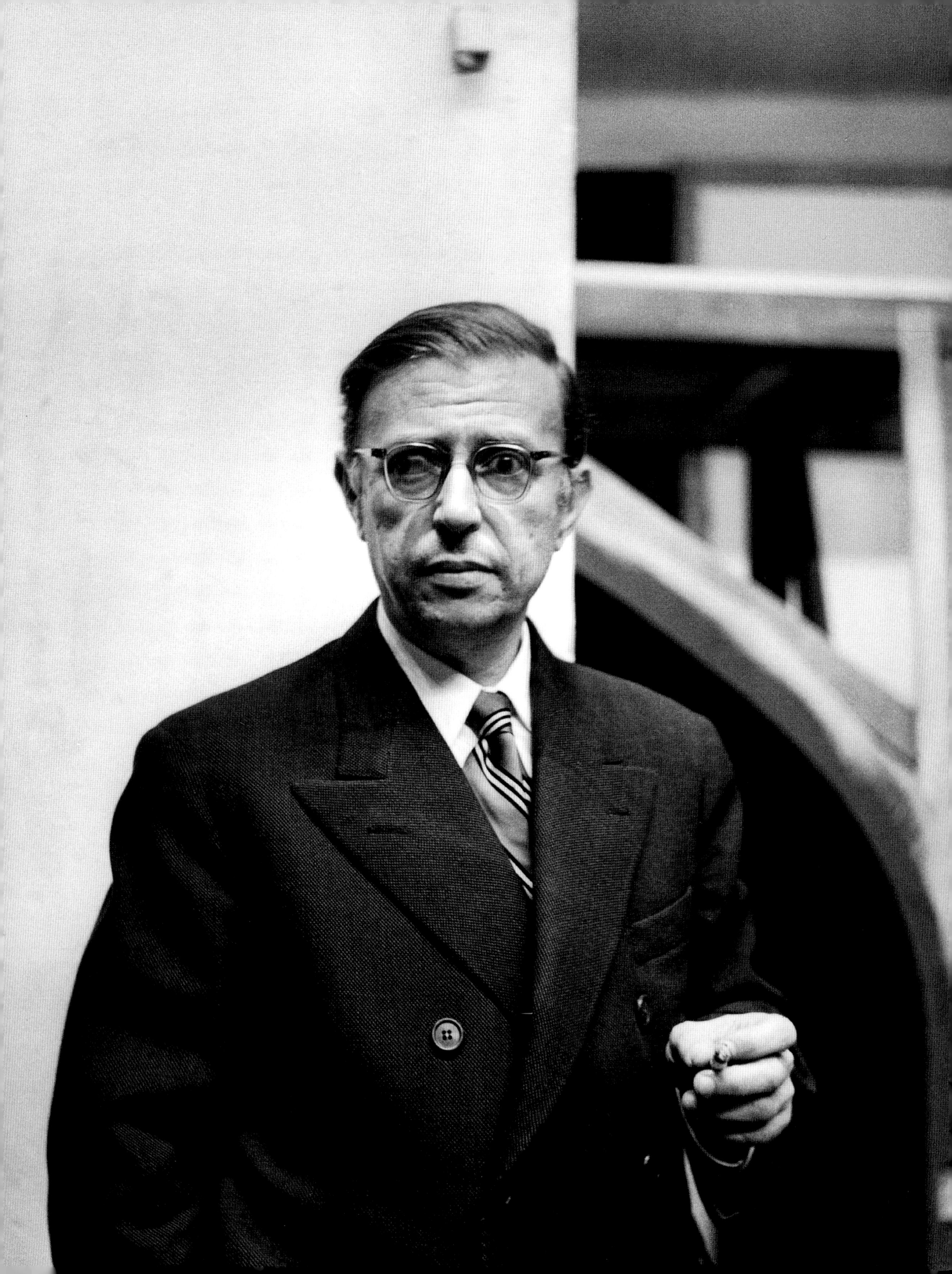

Paris

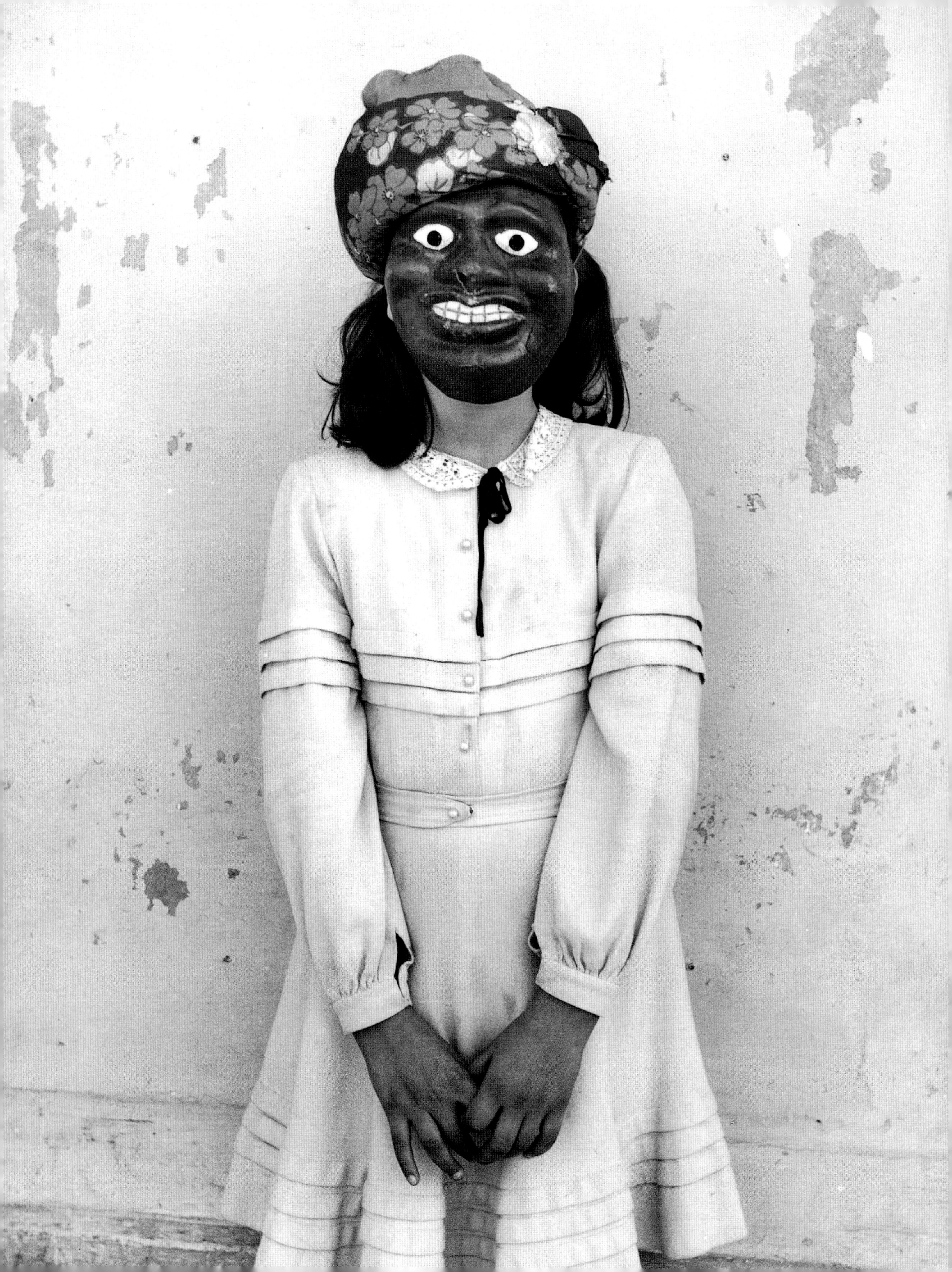

Deakin first visited Paris in the 1930s as an itinerant painter. It was here, in 1939, that he found a camera, left behind in his apartment after a party, and took his first pictures. Encouraged by Christian Bérard, the stage designer, fashion illustrator and full-time bohemian, he began to photograph the city. Pointing his camera into doorways, cemeteries, restaurant windows and alleyways, onto solitary pedestrians and the sleeping bodies of street people, and over fleamarkets, shops and travelling fairs, he produced a frequently dark evocation of Paris that has some of the power of Rimbaud's, or George Orwell's.

Although his career as a staff photographer for British *Vogue* kept him for the most part in London, Deakin returned to Paris whenever he could and continued his record of the city. Following the regime of Eugène Atget, the famous chronicler of nineteenth-century Paris, he rose at five o'clock each morning to photograph in whatever light was available, regardless of weather conditions.

In July 1956 he held an exhibition of these photographs in the Parton Gallery, in the basement of David Archer's Bookshop in Soho. Elizabeth Smart compiled the catalogue. She observed that Deakin's vision of the French capital betrayed no Gallic wit: 'No, only the joke that breaks your heart. John Deakin's Paris is vulgar, touching, beautiful. It is, in fact, true.' And she warned: 'You certainly won't feel rested after a time in John Deakin's Paris. These pictures take you by the scruff of the neck and insist that you see. And feel. If you have never been to Paris you will find it haunted when you arrive…'[1]

Opposite: Girl in a mask, 1950s

Page 84: Jean-Paul Sartre, philosopher, 1950s

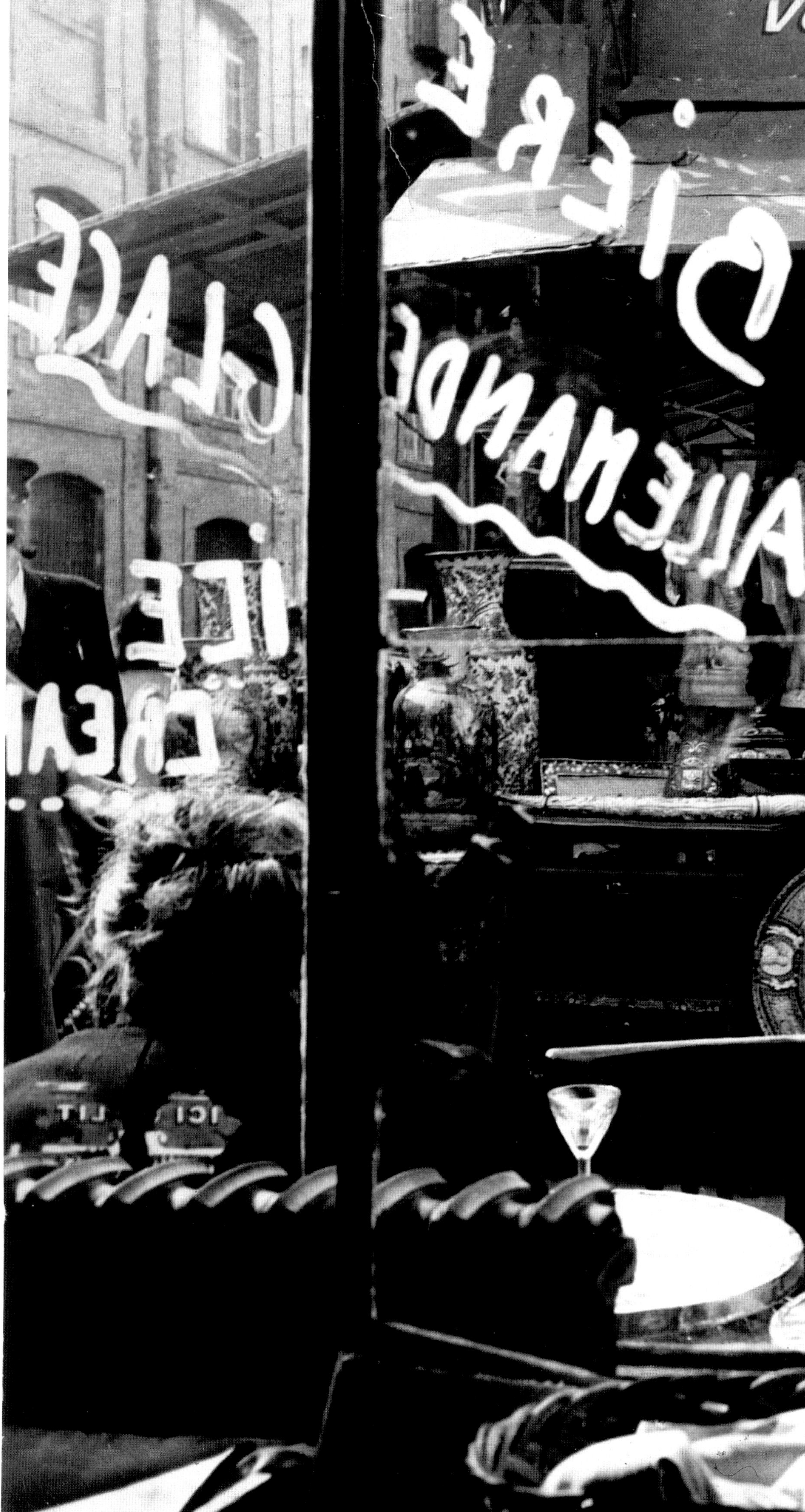

Fleamarket bistro, 1955

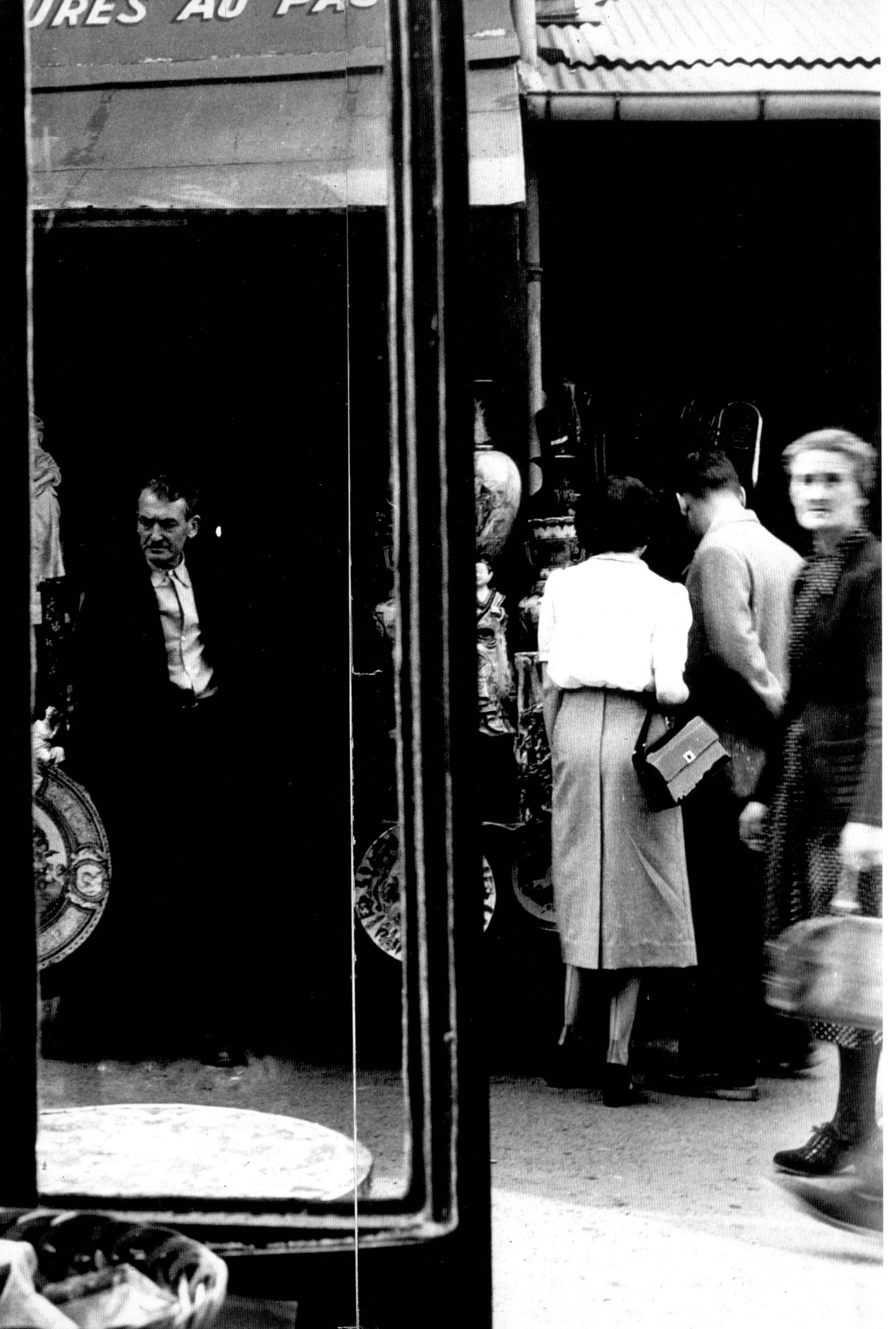
URES AU PA

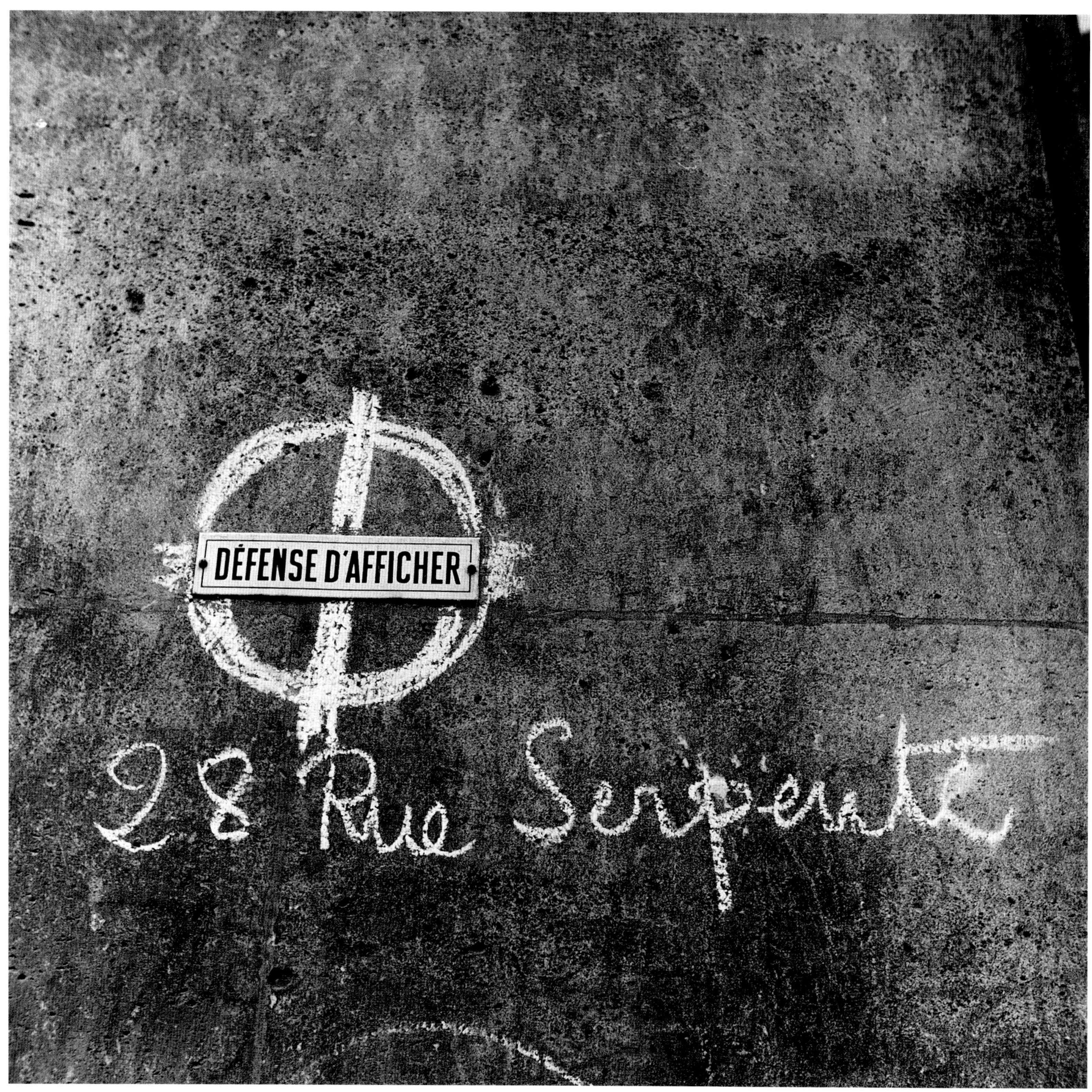

'No posters', 28 Rue Serpente, 1950s

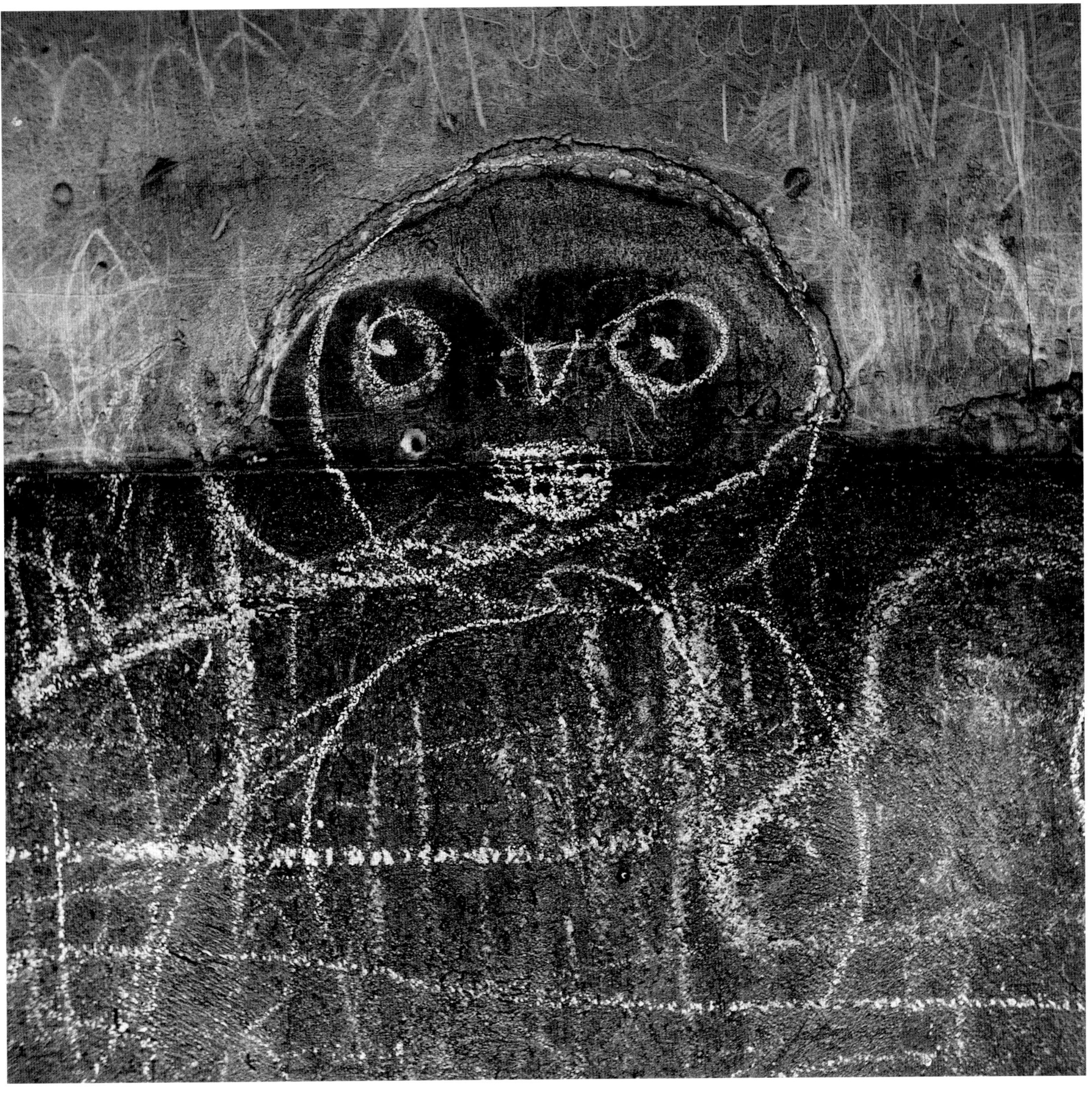

Graffiti, 1950s

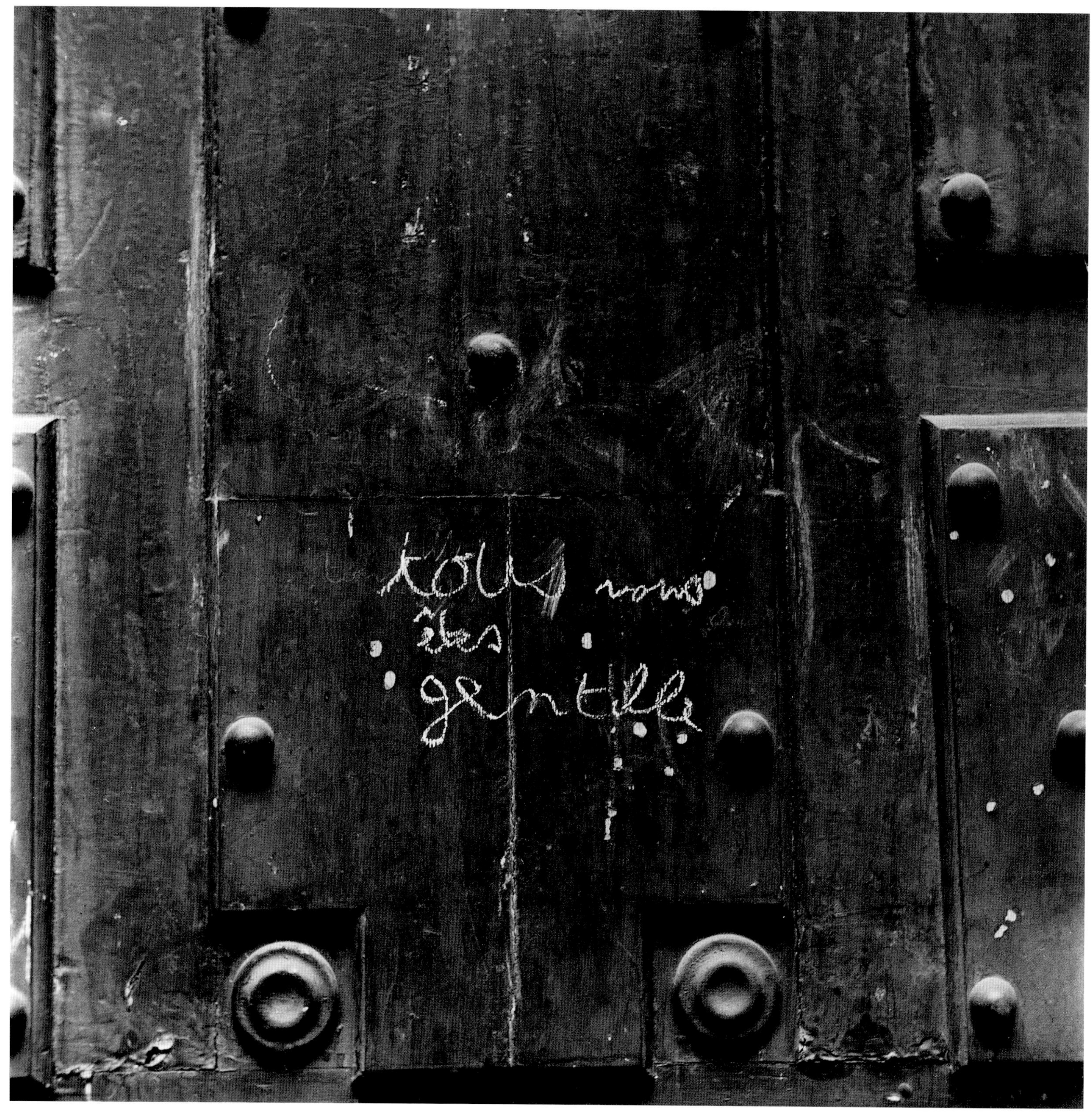

'You are all nice,' graffiti, 1950s

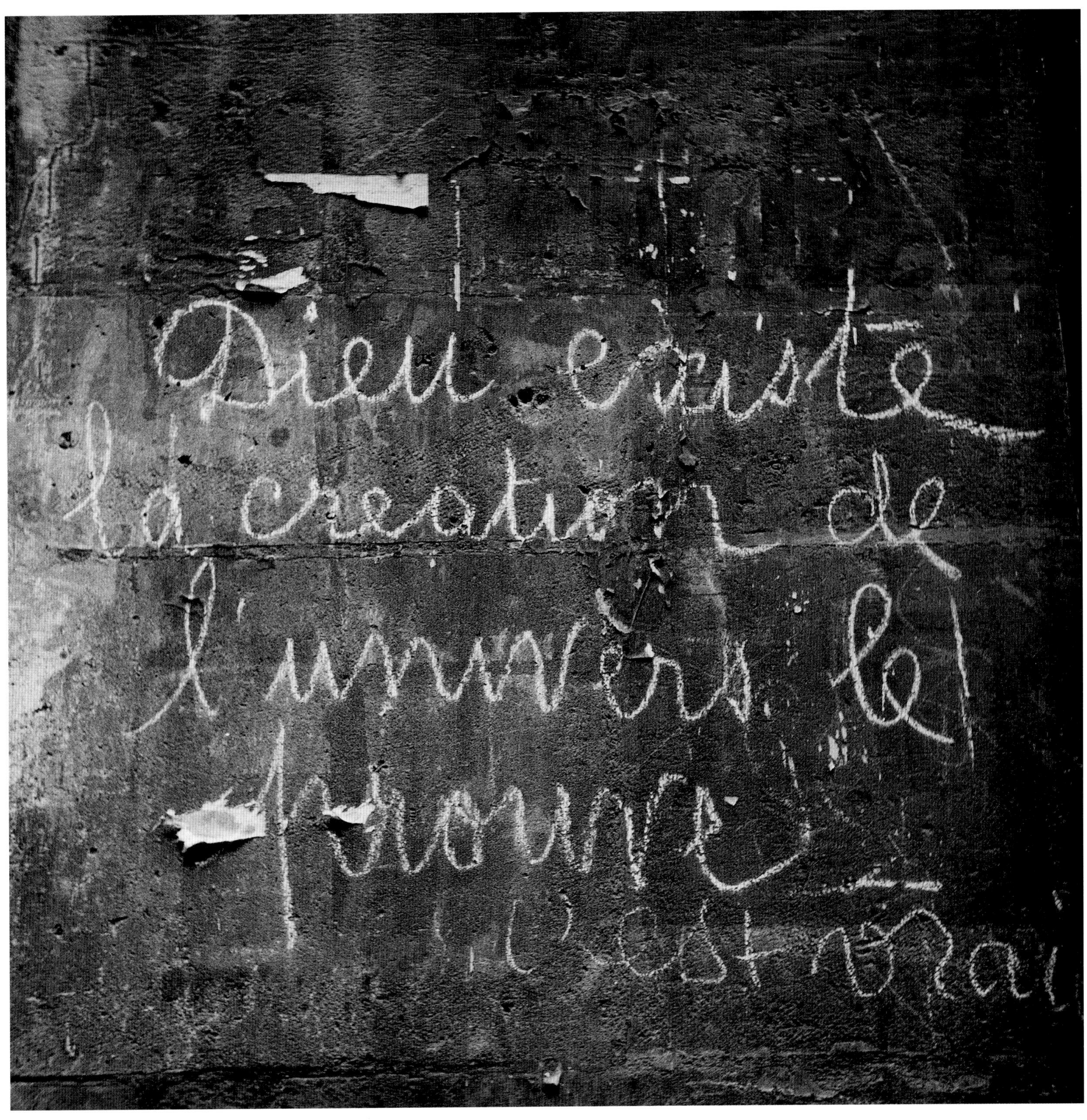

'God exists – the creation of the universe proves it' – 'That's true,' graffiti, 1950s

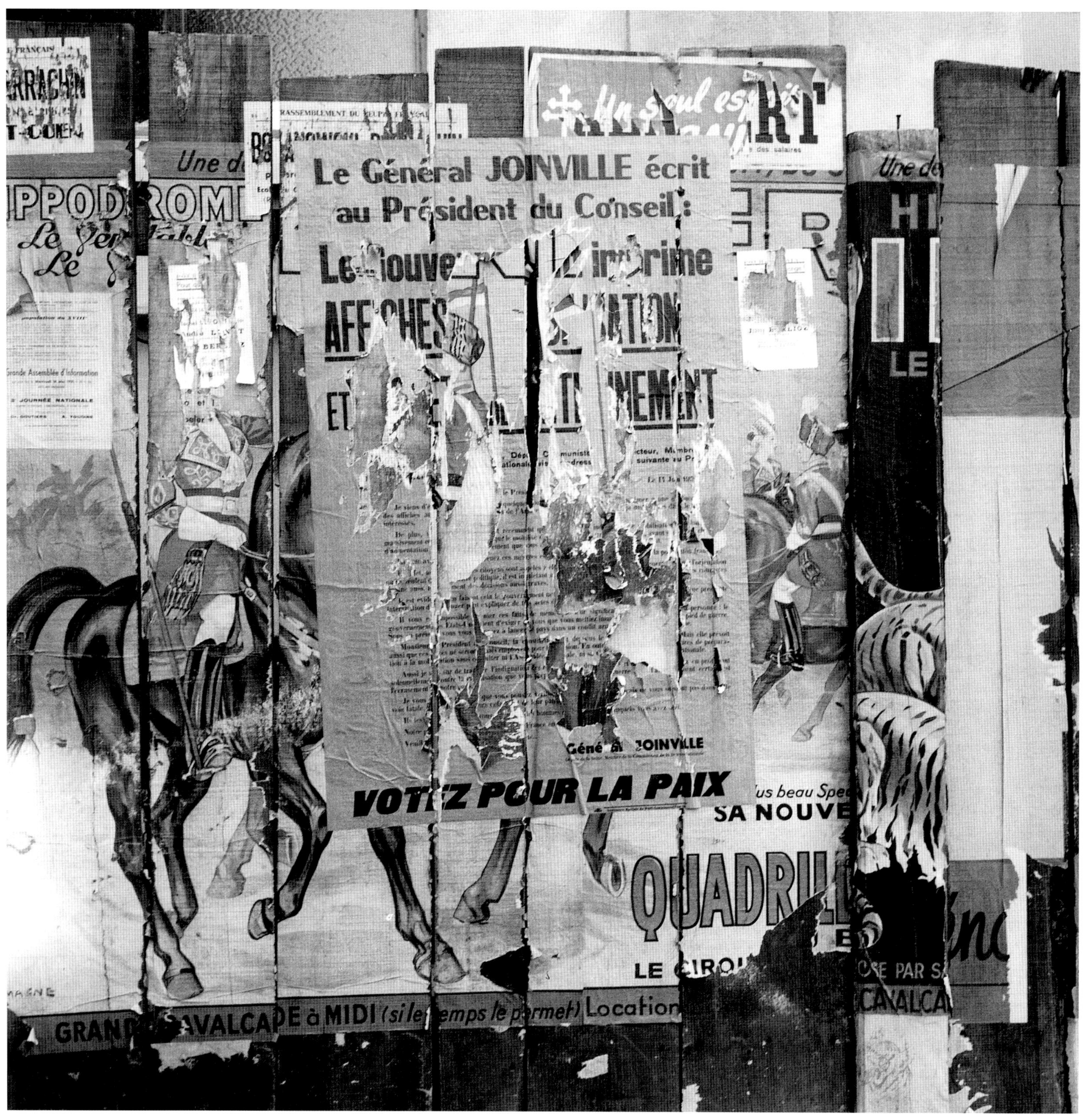

'Vote for Peace', 1950s

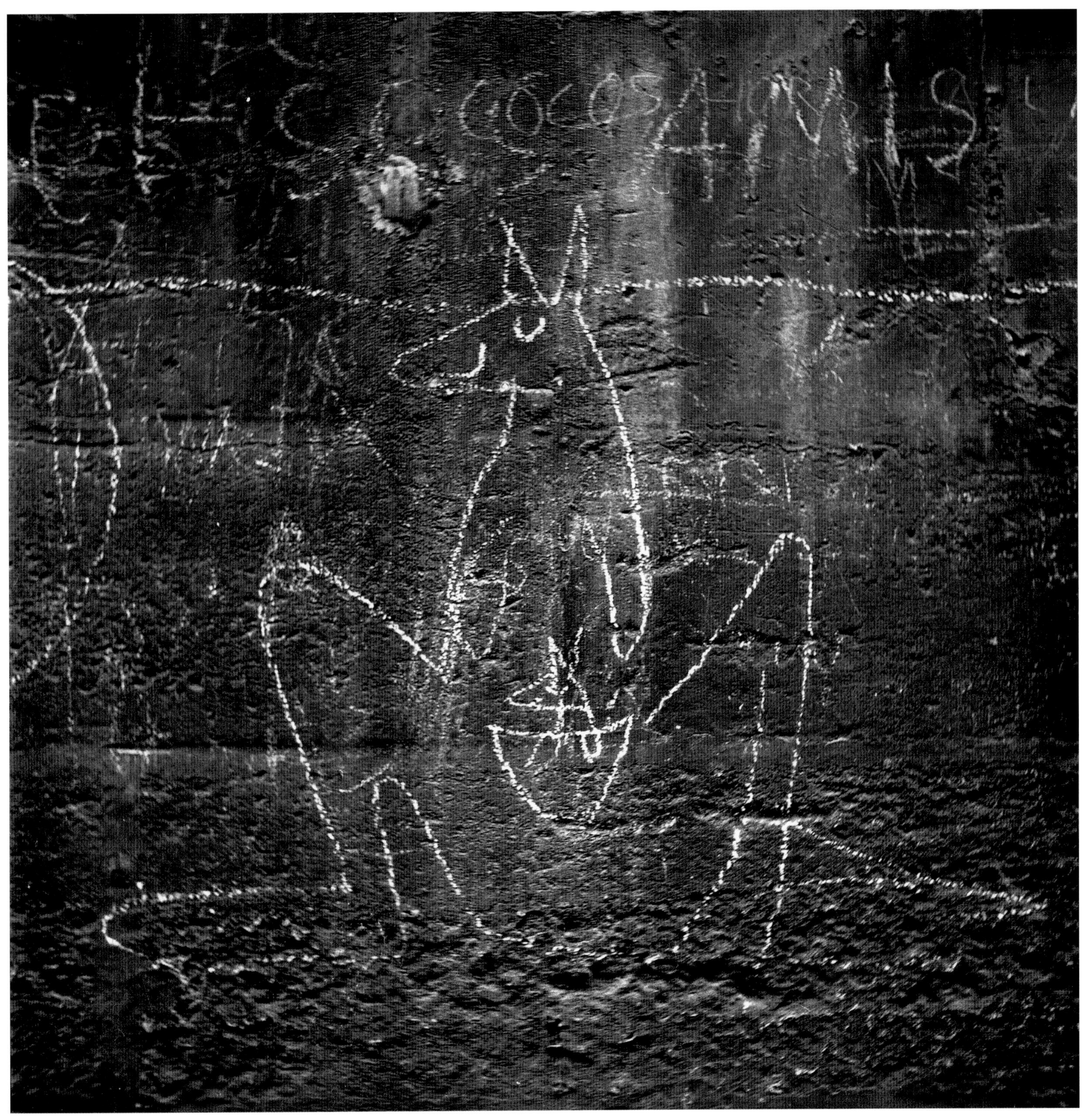

Kangaroo graffiti, 1950s

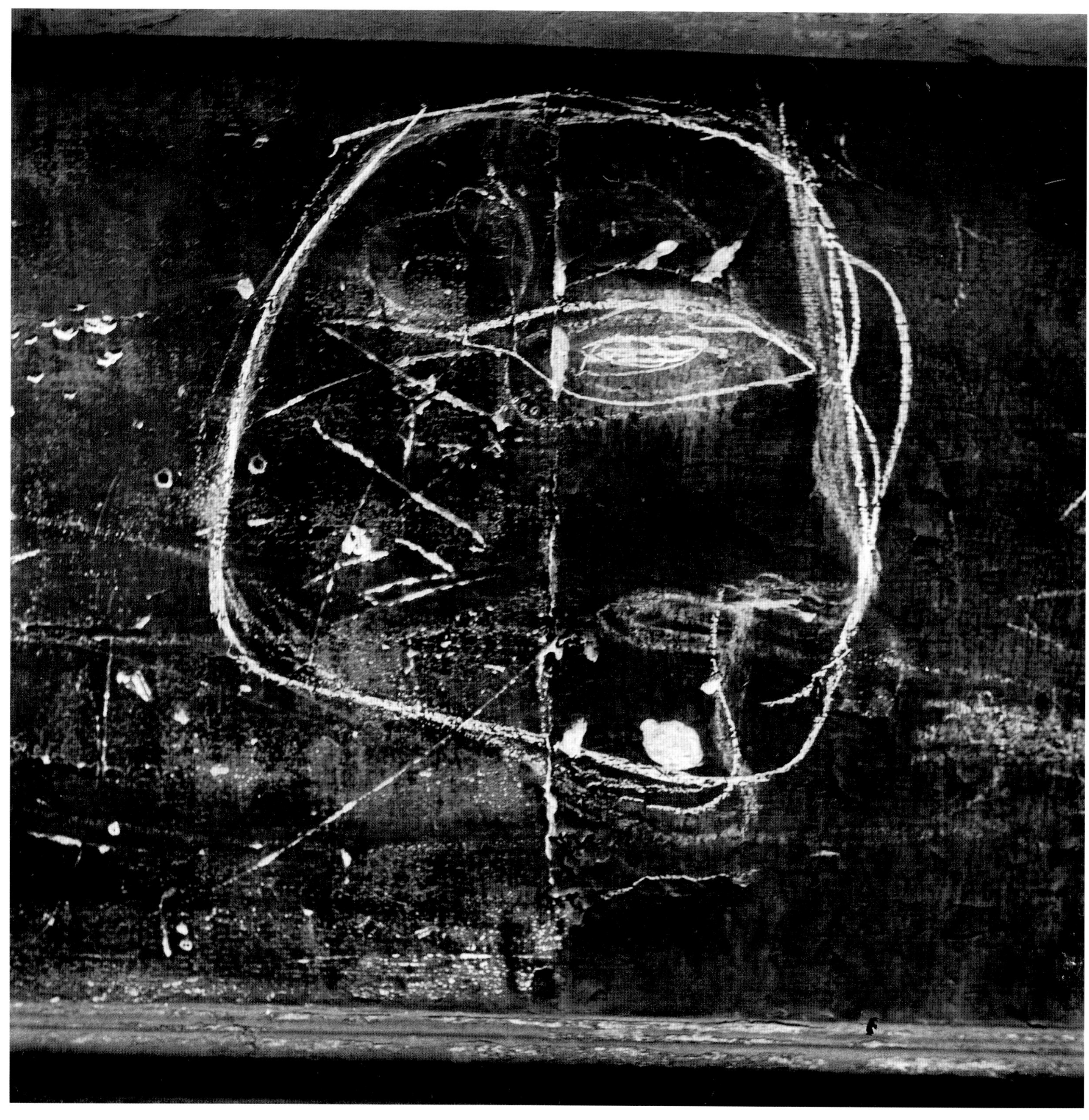

Graffiti face, 1950s

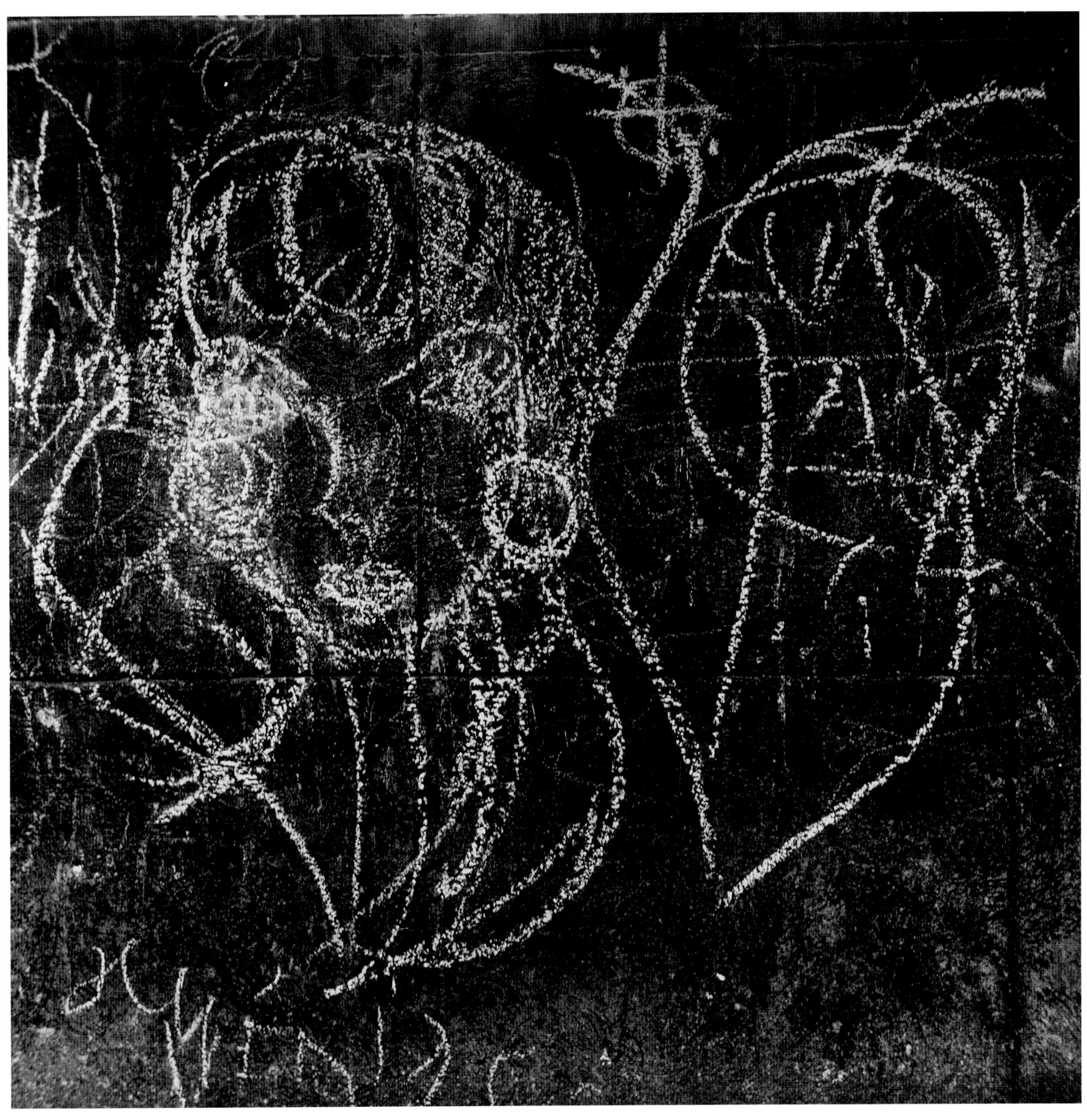

Graffiti faces, 1950s

Opposite: Graffiti, 1950s

Page 100: Shop window, 1950s

Page 101: Optician's window, 1950s

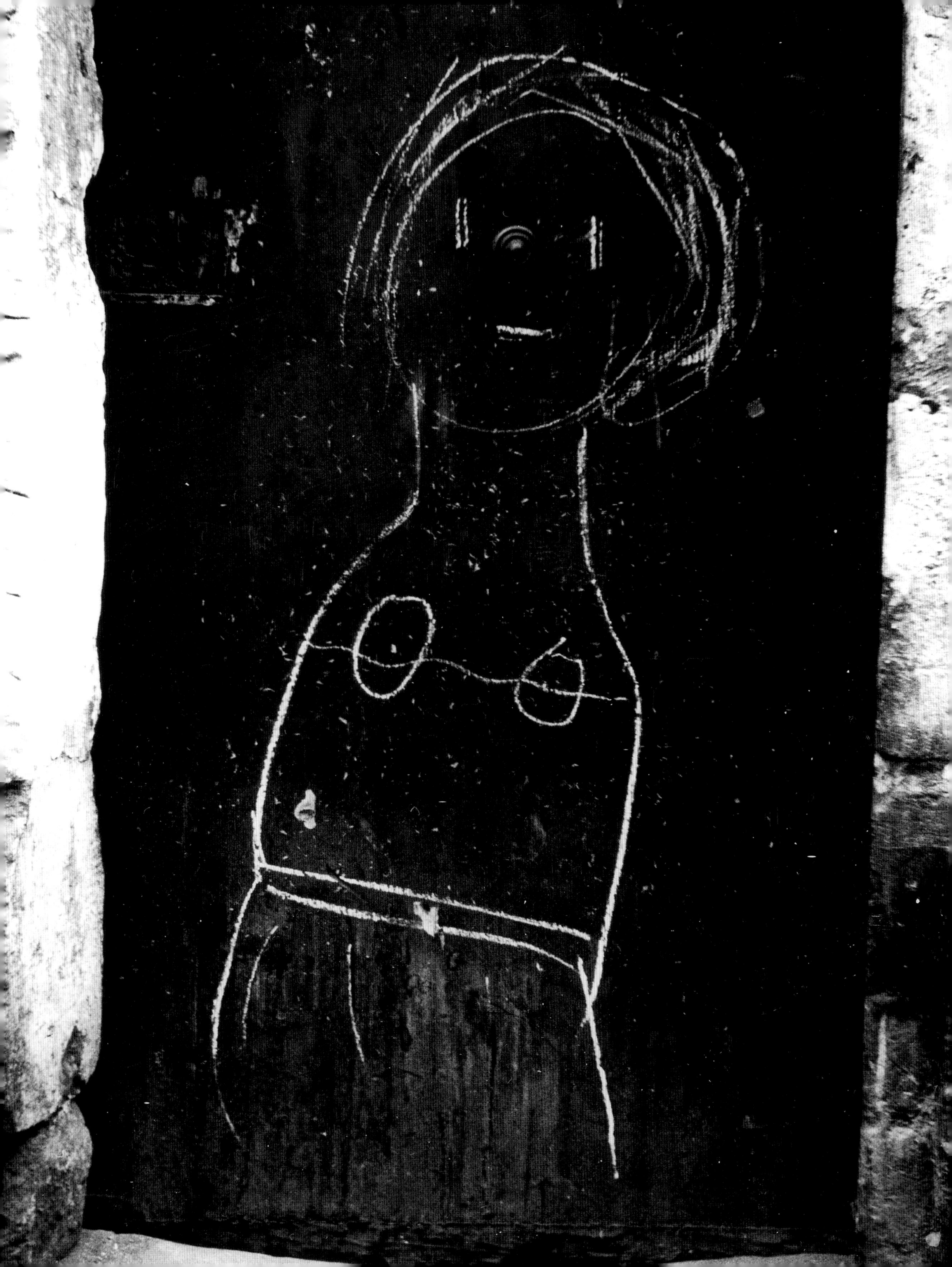

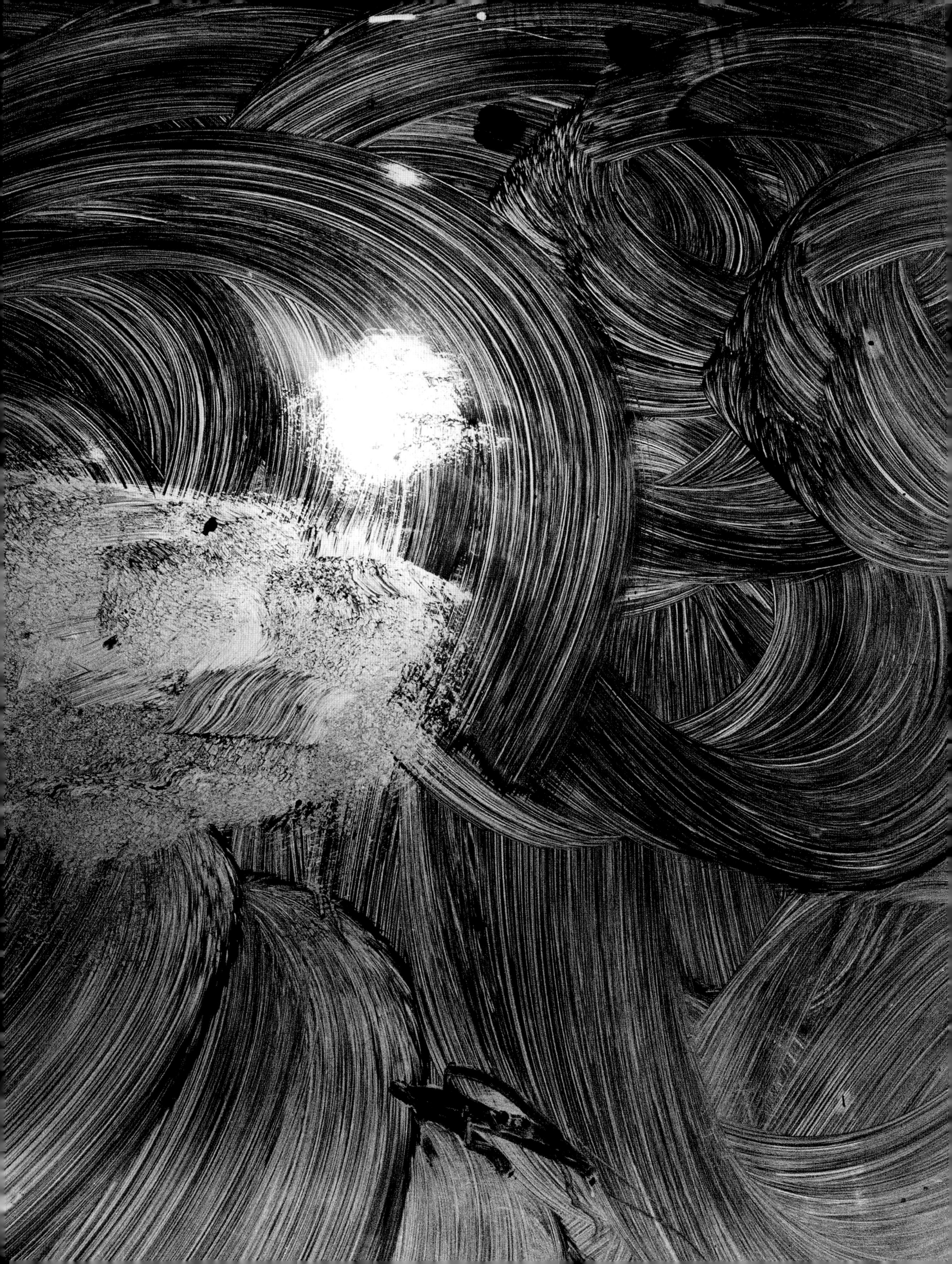

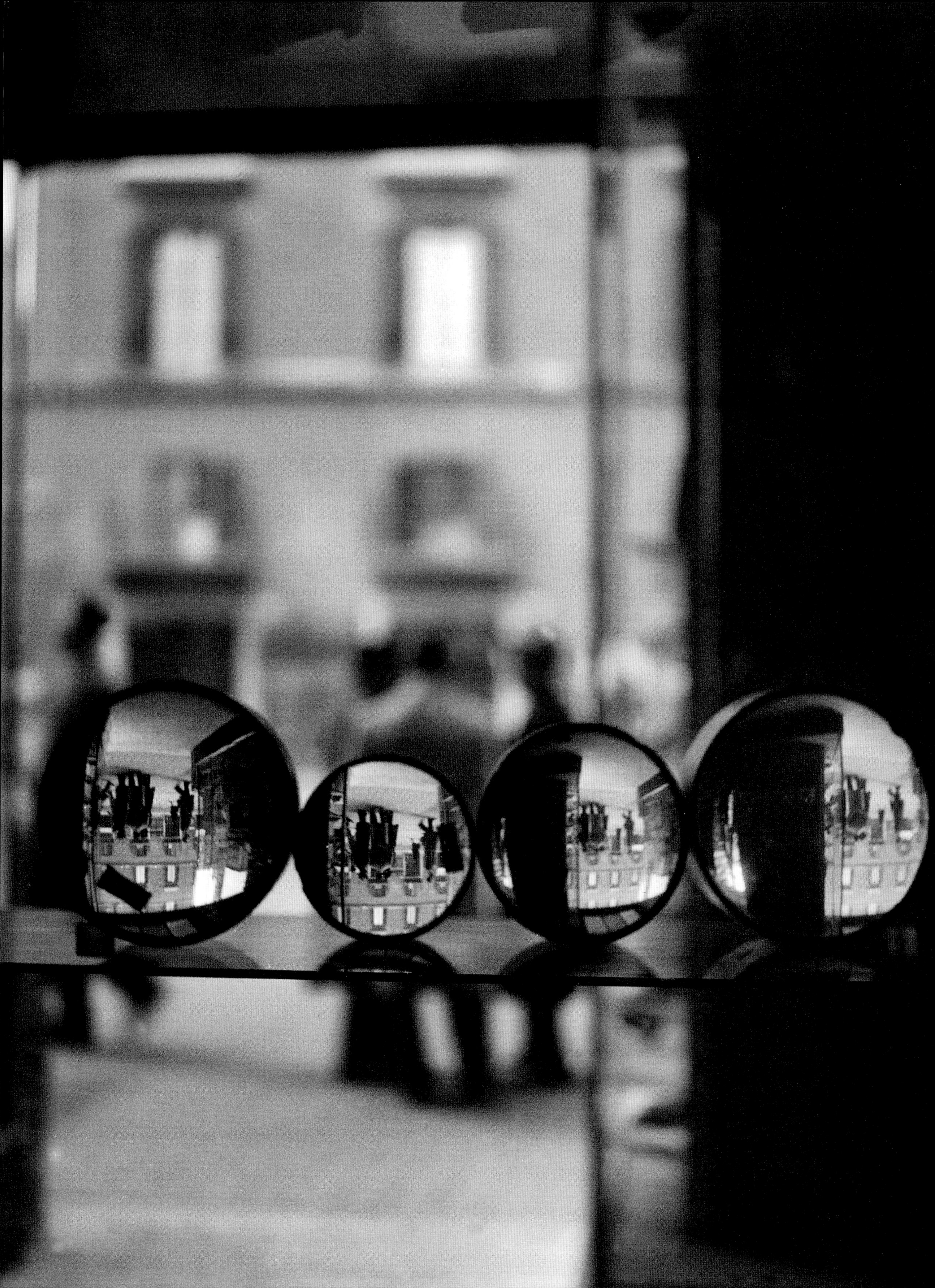

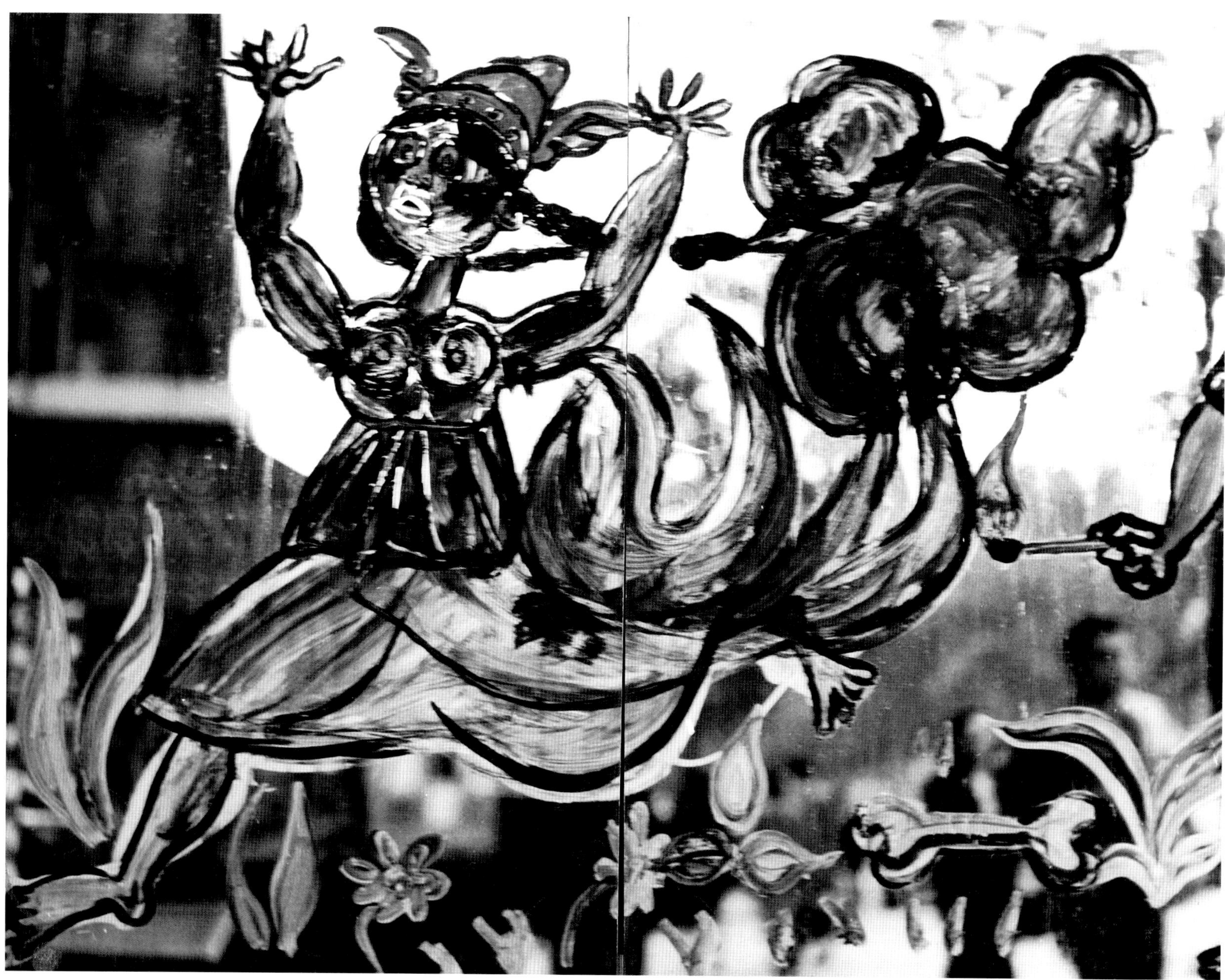

Bistro window, Montparnasse, 1950s

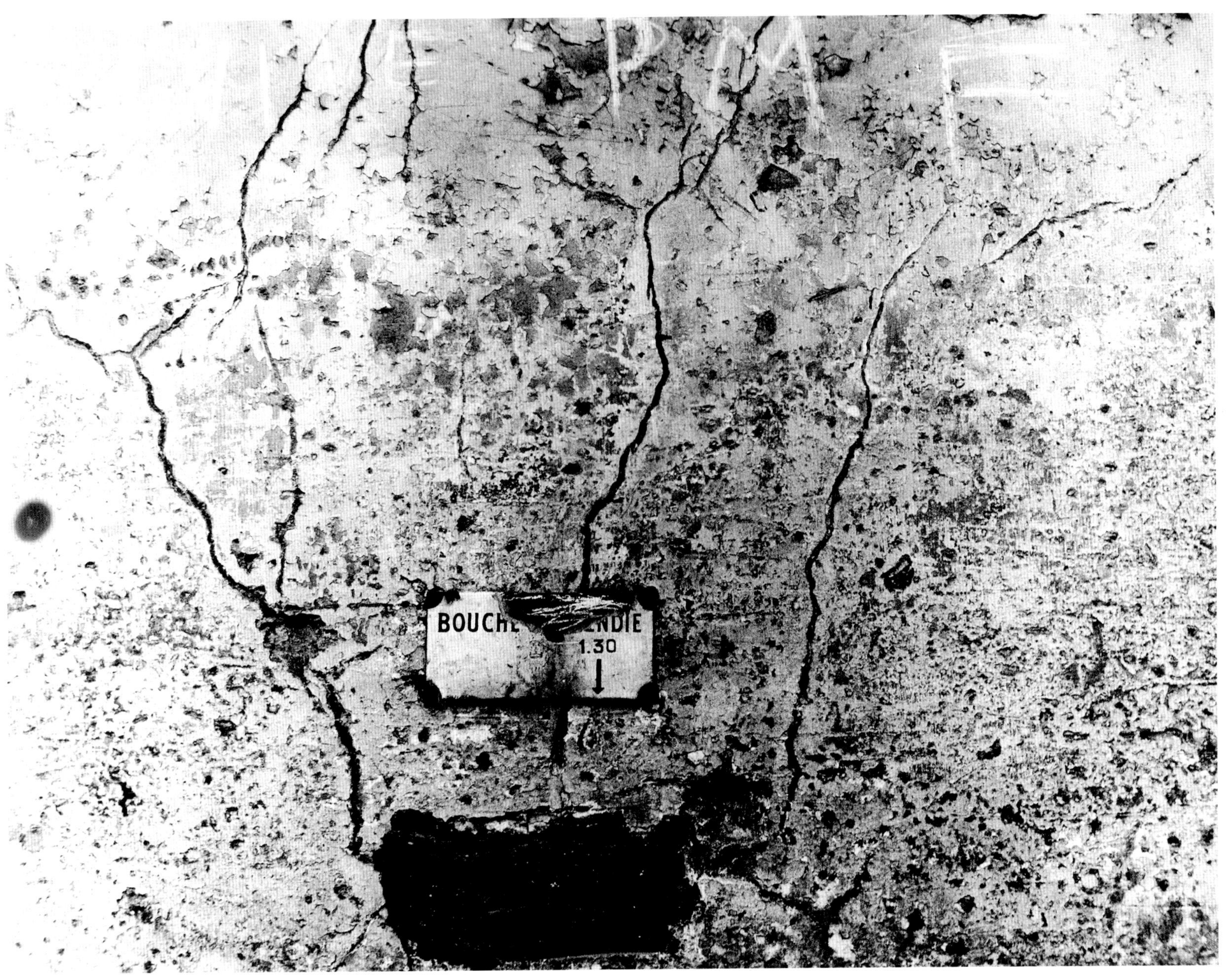

'Fire hydrant', from 'Paris Walls', 1950s

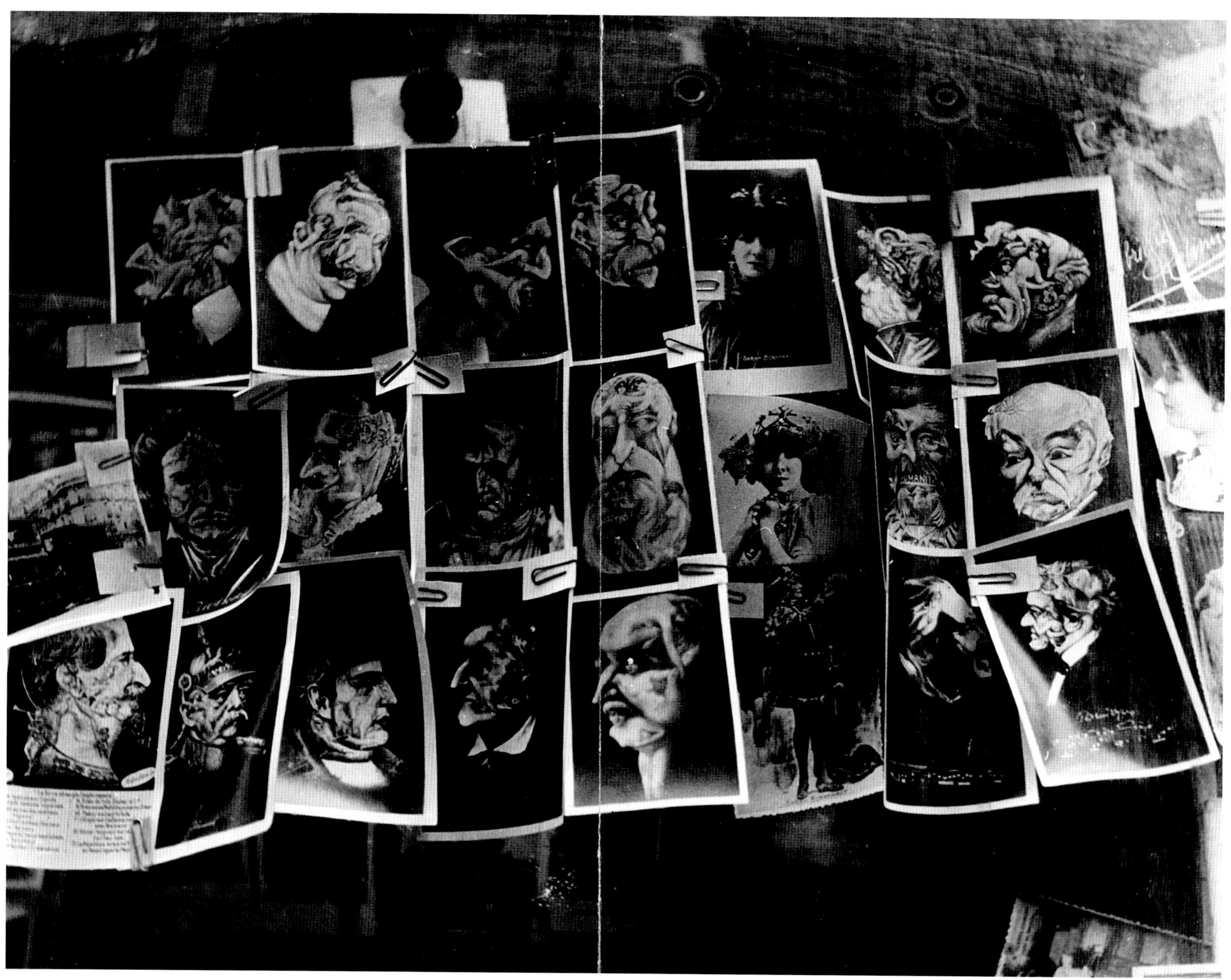

Postcard shop, 1950s

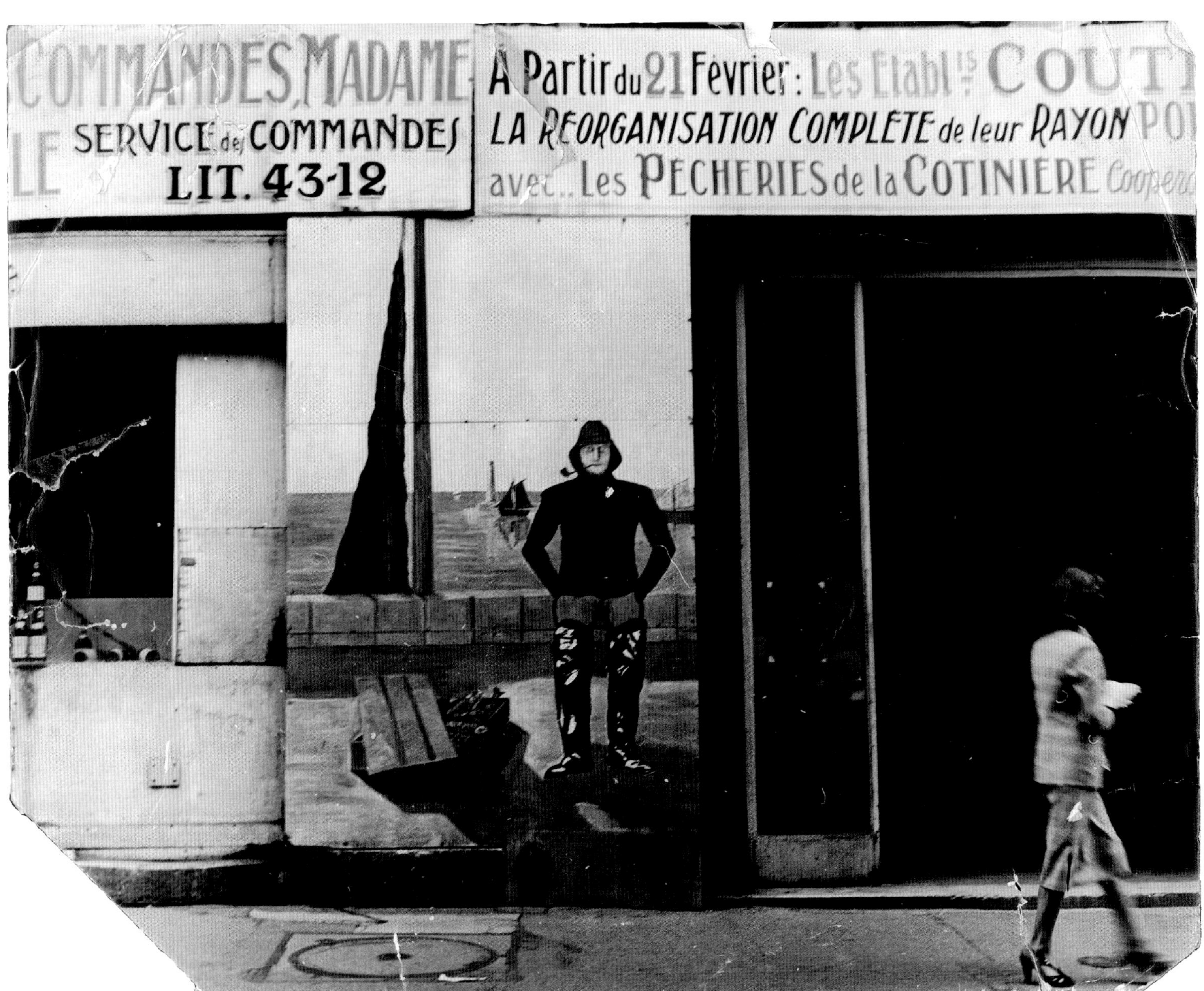

Fishmonger's awaiting rebuilding, 1950s

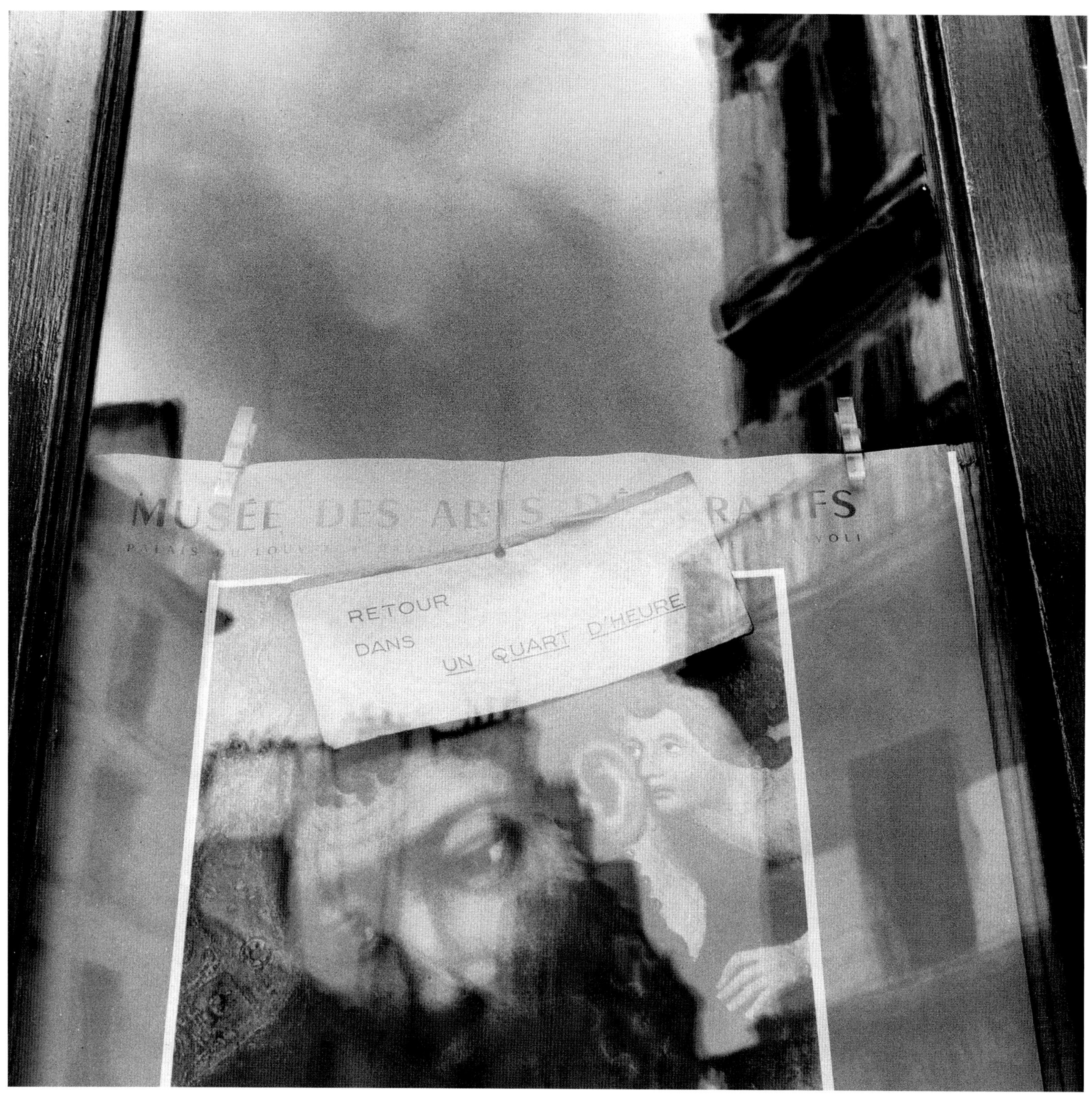

Shop window, 1950s

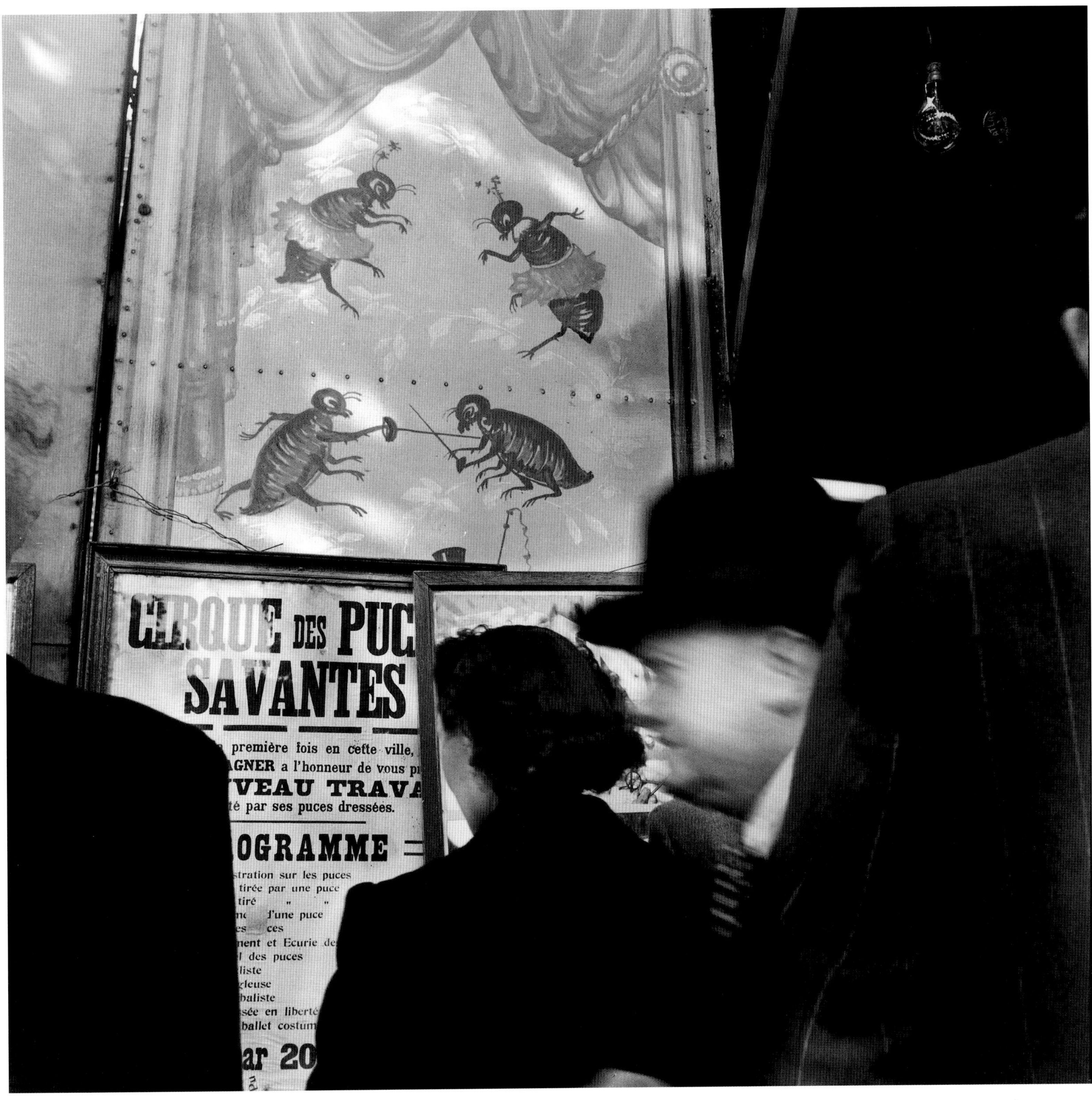

Flea circus, 1950s

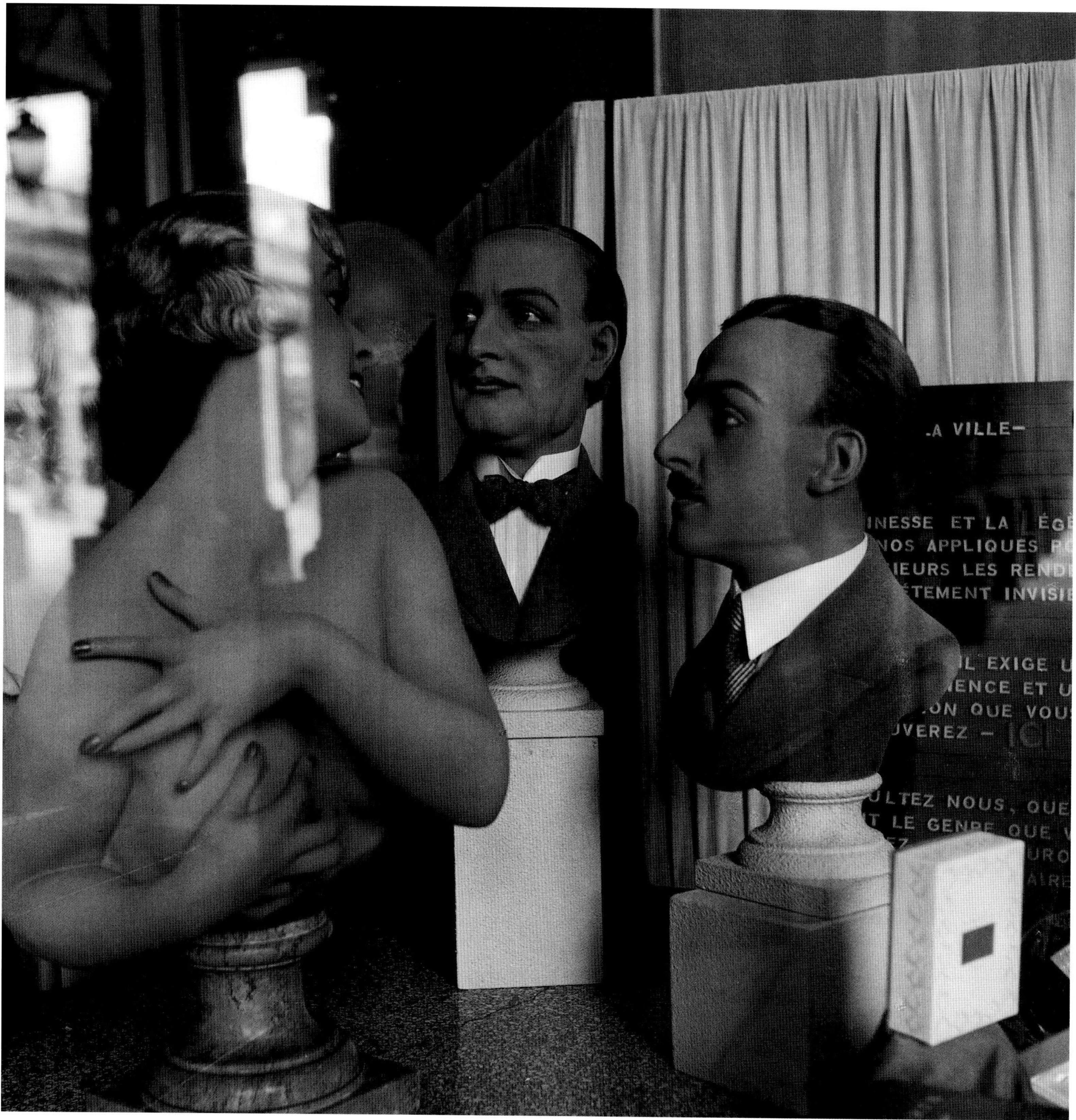

Wig shop, 1950s

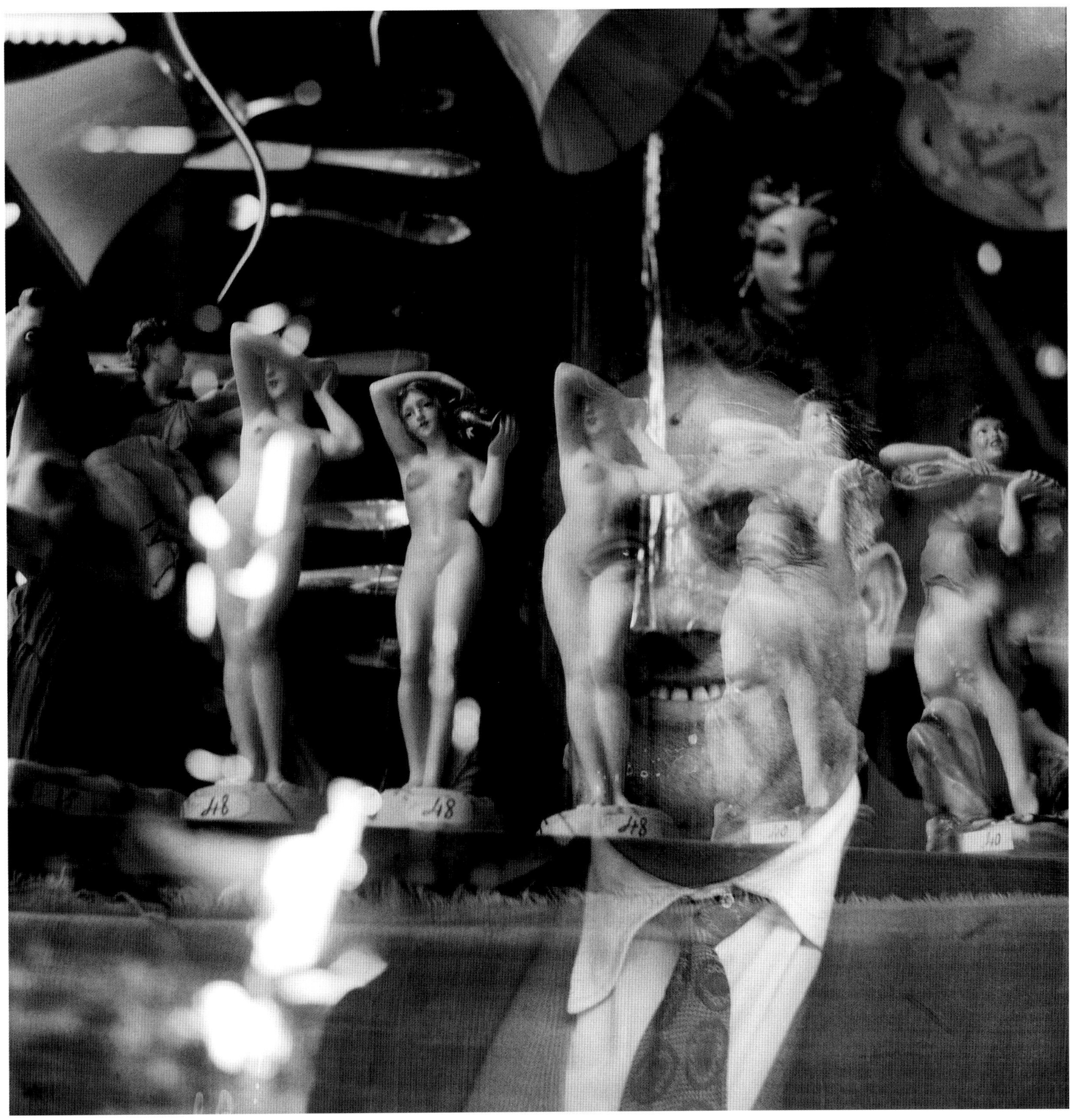

Shop window, 1950s

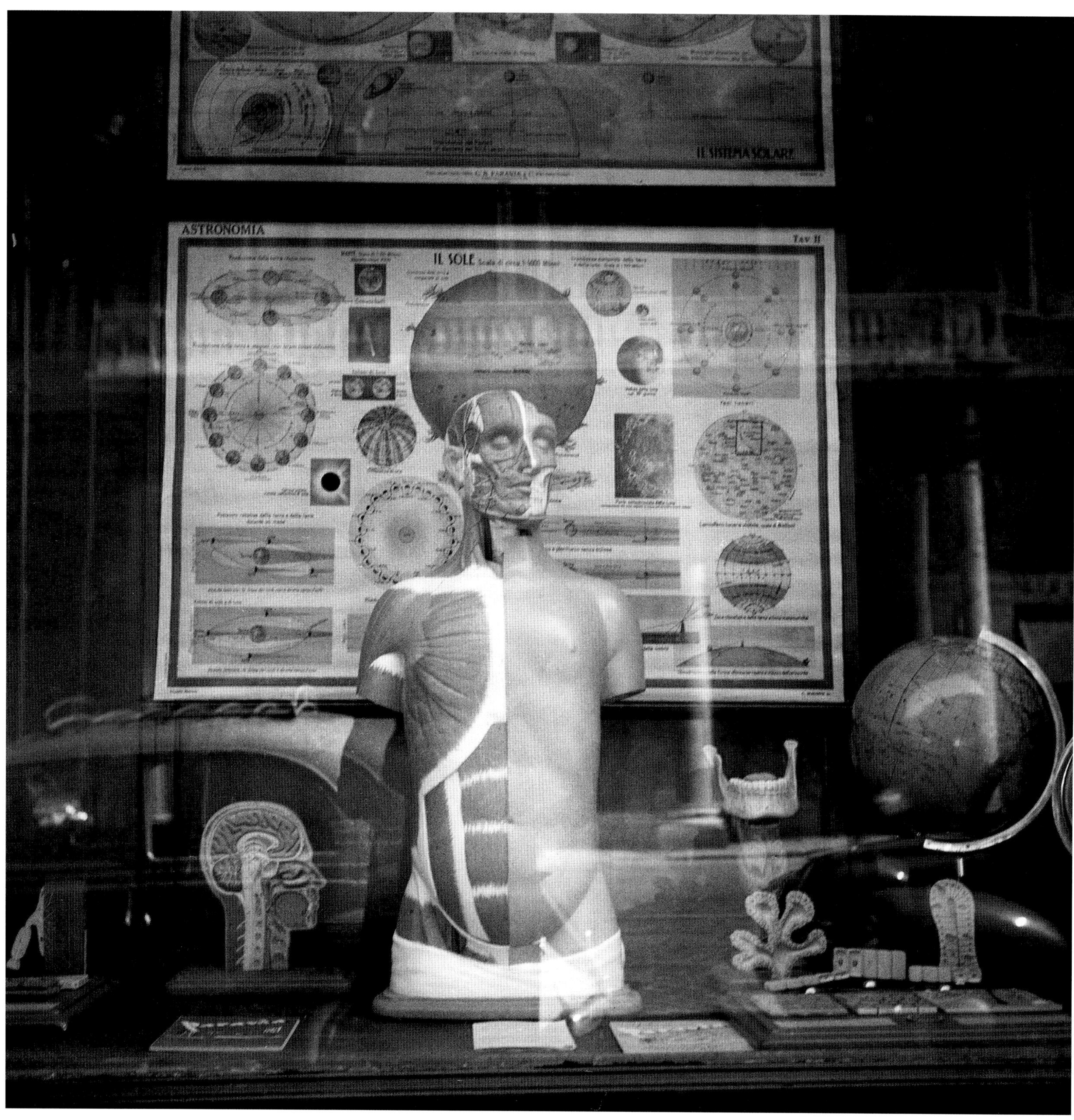

Surgical supplies shop, 1950s

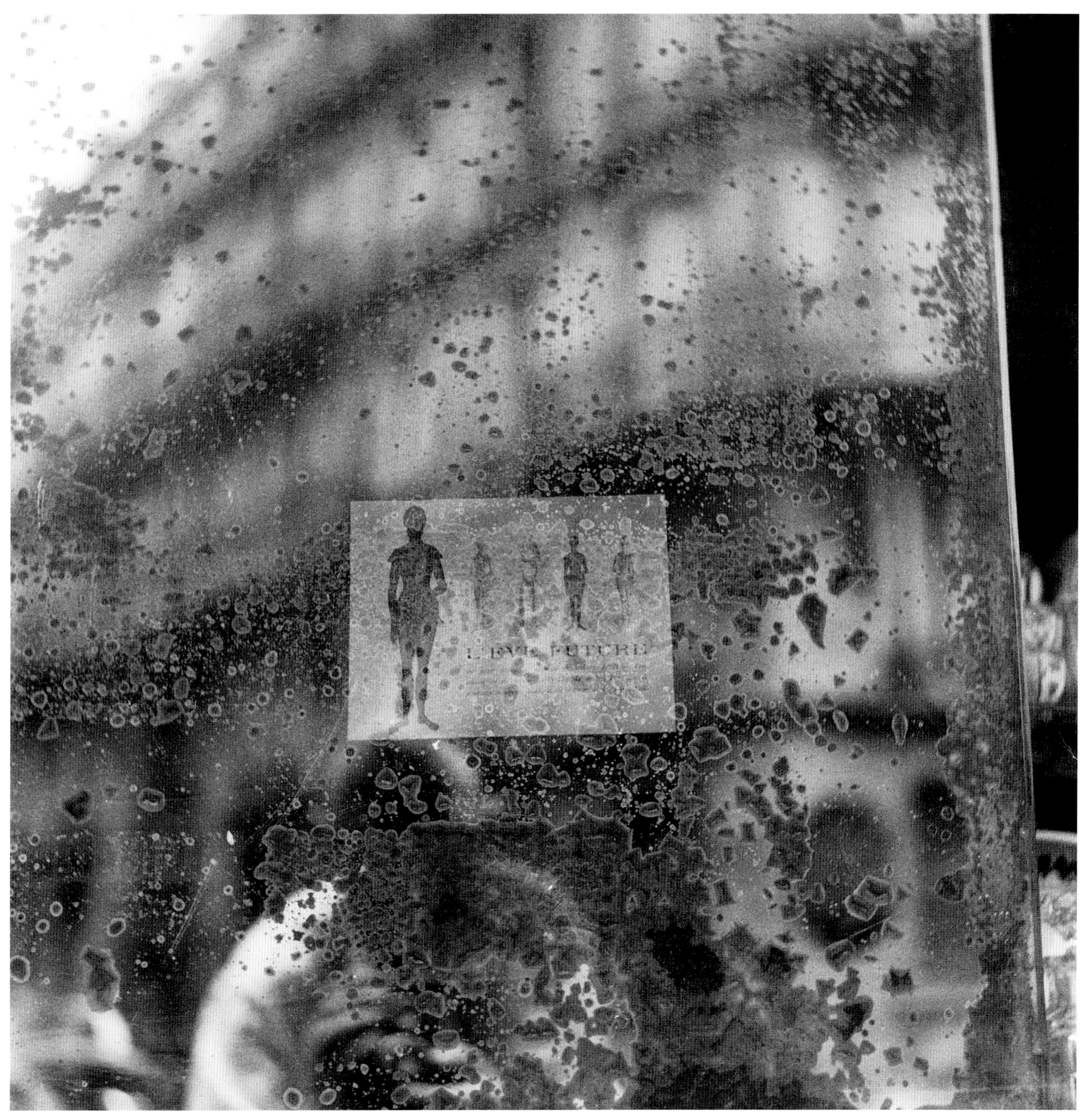

Shop window with Deakin's reflection, 1950s

Opposite: Marie Powers, opera singer, 1951

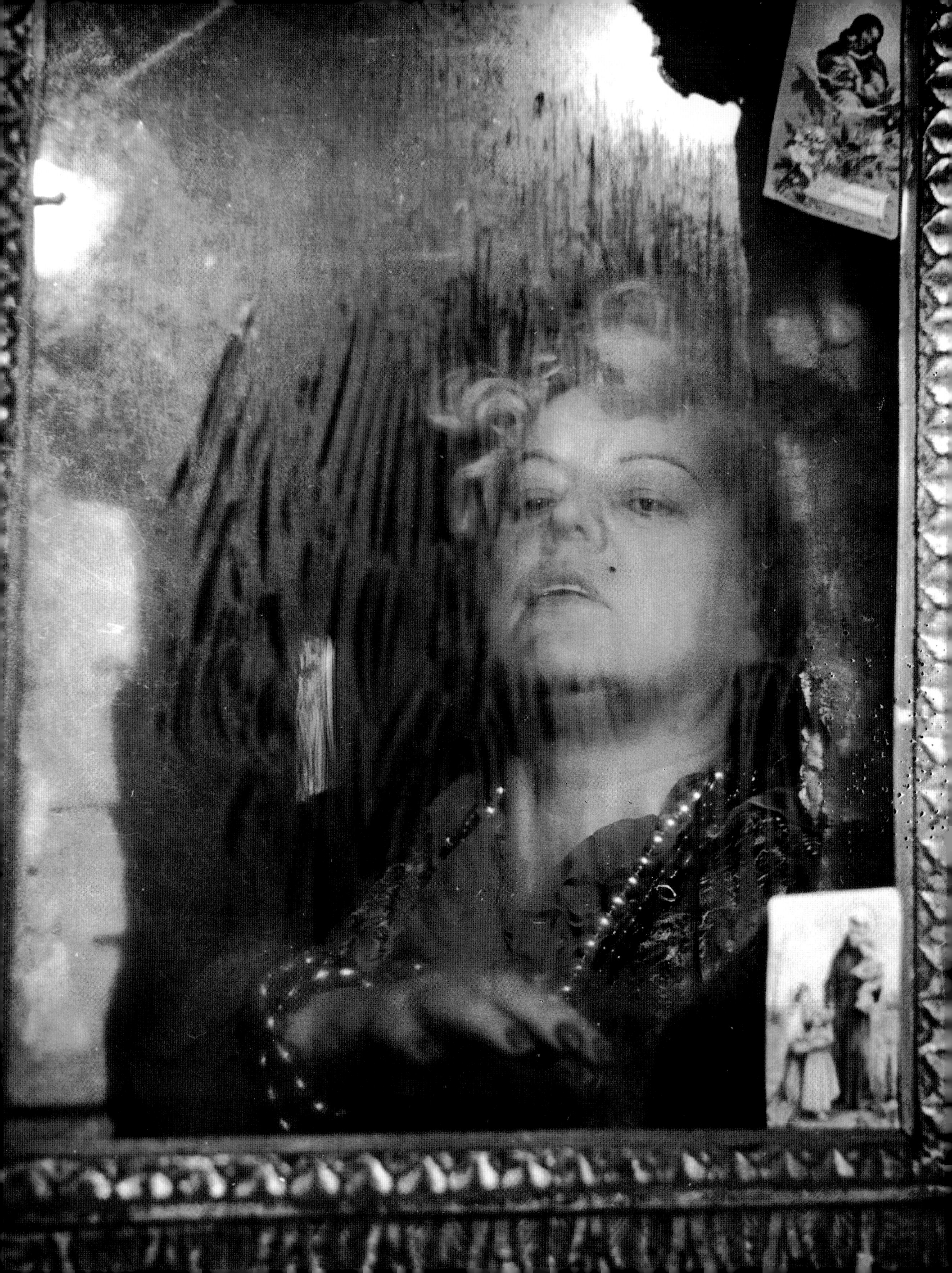

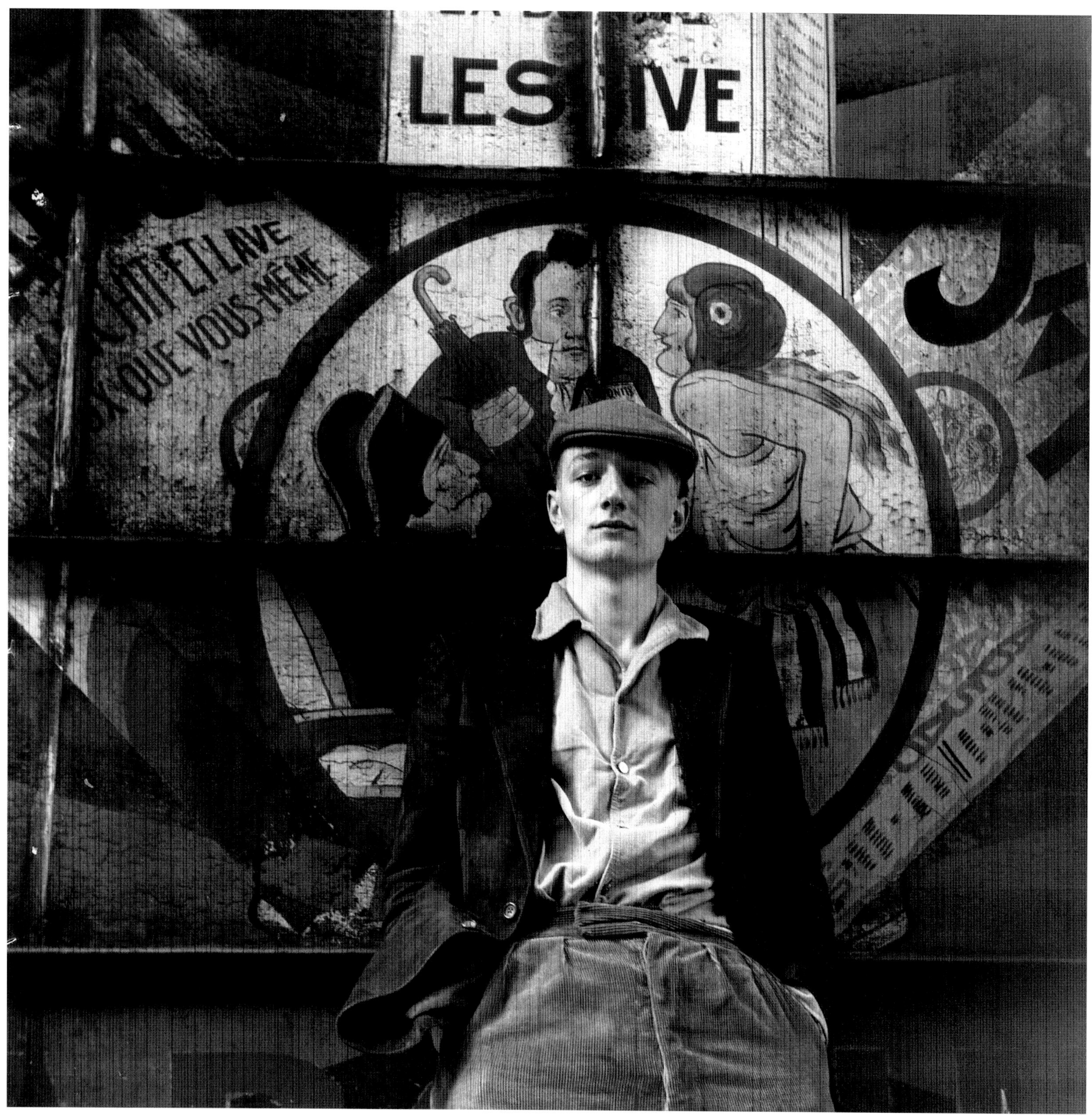

Ralph Rumney, painter, 1950s

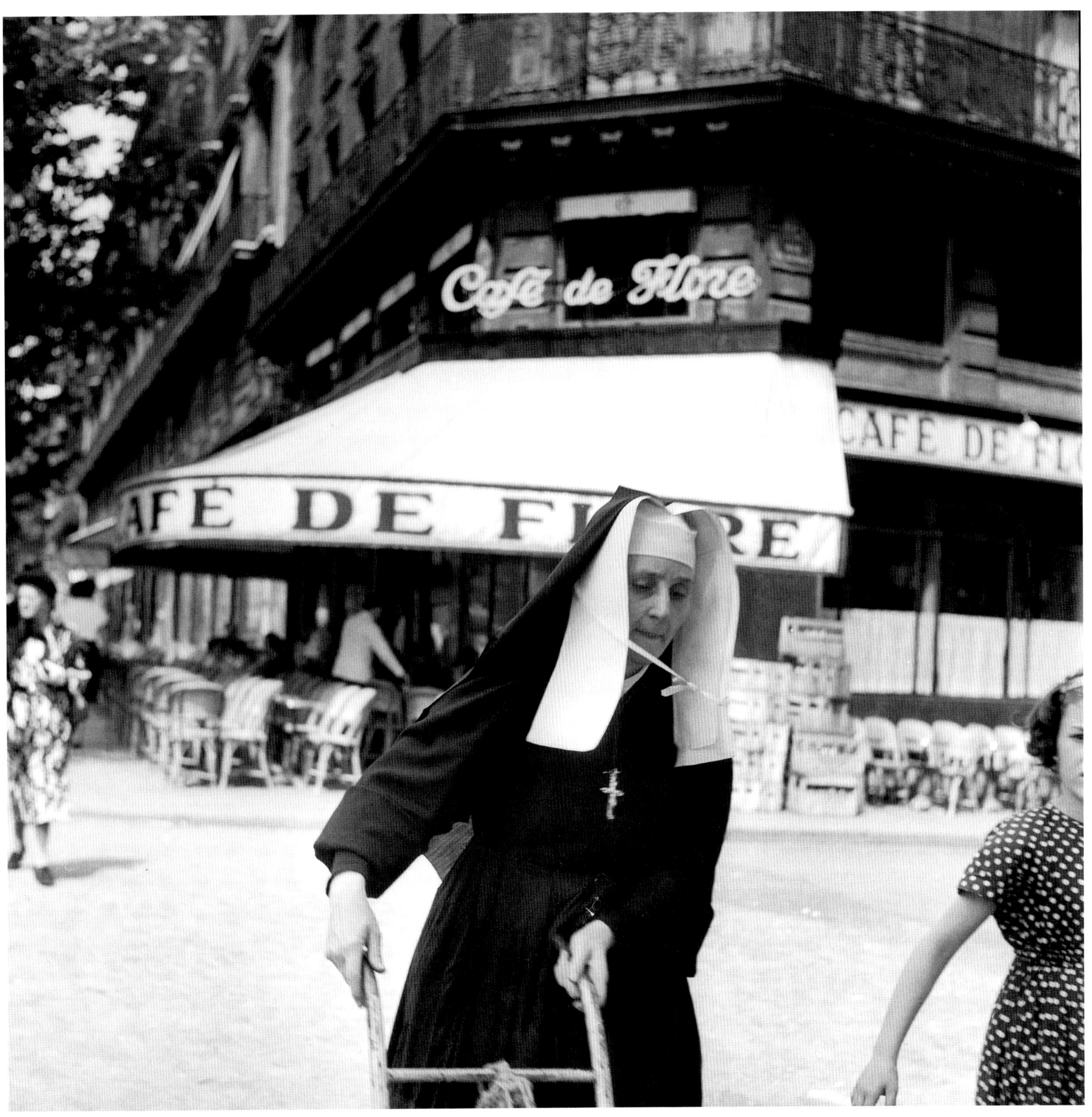

Café de Flore, Blvd Saint Germain, 1950s

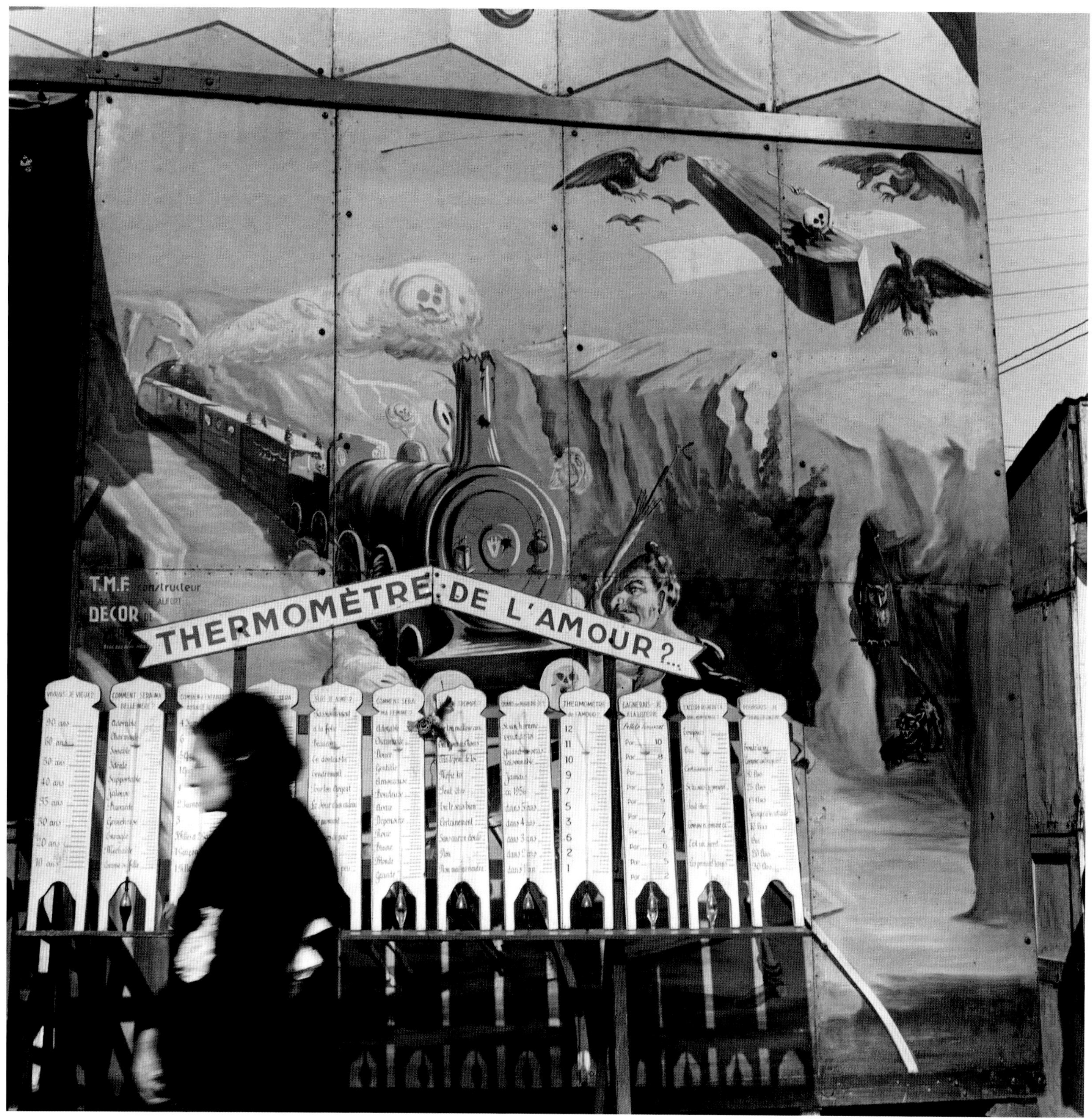

Fairground, Neuilly, 1950s

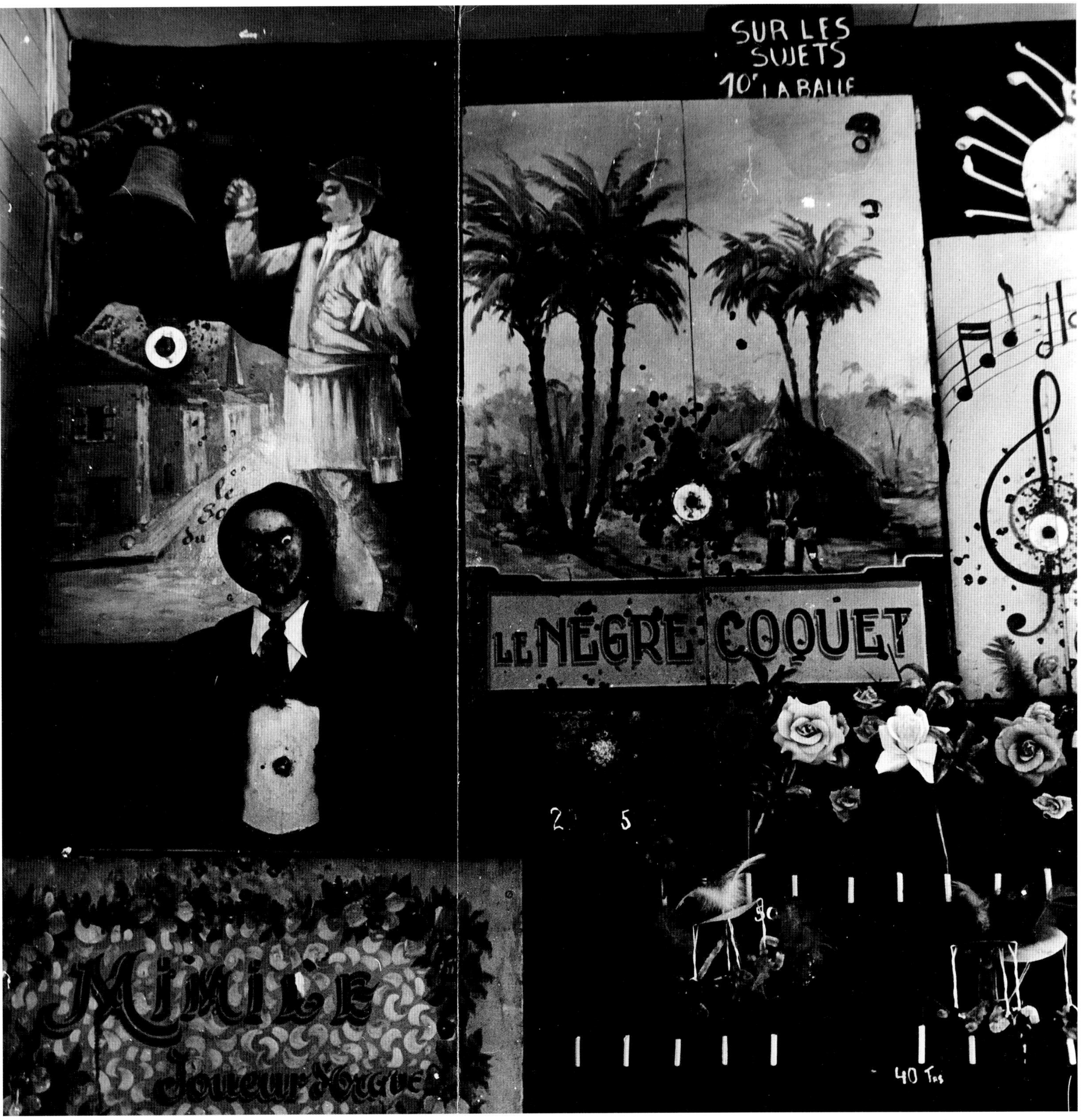

Shooting gallery, Neuilly, 1950s

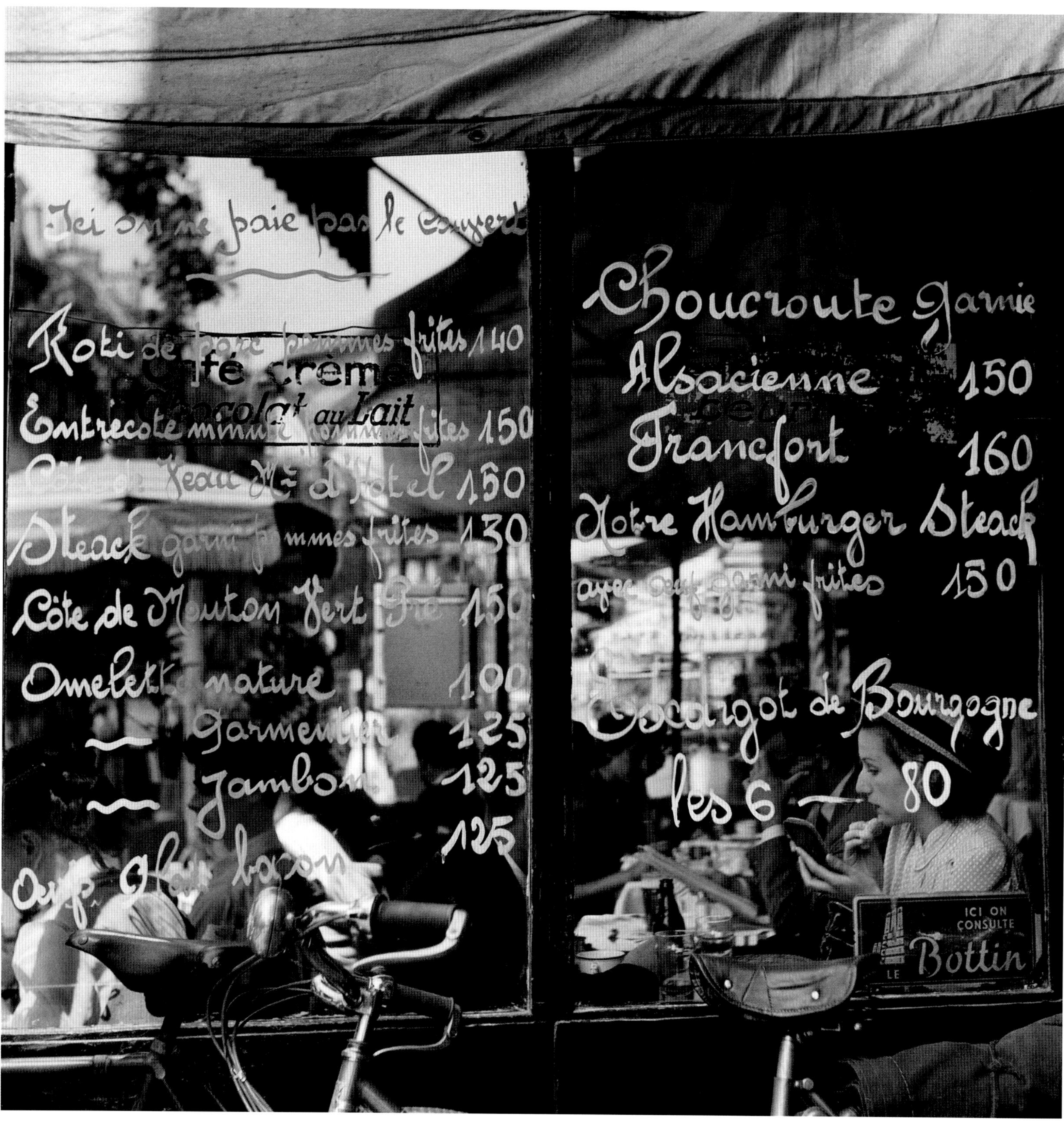

Restaurant, Blvd Saint Michel, c. 1954–55

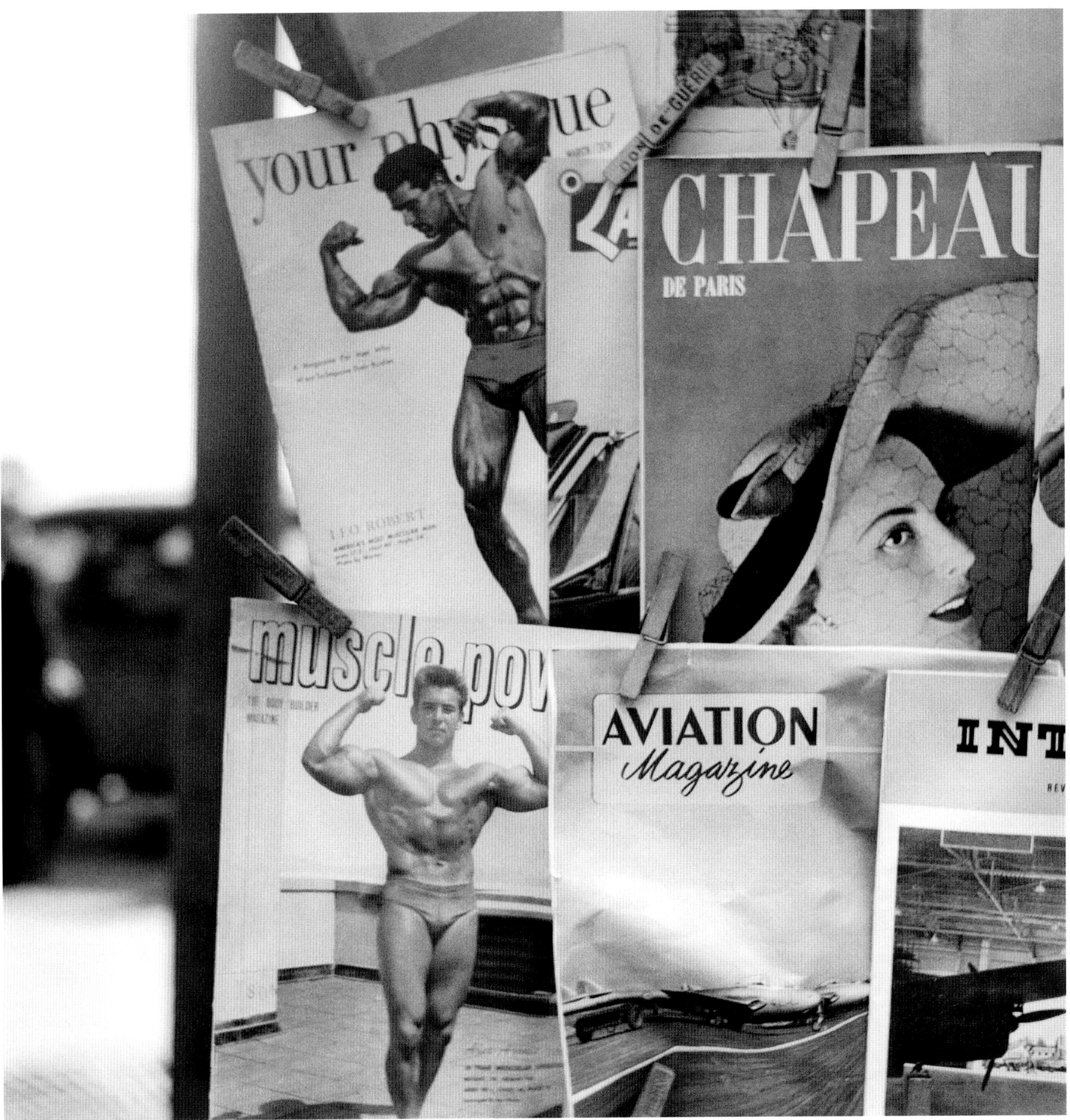

Magazine kiosk, 1950s

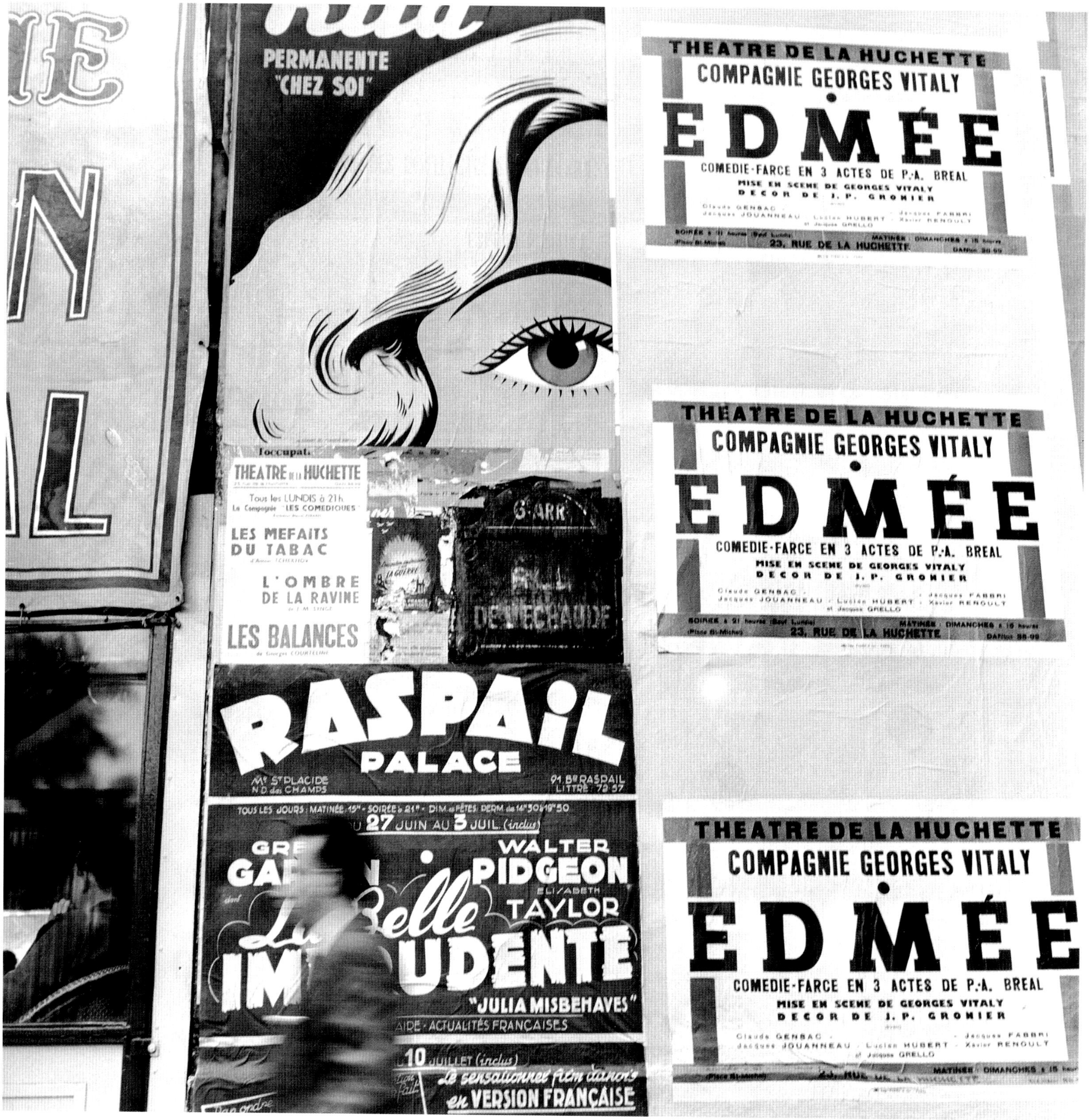

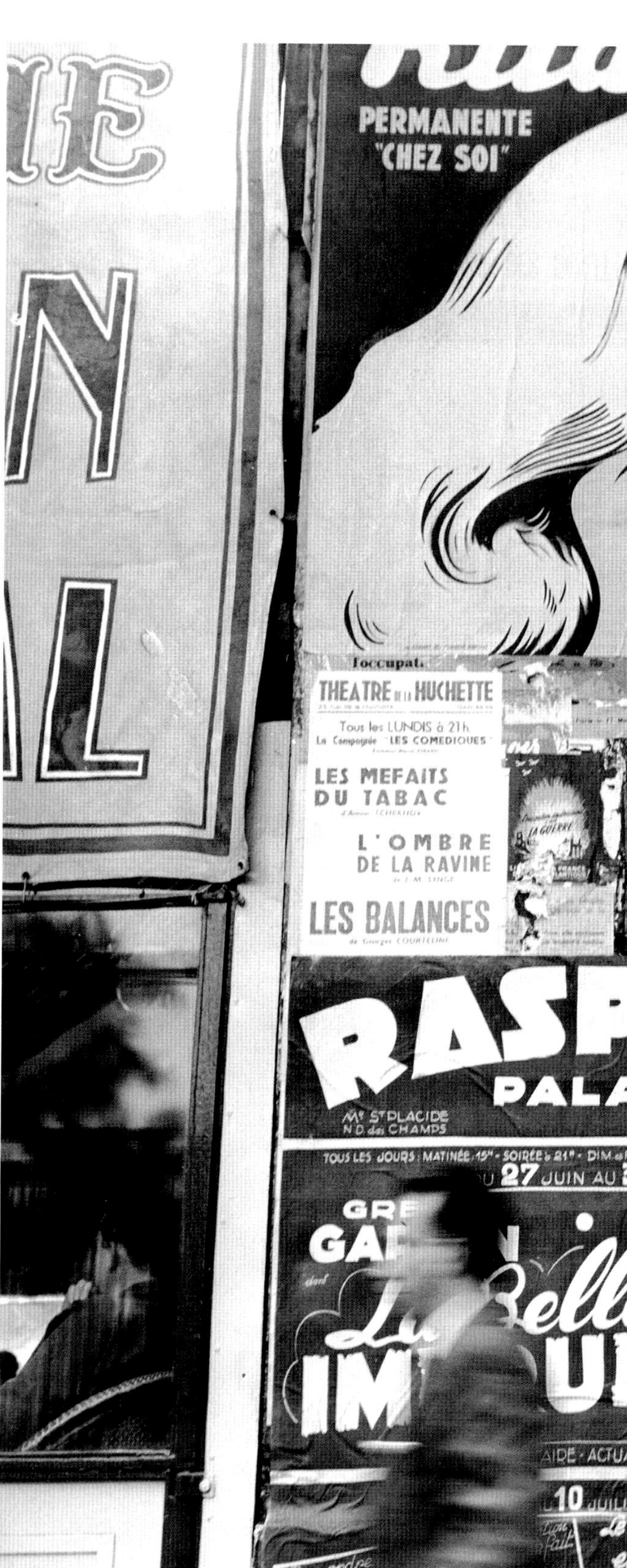

From 'Paris Walls', 1950s

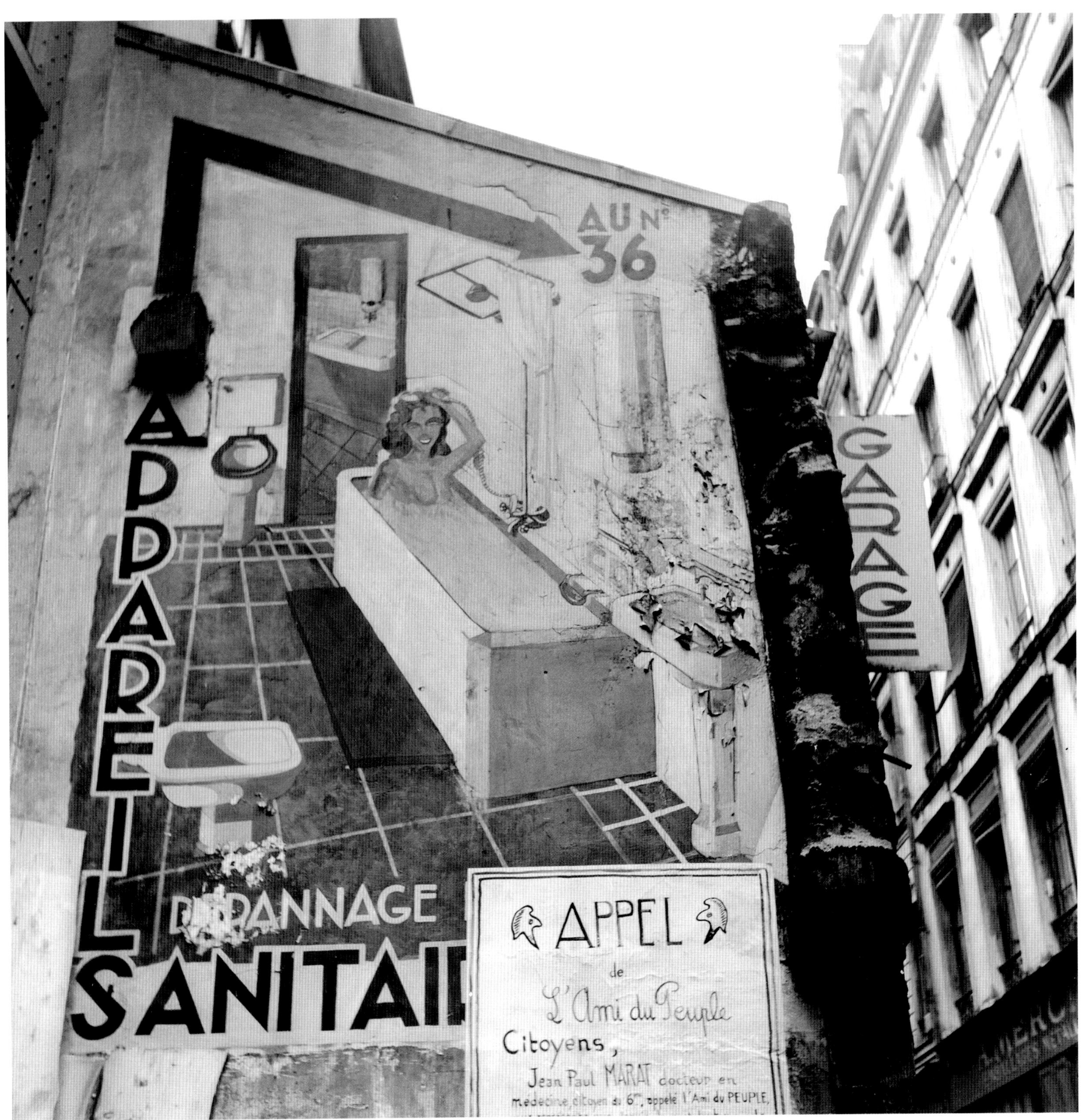

From 'Paris Walls', 1950s

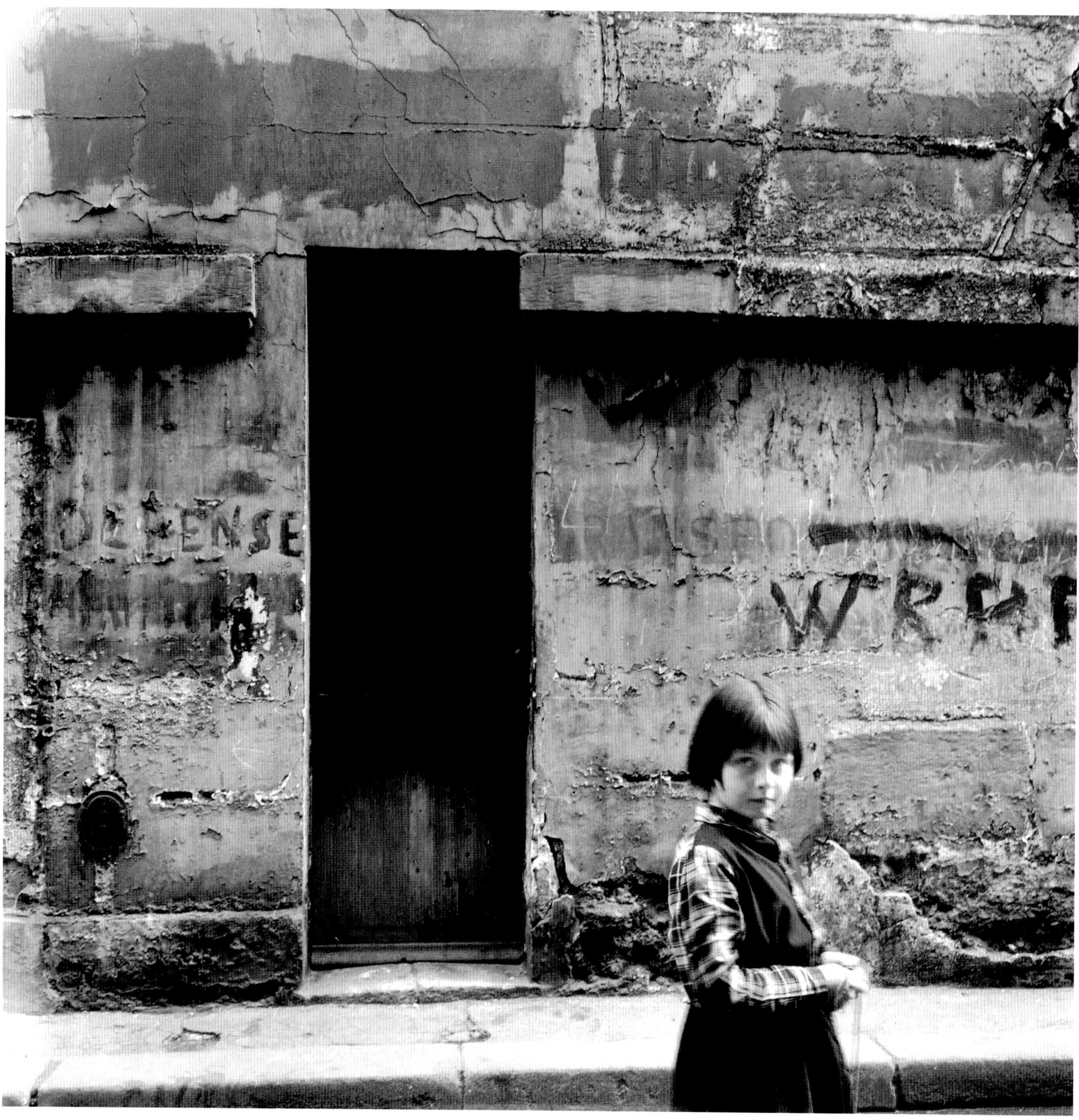

Girl in the street, 1950s

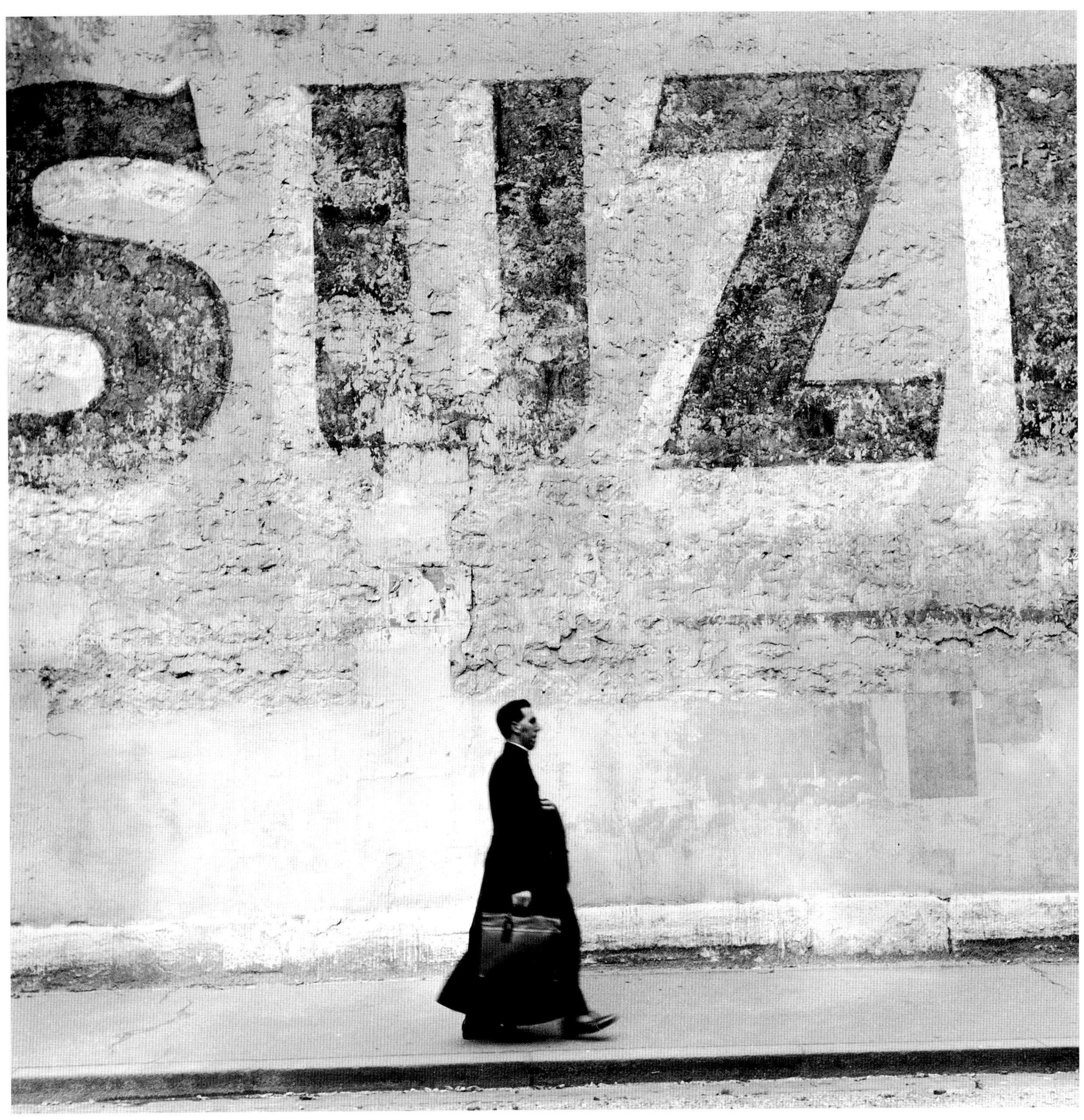

The Suze sign, 1950s

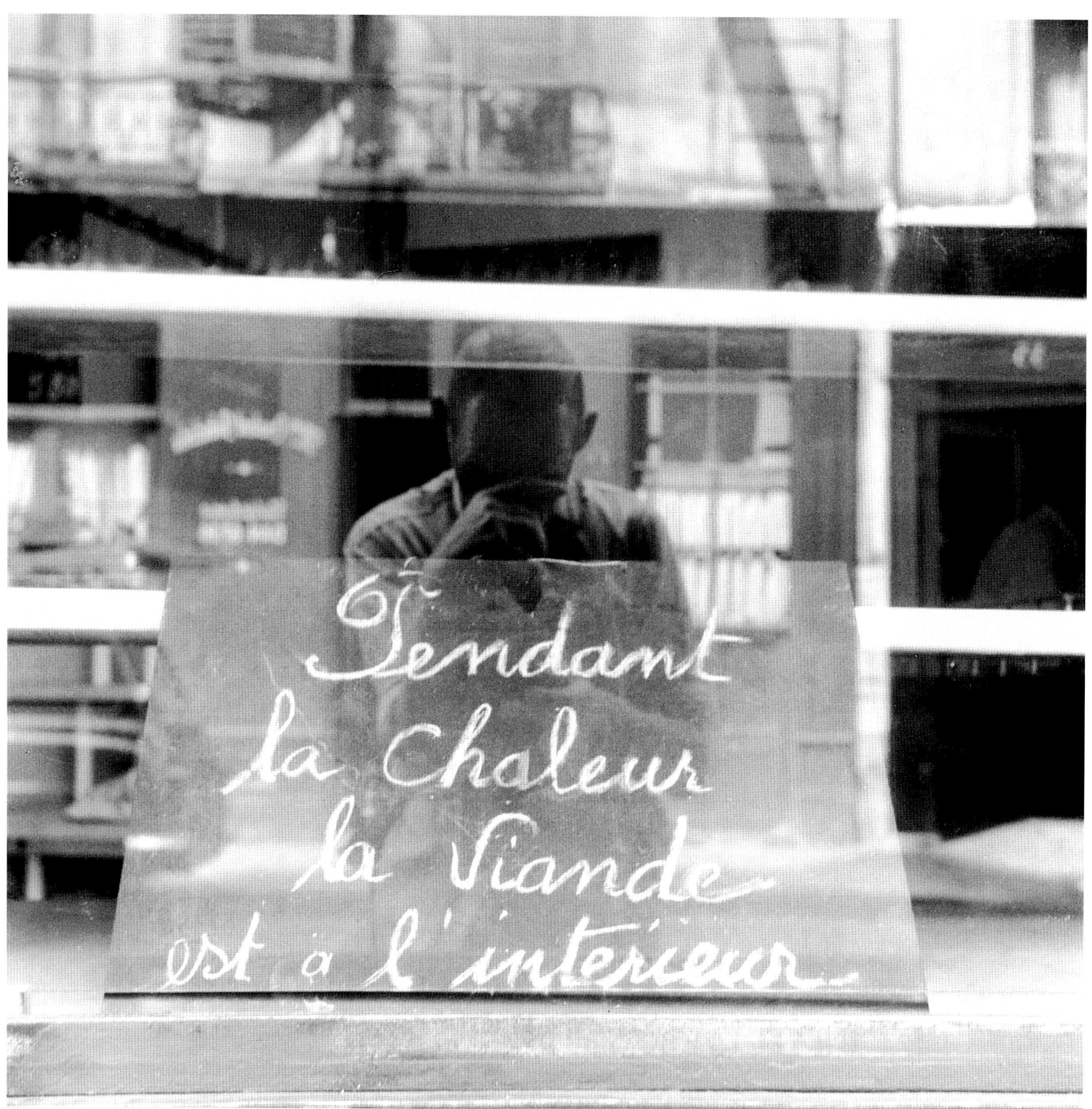

'In Warm Weather the Meat Is Kept Inside', butcher's shop window, with reflection of John Deakin, 1950s

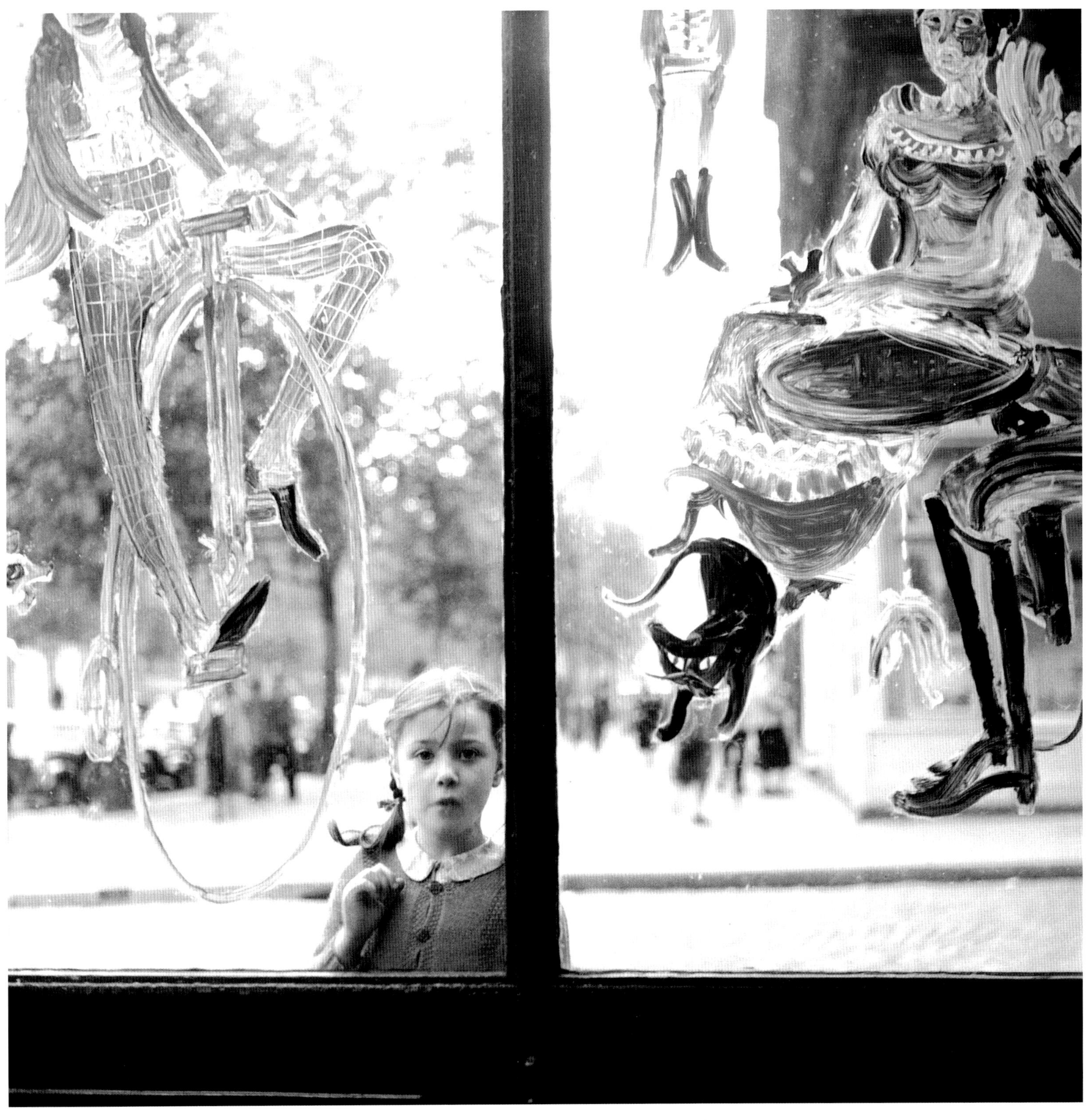

Girl at a bistro window, Montparnasse, 1950s

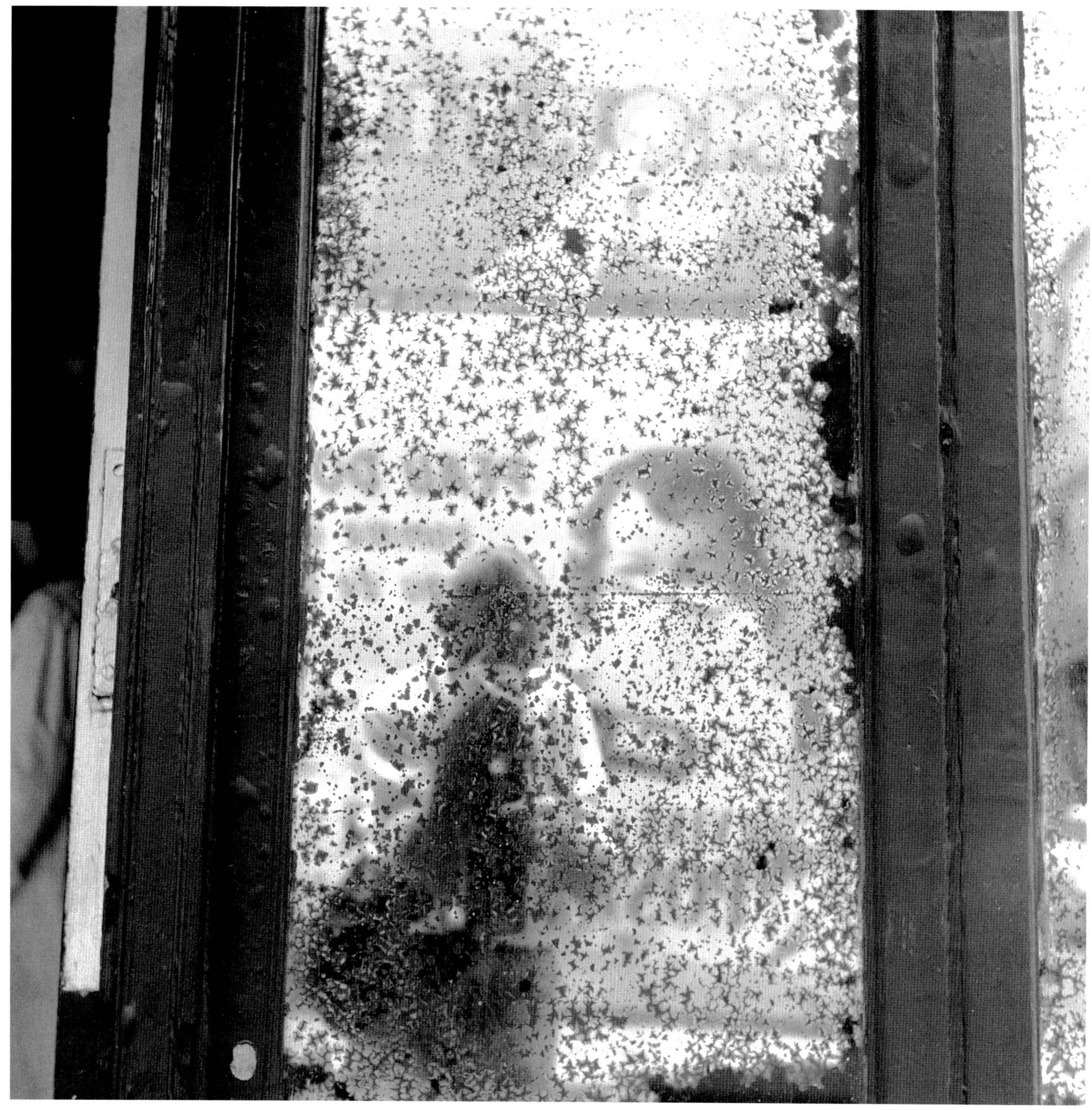

John Deakin reflected in cracked glass, 1950s

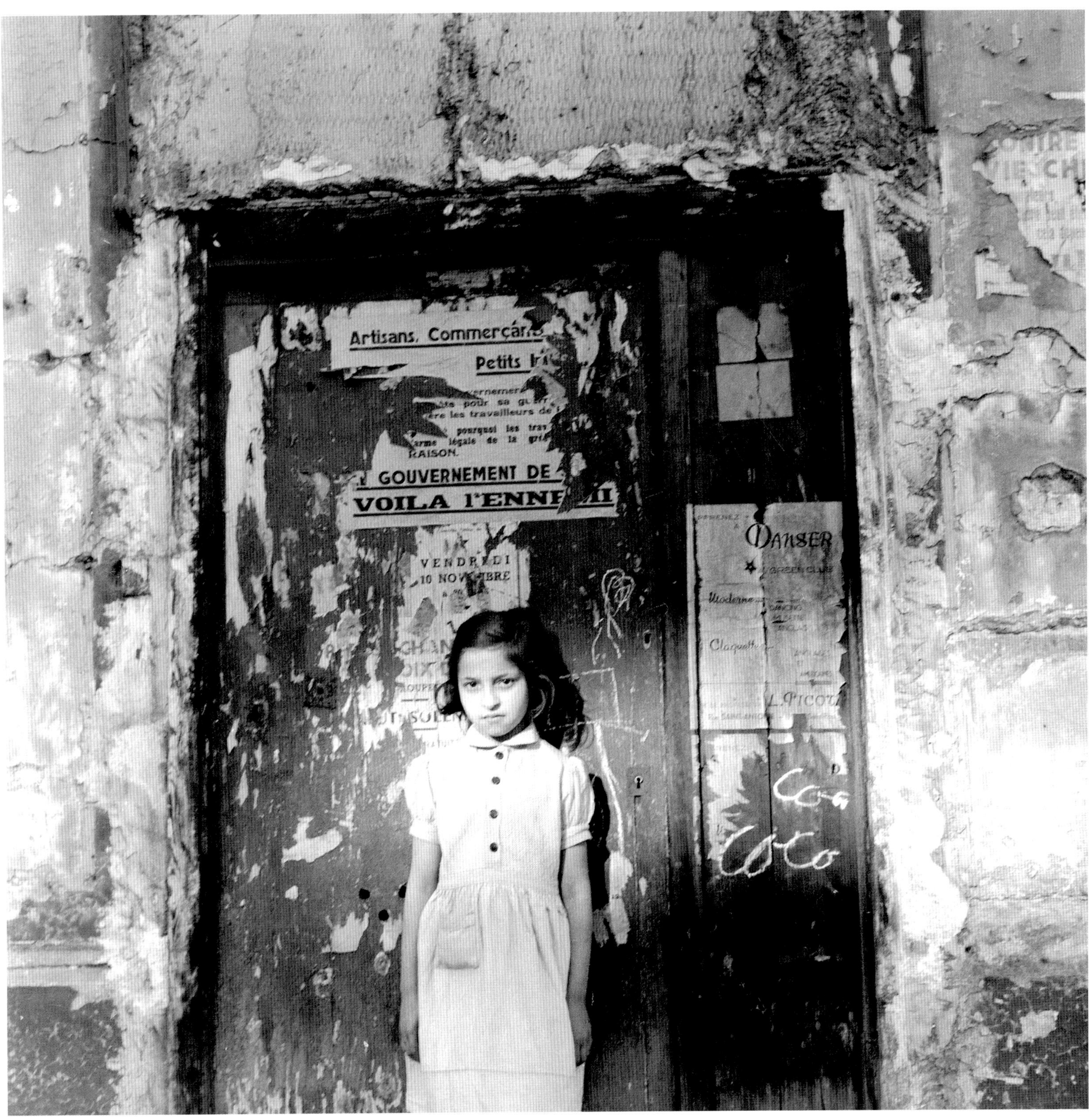

Girl in a blocked-up doorway, 1950s

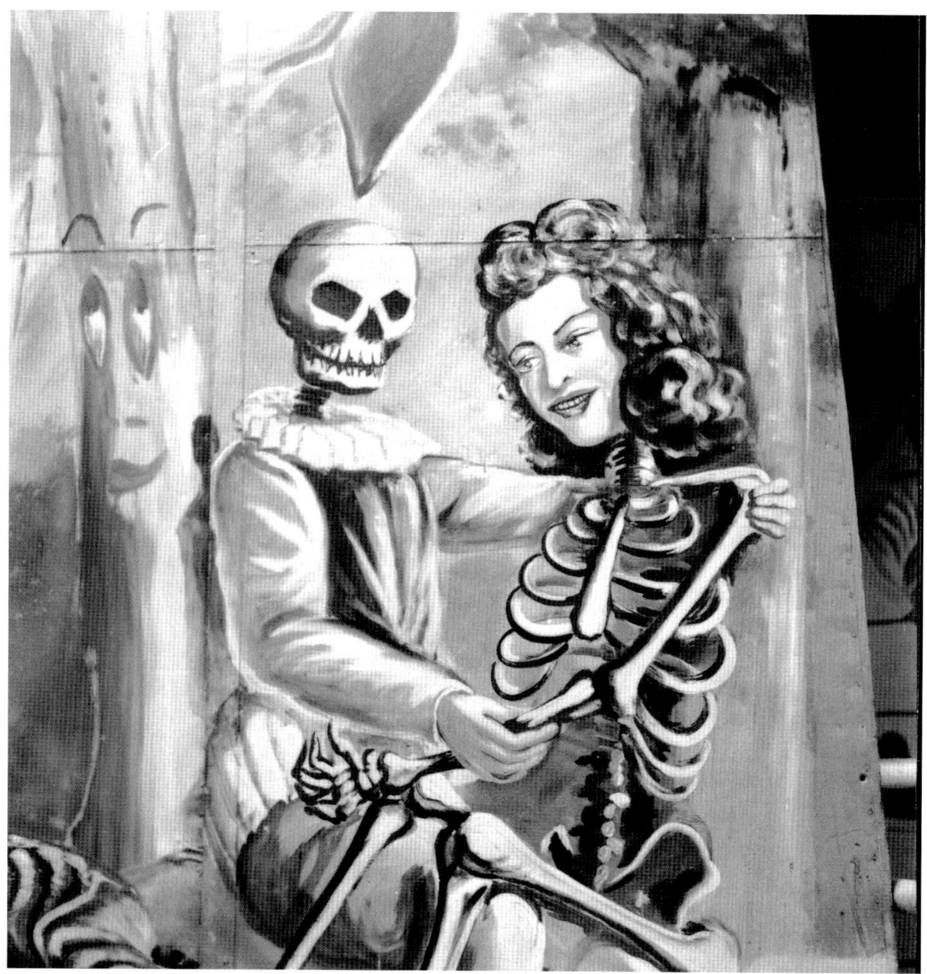

Fairground motif, 1950s

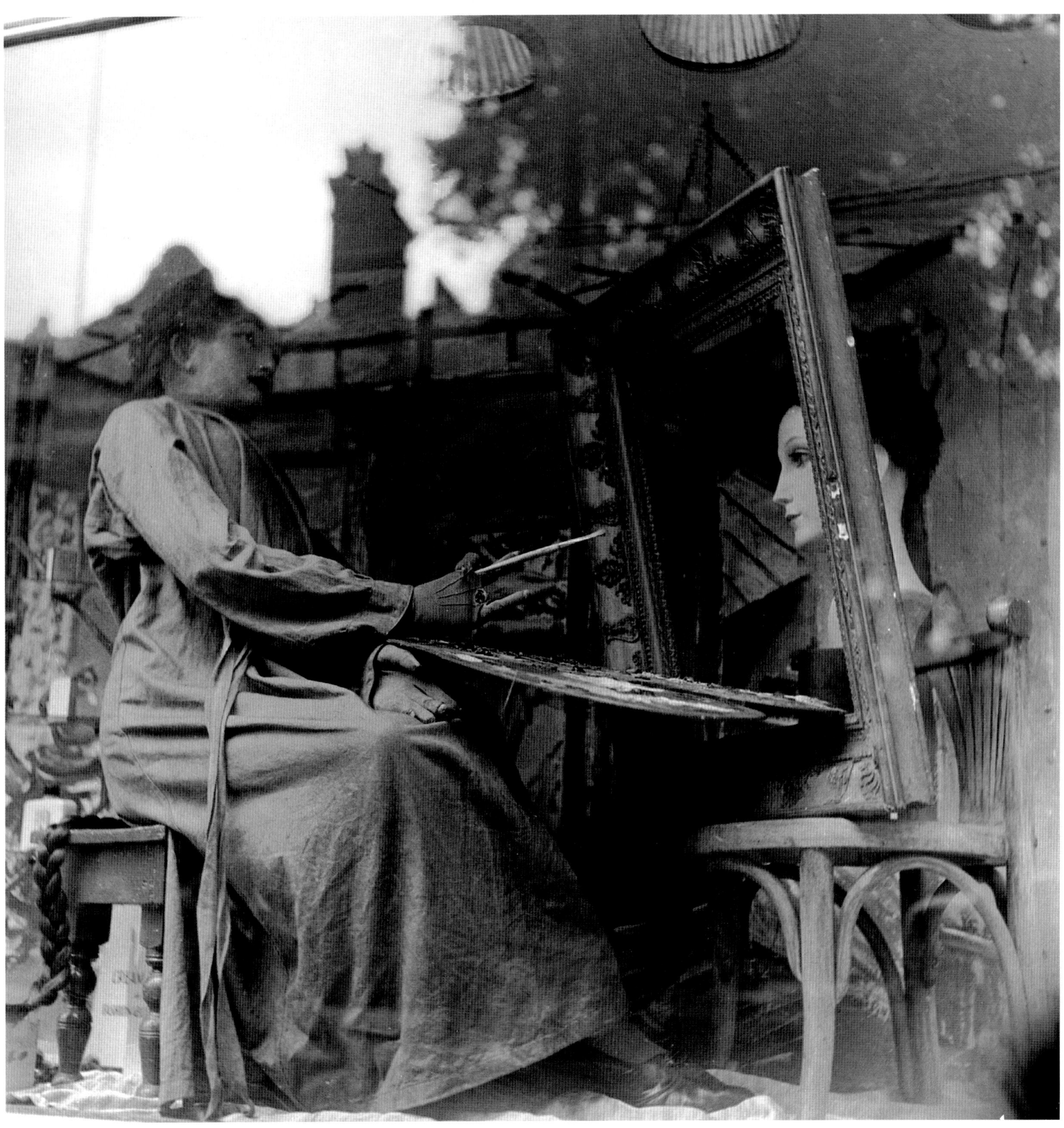

Junk shop window, 1950s

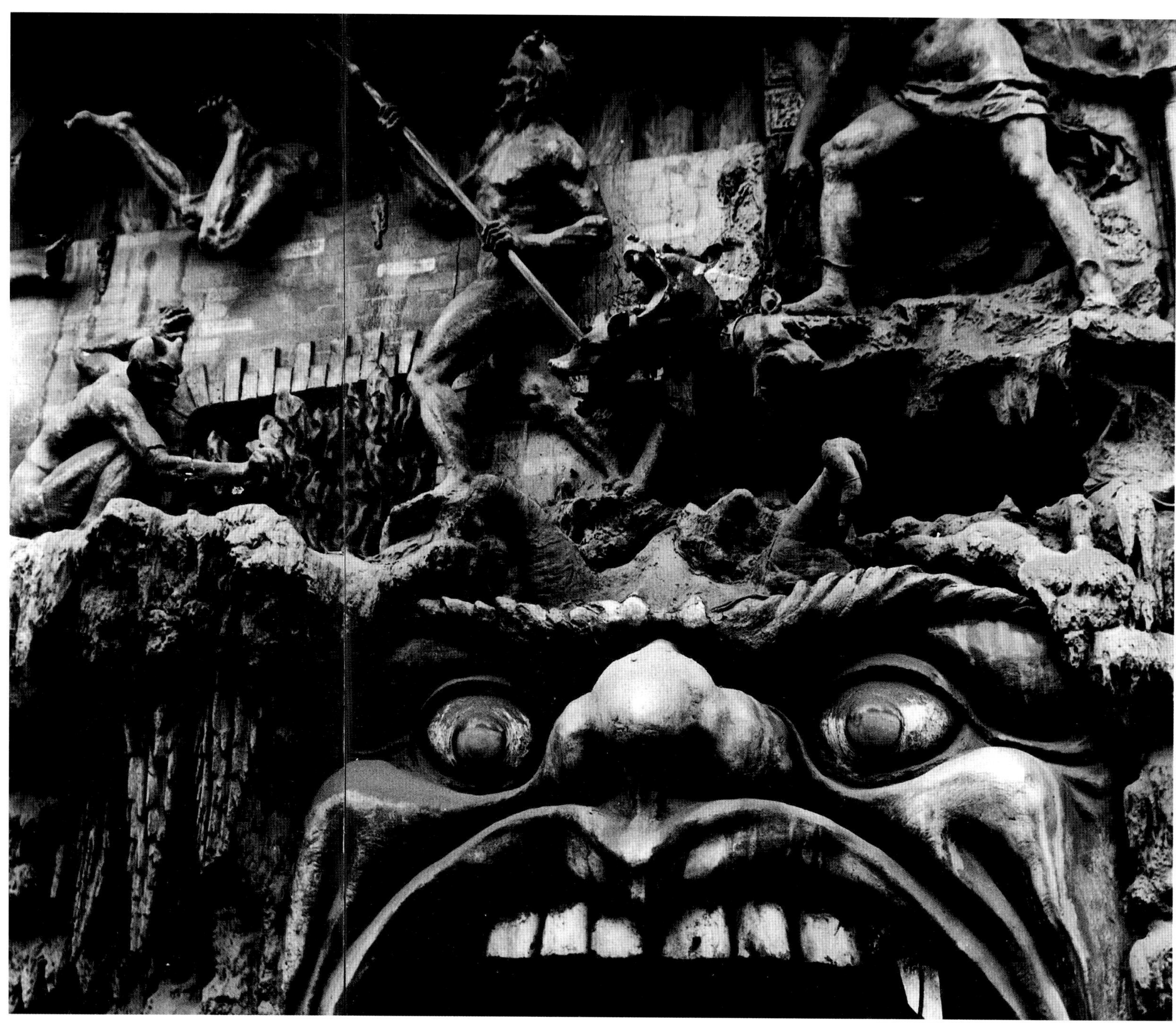

'L'Enfer', 1950s

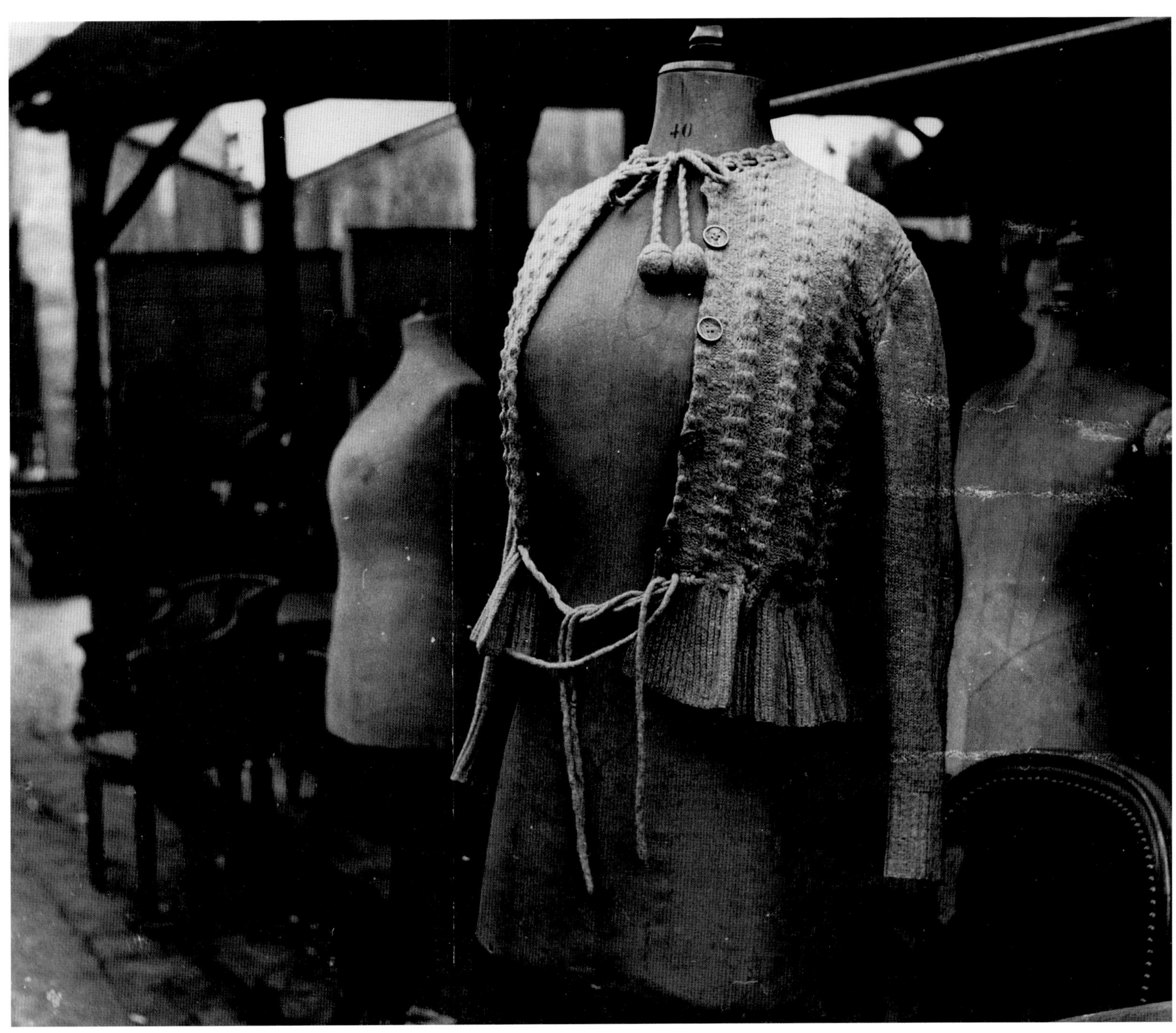

Dressmaker's mannequins, 1950s

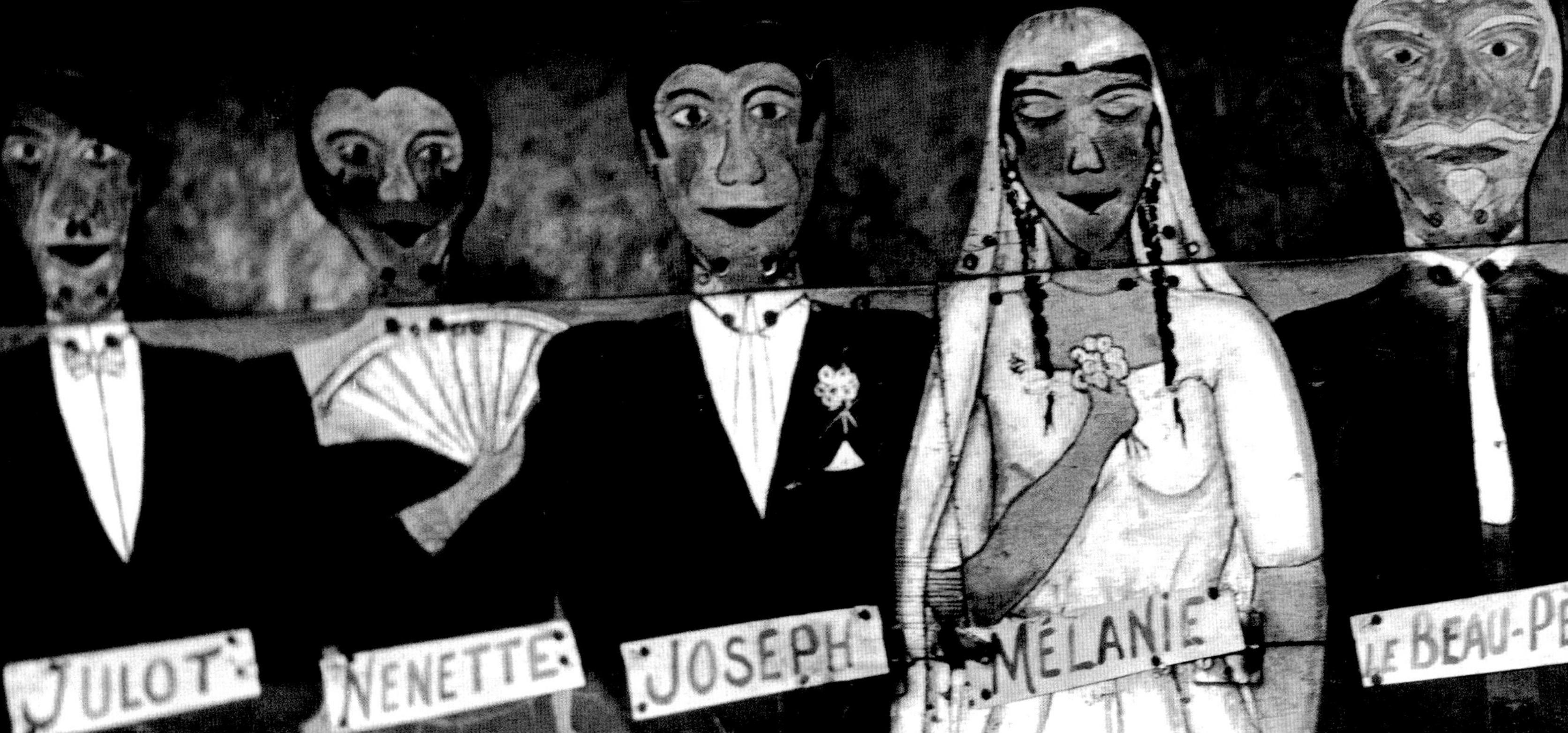
JULOT
NENETTE
JOSEPH
MÉLANIE
LES BALLES
REVENANT AU JOUEUR
NE COMPTENT PAS
2
LOTS

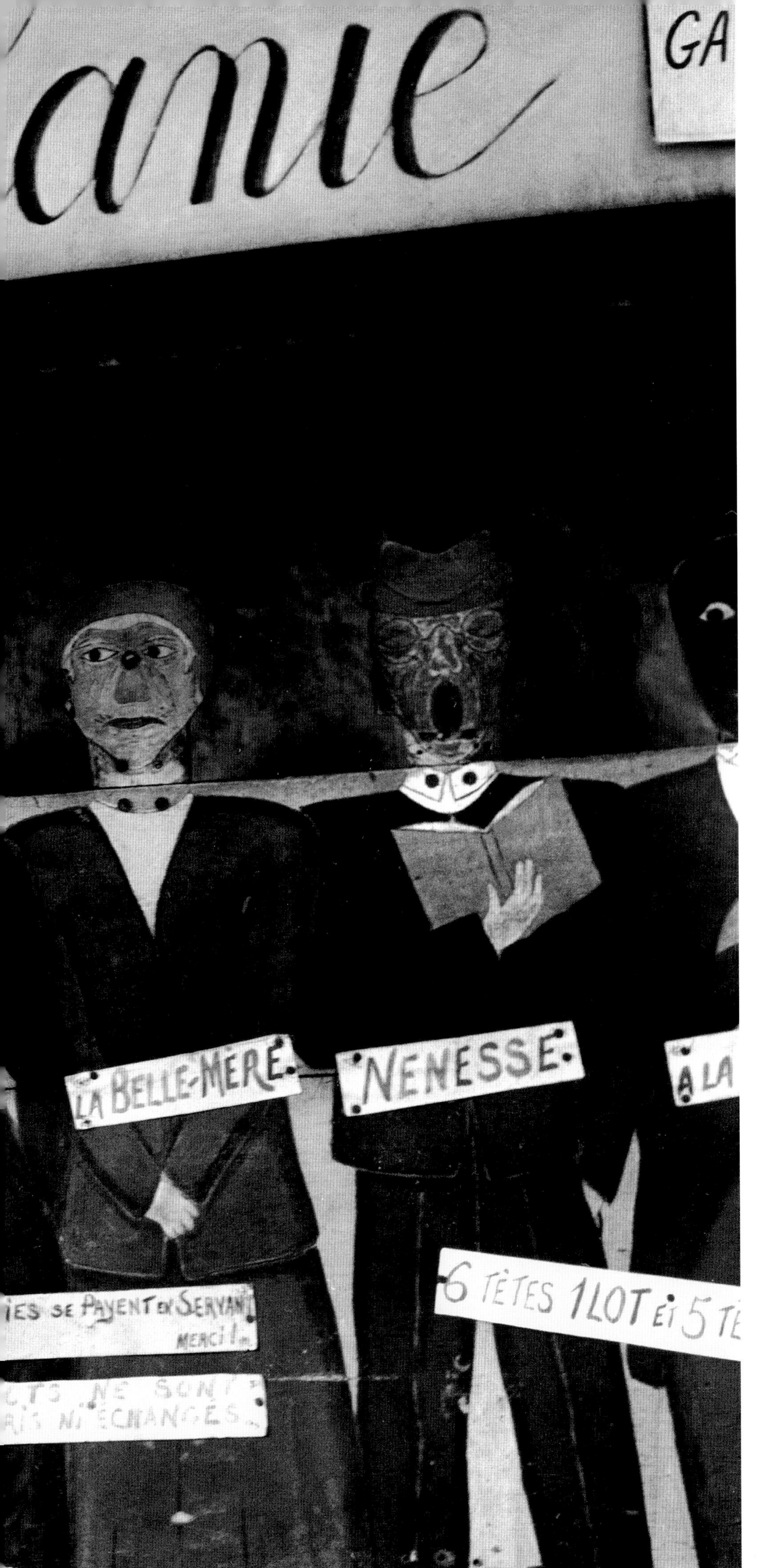

'Melanie's wedding', fairground stall, 1950s

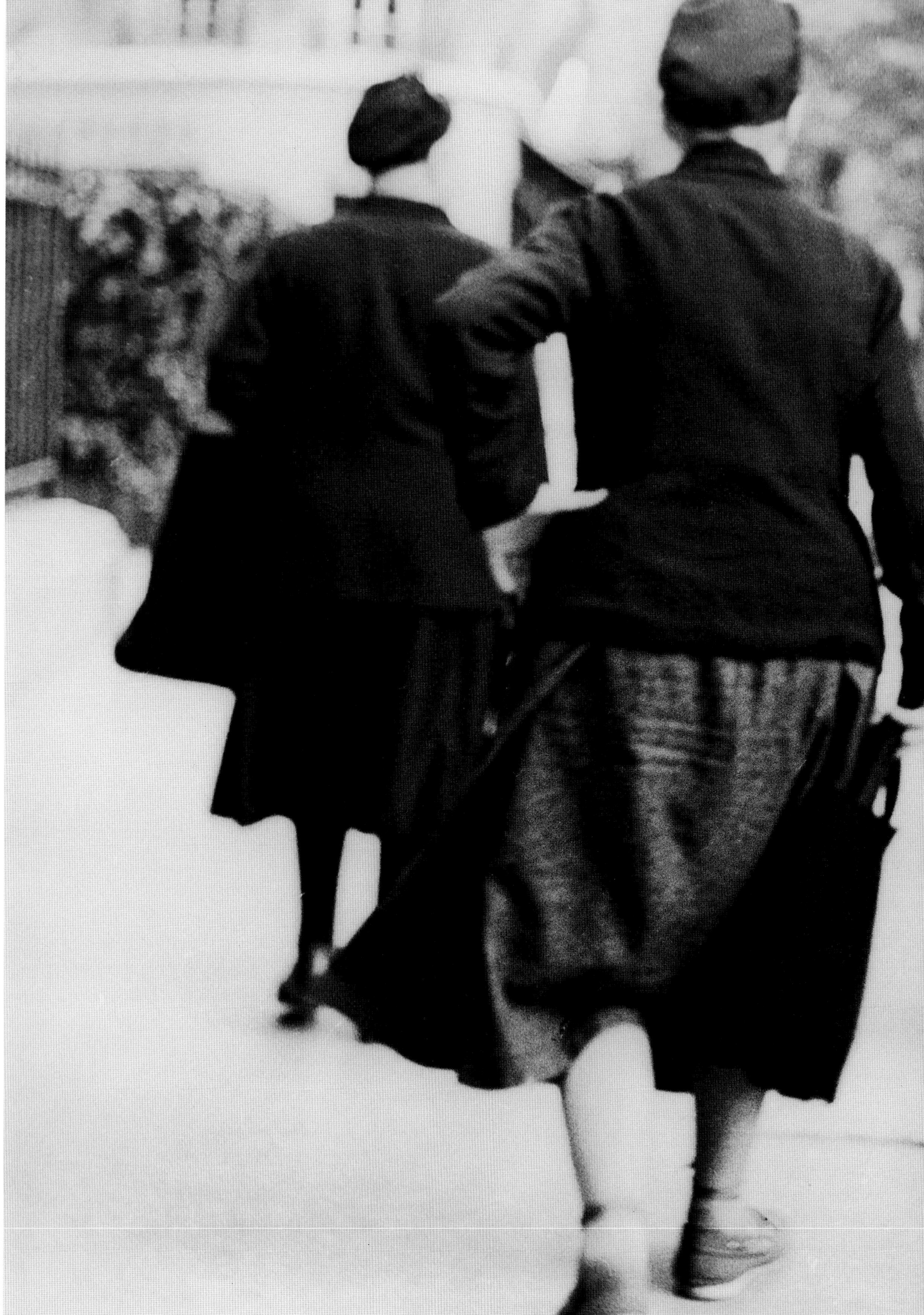

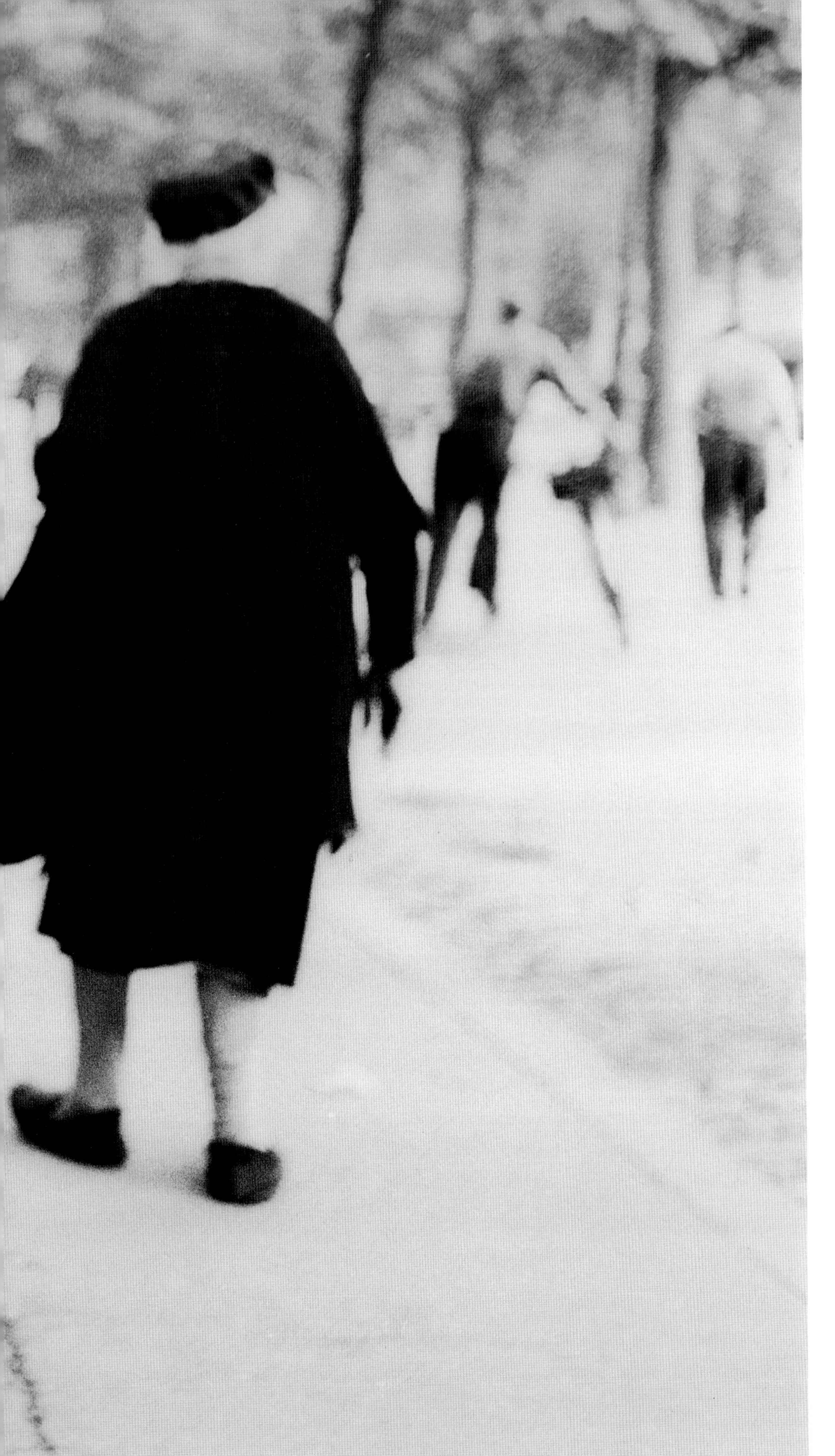

Walkers on the Champs-Elysées, 1950s

Early morning walker, off the Champs-Elysées, 1950s

Pages 138–139: 'Paris umbrella', c. 1954–55

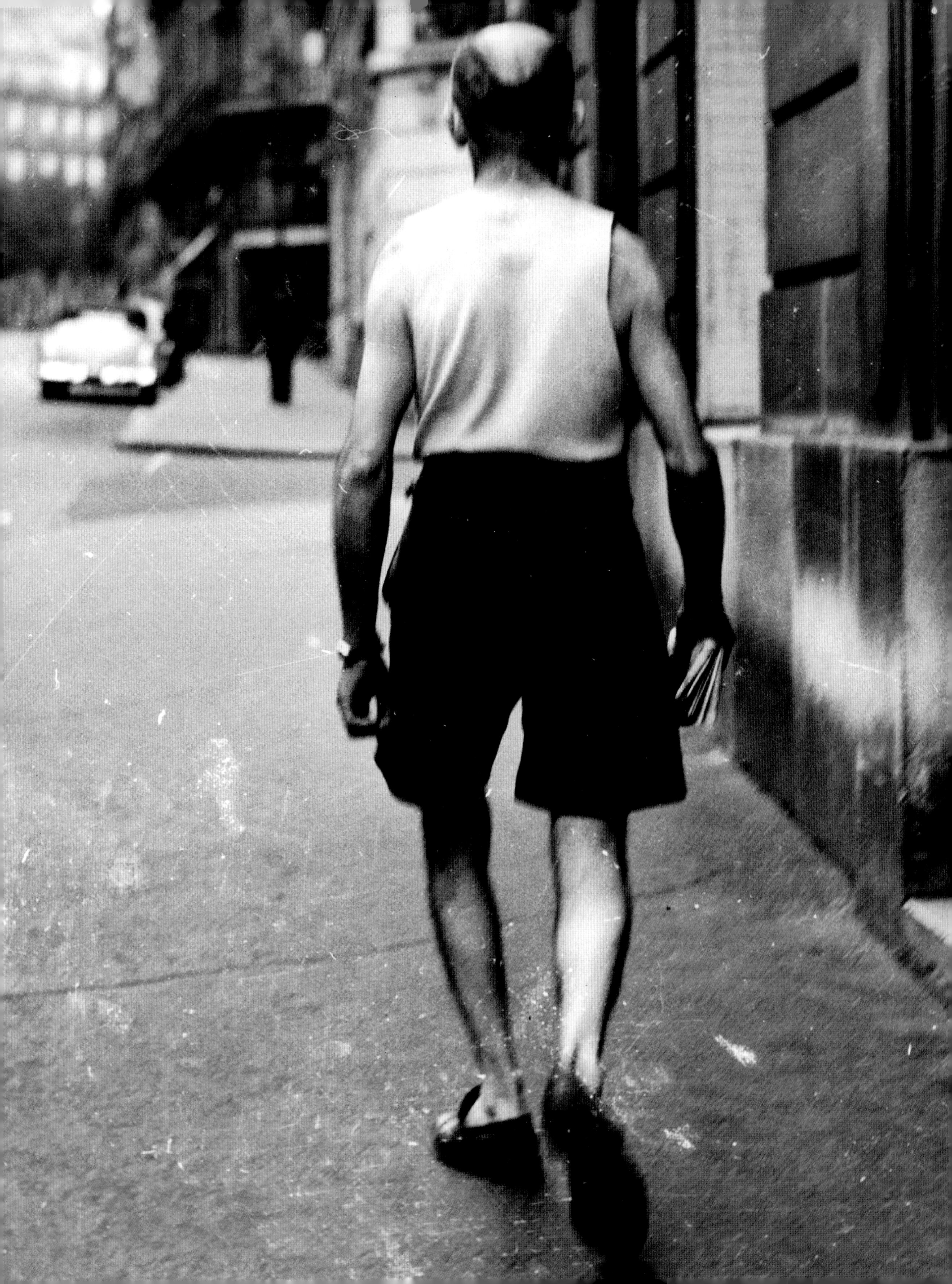

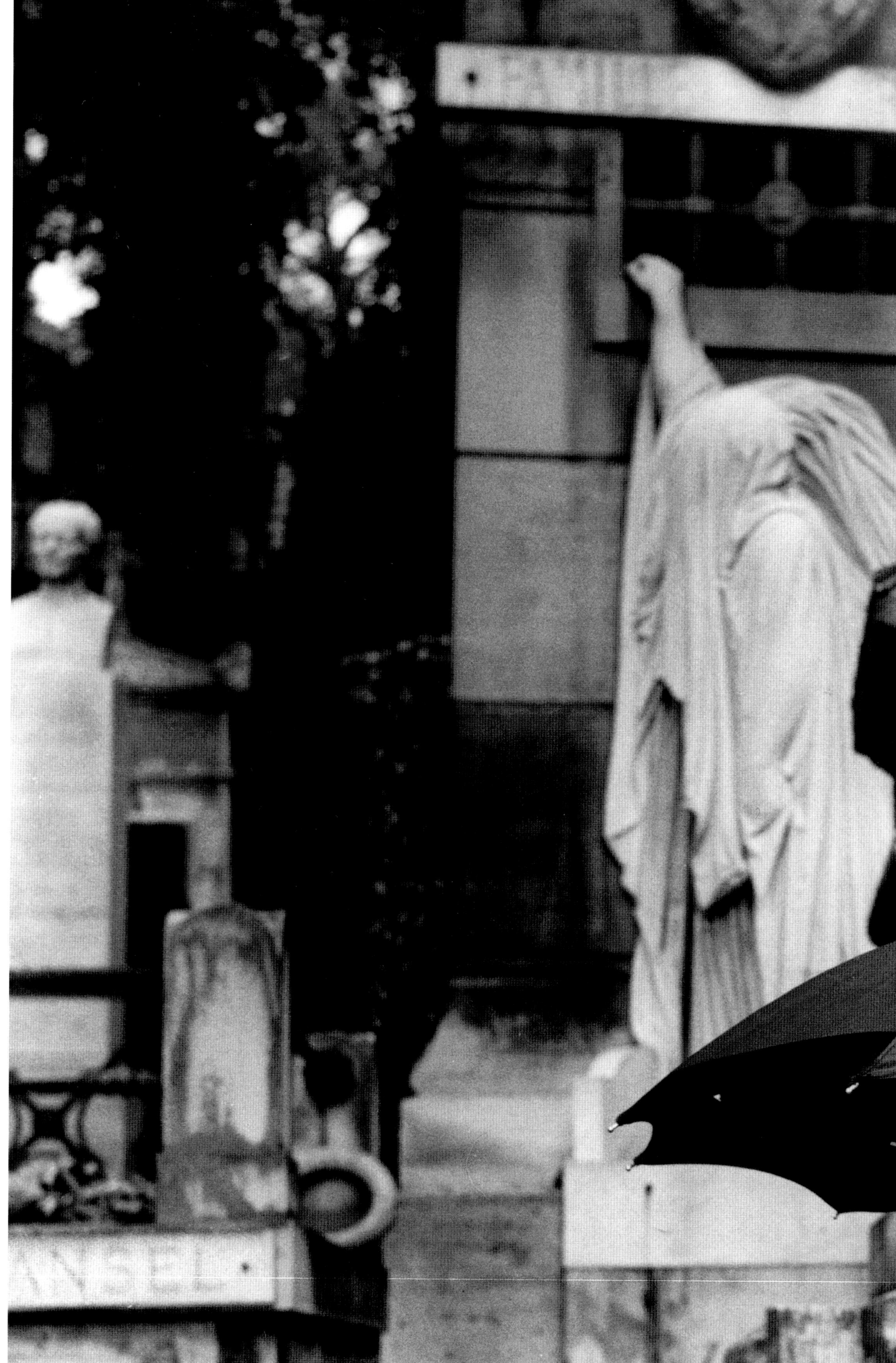

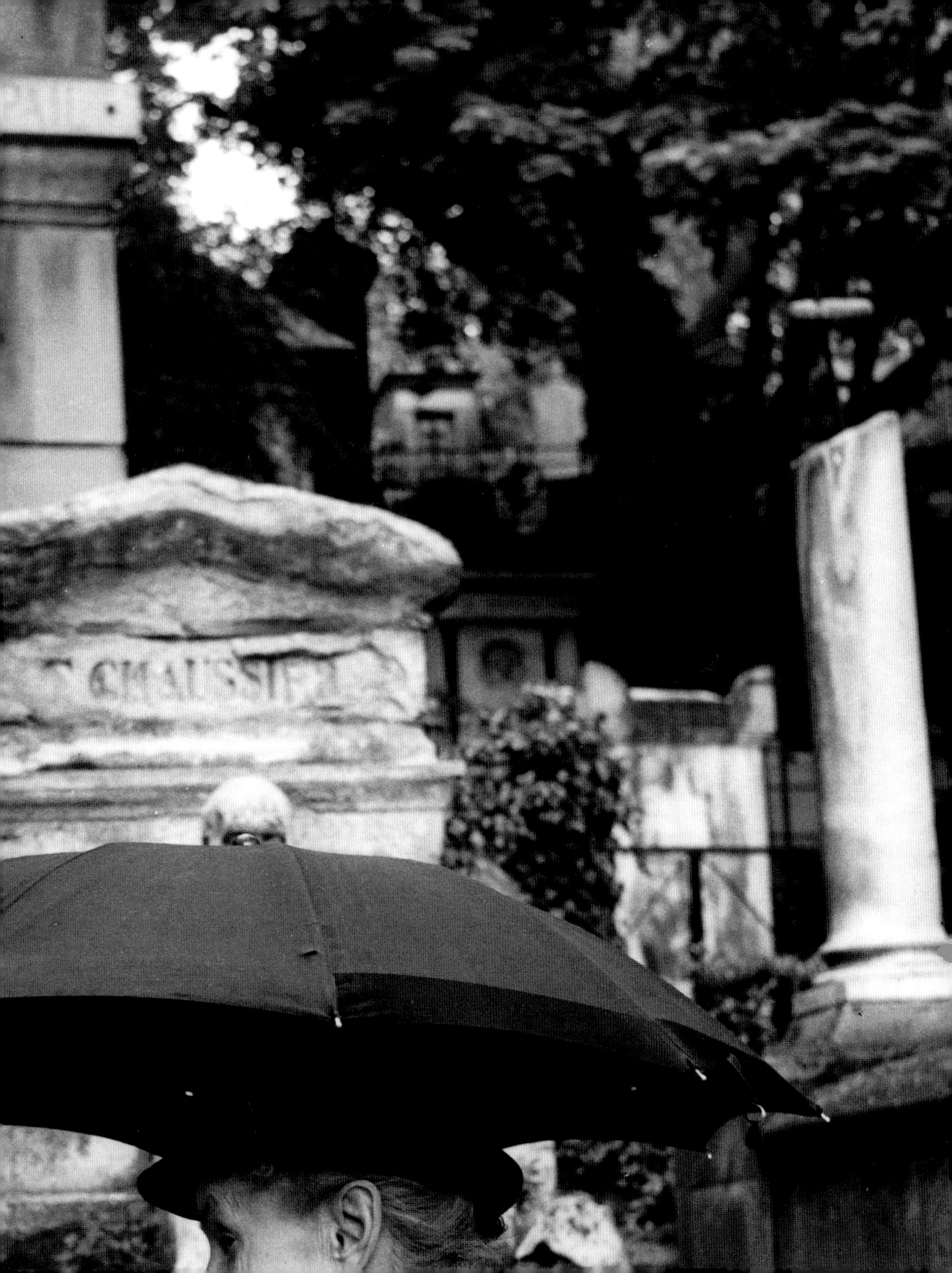

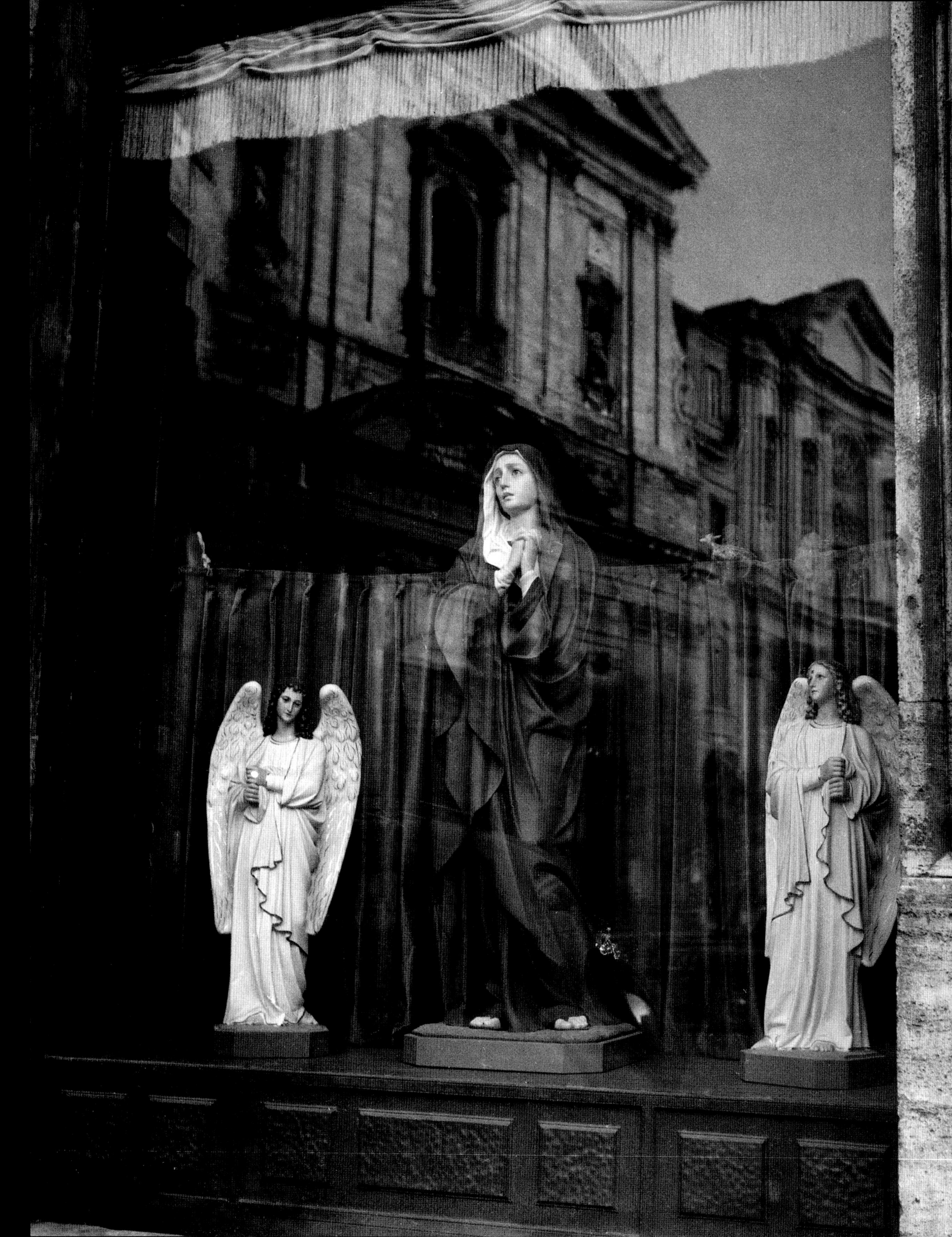

Rome

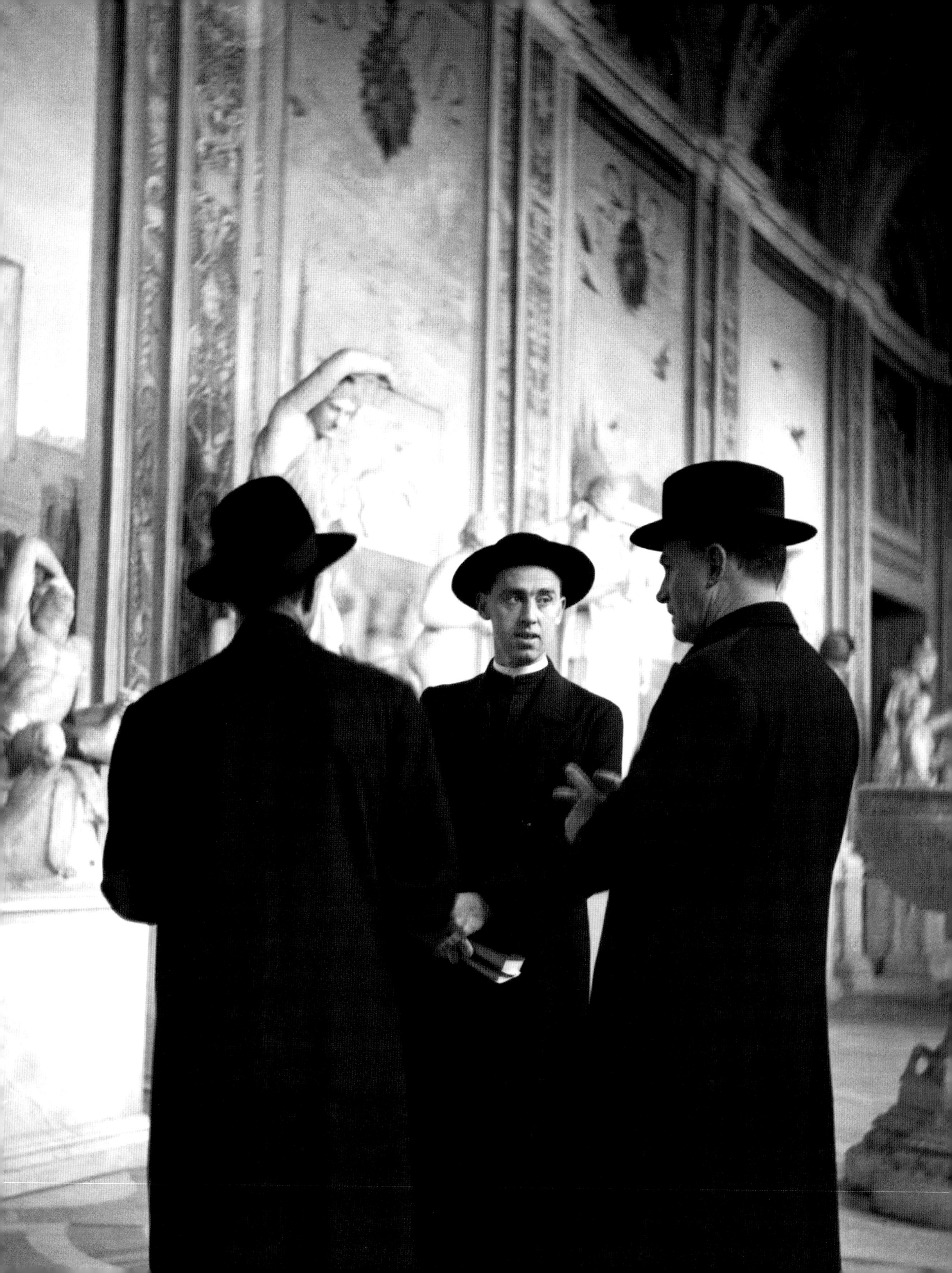

In September 1956, two months after Deakin's Paris show, the exhibition 'John Deakin's Rome' opened at the Parton Gallery, below David Archer's Bookshop. Around this time Deakin's drinking had become almost uncontrollable: 'We had to keep him captive to get it all done,' James Mortimer, a fellow photographer, recalls.[1]

Deakin knew Rome well, had visited it in the 1930s, returned after the war and for a while – dismissed from *Vogue* for the last time – had made his home in the via dei Greci. The exhibition contained the results of all those trips, together with out-takes of the plates section of Christopher Kininmonth's travel book *Rome Alive* (1951). Deakin had planned a book around his most recent trip, sometime in 1954, and had photographed there for a few weeks with uncharacteristic urgency on discovering that the German photographer Herbert List was doing the same. But he lost interest and, like so many of Deakin's projects, the book failed to materialize. List's book *Rom* appeared in 1955, some of the photographs eerily similar to Deakin's surviving frames and all taken on the square-format Rolleiflex, also Deakin's camera of choice.

In the 1940s, Deakin's pictures of Paris had been his calling card – a portfolio had persuaded *Vogue*'s editor, Audrey Withers, of his talent as a photographer. Although she fired him for bad behaviour, she rehired him on seeing his photographs on the streets of Rome, the work, she believed, of a genius.

Opposite: In the Vatican museum, 1950s

Page 140: Church reliquary shop with the reflection of the Chiesa Nuova, c. 1950

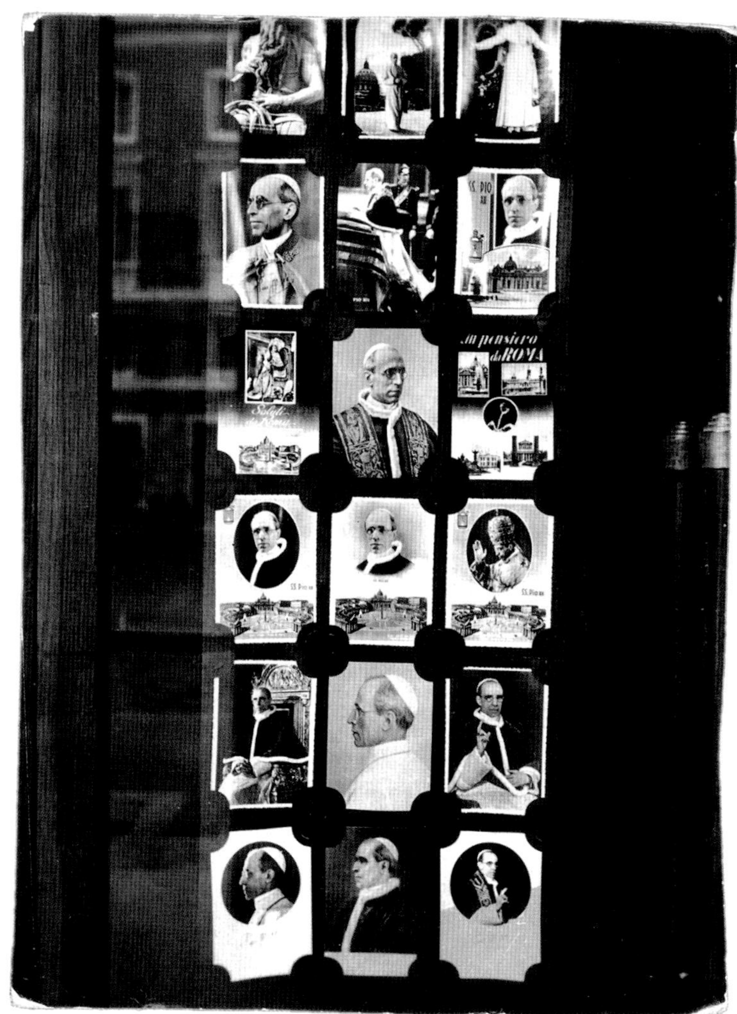

Postcards of Pope Pius XII, 1950s

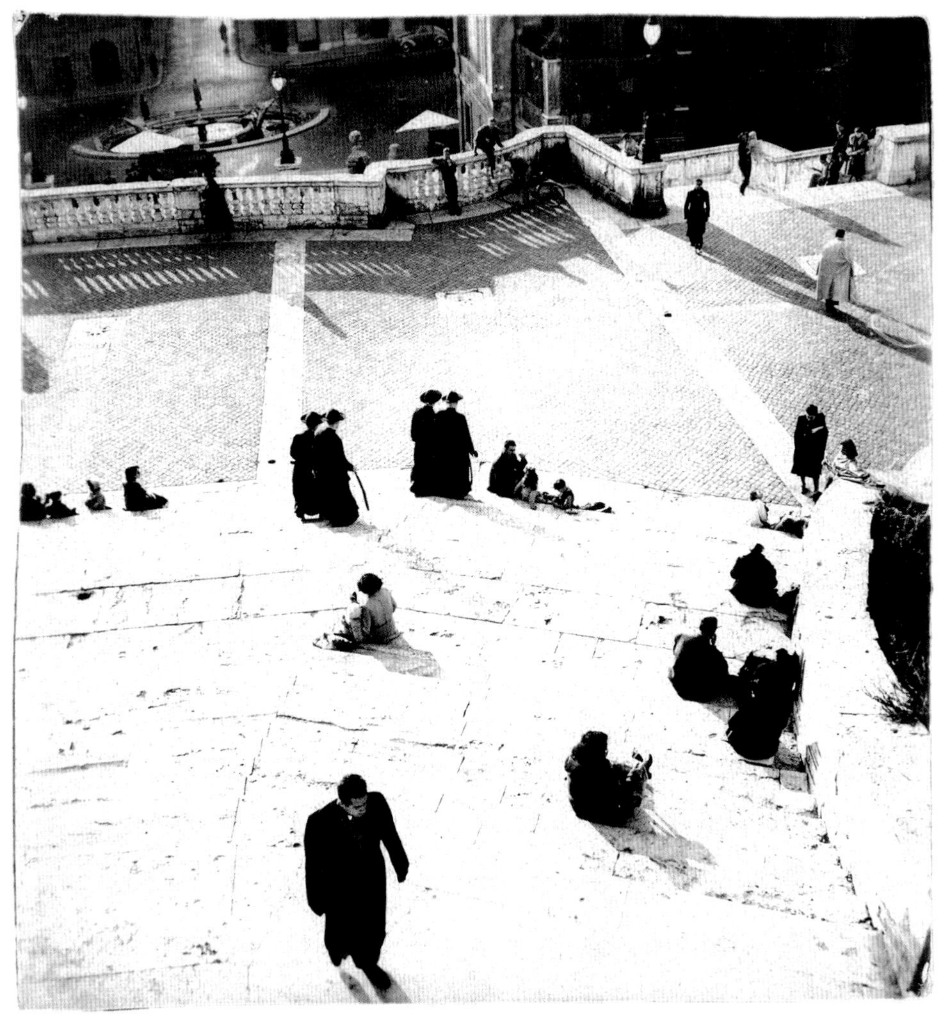

The Spanish steps, Piazza di Spagna, c. 1950

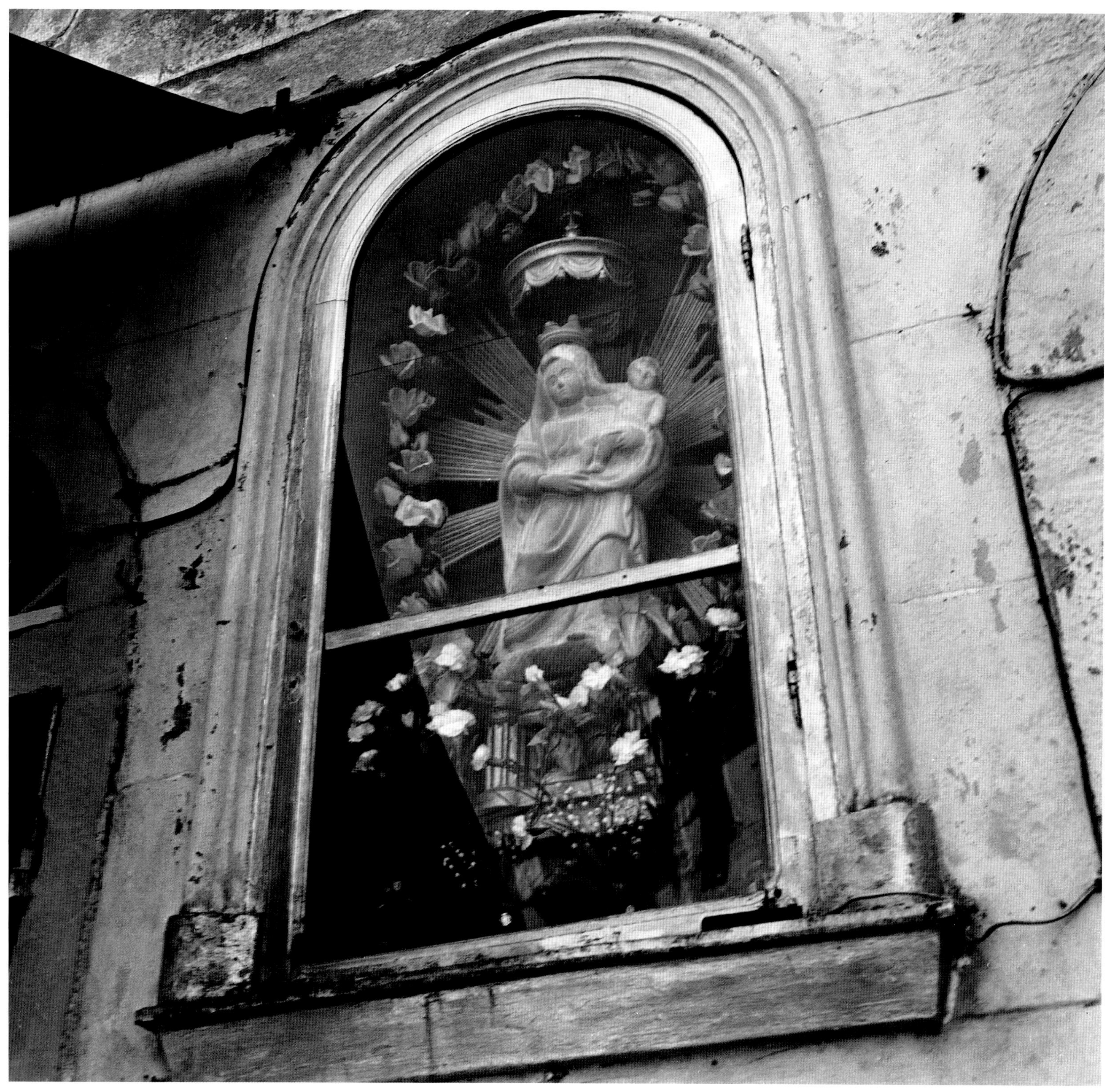

Street shrine to the Blessed Virgin Mary, 1950s

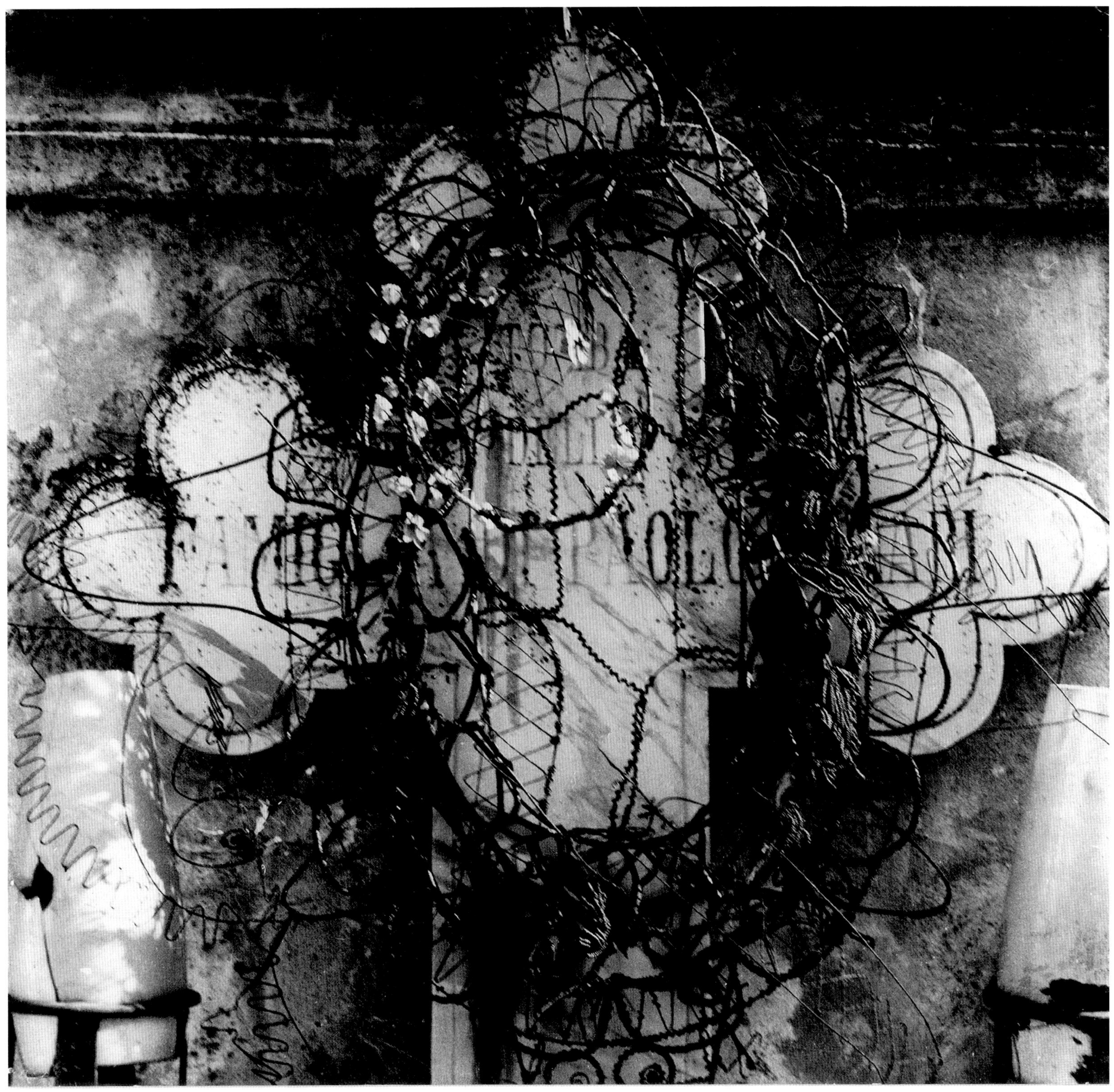

Remains of wreaths, 1950s

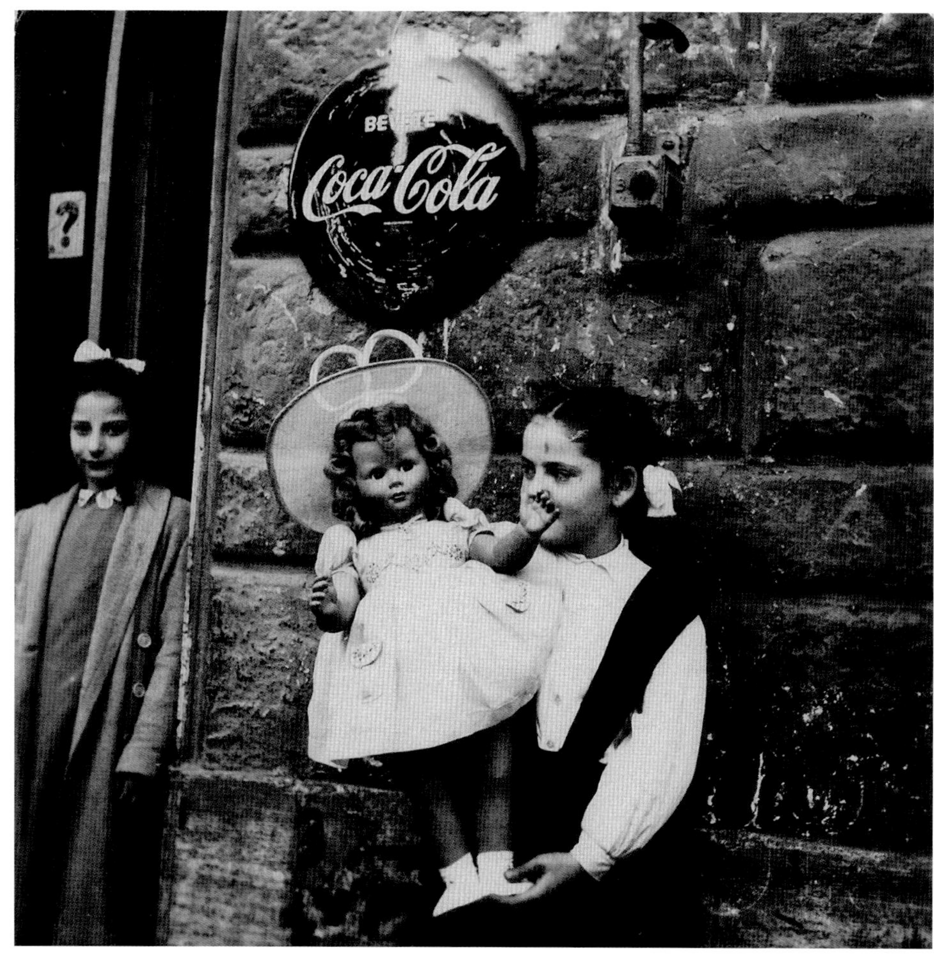

Girl with a doll, Trastavere, 1950s

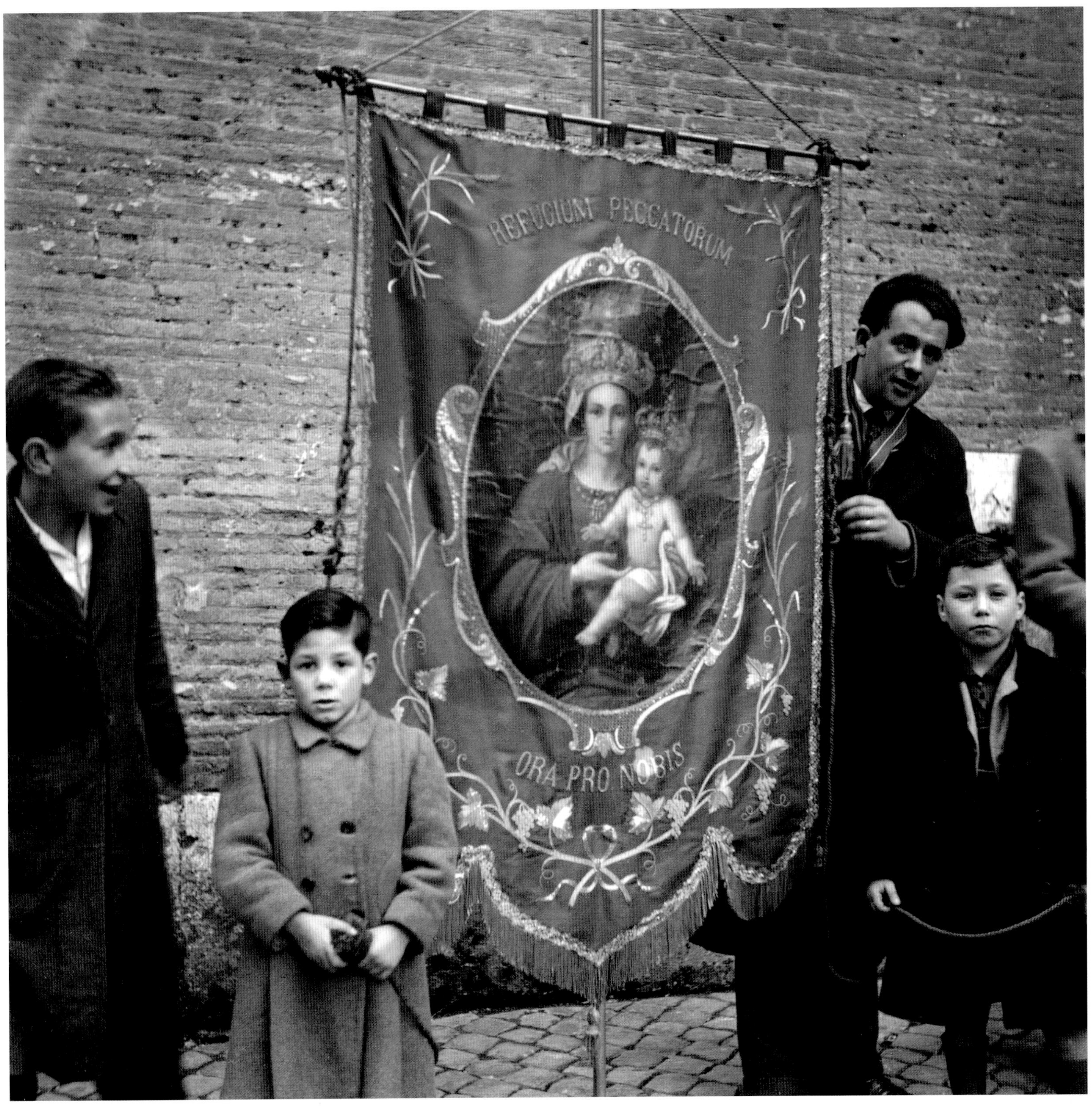

Boys with a banner, 1950s

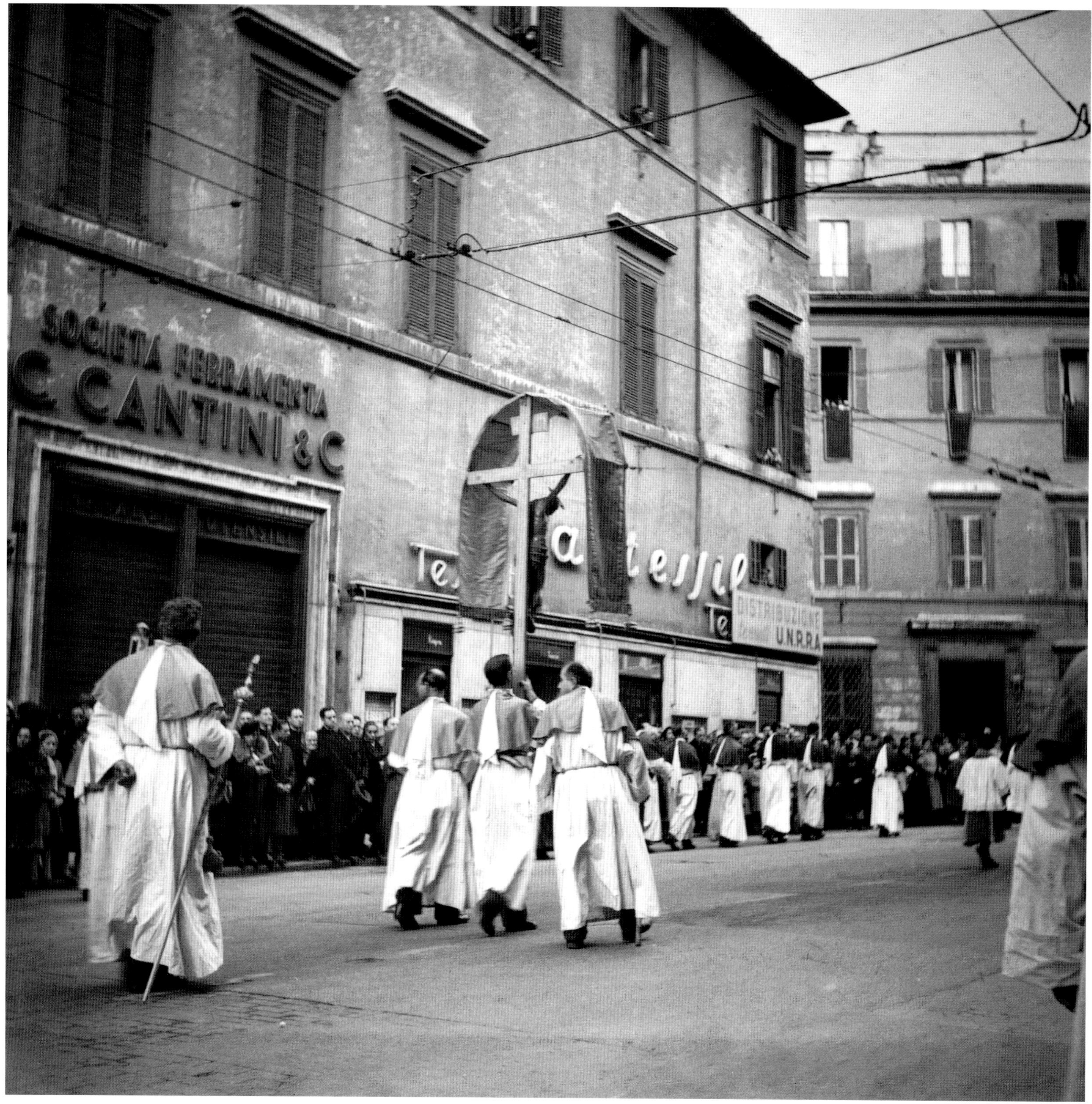

Religious procession, 1950s

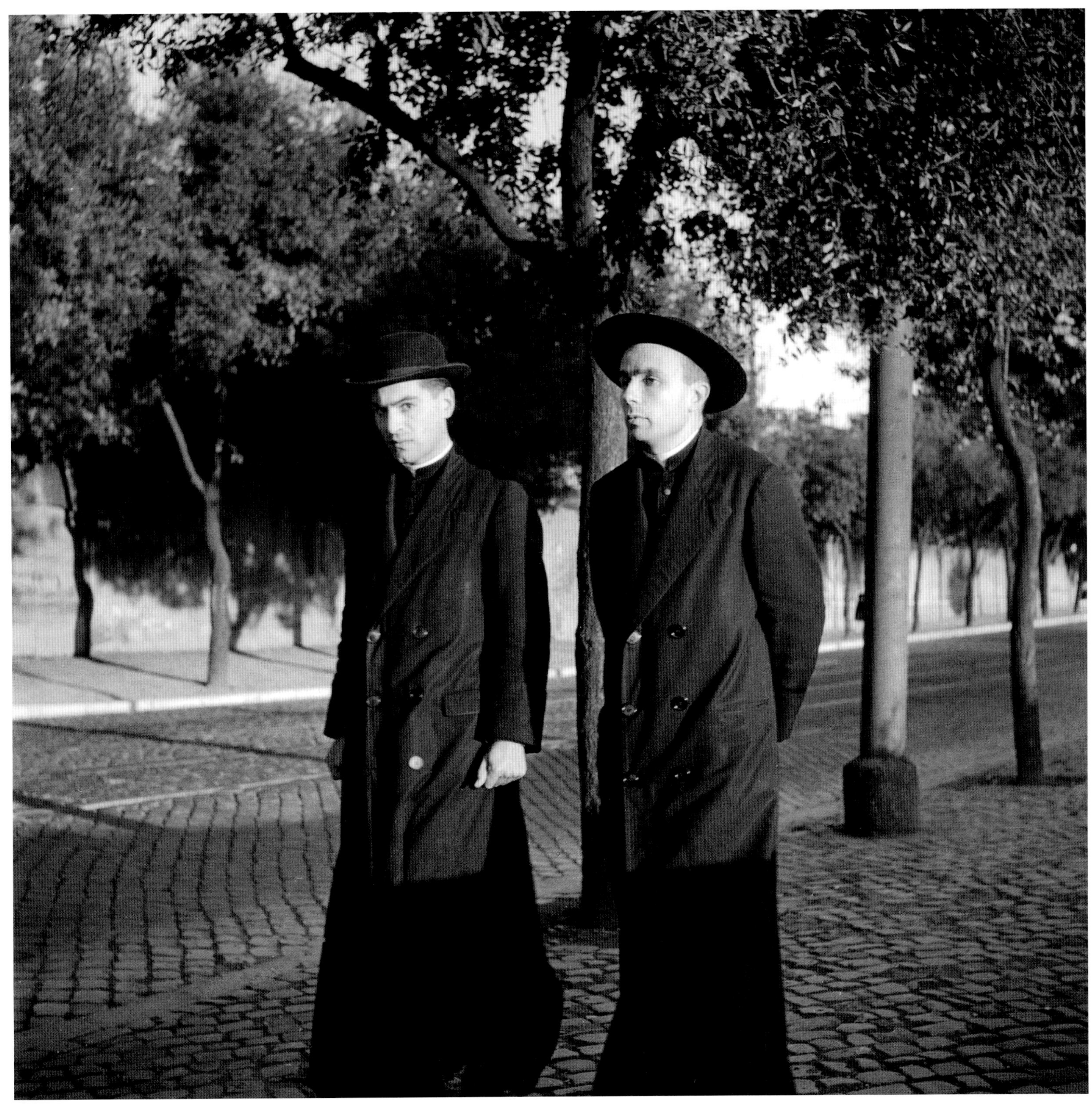

In the park of the Villa Borghese, 1950s

Page 153: Girl at a mirror, 1950s

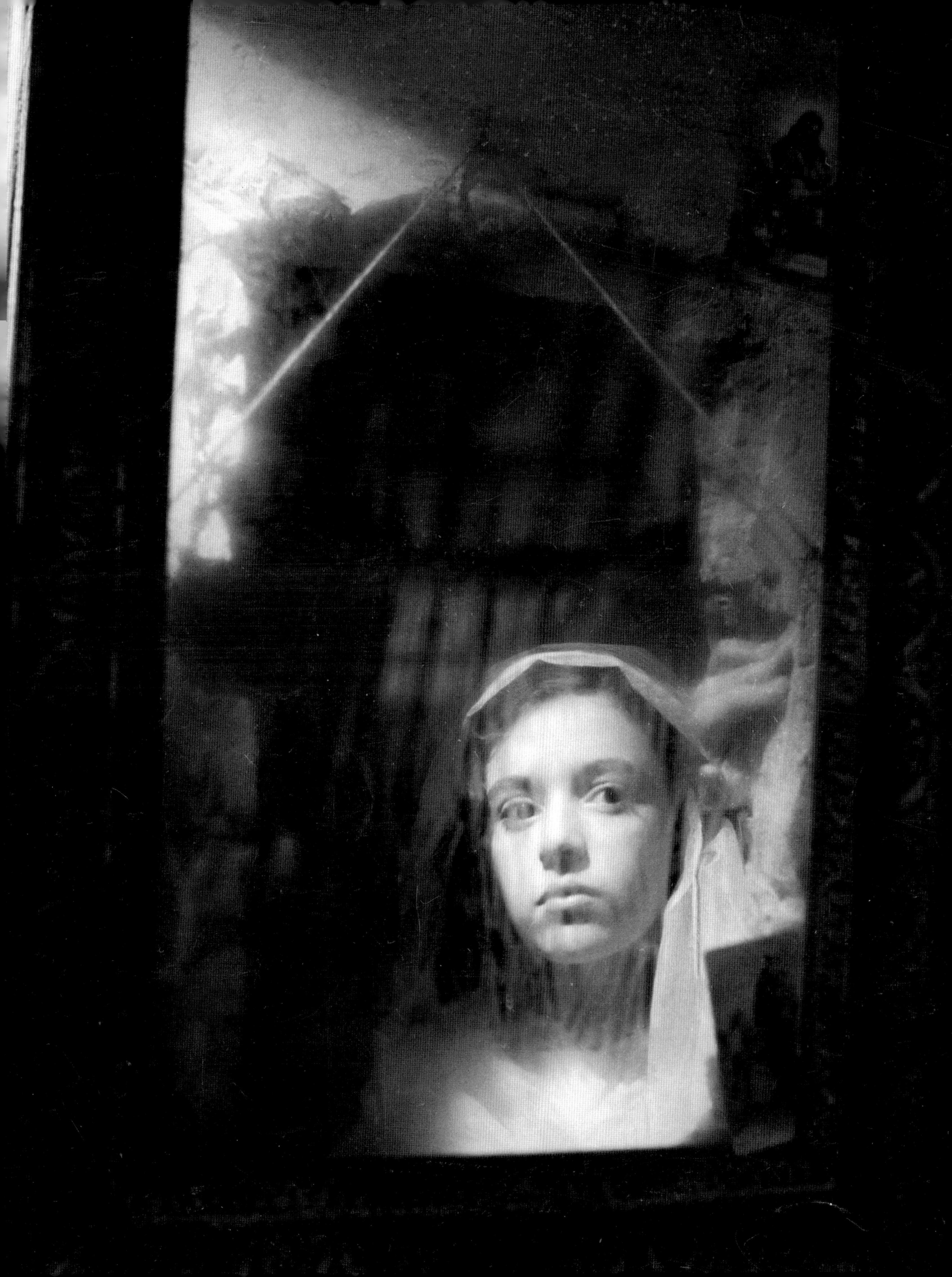

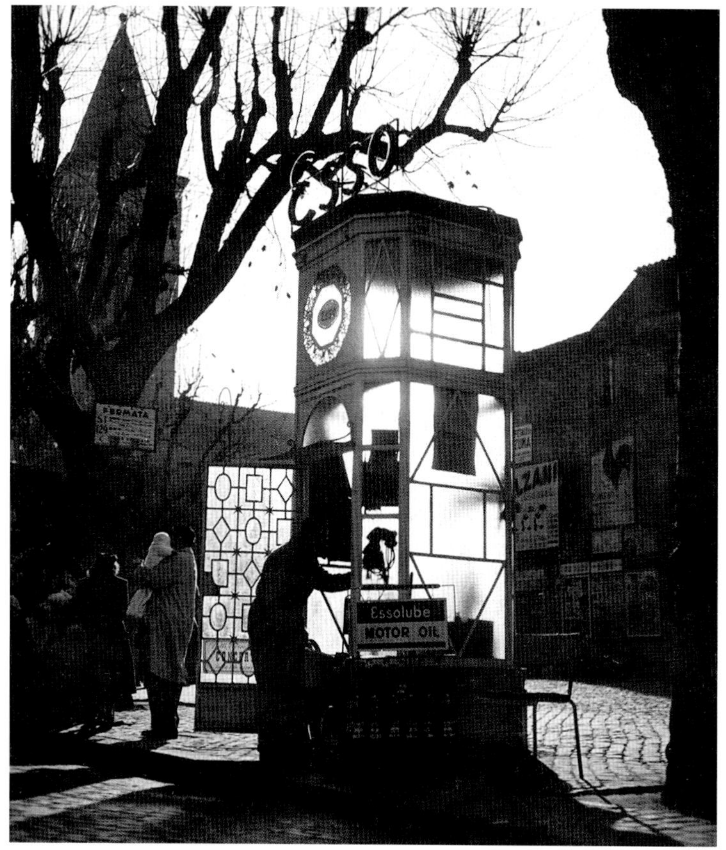

Petrol pump, 1950s

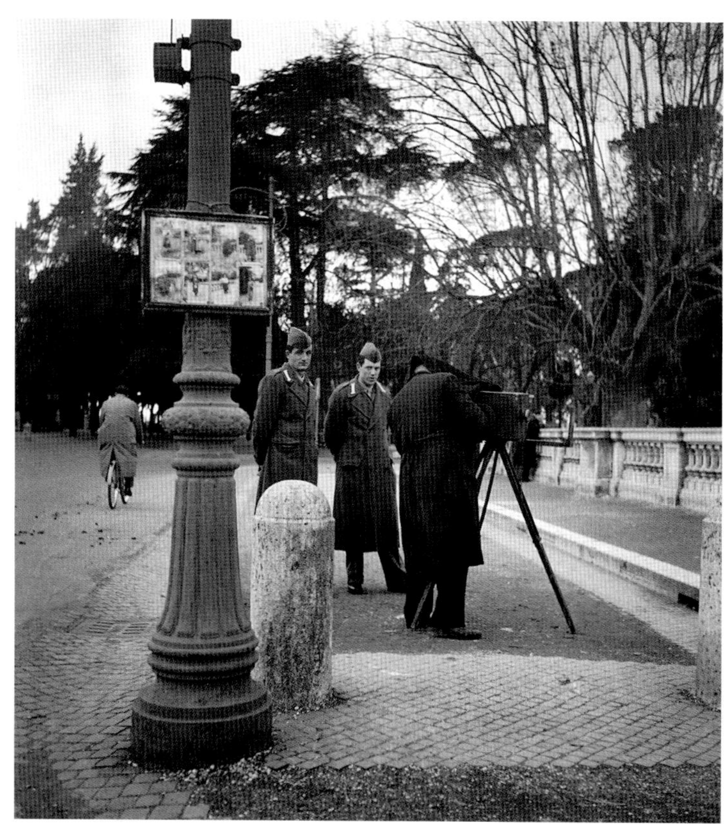

Street photographer, 1950s

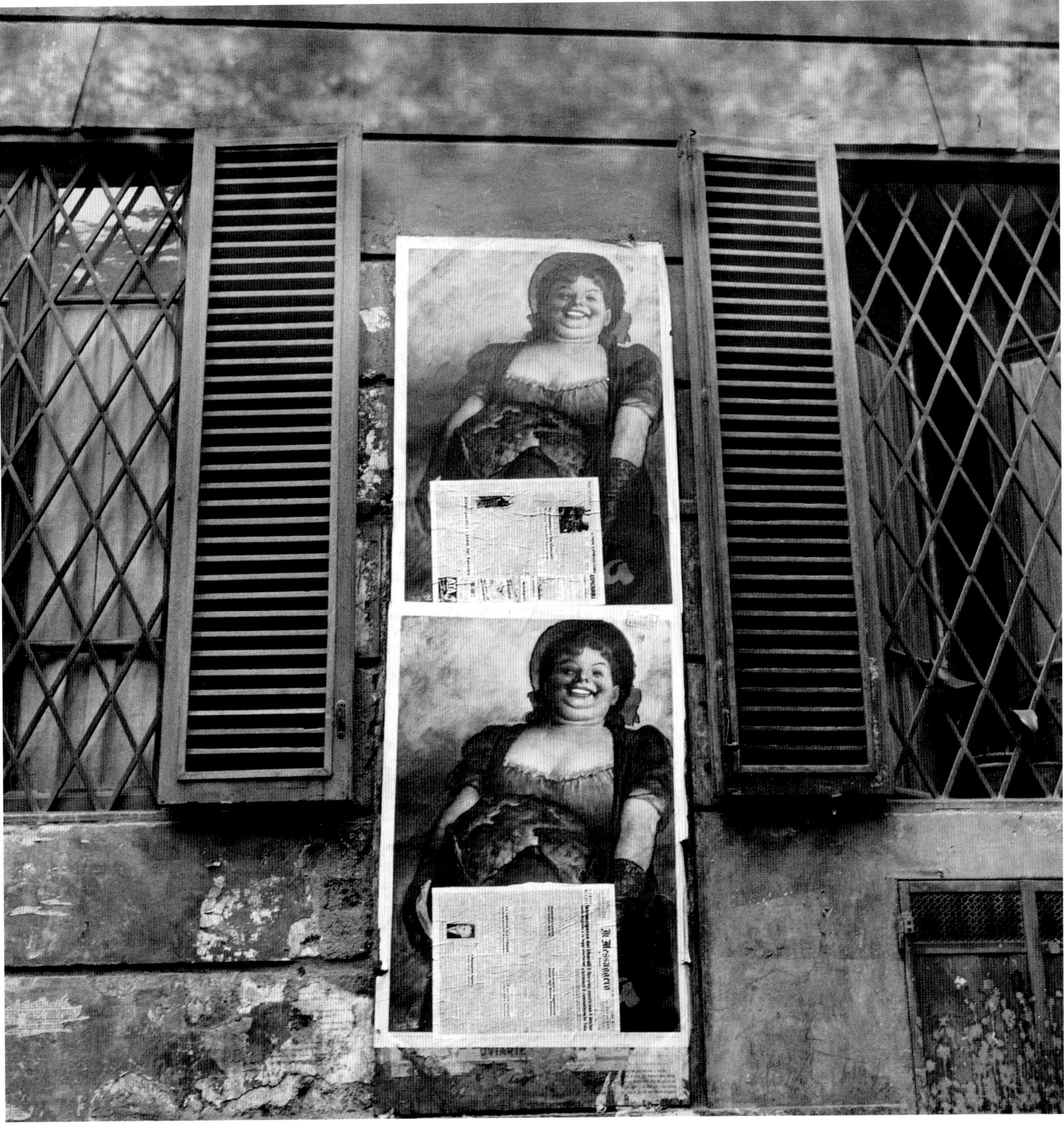

Posters, 1950s

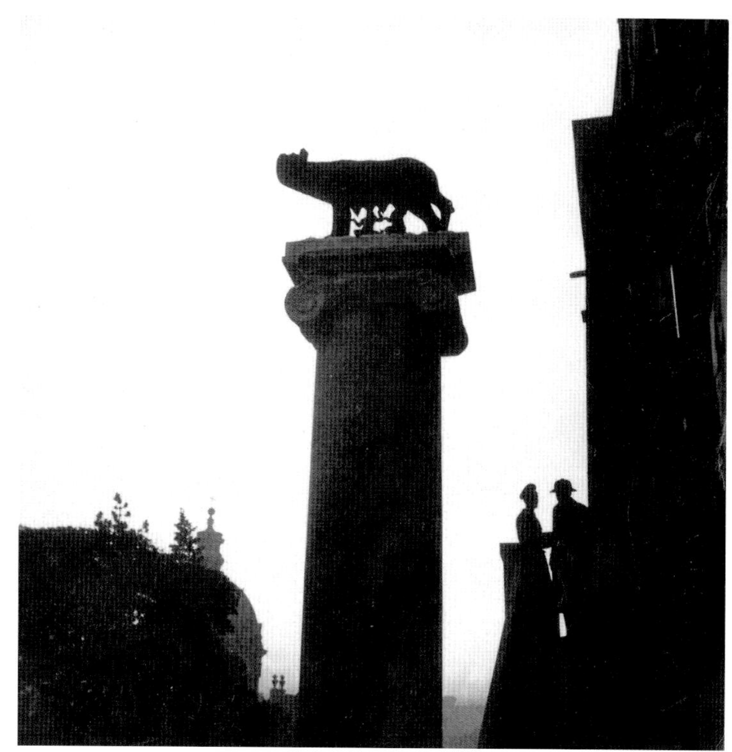

Statue of Romulus and Remus, 1950s

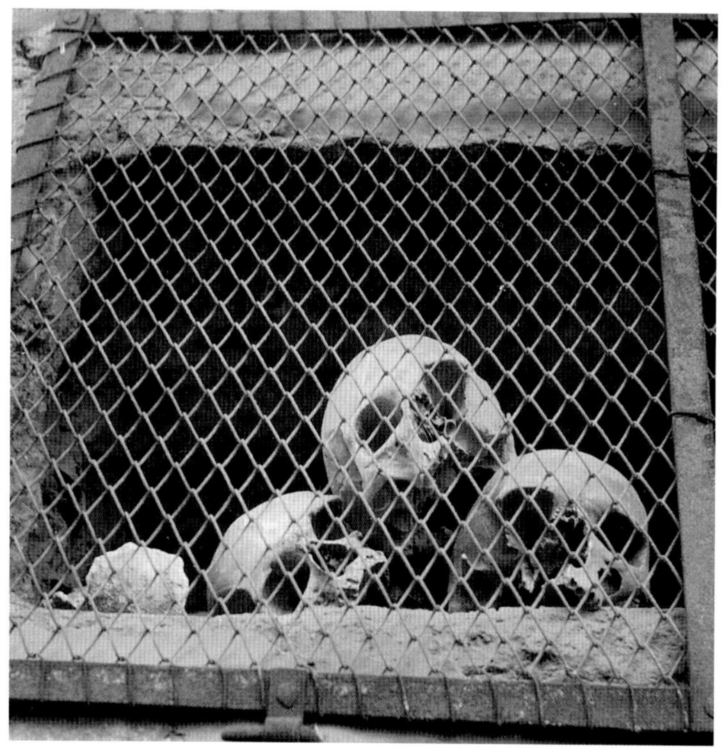

Skulls of the Martyrs, the Forum, 1950s

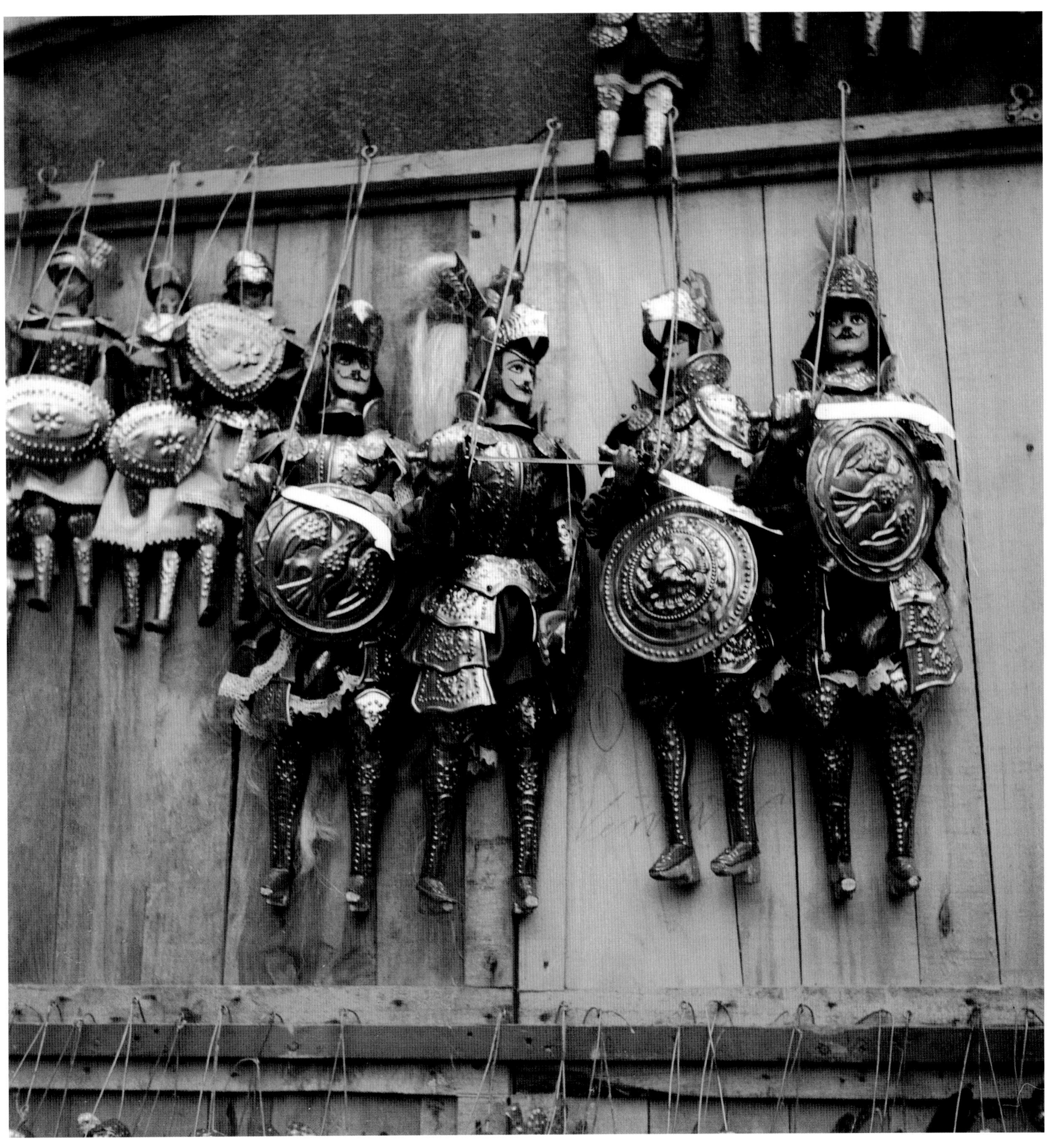

Sicilian marionettes at the Epiphany fair, c. 1950

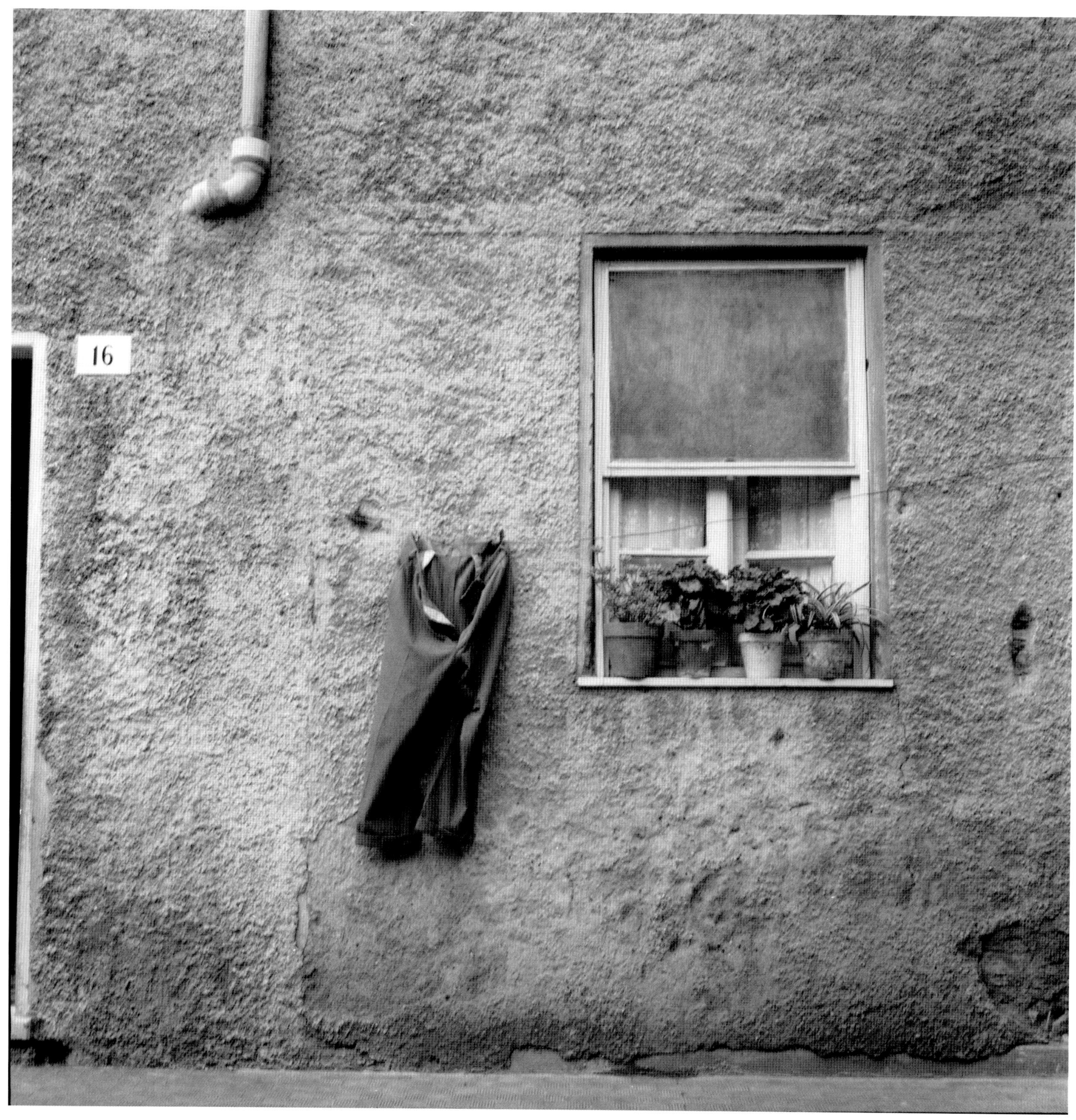

Out to dry, 1950s

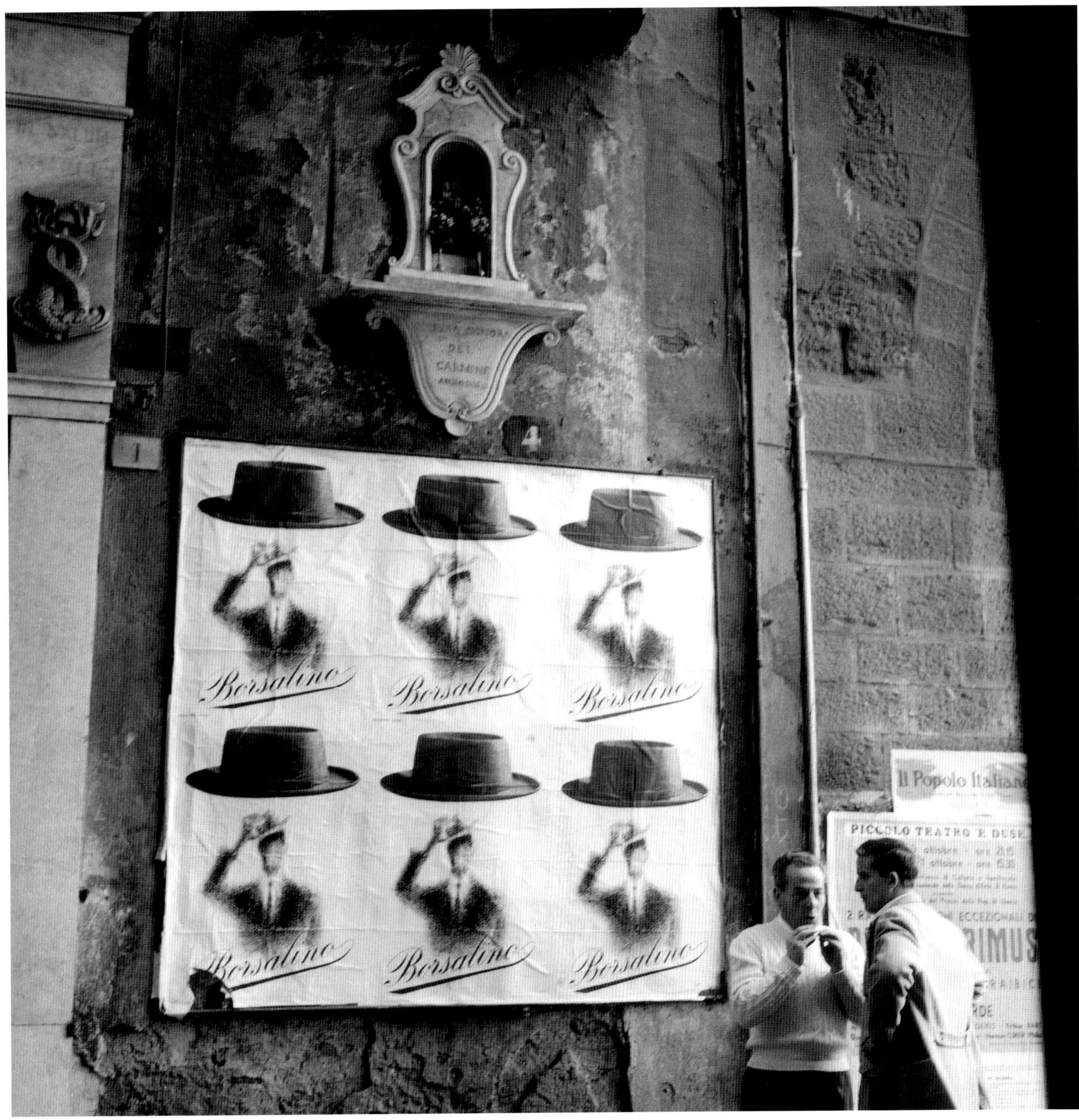

Street poster advertising Borsalino hats, 1950s

Page 161: Girl in carnival costume, *c.* 1950

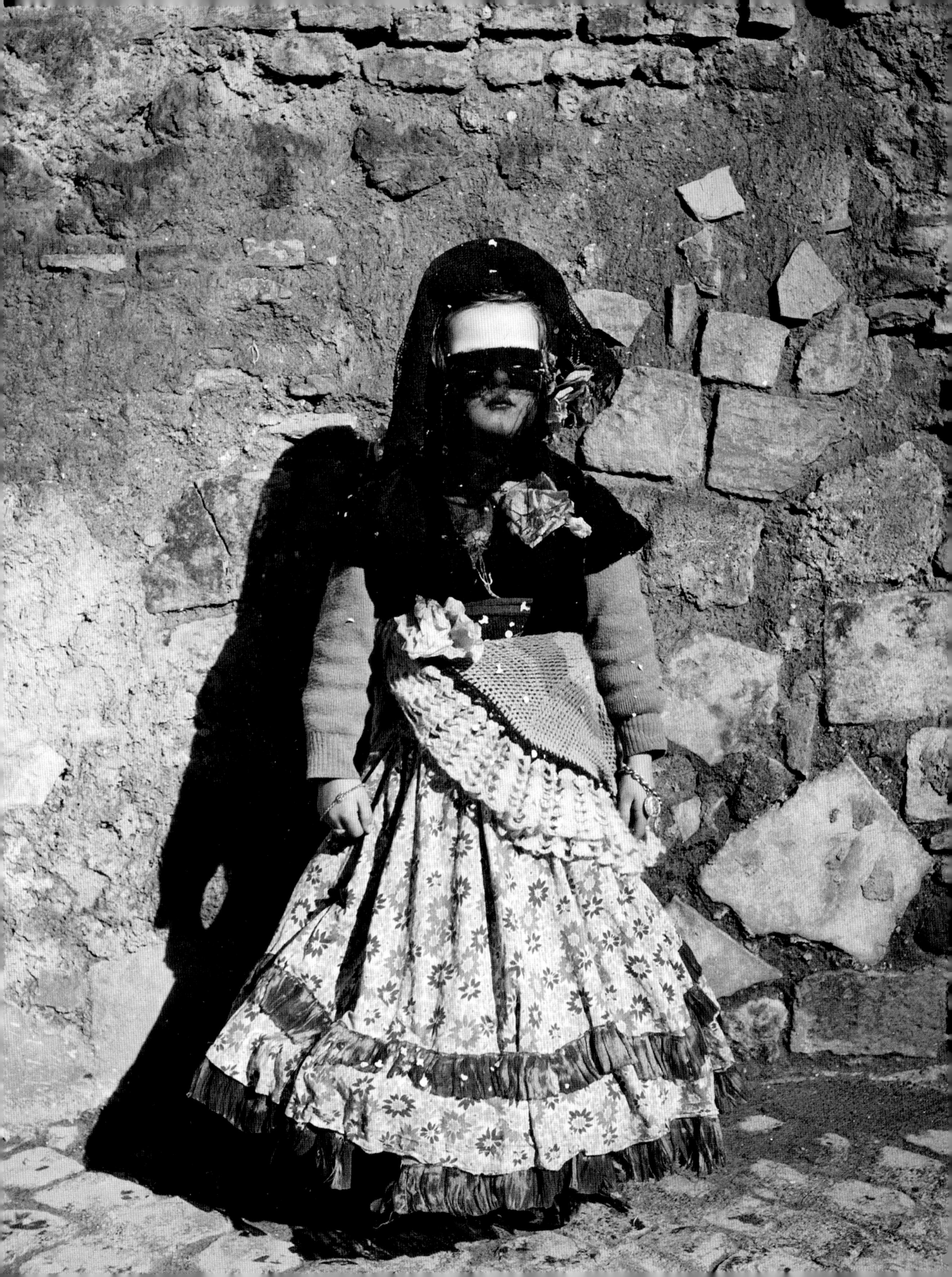

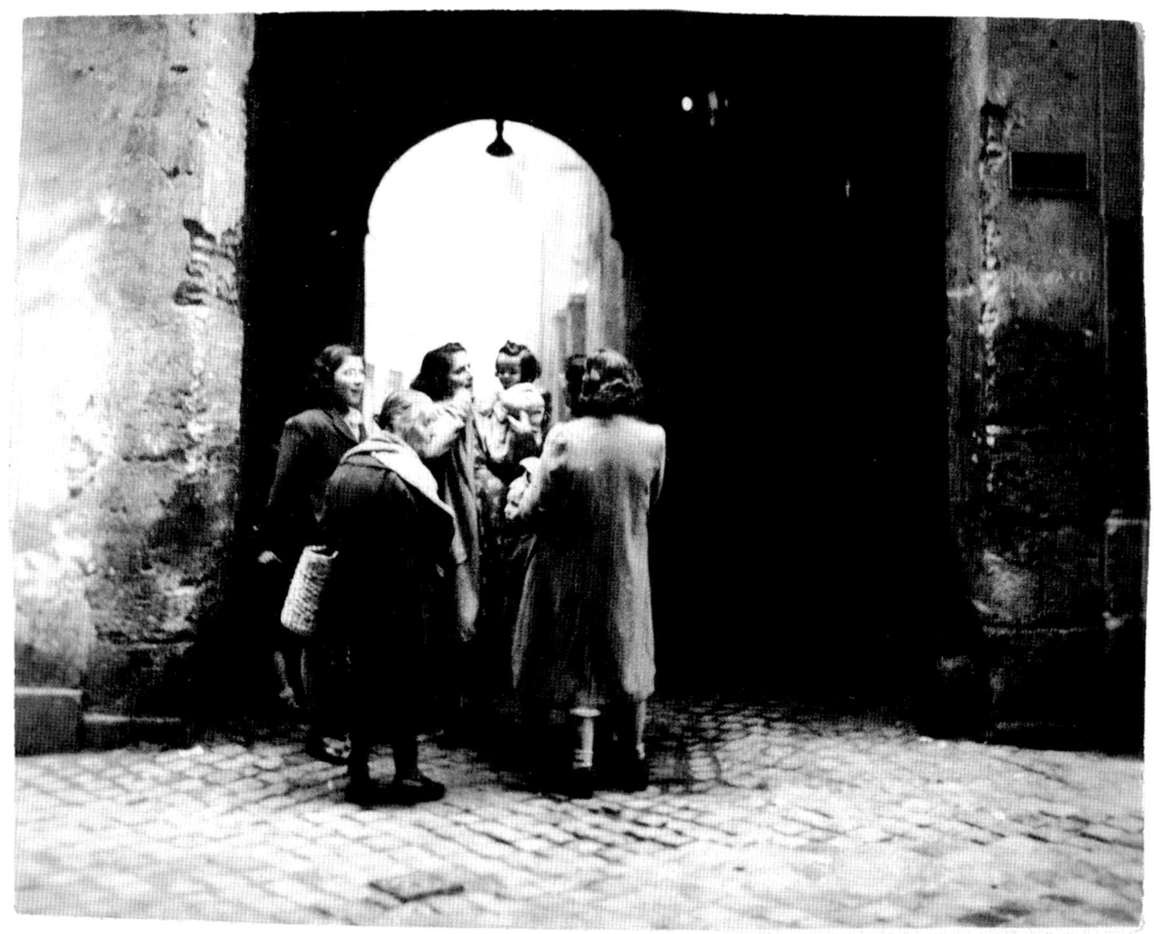

On the way to the market, 1950s

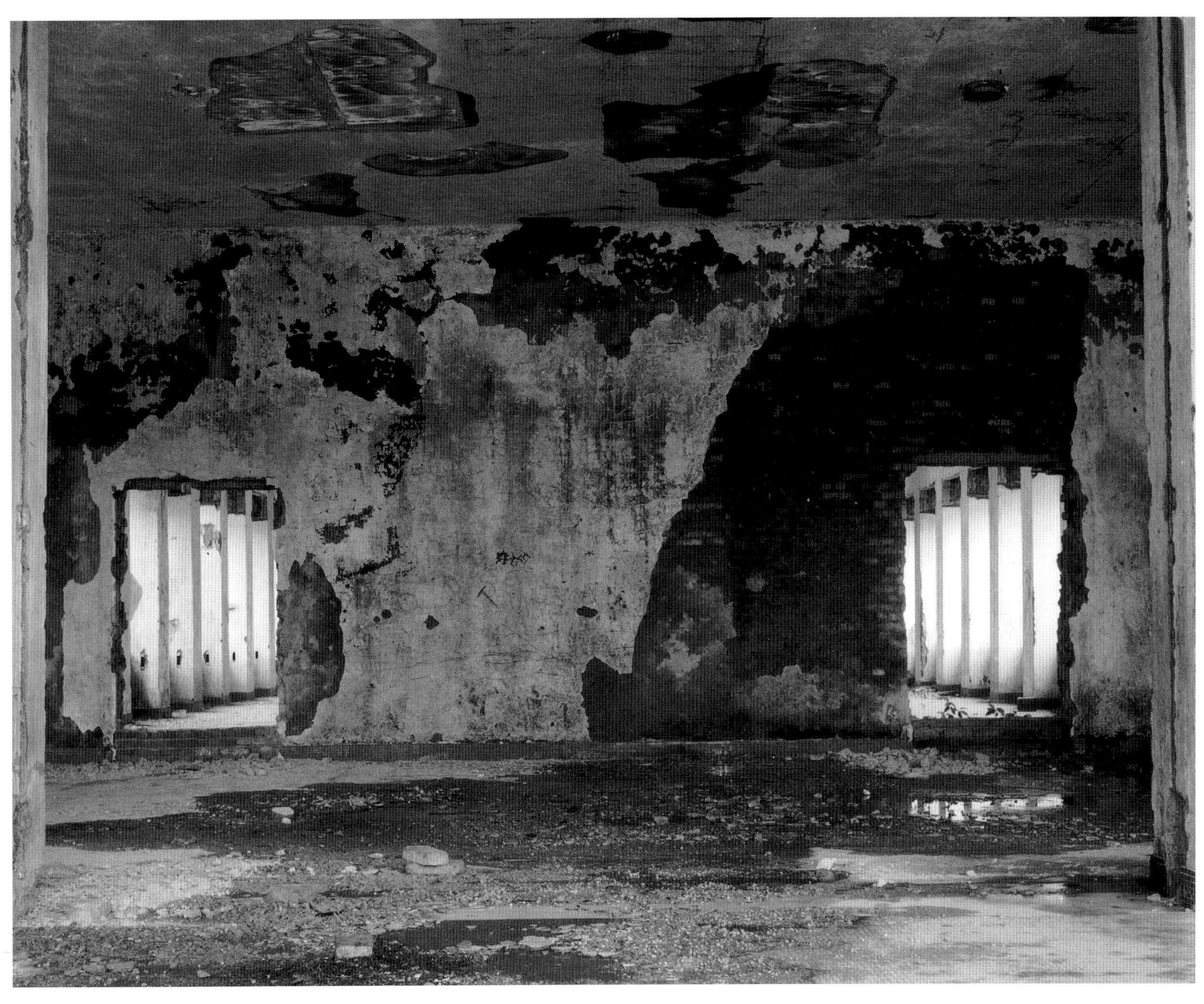

Ruined fascist stadium, c. 1950

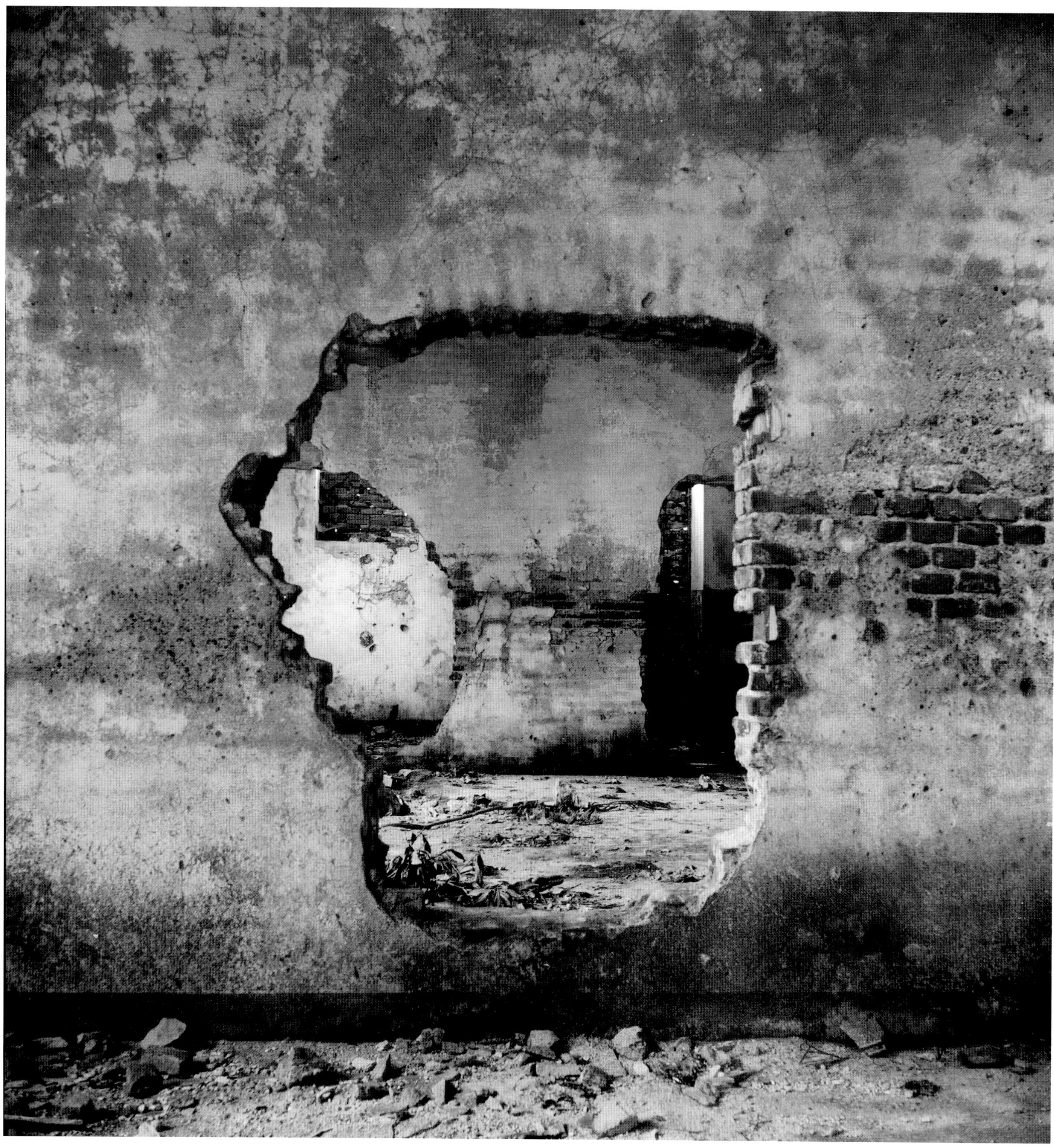

Ruined fascist stadium, c. 1950

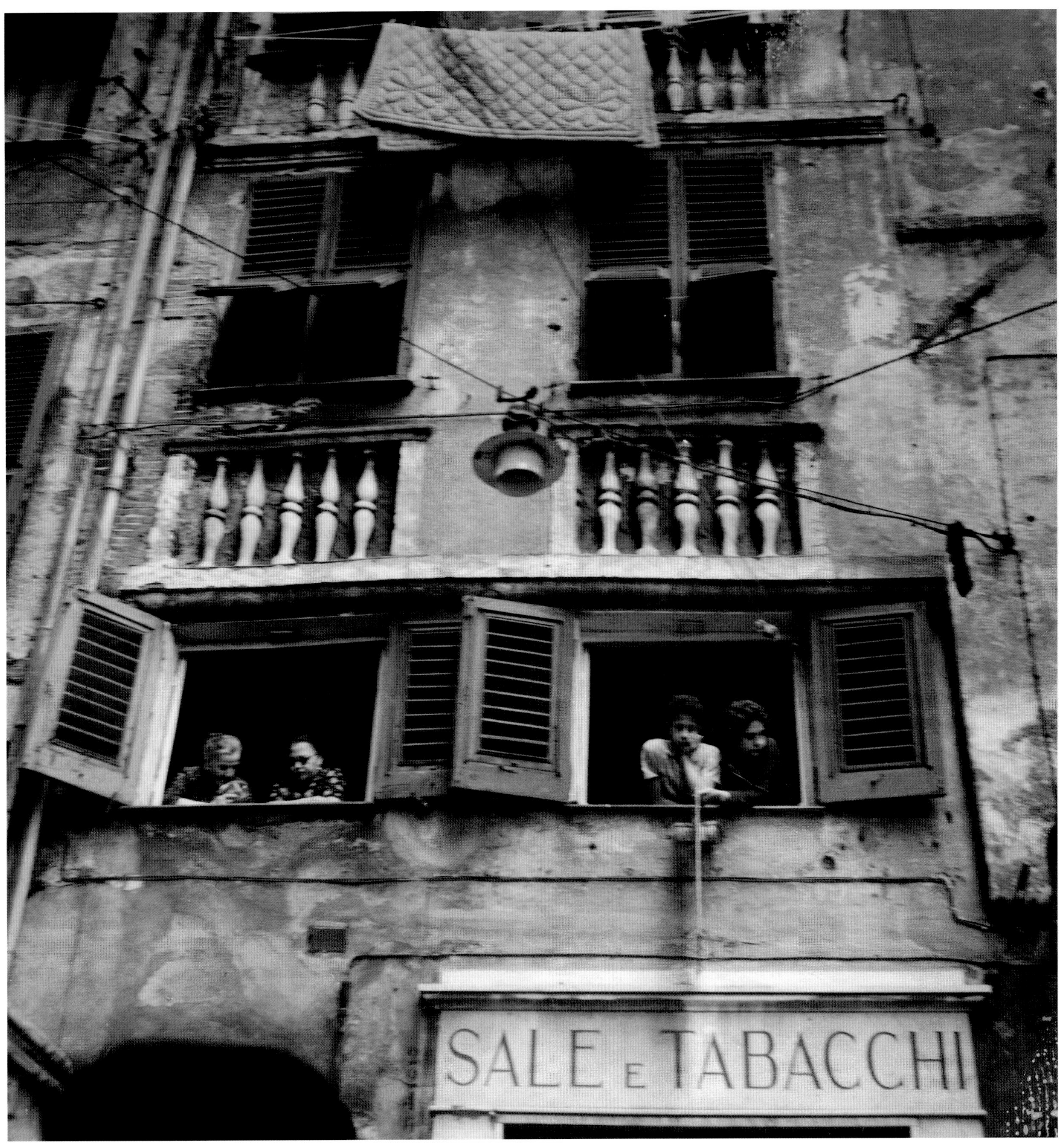

Above the tobacconist's, 1950s

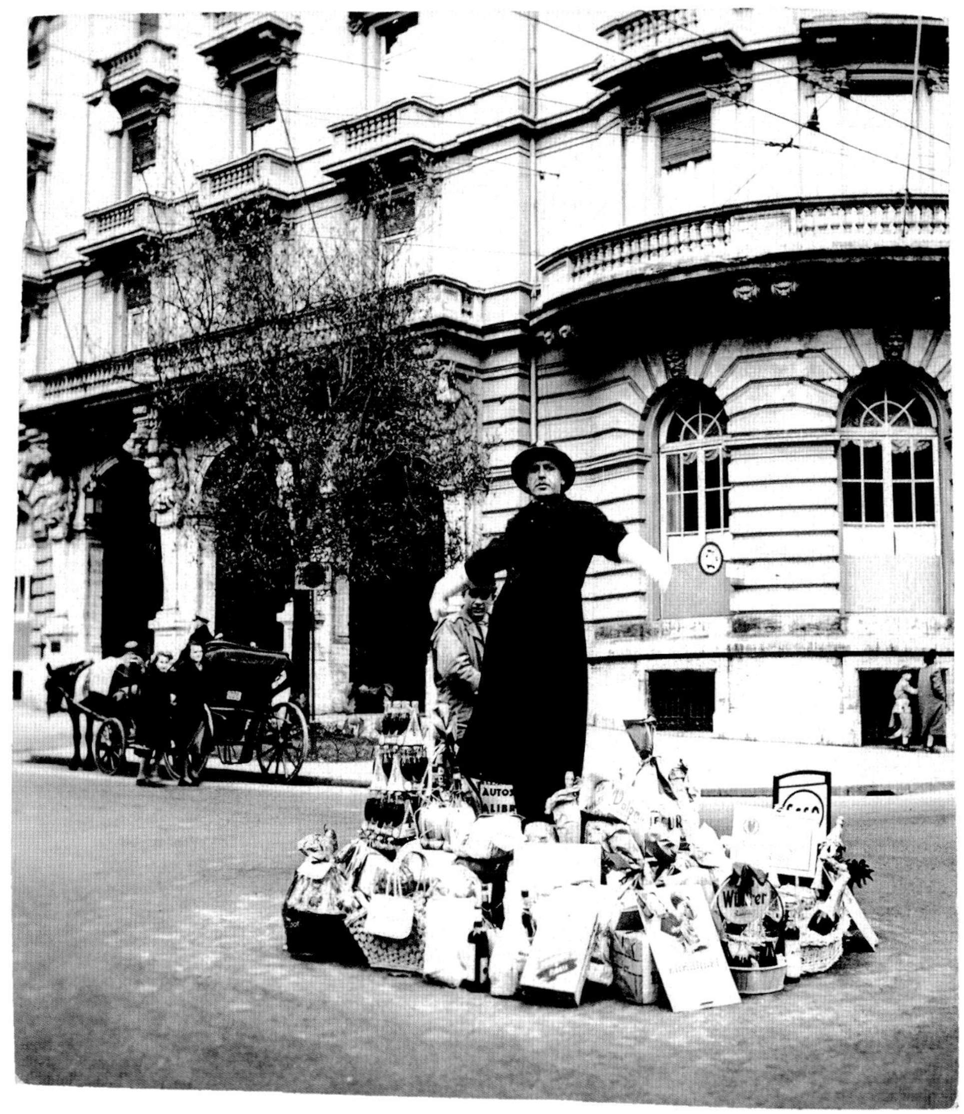

Traffic policeman, 1950s

Opposite: Boys on an ancient Roman ruin, 1950s

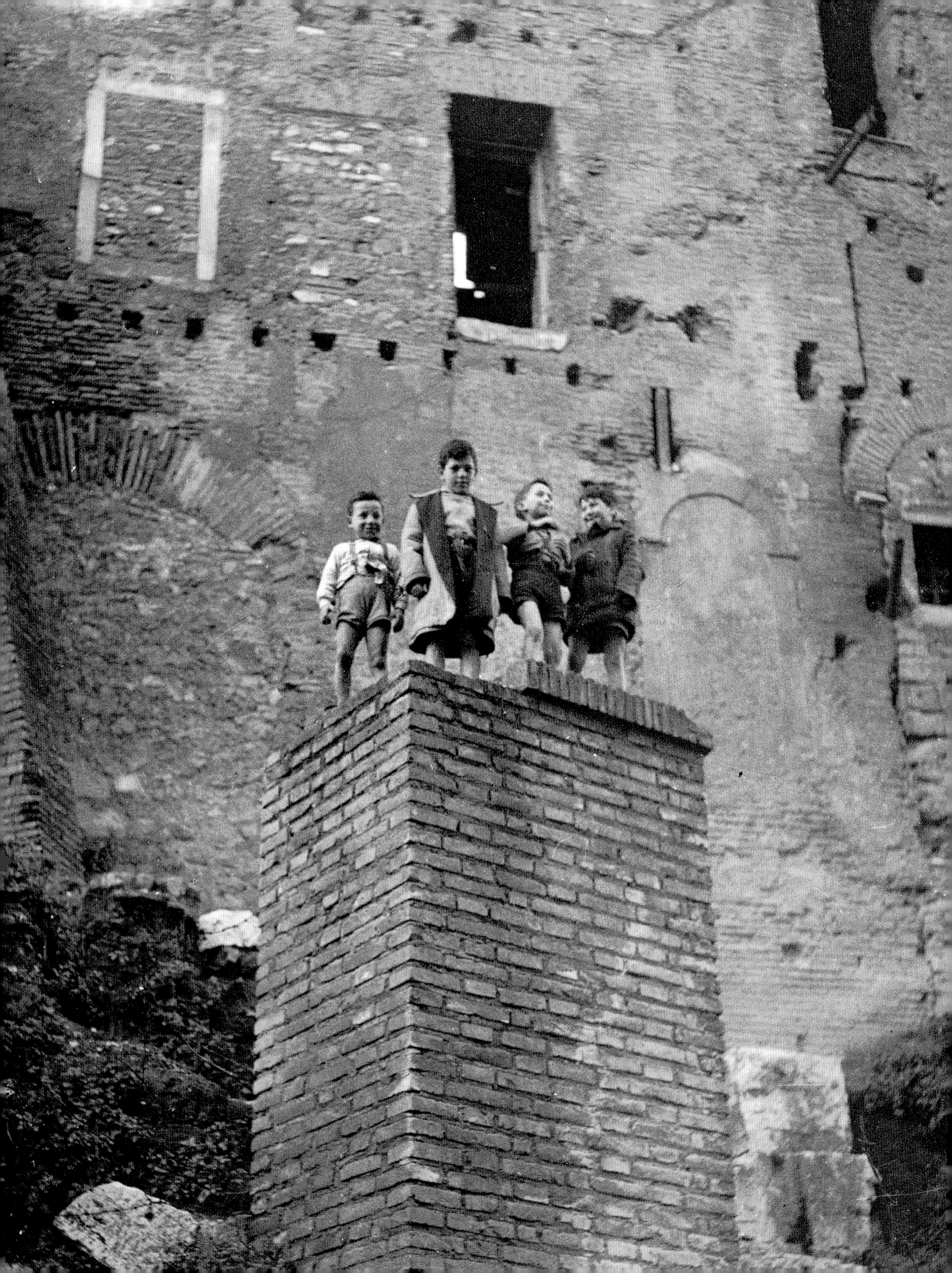

Opposite: Piazza del Campidoglio, Capitoline Museum, 1950s

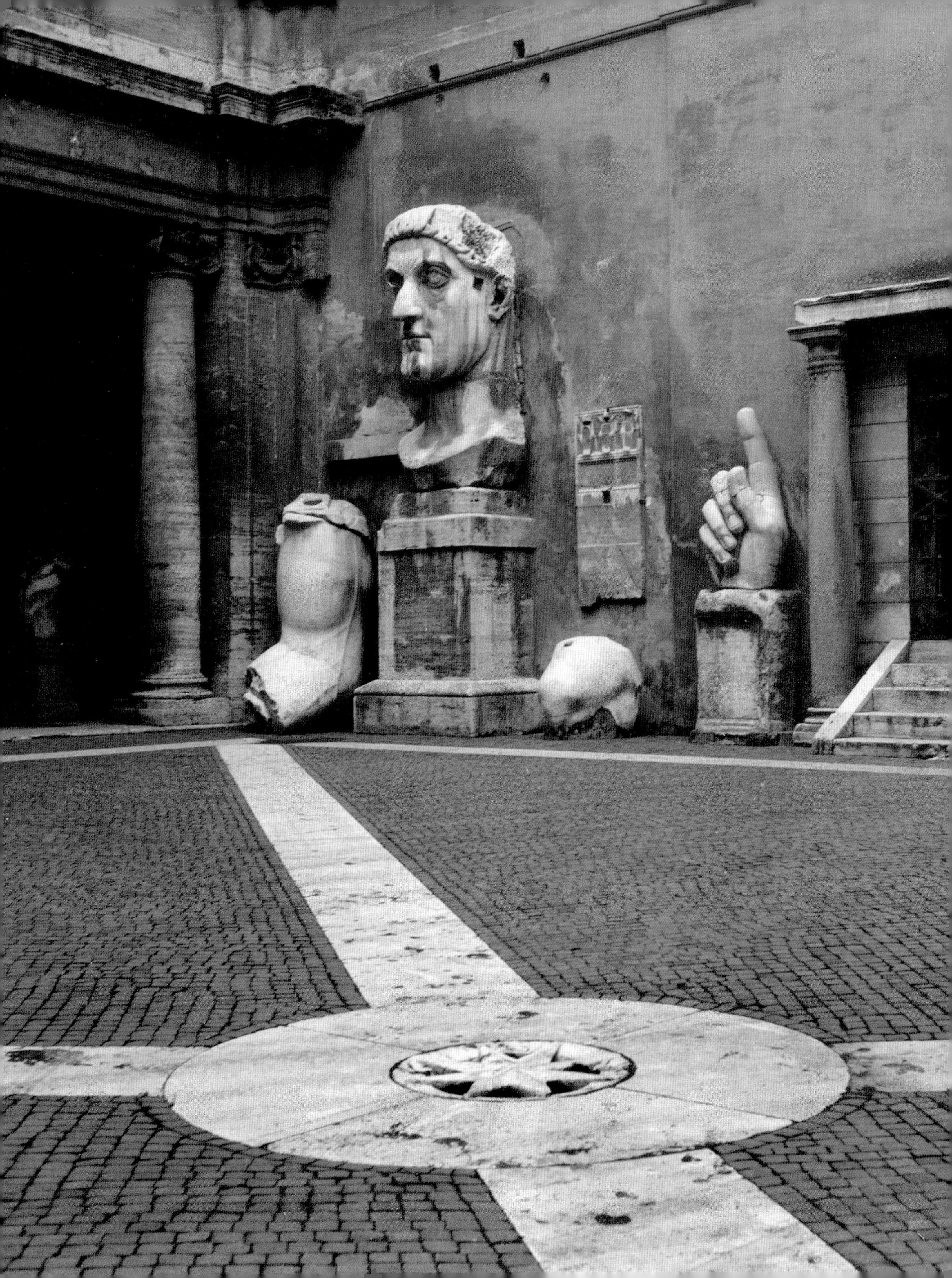

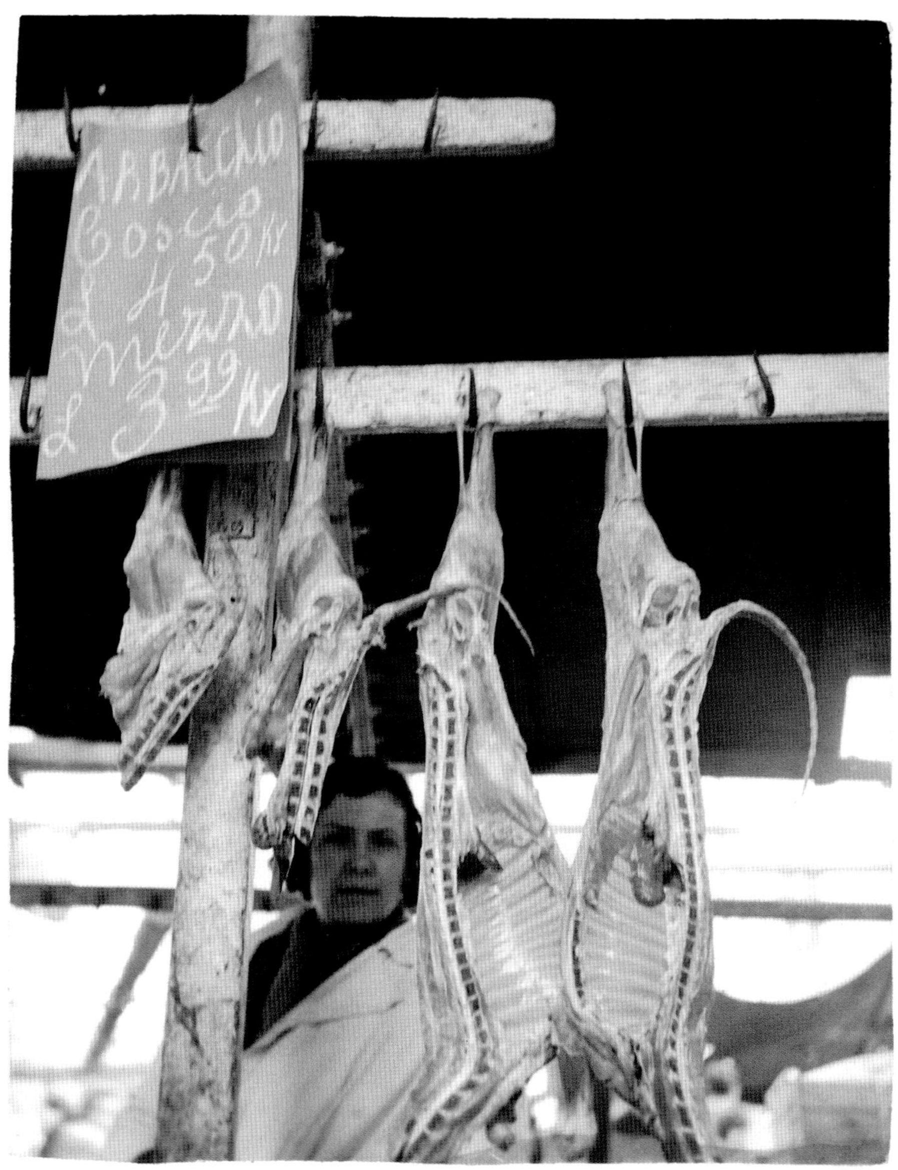

Spring lamb for sale, Campo dei Fiori, 1950s

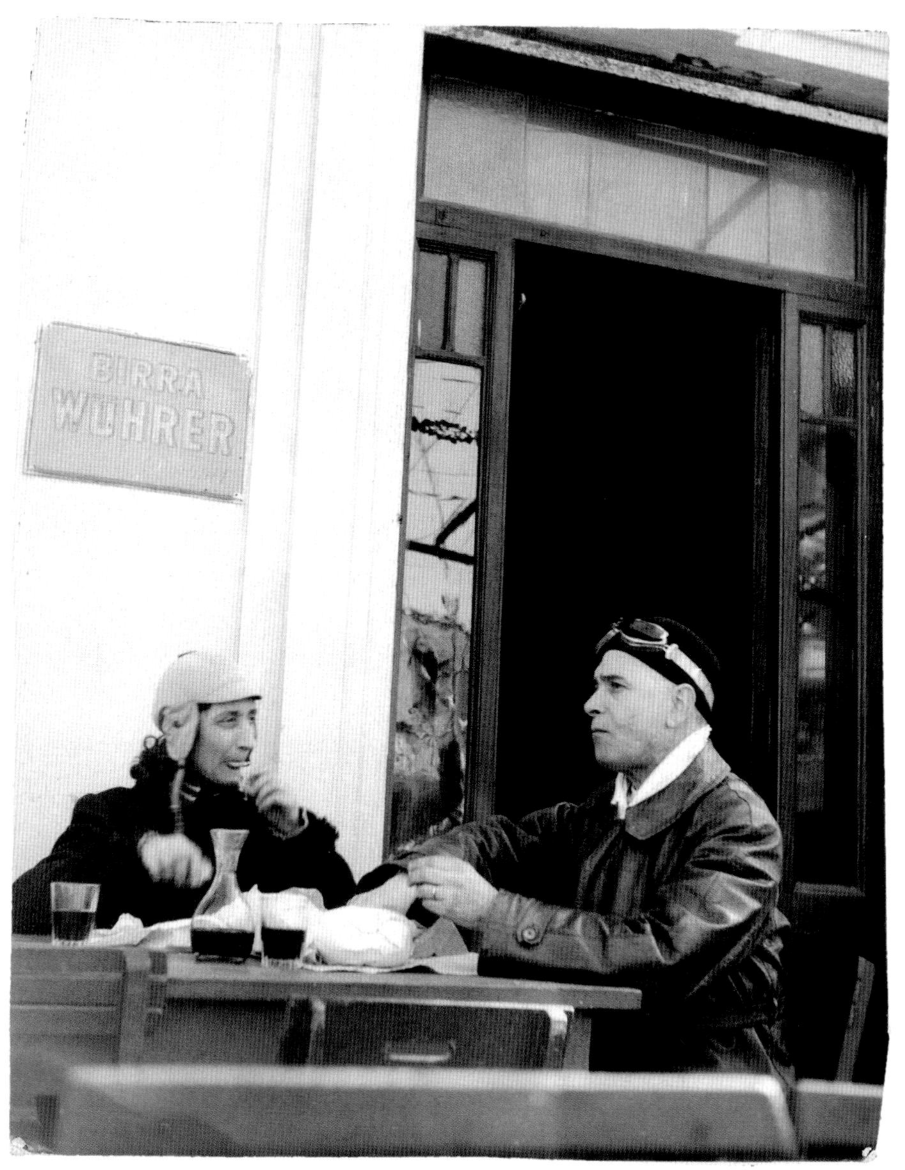

Cyclists at a café table, 1950s

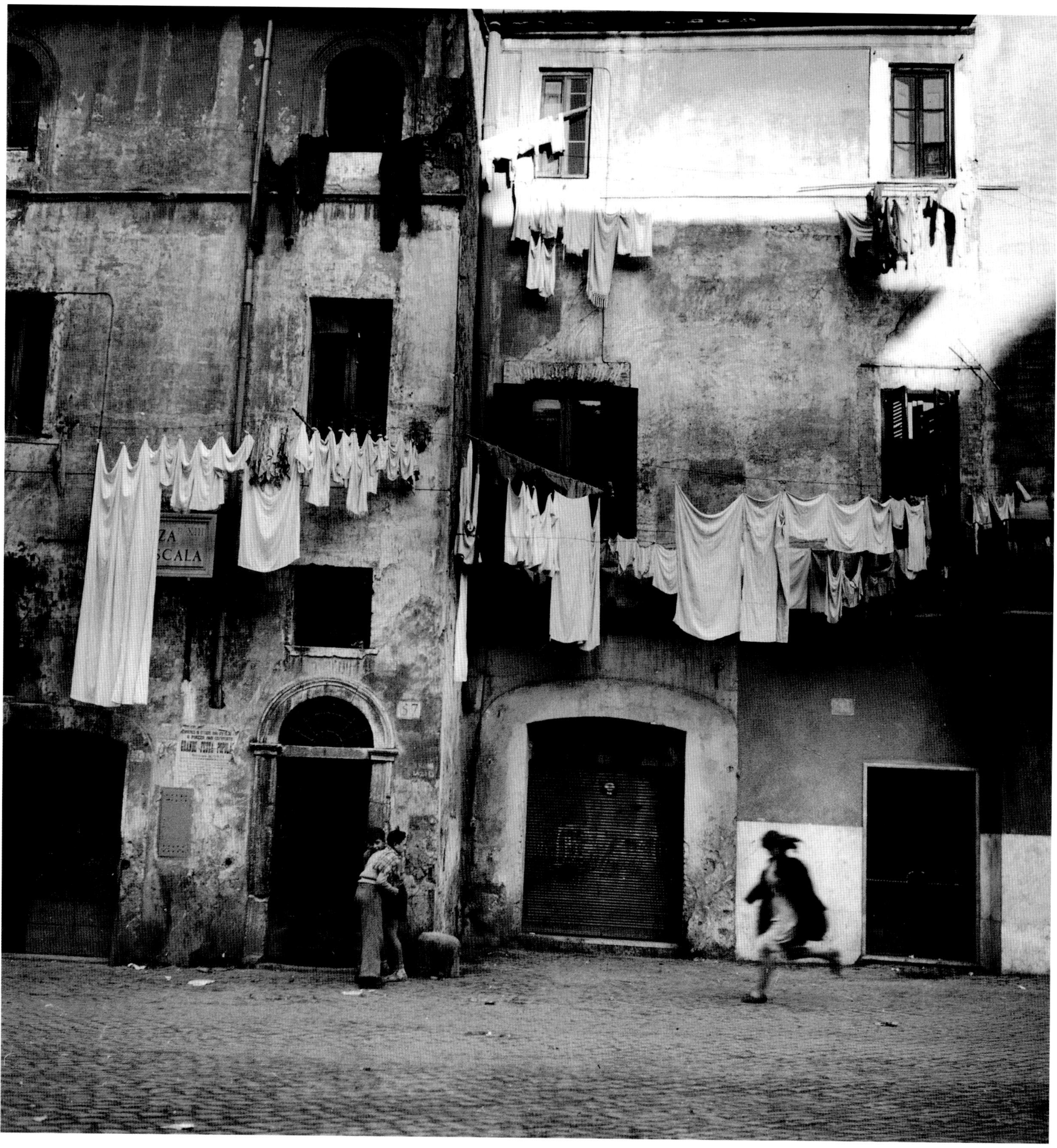

Piazza della Scala, Trastavere, c. 1950

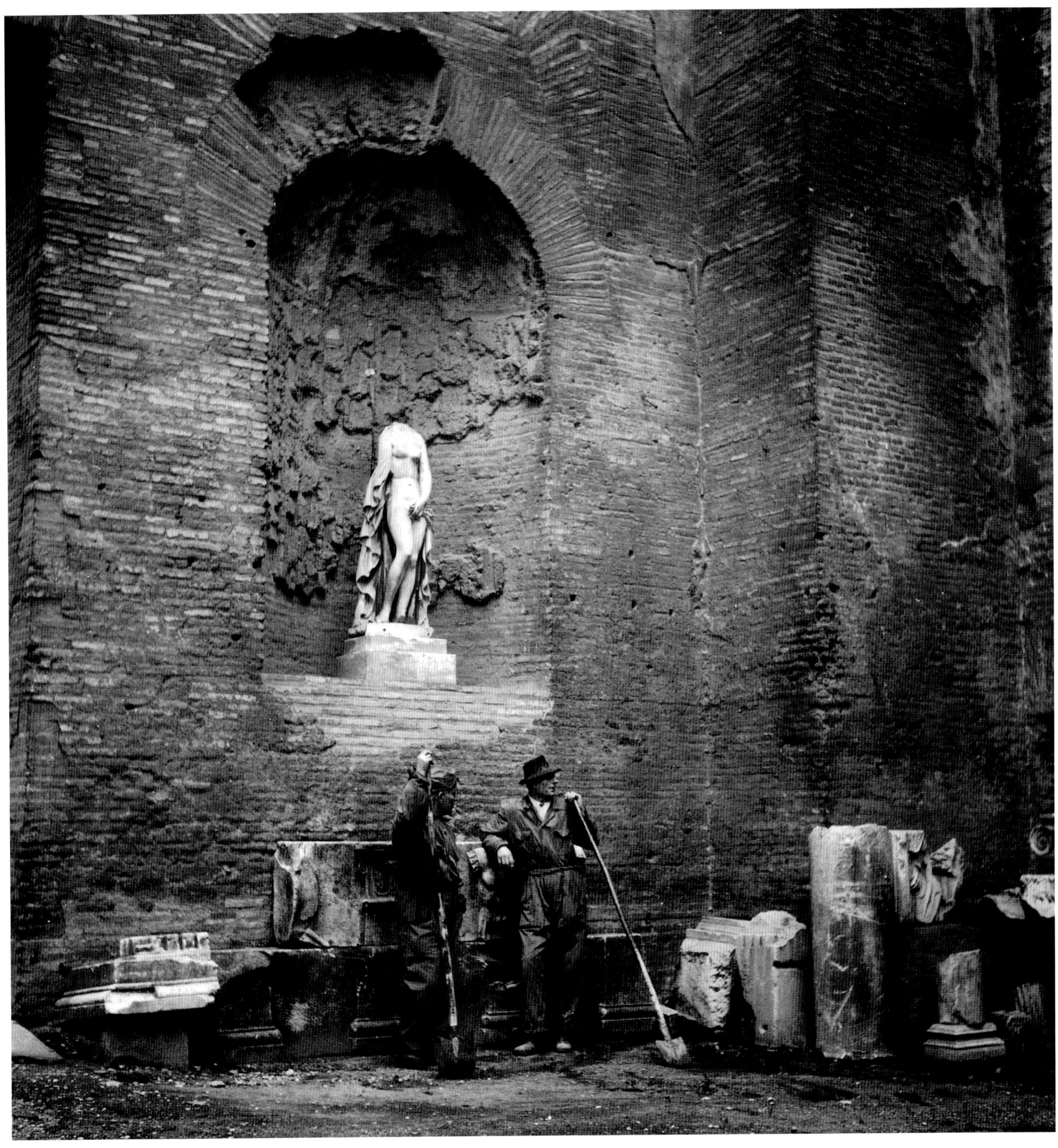

Cleaners at the Terme di Dioclezianus, 1950s

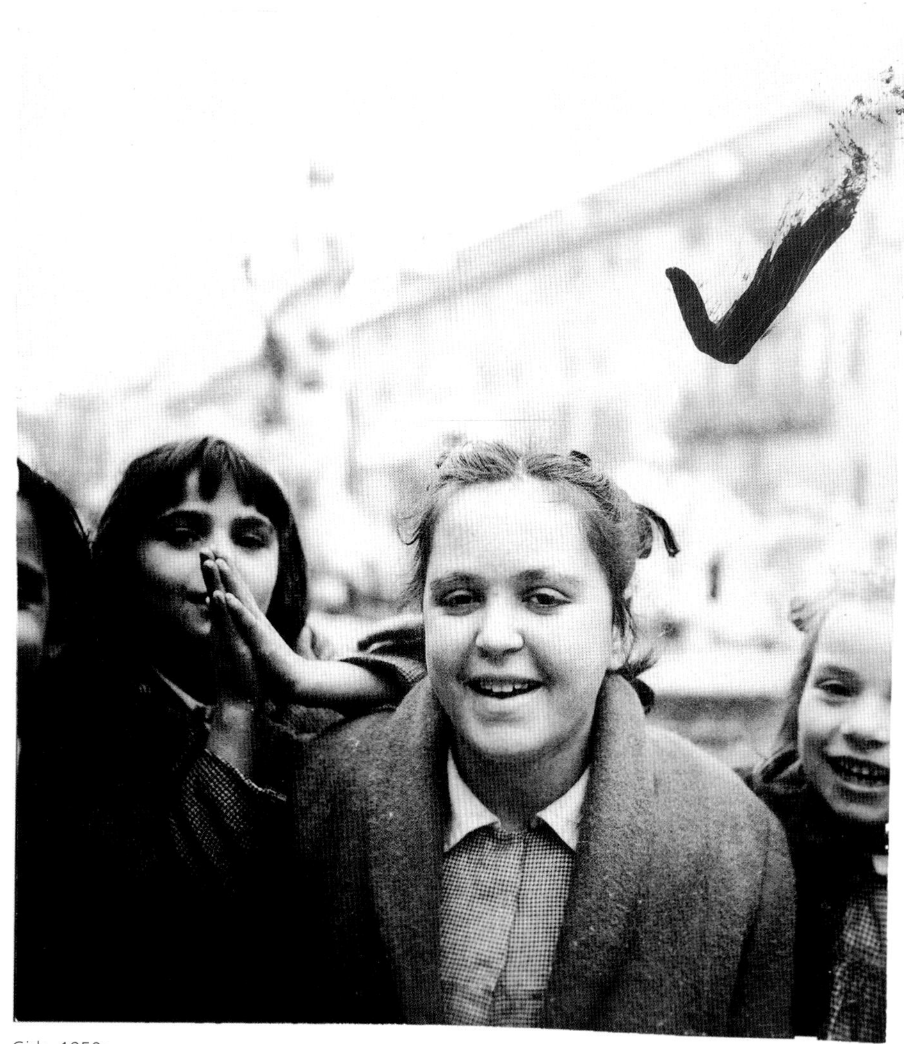

Girls, 1950s

Opposite: Fountain in the courtyard of the Capitoline Museum, 1950s

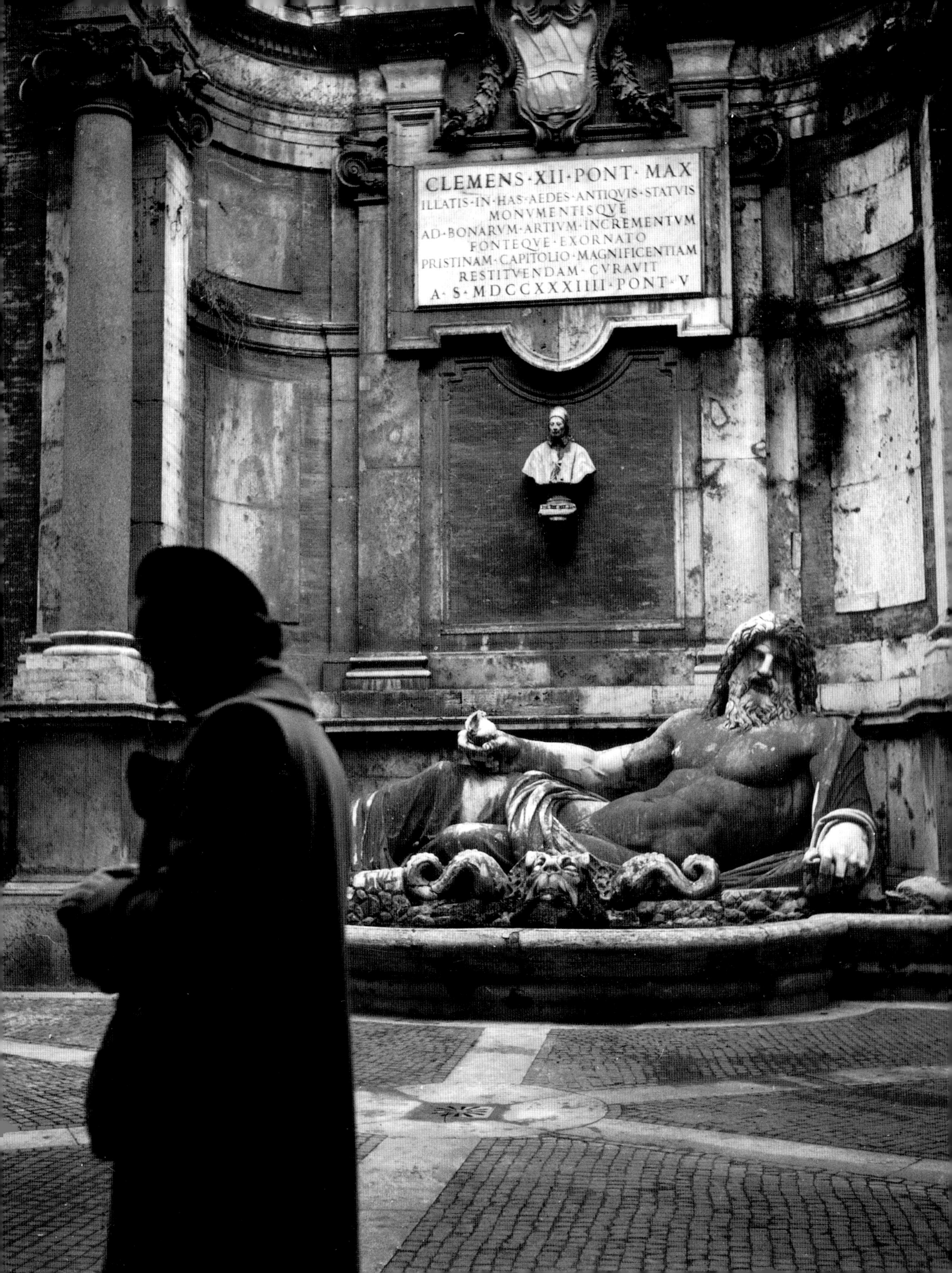
CLEMENS·XII·PONT·MAX
ILLATIS·IN·HAS·AEDES·ANTIQVIS·STATVIS
MONVMENTISQVE
AD·BONARVM·ARTIVM·INCREMENTVM
FONTEQVE·EXORNATO
PRISTINAM·CAPITOLIO·MAGNIFICENTIAM
RESTITVENDAM·CVRAVIT
A·S·MDCCXXXIIII·PONT·V

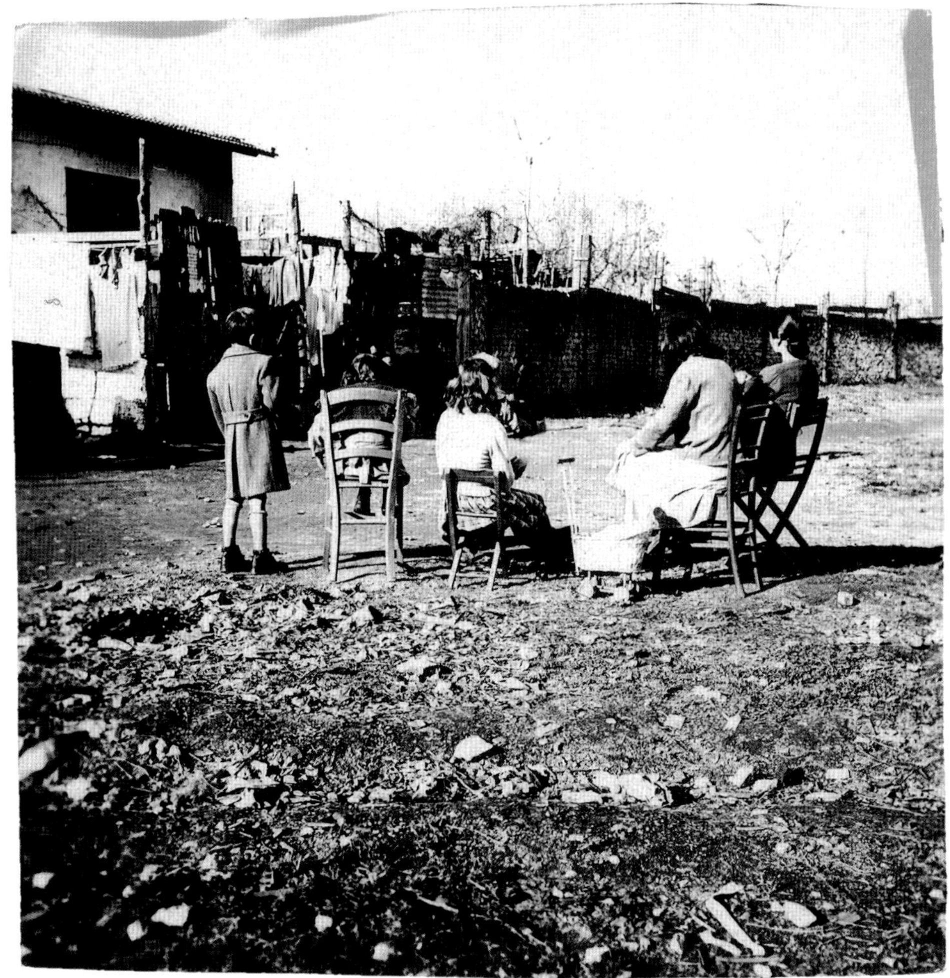

Terme di Caracalla, 1950s

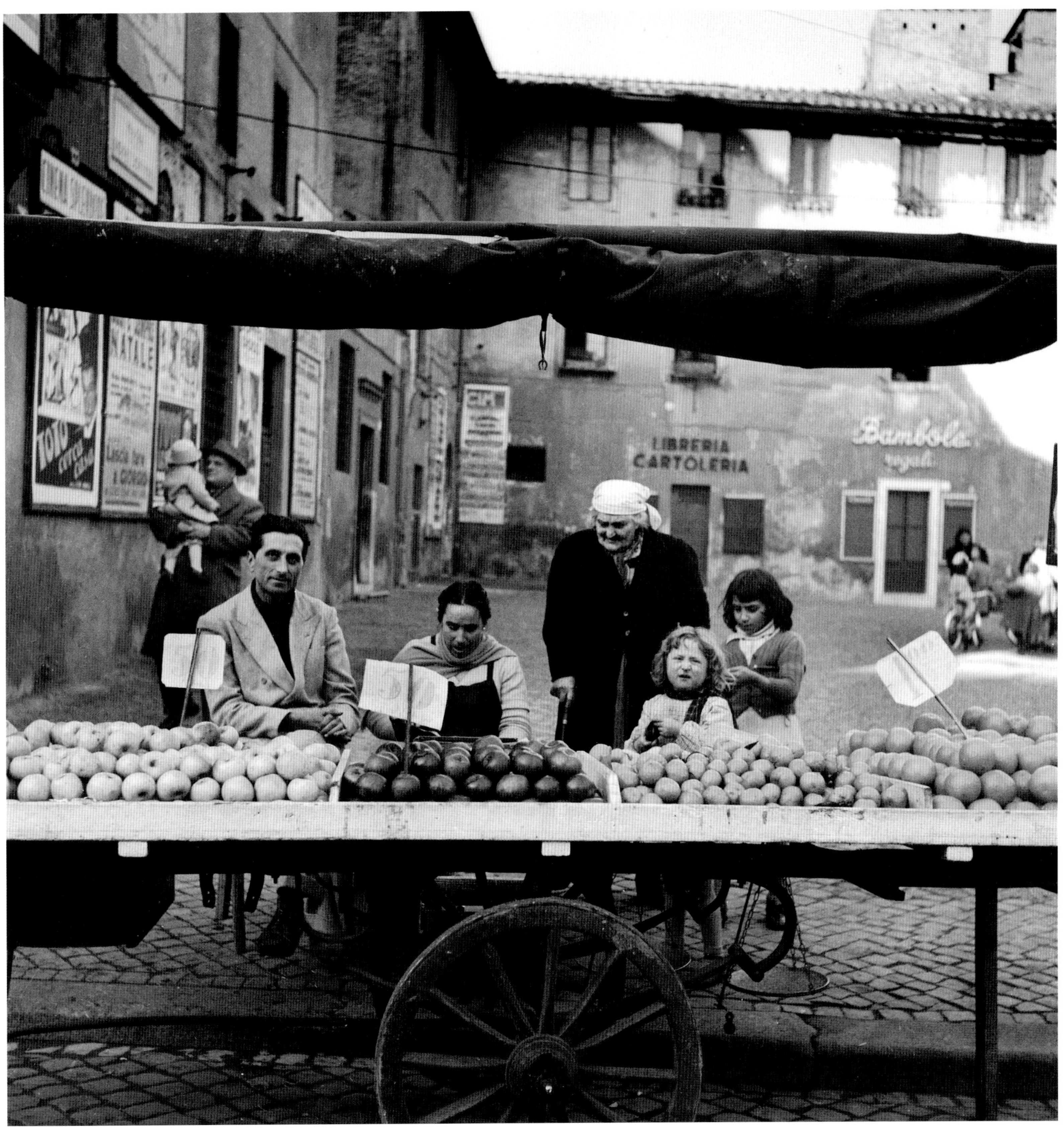

Market stall, 1950s

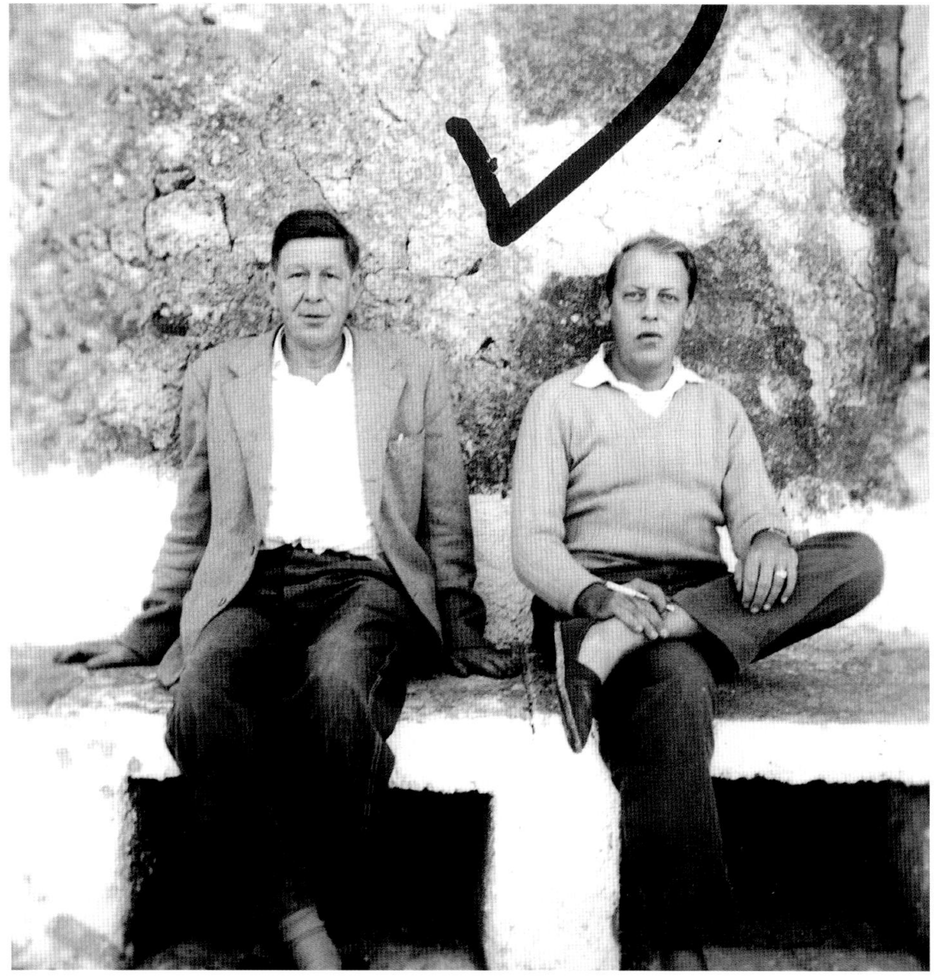

The poets W. H. Auden and Chester Kallman, 1950s

Opposite: Luchino Visconti, film director, 1950

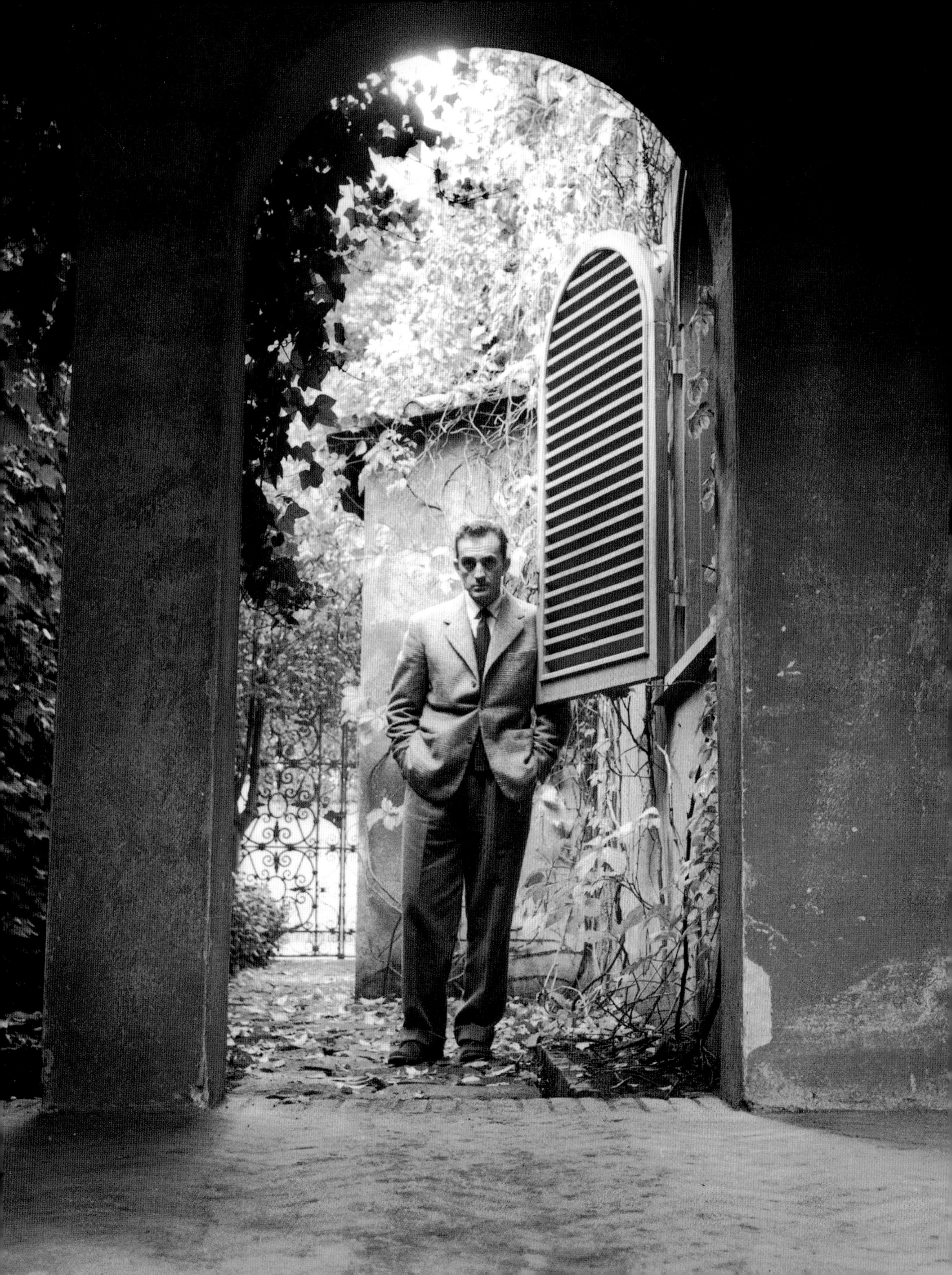

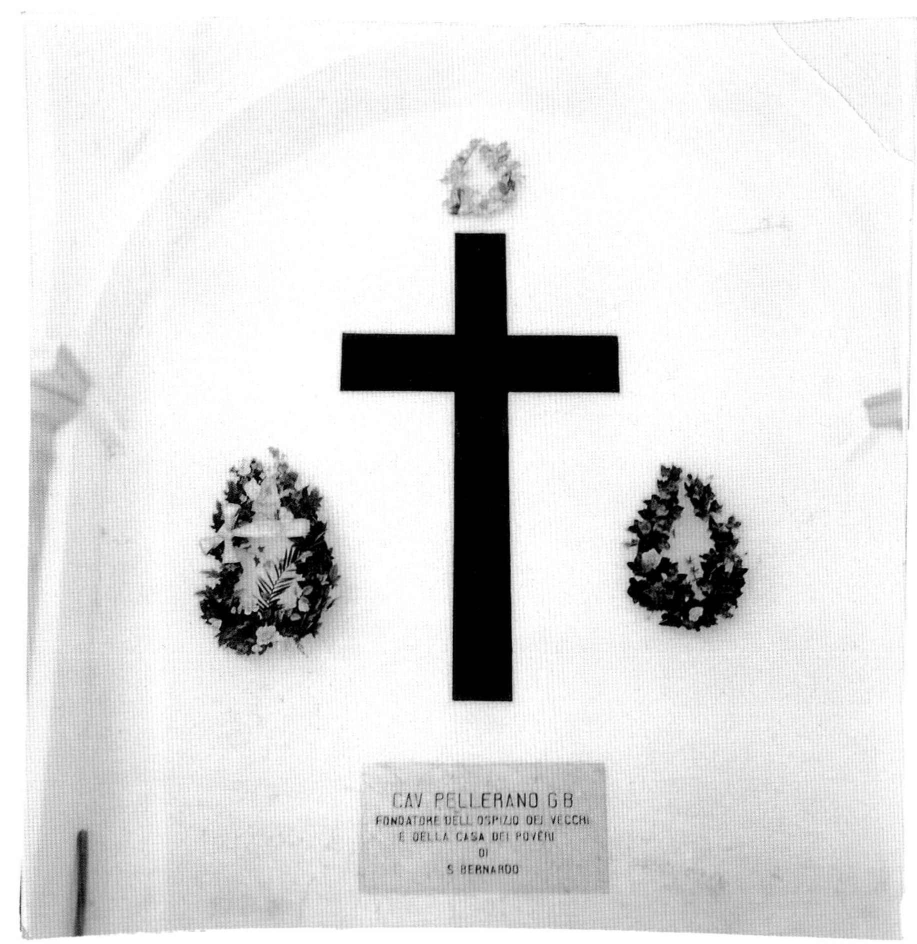

Santa Margharita cemetery, 1950s

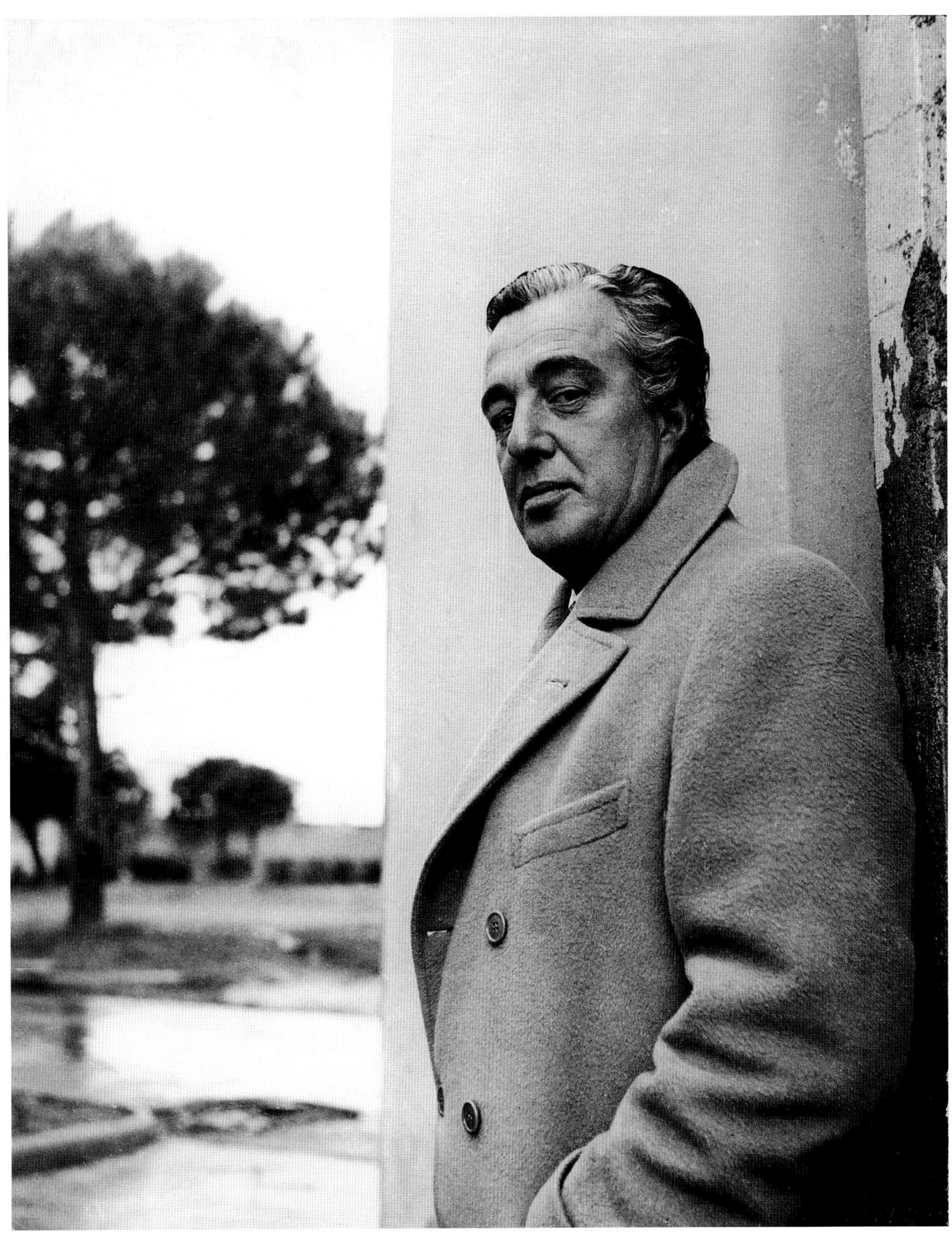

Vittorio de Sica, film director, 1951

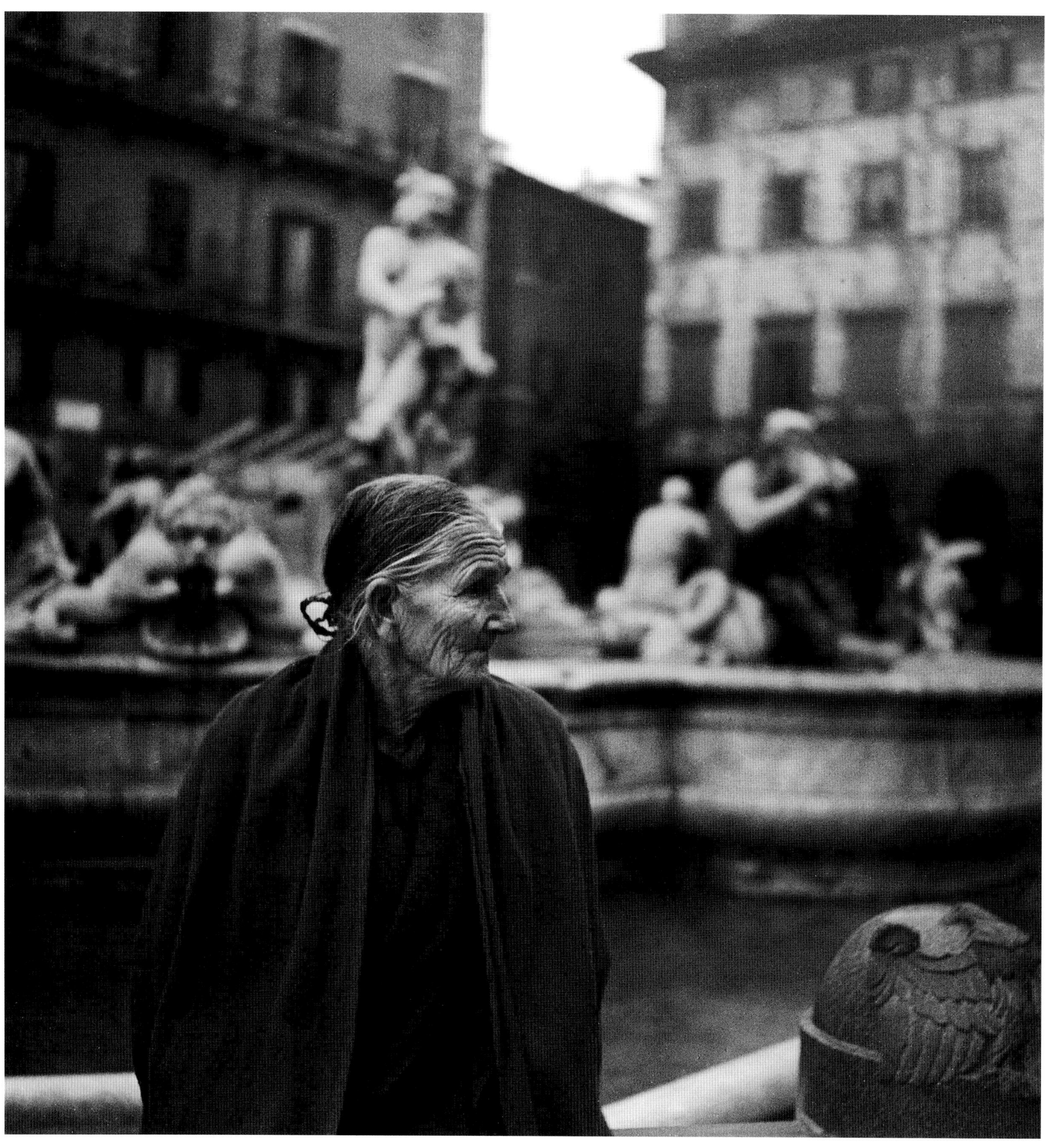

Beggar at the Piazza Navona, 1950s

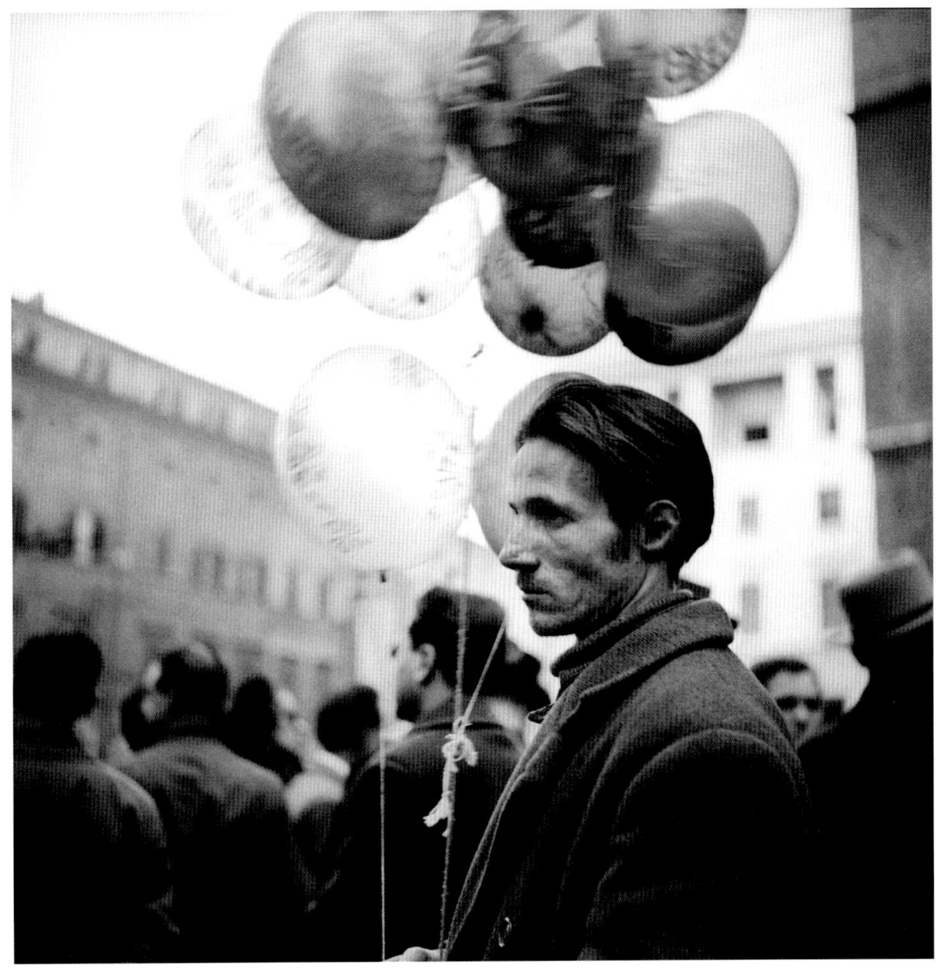

Balloon seller, 1950s

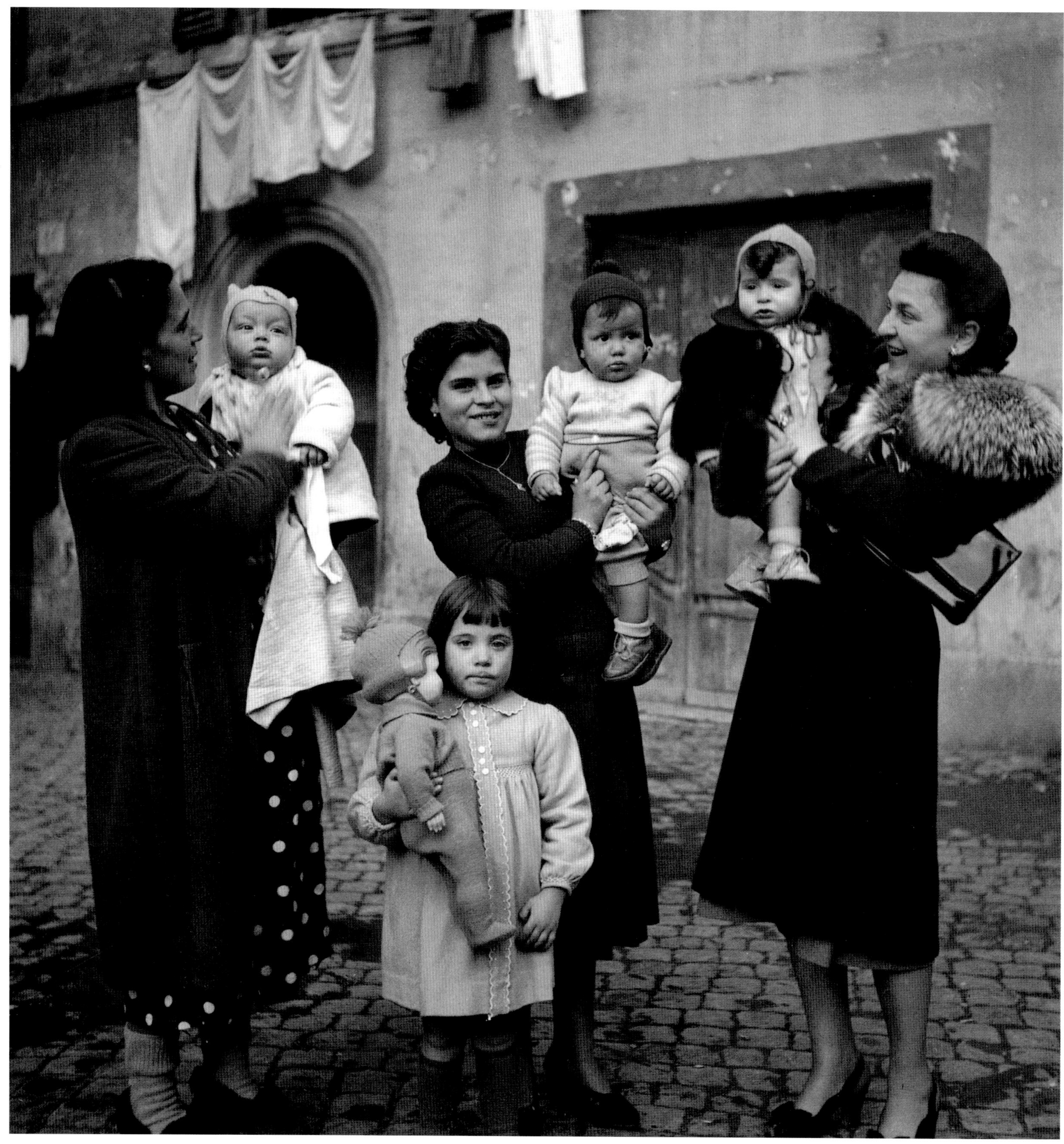

Proud mothers, Trastavere, 1950s

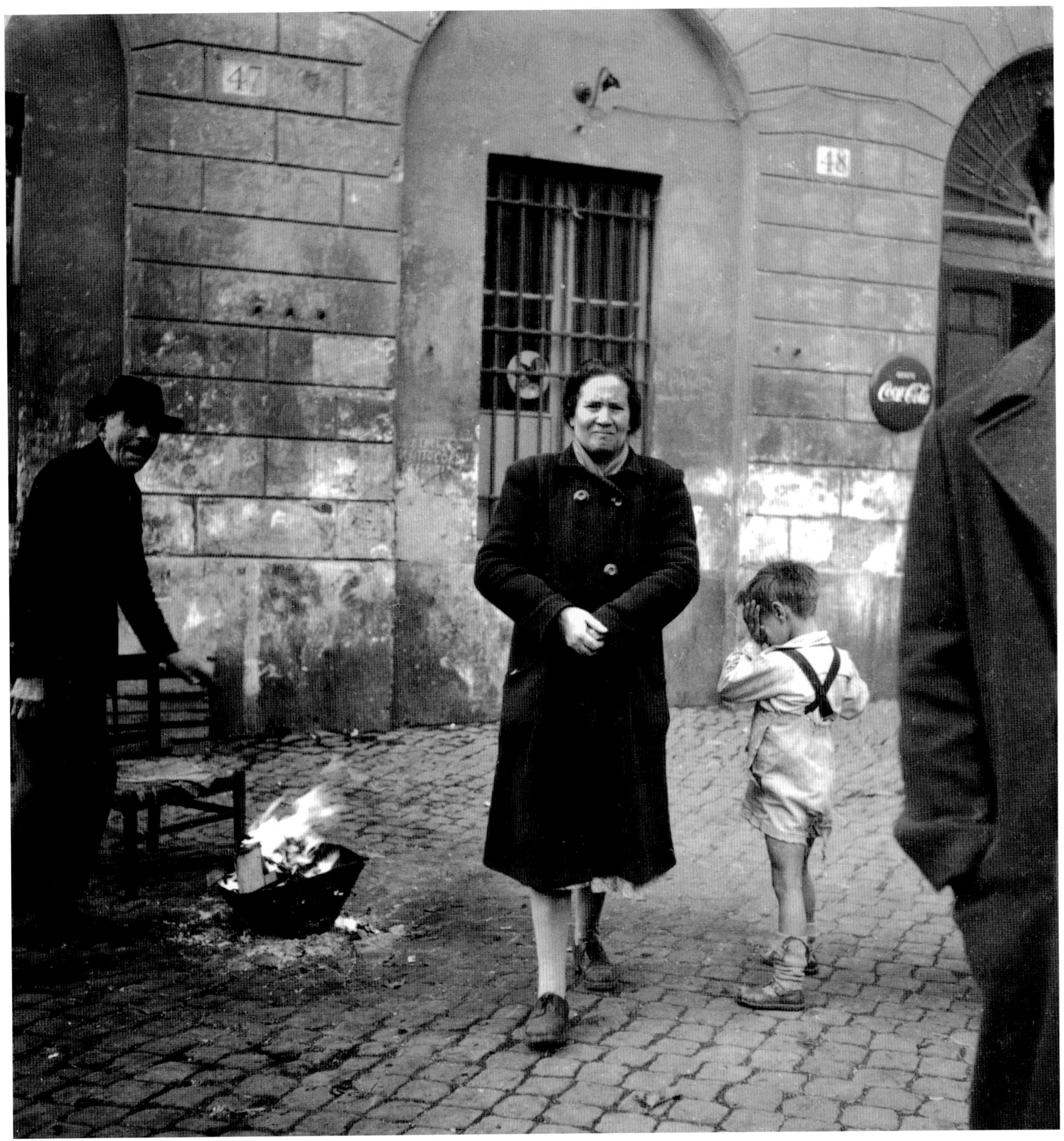

Street bonfire, Trastavere, 1950s

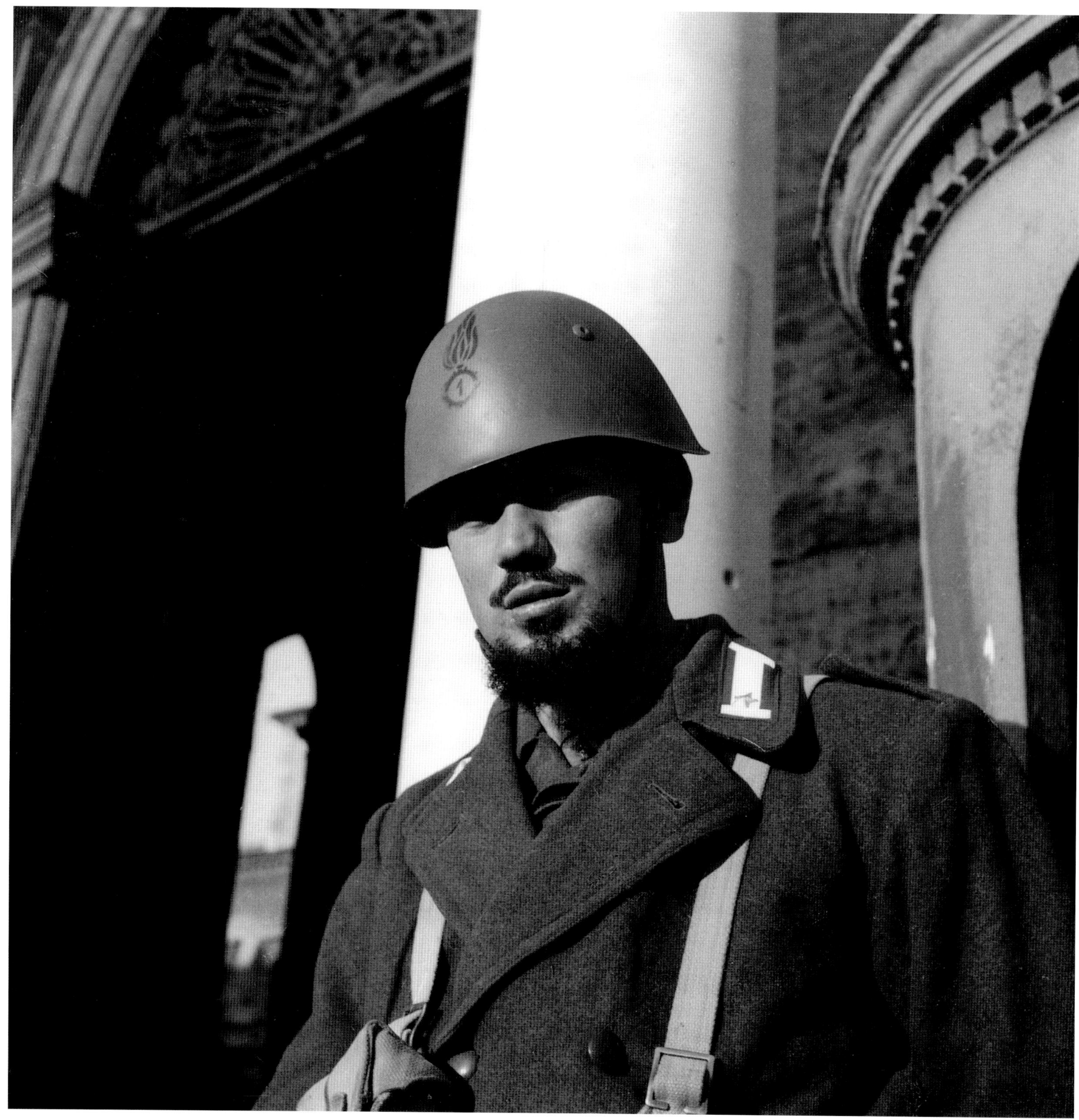

Quirinal guard, 1950s

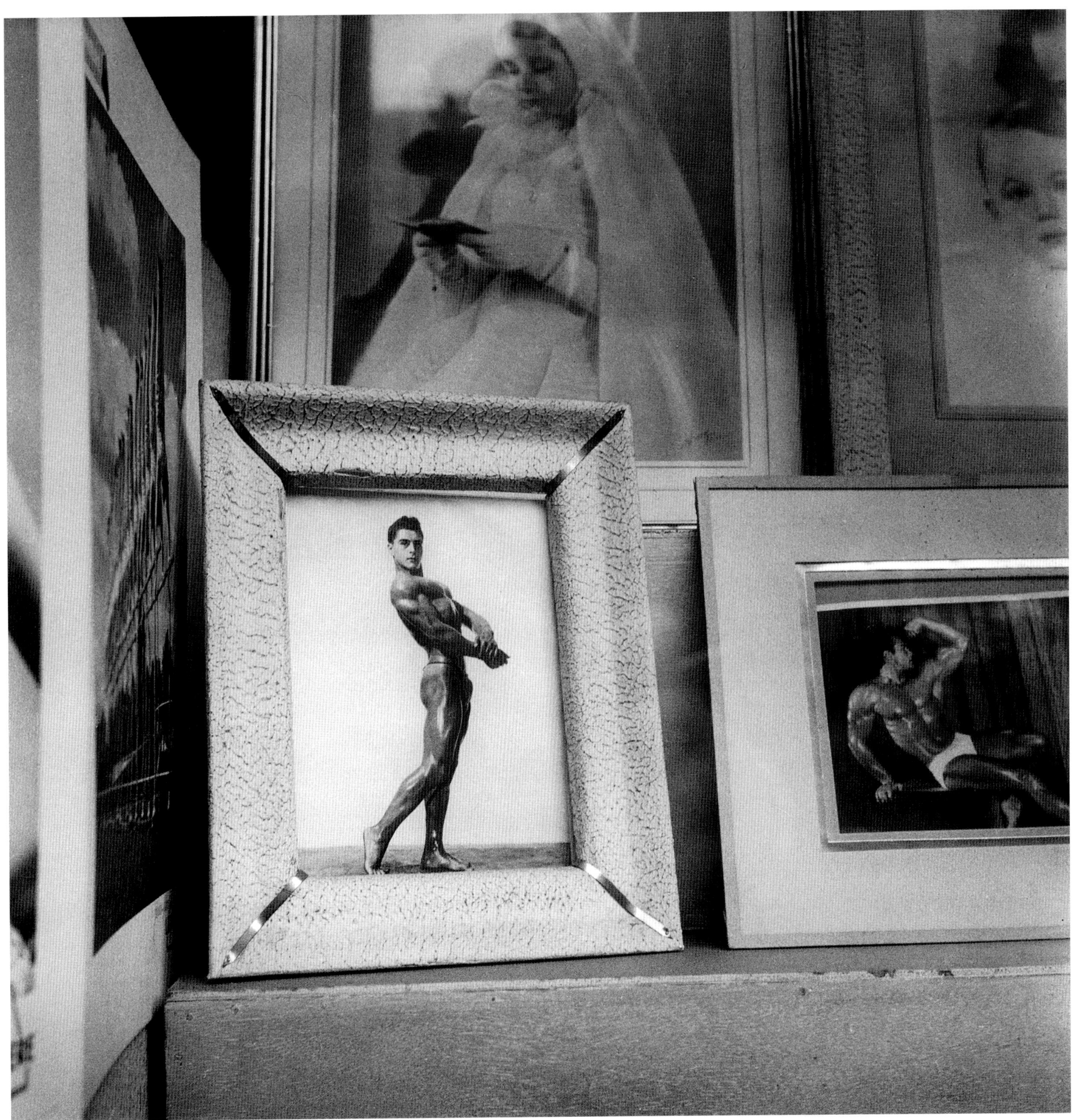

Photographer's window, 1950s

Opposite: Man in the street, 1950s

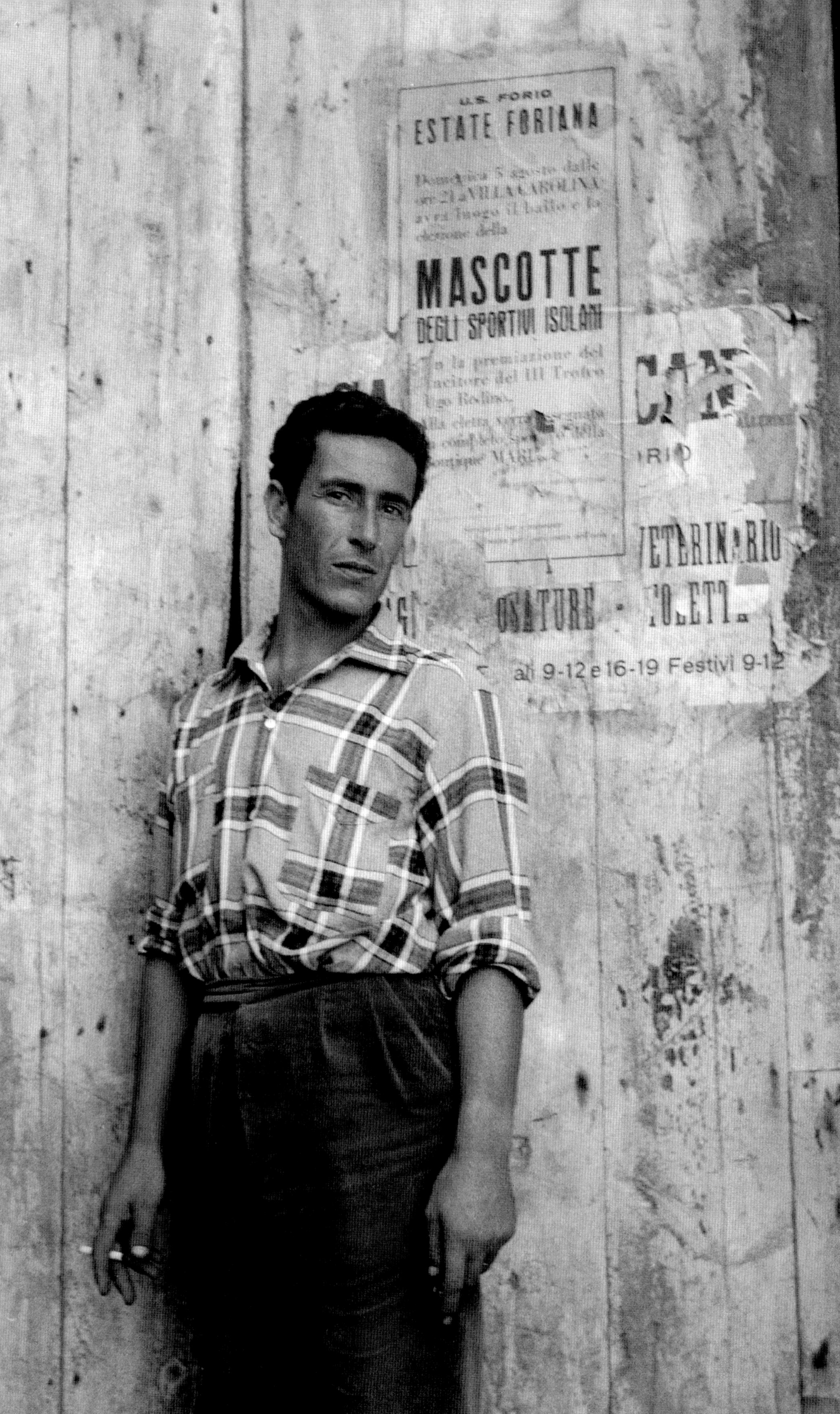
U.S. FORIO
ESTATE FORIANA
MASCOTTE
DEGLI SPORTIVI ISOLANI
VETERINARIO
al 9-12 e 16-19 Festivi 9-12

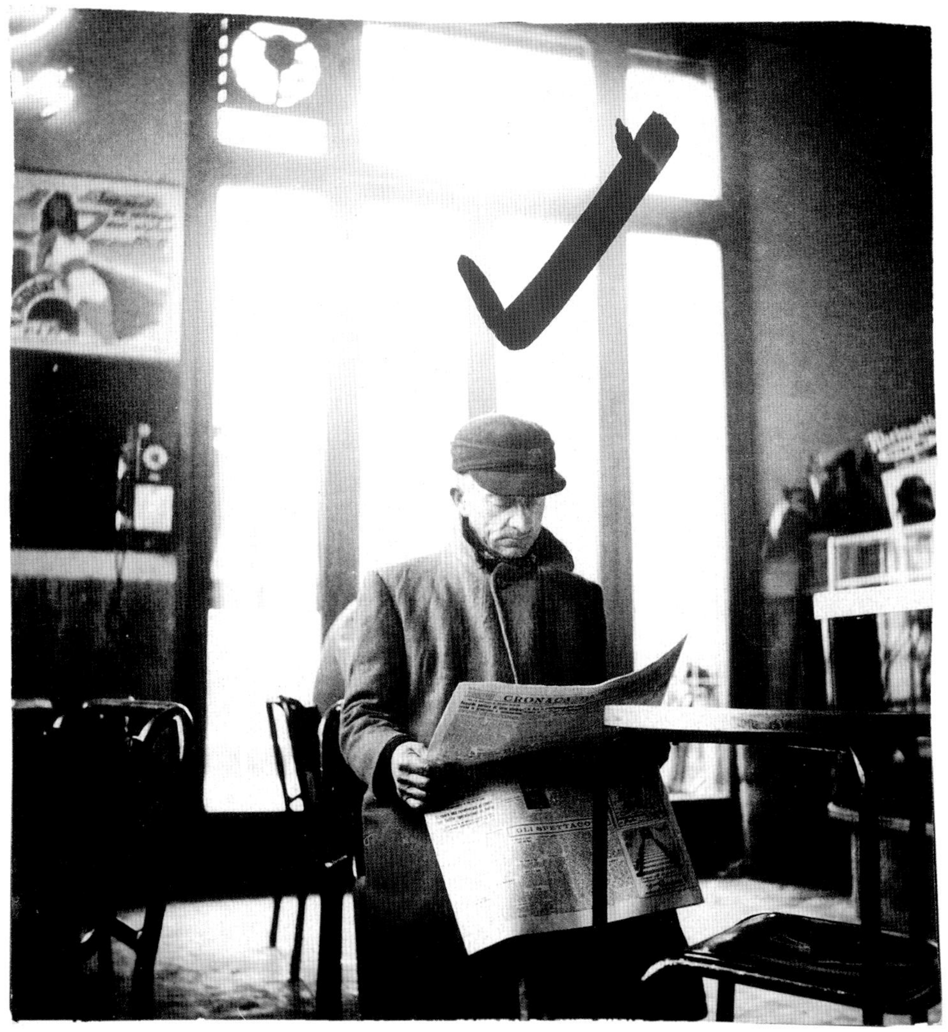

Reading the evening paper, 1950s

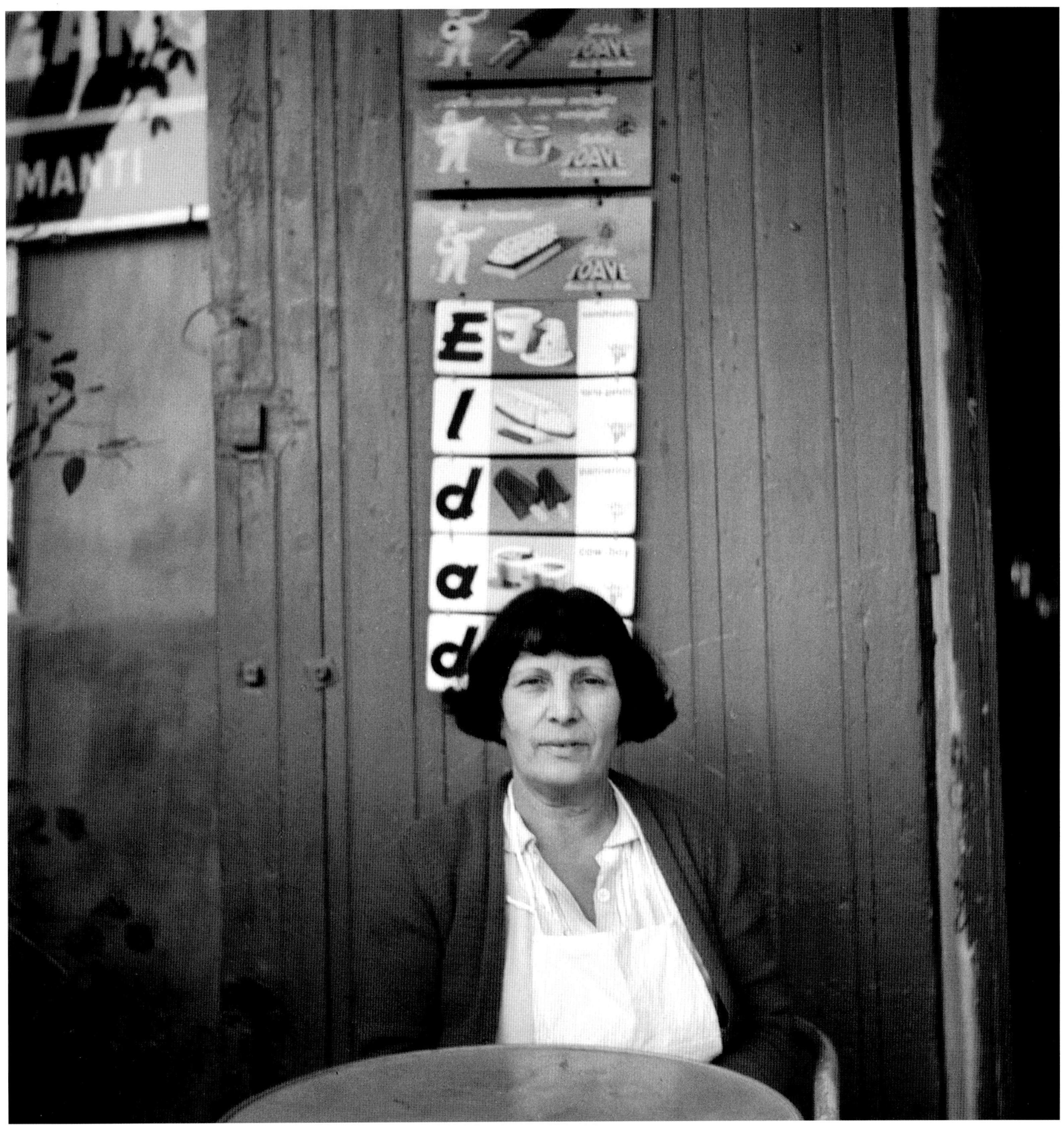

Woman in a café, 1950s

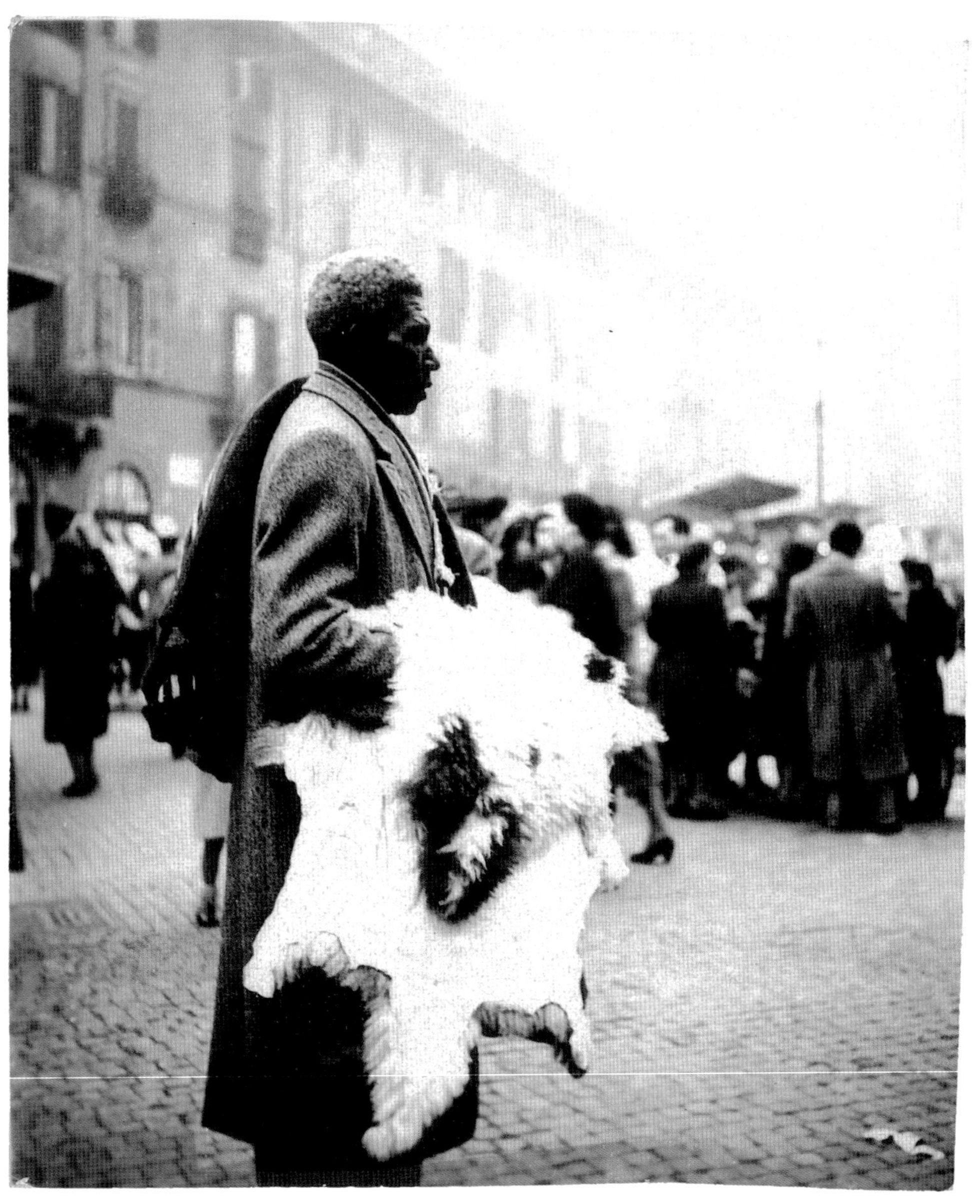
Hide seller, 1950s

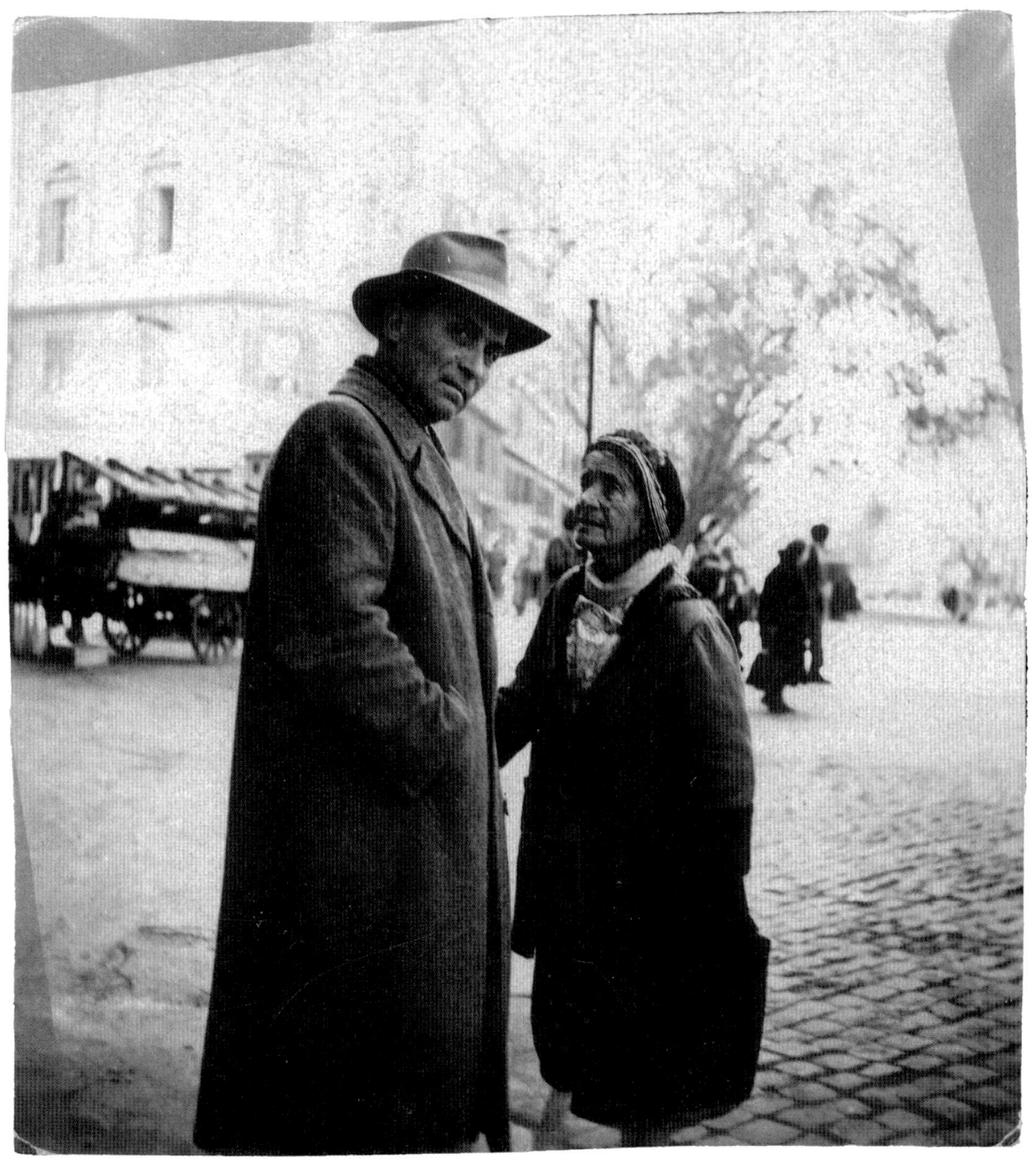

Woman begging, 1950s

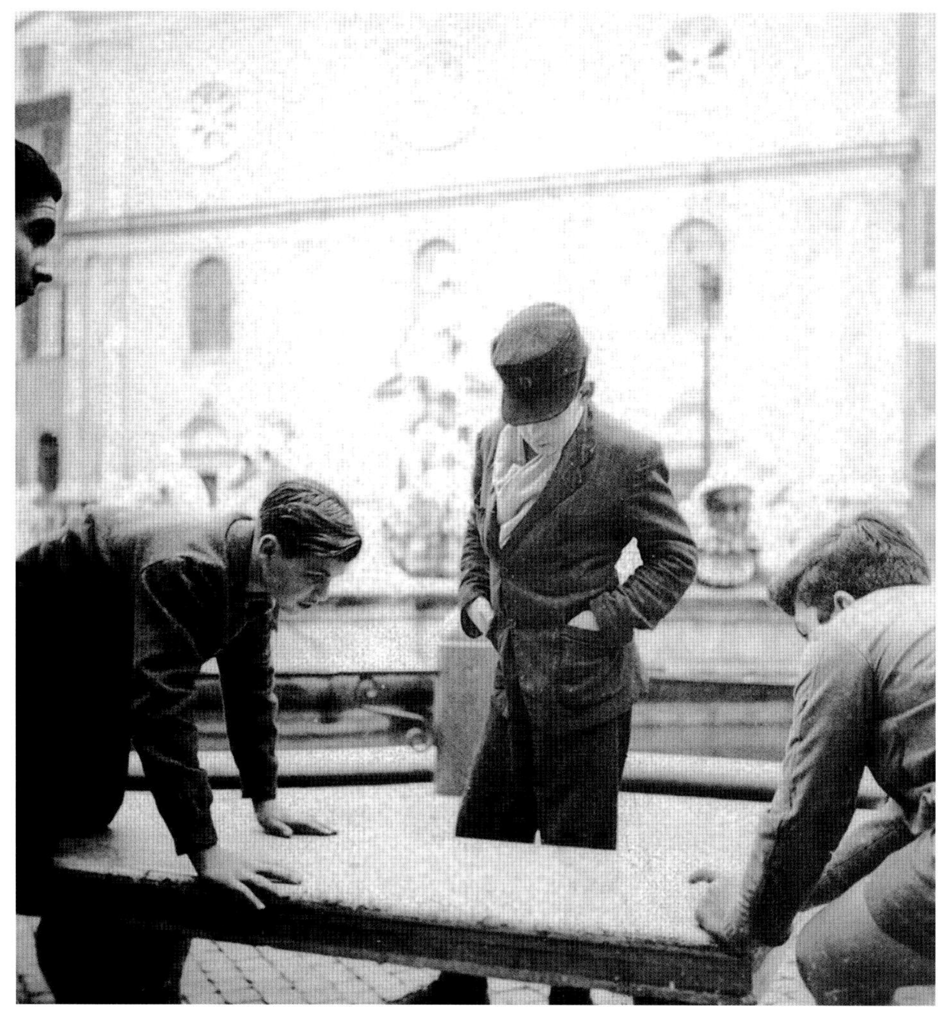

Poor boys, Piazza Navona, 1950s

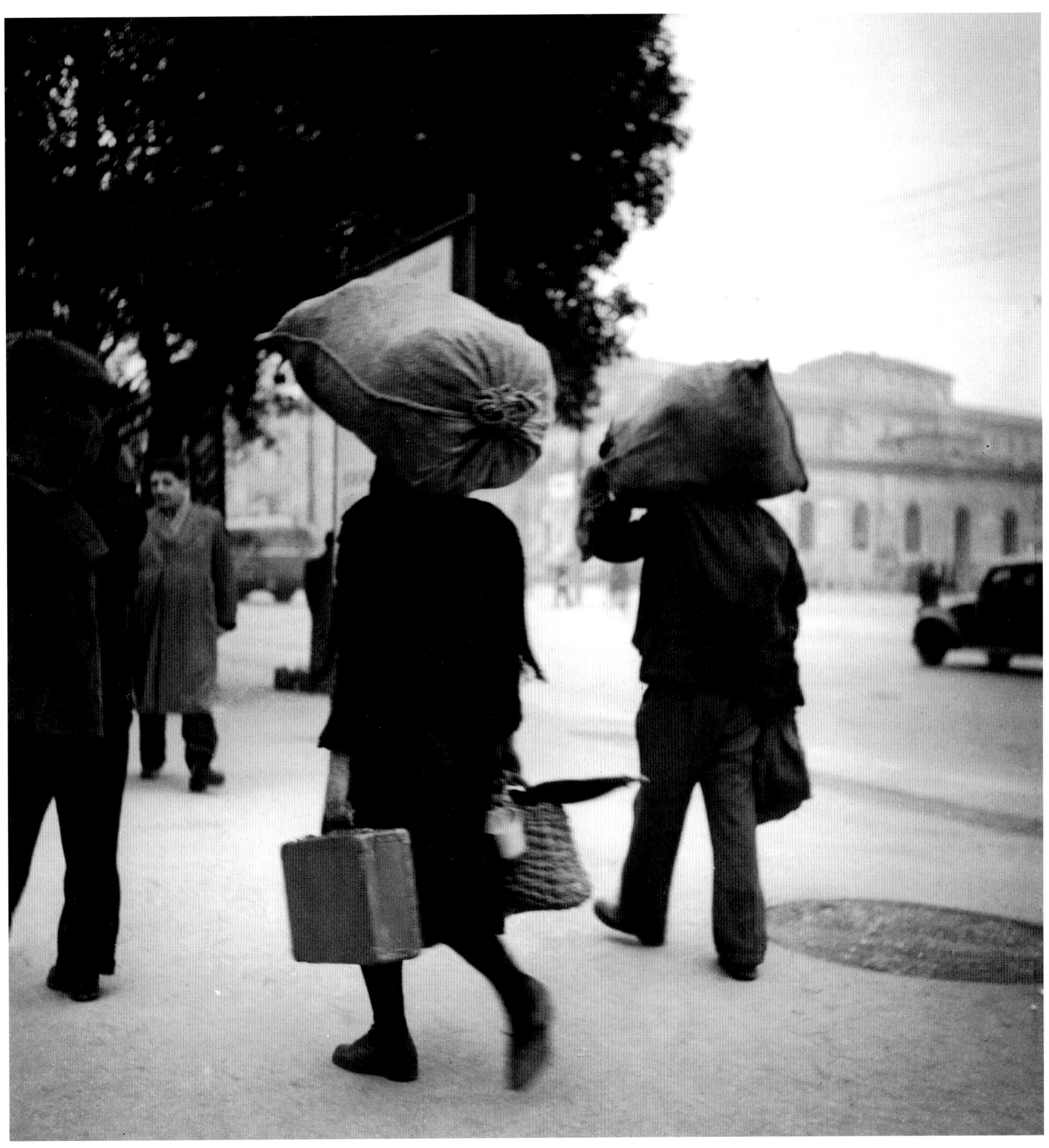

Near the railway station, 1950s

Nun near St Peter's, 1950s

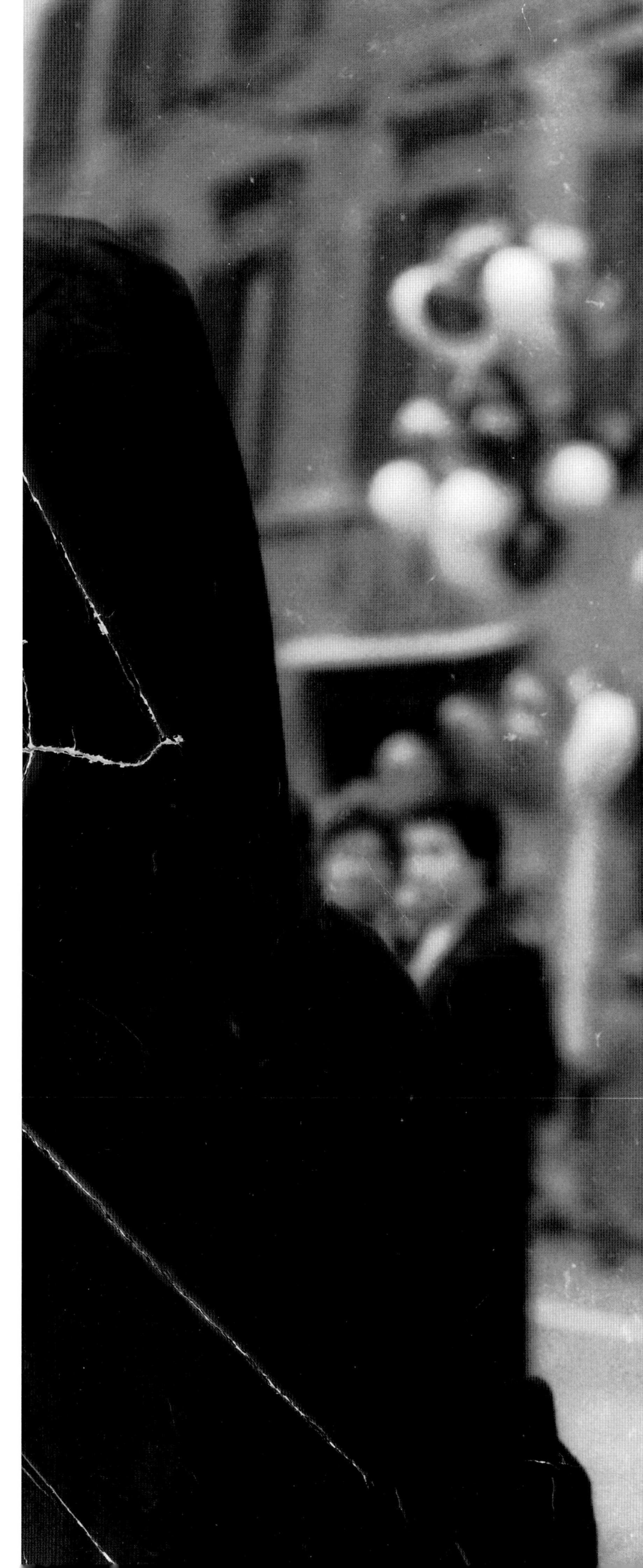

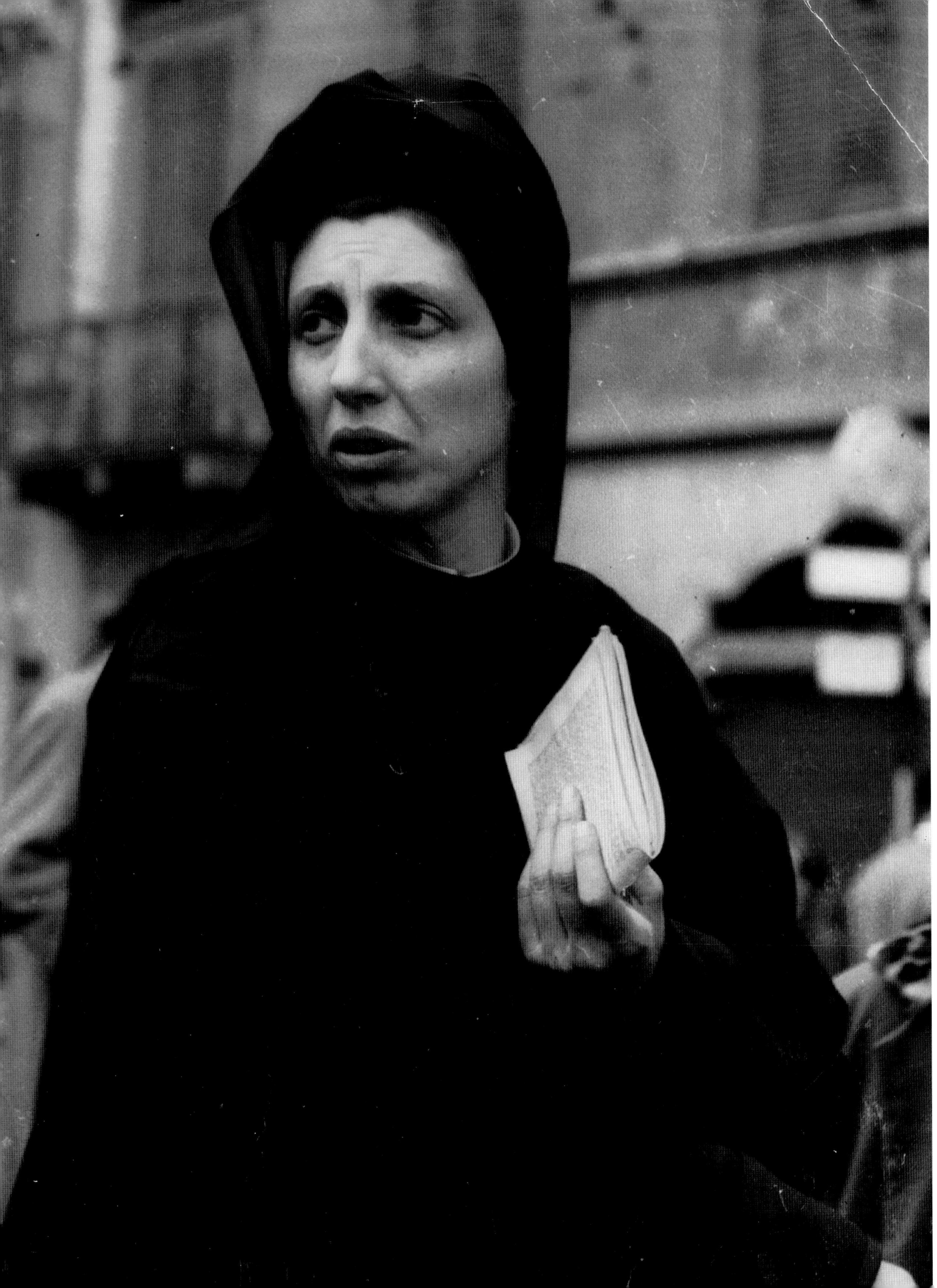

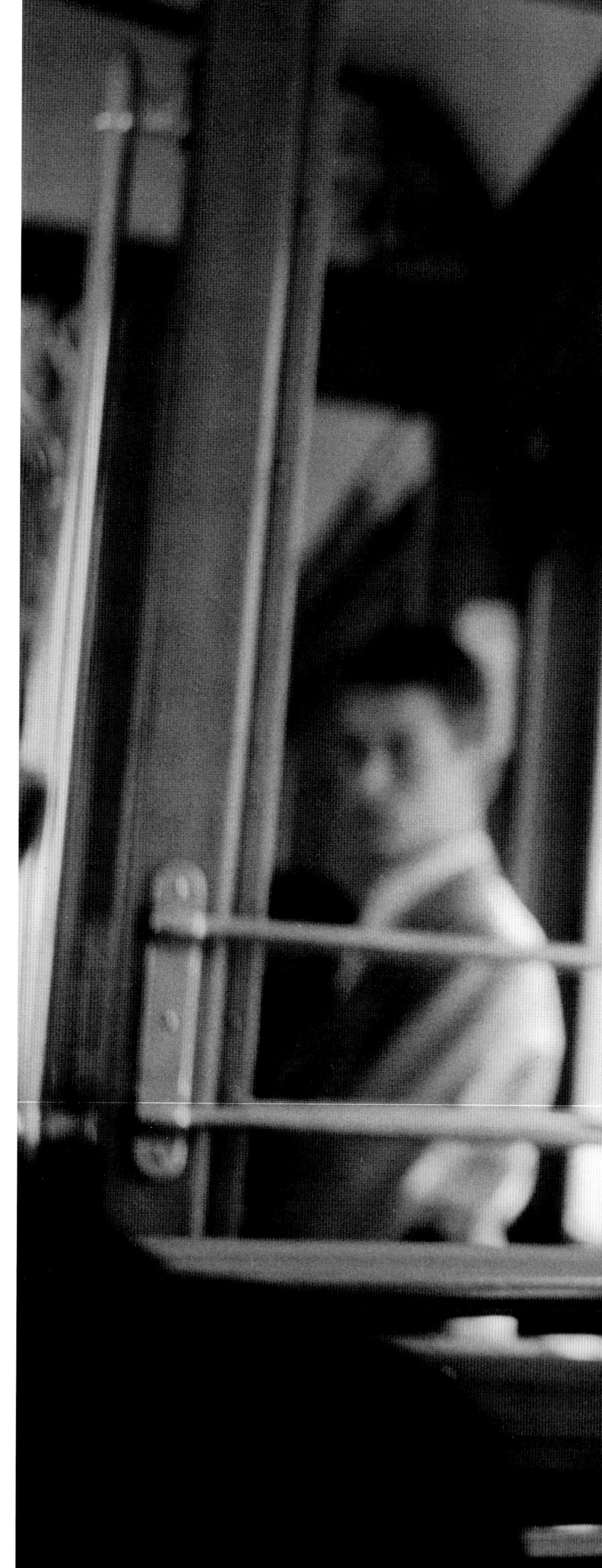

On the tram, 1950s

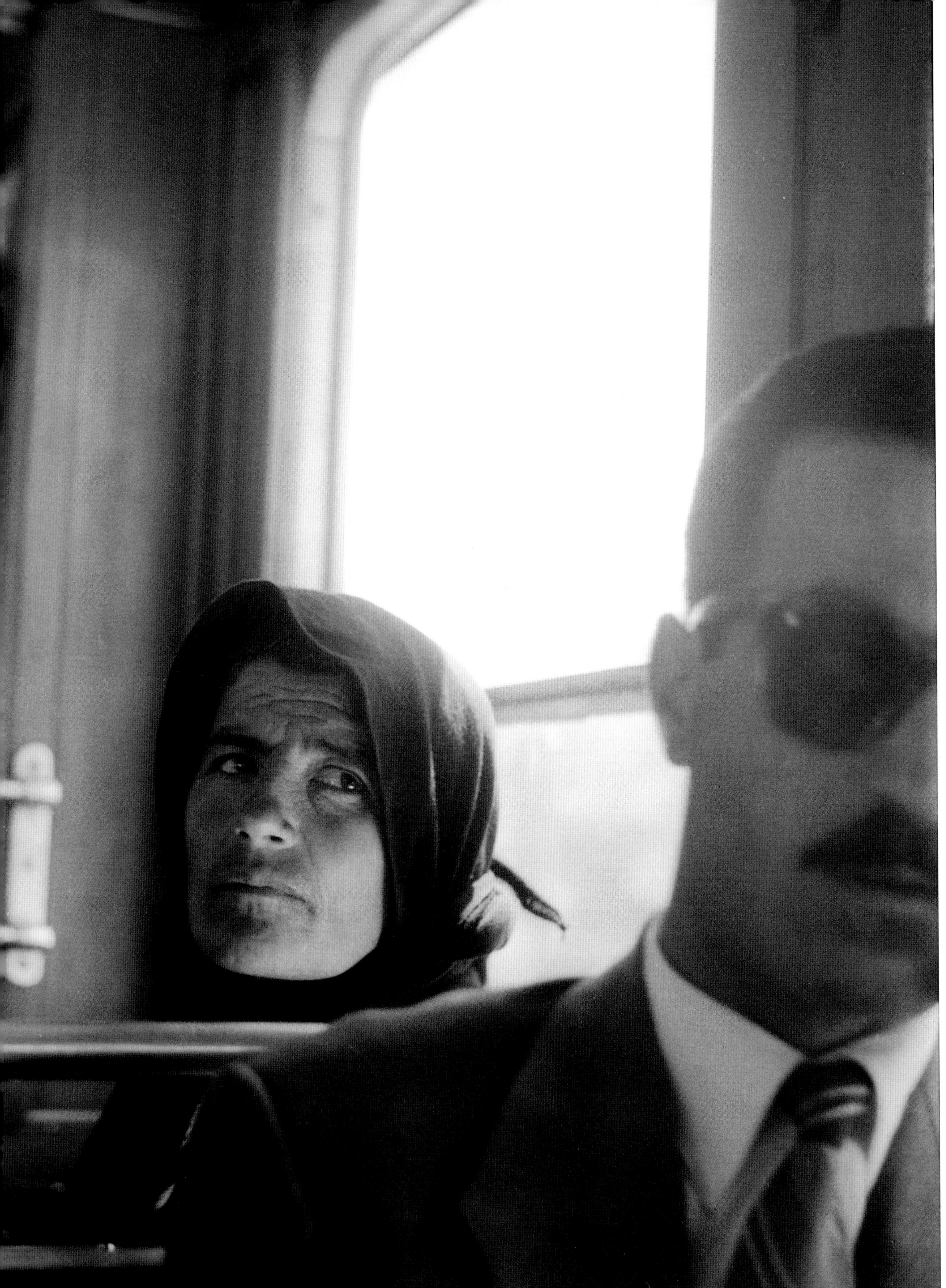

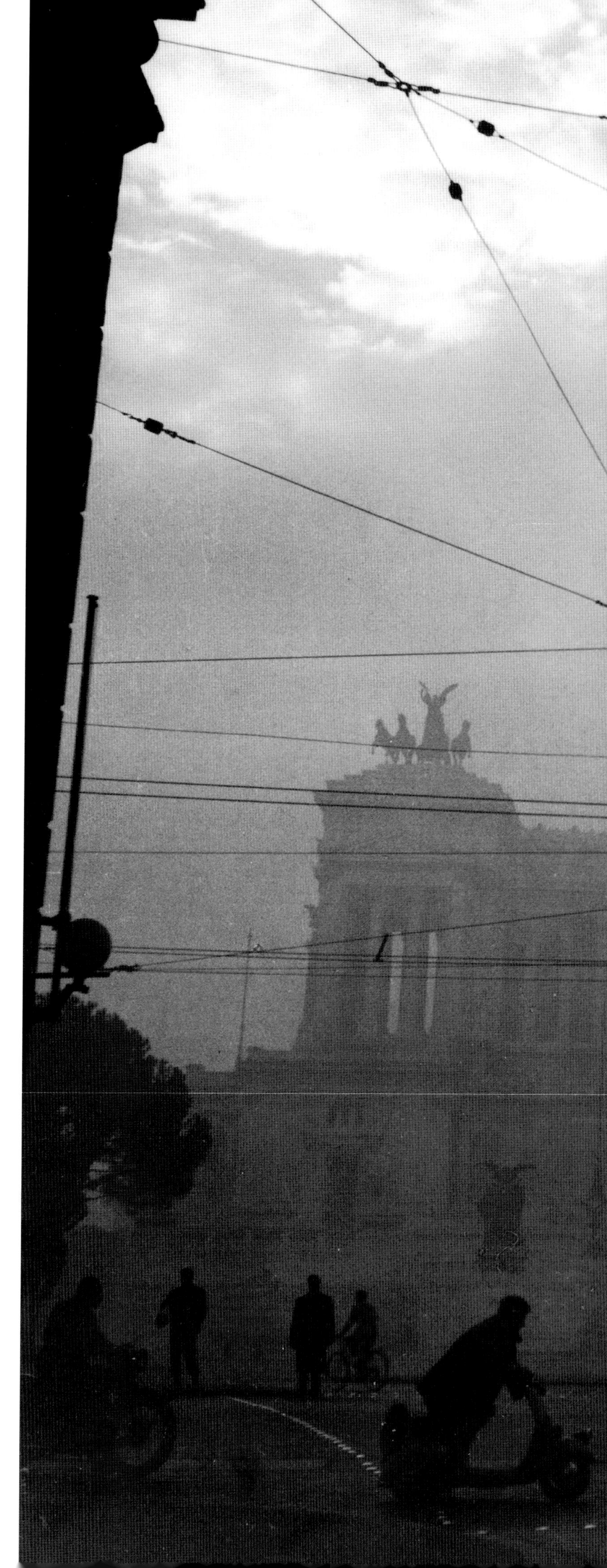

The Victor Emmanuel monument, 1950s

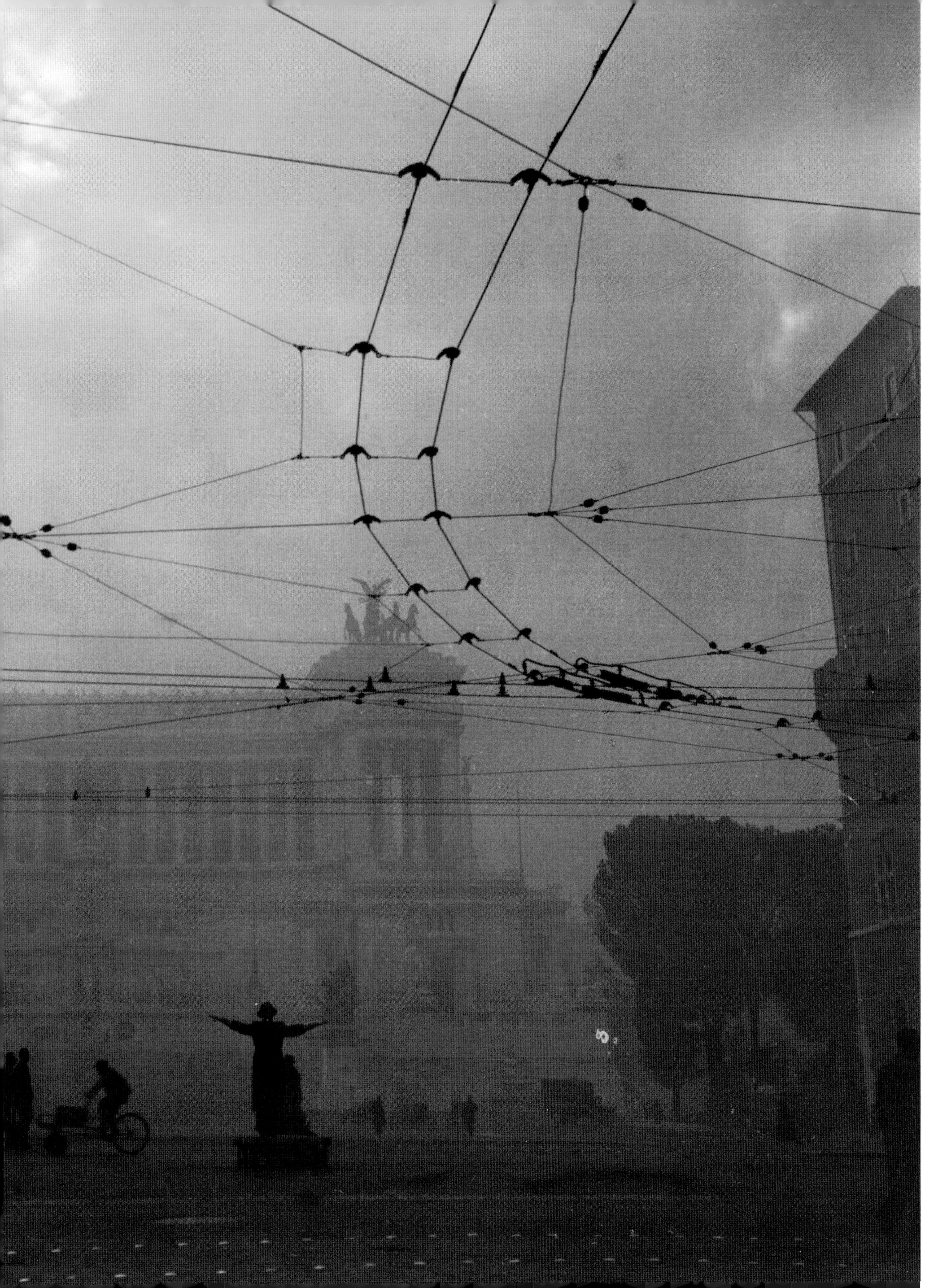

Notes

A Maverick Eye

1. Daniel Farson, *The Gilded Gutter Life of Francis Bacon*, Century, London, 1993, p. 190.
2. Ibid.
3. 'John Deakin: The Salvage of a Photographer', Victoria and Albert Museum, London, 26 September 1984 – 20 January 1985.
4. George Melly, introduction to Daniel Farson, *Soho in the Fifties*, Michael Joseph, London, 1987, p. xiv.
5. Quoted in 'John Deakin Chose Cassie Chaney' (the results of Vogue's model contest), *Vogue*, June 1952, p. 63.
6. Audrey Withers, letter to Alexander Liberman, 21 November 1952.
7. Sheila Wetton, in conversation with author, 1994. A former showroom model for Molyneux, Wetton (1911–1997) was *Vogue*'s longest-serving fashion editor. She was a self-confessed lover of 'difficult people'.
8. Paul Scofield, letter to author, 9 September 1994.
9. Farson wrote in *Out of Step*, Michael Joseph, London, 1974: 'They were photographs to recoil from, brutal portraits – intimate close-ups of the face – emphasising every blemish, with the stark reality of identification shots taken in prison,' p. 70.
10. Bruce Bernard in *John Deakin: The Salvage of a Photographer*, Victoria and Albert Museum, London, 1984, catalogue, p. 7.
11. John Deakin (JD), letter to Daniel Farson (DF), 11 April 1972.
12. Daniel Farson, *Out of Step*, Michael Joseph, London, 1974, p. 240.
13. John Deakin, 'Eight Portraits', unpublished manuscript, n.d., pp. 3–4.
14. Bernard regarded the tattered remains of the skin decoration photographs as 'joylessly self-indulgent but obliquely confessional'. See Bruce Bernard, 'John Deakin: Tattoo Portraits', Philharmonic Pub, Liverpool, 1999, handlist.
15. Deakin, 'Eight Portraits' (note 13 above), pp. 1–2.
16. Daniel Farson, *Never a Normal Man*, HarperCollins, London, 1997, pp. 113–14.
17. Jeffrey Bernard in *John Deakin: The Salvage of a Photographer* (note 10 above), p. 10.
18. Oliver Bernard, undated letter to author, 1995.
19. Dylan Thomas, letter to Helen and Bill MacAlpine, 12 November 1949. The photograph appeared first in *Flair* magazine.
20. Francis Bacon in *John Deakin: The Salvage of a Photographer* (note 10 above), p. 8.
21. Farson, *Out of Step* (note 12 above), p. 58.
22. Quoted in Farson, *Soho in the Fifties* (note 4 above), p. 138. The painting, *John Deakin 1963/4*, was sold at auction at Christie's, London, on 25 June 1997 for $1,472,625, three times the pre-sale estimate. It was allegedly acquired by the Newhouse family, owners of, among other newspaper and magazine companies, The Condé Nast Publications Inc., publishers of *Vogue*.
23. Quoted in Bruce Bernard, 'Fearless Exposures', *The Independent Magazine*, 23 March 1991.
24. Deakin, 'Eight Portraits' (note 13 above), p. 3.
25. Ibid., p. 1.
26. JD, letter to DF, 17 November 1971.
27. Ibid.
28. Farson, *Out of Step* (note 12 above), p. 72.
29. JD, letter to DF, 17 November 1971.
30. JD, letter to DF, 9 November 1971.
31. Ibid.
32. JD, letter to DF, 17 November 1971.
33. The exhibition ran from 29 February to 31 March 1956.
34. George Melly, quoted in *John Deakin: The Salvage of a Soho Photographer*, Annalogue Productions for Channel Four, 1991.
35. Farson, *Never a Normal Man* (note 16 above), p. 323.
36. Audrey Withers, letter to Paul Dieu, 26 January 1956.
37. Eric Lister, *Portal Painters: A Survey of British Idiosyncratic Artists*, Alpine Fine Arts Collection, London, 1982, revised Jess Wilder, 1992, pp. 105–106.
38. Farson, *Never a Normal Man* (note 16 above), p. 323.
39. Quoted in Daniel Farson, 'Clown with a Camera', *The Spectator*, 29 September 1984, p. 33.
40. A reference to Deakin's early career as a painter appears in *Vogue*, June 1952, p. 63, in a short biography accompanying the results of Vogue's model contest. The poet Dom Moraes also mentions it in passing in his memoirs, *My Son's Father*, Secker & Warburg, London, 1968, pp. 71–72.
41. *The Studio*, January 1939.
42. David Cozens, *The Architect's Journal*, 10 November 1938.
43. *The Sunday Times*, 6 November 1938.
44. Jan Gordon, *The Observer*, 6 November 1938.
45. *The Evening Standard*, 26 October 1938.
46. Jeffrey Bernard in *John Deakin: The Salvage of a Photographer* (note 10 above), p. 10.
47. Jeffress co-owned the Hanover Gallery, Mayfair, with Erica Brausen, Bacon's first dealer from the mid-1940s to the end of the 1950s.
48. For further details, see Farson, *Out of Step* (note 12 above), pp. 74–75.
49. Obsessed by uniforms, Jeffress was alerted by Graham Sutherland whenever the US fleet sailed into Villefranche and took care to be in London for the Royal Tournament in Earl's Court (he referred to it as the 'Royal Torment'). Unsurprisingly, perhaps, much of his estate was left to a Royal Navy fund for ratings – on the condition none was spent on the WRNS.
50. Elizabeth Smart, *John Deakin's Paris*, Parton Gallery, London, 1956, unpaginated catalogue.
51. By 1956 his fortunes had changed. He lived in an apartment on Third Avenue in Manhattan, see Audrey Withers, letter to Paul Dieu (note 36 above); and by 1972 he lived in Switzerland, see JD, letter to DF, 11 April 1972.
52. Edna Woolman-Chase, *Always in Vogue*, Gollancz, London, 1954, p. 233. Though Condé Nast, *Vogue*'s proprietor, could not abide Bérard's faceless drawings, he was among the magazine's stars. He had been Vuillard's favourite pupil and influenced the designs of both Schiaparelli and Dior.
53. Warwick Charlton, 'Deakin at War', letter to *The Times*, 21 May 1996.
54. Jeffrey Bernard in *John Deakin: The Salvage of a Photographer* (note 10 above), p. 10.
55. Daniel Farson, *Sacred Monsters*, Bloomsbury, London, 1988, p. 59.

56. Charlton, 'Deakin at War' (note 53 above).
57. Elizabeth Smart has written of his having documented leper colonies and tribes with sleeping sickness there, but these photographs appear not to have survived. See Smart, *John Deakin's Paris* (note 50 above).
58. Some Malta pictures were reproduced in John Pudney's *Whom Only England Know*, John Lane/The Bodley Head, London, 1943.
59. Farson, *Out of Step* (note 12 above), p. 59.
60. Moraes, *My Son's Father* (note 40 above), pp. 171–72.
61. See the dustjacket flap to Dom Moraes, *A Beginning*, Parton Press, London, 1957.
62. Bruce Bernard in *John Deakin: The Salvage of a Photographer* (note 10 above), p. 6.
63. Alex Noble mentions Anthony Armstrong-Jones and Harold Chapman ('A New Beginning' in *John Deakin: The Salvage of a Photographer* [note 10 above]). Roger Mayne recalls having commissioned Deakin to take a portrait of him, just to see how he did it (he learnt nothing at all).
64. 'People Are Talking About...', *Vogue*, October 1956, p. 244.
65. David Sylvester, 'Round the London Galleries', *The Listener*, 2 August 1956, pp. 166–67.
66. Colin MacInnes, 'The Photographer as Artist', *The Times*, 13 July 1956.
67. Alexander Liberman, letter to Audrey Withers, 28 November 1952.
68. Deakin would surely have agreed with Brassaï in respect of street reportage: 'there is nothing more horrifying than to be taken for a professional photographer.' See preface to Brassaï, *Camera in Paris*, Focal Press, London, 1949.
69. 'Language of the Wall: Parisian Graffiti Photographed by Brassaï', ICA, London (opened 17 October 1958). Brassaï, *Graffiti*, Belser Verlag, Stuttgart, 1960.
70. John Deakin, *London Today*, Saturn Press, London, 1949, unpaginated.
71. Farson, *Out of Step* (note 12 above), p. 56.
72. The essay is reproduced in Colin MacInnes, *England Half English*, McGibbon & Kee, London, 1961, reprinted by the Hogarth Press, London, 1986. Dom Moraes expressed a similar view, writing of 'lonely men in corners, staring, and sad patterns squinted up from the carpet'; see Moraes, *My Son's Father* (note 40 above), p. 170.
73. Bruce Bernard in *John Deakin: The Salvage of a Photographer* (note 10 above), p. 7. It is illustrated on p. 27. A variant, now at the Victoria and Albert Museum, London, appears in Robin Muir, *John Deakin Photographs*, Schirmer/Mosel Verlag, Munich, 1996, p. 83.
74. Alex Noble, 'A New Beginning', in *John Deakin: The Salvage of a Photographer* (note 10 above), p. 17.
75. Bruce Bernard in *John Deakin: The Salvage of a Photographer* (note 10 above), pp. 6–7. Now part of the collection of the Victoria and Albert Museum, London, it is illustrated on p. 11.
76. Farson, 'Clown with a Camera' (note 39 above), p. 32.
77. Farson, *Soho in the Fifties* (note 4 above), p. 133.
78. Christopher Kininmonth, *Rome Alive*, John Lehmann, London, 1951.
79. His halfheartedness may have had something to do with the publication in 1955 by the German photographer Herbert List of *Rom*, his own book of photographs of Rome.

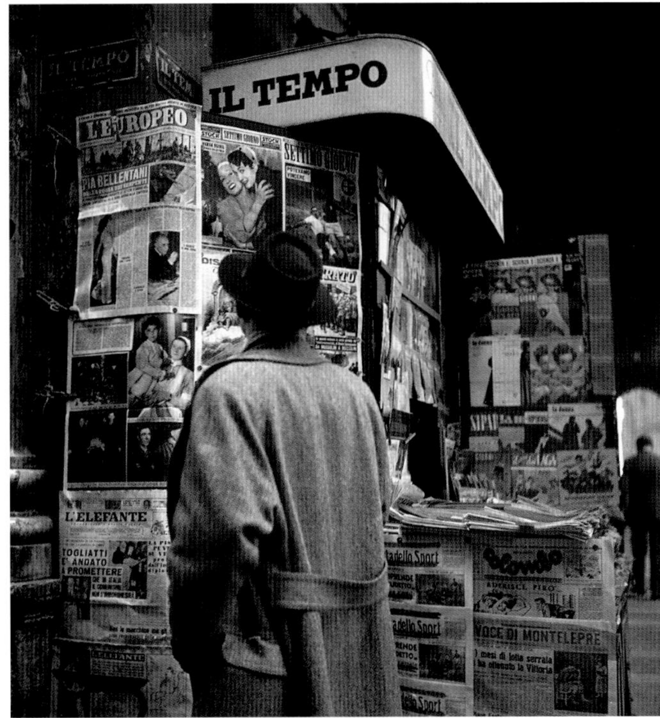

Newsagent's kiosk, Rome, 1950s

80. *The Observer*, 2 December 1956.
81. Farson, *Never a Normal Man* (note 16 above), p. 224.
82. Kininmonth, *Rome Alive* (note 78 above), p. 27.
83. Farson, *Out of Step* (note 12 above), p. 238.
84. JD letter to DF, 17 November 1971.
85 Deakin, 'Eight Portraits' (note 13 above), p. 6.
86 Farson, 'Clown with a Camera' (note 39 above), p. 33.
87. Deakin's encounter with Hutton is related in the essay, 'An Incident in the Casbah', in Farson, *Sacred Monsters* (note 55 above), pp. 56–63.
88. Elaine Dundy, *The Old Man and Me*, Gollancz, London, 1964.
89. Colin Wilson, *Ritual in the Dark*, Gollancz, London, 1960.
90. Iain Sinclair, *Downriver*, Paladin, London, 1991; Nigel Richardson, *Dog Days in Soho*, Gollancz, London, 2000.
91. Martin Green, *The French House and The Snows of Yester-Year*, Green Rivers Press, place of publication unknown, 1996.
92. Bruce Bernard in *John Deakin: The Salvage of a Photographer* (note 10 above), p. 7.

London

1. John Deakin, *London Today*, Saturn Press, London, 1949, unpaginated.

Paris

1. Elizabeth Smart, *John Deakin's Paris*, Parton Gallery, London, 1956, unpaginated catalogue.

Rome

1. James Mortimer, in conversation with author, 1994.

Chronology

Deakin skilfully deflected inquiries into his background and left no papers and little biographical detail. The following chronology, though sketchy, is probably the most that can be ascertained from the memoirs, written and oral, of the friends who survived him, from newspaper and magazine clippings and from the archives of *Vogue*.

1912
8 May: born in Bebington, Cheshire, to Elsie Mary Bond and John Henry Deakin, a factory checker for Lever Brothers. They had moved from Liverpool shortly before the birth.

Educated locally at a school in Chester Road.

1923
September: enters Calday Grange Grammar School, West Kirby.

1928
A testimonial dated 18 October, presumably on his leaving grammar school, notes that 'his behaviour in class was excellent. He was attentive to instructions and worked steadily. He was always polite and courteous and got on with his fellows.'

c. 1930
Moves to Dublin, takes a position as a window dresser for a display company, and, according to Daniel Farson, becomes 'involved with theatricals in some capacity never fully explained'.

1937–38
Tours the world with the art collector and patron Arthur Jeffress (they travel to Italy, Hollywood, Mexico, Tahiti, New Caledonia and Fiji). Paints.

November 1938: exhibits his paintings for the first time at the Mayor Gallery, London.

1939
Starts photographing in Paris. Introduced to Michel de Brunhoff, editor of French *Vogue*, by the set designer and fashion illustrator Christian Bérard.

1939–45
Seconded to the Army Film Unit as a photographer. Covers the aftermath of the siege of Malta (1942) and is posted to East Africa. Involved in aerial reconnaissance of enemy troops. Also attached to the Eighth Army, attending Field-Marshal Montgomery's briefings before the battle of El Alamein. Comes under enemy fire off the Libyan coast and on the outskirts of Tripoli.

1945–46
Contributes photographs to the magazines *Lilliput*, *Picture Post* and the British edition of *Harper's Bazaar*.

1947
July: hired as a staff photographer for *Vogue*. First pictures published in the September edition.

September: closes his studio with considerable debts.

October 31: first reported loss of equipment that would eventually lead to his dismissal.

1948
September 3: Fired from *Vogue*.

Contributes portraits to *The Sketch* and *Tatler* magazines.

1949
London Today, with text and photographs by Deakin, published by the Saturn Press.

1950
Contributes to the shortlived magazine *Flair*.

1951
August: hired again by *Vogue* and based for a few months in Paris.

September: *Rome Alive* published, with a text by Christopher Kininmonth and photographs by Deakin.

1952
Contract renewed again by *Vogue*.

1954
March: fired again from *Vogue* and paid off generously. Plans to settle in Europe and ends up in Rome at 6 via dei Greci.

1955
Spring: living in Penzance, having taken up painting once again.

February: hospitalized in London, suffering from pneumonia.

1956
29 February – 31 March: exhibition of paintings at St George's Gallery, London.

July 9: 'John Deakin's Paris', an exhibition of photographs, opens at the Parton Gallery, in David Archer's Bookshop in Soho.

September 18: the follow-up exhibition, 'John Deakin's Rome', opens, also at the Parton Gallery.

Kept on a retainer by *The Observer* (until 1958).

1960
Travels to Tangier with Daniel Farson and Lady Rose McLaren.

1961
Living in Rome. Marries Anna, a stateless Hungarian refugee, in Milan.

Contributes occasional photographs to *Harper's Bazaar* (UK edition).

1961–62
Undertakes photographic commissions for Francis Bacon.

1963
Is painted by Lucian Freud and Michael Andrews.

1969
Is commissioned by Alan Aldridge to provide the accompanying illustration to 'P. S. I Love You' for *The Beatles' Illustrated Lyrics*.

c. 1970
Works alongside Bruce Bernard as a picture researcher on a partwork, *A History of the Twentieth Century*.

1971
October: in Paris for Francis Bacon's retrospective at the Grand Palais.

November: hospitalized with suspected lung cancer.

1972
April: hospitalized for an operation for lung cancer.

May 25: dies of heart failure at the Old Ship Hotel, Brighton.

Francis Bacon named as next-of-kin.

1984
26 September 1984 – 20 January 1985; exhibition 'John Deakin: The Salvage of a Photographer' at the Victoria and Albert Museum, London.

1996
12 April – 14 July: exhibition 'John Deakin Photographs' at the National Portrait Gallery, London. The book *John Deakin Photographs*, by Robin Muir, published by Schirmer/Mosel Verlag, Munich.

1999
24 September – 6 November: exhibition of tattoo portraits opens at the Philharmonic Pub, Hope Street, Liverpool.

Bibliography

Exhibitions

'John Deakin's Paris', Parton Gallery, London, 1956
'John Deakin's Rome', Parton Gallery, London, 1956
'John Deakin: The Salvage of a Photographer', Victoria and Albert Museum, London, 1984–85
'John Deakin Photographs', National Portrait Gallery, London, 1996
'John Deakin: Tattoo Portraits', Philharmonic Pub, Liverpool, 1999

Books

by John Deakin
Deakin, John, *London Today*, The Saturn Press, 1949
---,'Eight Portraits', unpublished manuscript

John Deakin as contributor
Pudney, John, *Whom Only England Know*, John Lane/The Bodley Head, 1943
Kininmonth, Christopher, *Rome Alive*, John Lehmann, 1951

about John Deakin
Farson, Daniel, *Out of Step*, Michael Joseph, London, 1974
---, *Soho in the Fifties*, Michael Joseph, London, 1987
---, *The Gilded Gutter Life of Francis Bacon*, Century, London, 1993
---, *Sacred Monsters*, Bloomsbury, London, 1988
---, *Never a Normal Man*, HarperCollins, London, 1997
John Deakin: The Salvage of a Photographer, Victoria and Albert Museum, 1984
Lister, Eric, *Portal Painters: A Survey of British Idiosyncratic Artists*, Alpine Fine Arts Collection, London, 1982, rev. Jess Wilder 1992
Moraes, Dom, *My Son's Father*, Secker & Warburg, London, 1968
Moraes, Henrietta, *Henrietta*, Hamish Hamilton, London, 1994
Muir, Robin, *John Deakin Photographs*, Schirmer/Mosel Verlag, Munich, 1996
Smart, Elizabeth, *John Deakin's Paris*, exhibition catalogue, London, 1956

Articles and Reviews

Anon., 'John Deakin Chose Cassie Chaney', *Vogue*, June 1952
Bernard, Bruce, 'Face to Face with John Deakin', *Sunday Times Magazine*, 7 October 1984
---, 'Fearless Exposures', *The Independent Magazine*, 23 March 1991
Charlton, Warwick, 'Deakin at War', letter to *The Times*, 21 May 1996
Farson, Daniel, 'Clown with a Camera', *The Spectator*, 29 September 1984
---, 'Through a Glass Darkly', *Sunday Telegraph Magazine*, 31 March 1996
Halpert, Peter Hay, 'Influence and Inspiration: Francis Bacon, John Deakin & Photography', *Aperture* 145, 1997
Koestenbaum, Wayne, 'Facing Reality', US *Vogue*, September 1997
Lane, Anthony, 'Malicious Eye', *New Yorker*, 14 July 1997
MacInnes, Colin, 'The Photographer as Artist', *The Times*, 13 July 1956
Moraes, Henrietta, 'The Curse of the Drinking Classes', *The Independent Magazine*, 6 April 1996
Sewell, Brian, 'Which Was First, the Camera or the Art?', *Evening Standard*, 25 April 1996
Sylvester, David, 'Round the London Galleries', *The Listener*, 2 August 1956

Acknowledgments

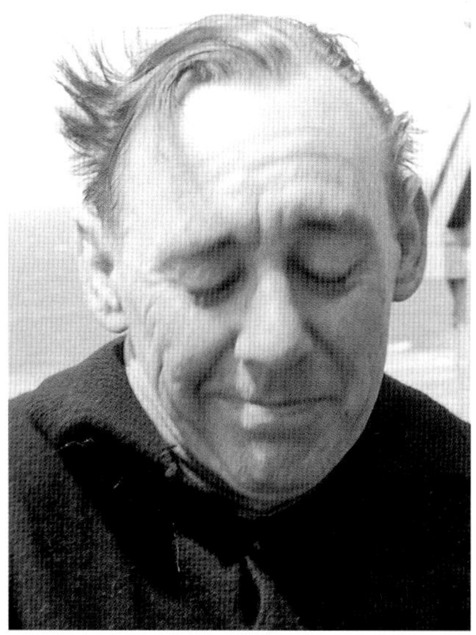

John Deakin by Daniel Farson, Devon, early 1960s

The photographs in this book were rescued from John Deakin's Soho flat in early summer 1972. That we are able to look at them at all is thanks to the foresight of the late Bruce Bernard, who carried out the rescue. A champion of photography, and a connoisseur in whatever sense makes it least pretentious, Bruce died in the week research for this book started in earnest. To many photographic enthusiasts he was something of a hero – which he would certainly have found appalling, but I can't think of a better word and he was certainly one to me.

From Bruce the boxes of negatives came to another remarkable man, James Moores, of whose collection of artworks they now form a part. He and his assistants, particularly Jane Rankin-Reid, Mo Campbell and currently Joanna Garfinkel, have turned daunting piles of unidentified negatives into the extraordinary archive it always promised to be. I am enormously in James's debt for allowing me to sift through the negatives any time I wanted and of course for allowing the photographs to appear in this book.

I would also like to acknowledge the contribution of the late Dan Farson, who encouraged my research into Deakin's life and who gave me his correspondence with him as well as several key photographs and paintings. I am deeply grateful too to Martin Harrison for agreeing to art direct and sequence the photographs and to his assistants Tony Waddingham and Ben Harrison. Steve Walsh at Downtown Darkroom made the black and white prints; I thank him and also Terry Davis and Bob Wiskin of Grade One Photographic.

The following offered help and encouragement, for which I am most grateful: Paul Lyon-Maris, Roger Mayne, Vince Aletti, Charlotte Cotton, Saul Fletcher, Philippe Garner, Amanda Harrison, Mr and Mrs Frank Monaco, Jane Ross and Virginia Verran. I would also like to pay tribute to the patience of the following members of the *Vogue* library, London: Lisa Hodgkins, Francesca Harrison, Nancy Kim, Chris Pipe and Regan Fletcher and also to Emma Mancroft, Emily Wheeler-Bennett and Harriet Wilson of The Condé Nast Publications Ltd.

Finally I would like to dedicate the text of the book to James Moores and to the memory of Bruce Bernard.

Index

Illustration references are in *italic* and follow the sequence of page numbers in each entry.